THE SECOND CENTURY

THE SECOND CENTURY

U.S.-LATIN AMERICAN RELATIONS SINCE 1889

Mark T. Gilderhus

A Scholarly Resources Inc. Imprint
Wilmington, Delaware

Scholarly Resources Inc.
104 Greenhill Avenue
Wilmington, DE 19805-1897
www.scholarly.com

Library of Congress Cataloging-in-Publication Data

Gilderhus, Mark T.
  The second century : U.S.-Latin American relations since 1889 /
Mark T. Gilderhus.
      p.   cm. — (Latin American silhouettes)
   Includes bibliographical references and index.
      ISBN 0-8420-2413-1 (cloth : alk. paper). — ISBN 0-8420-2414-X
(pbk. : alk. paper)
      1. Latin America—Foreign relations—United States. 2. United
States—Foreign relations—Latin America. 3. United States—Foreign
relations—20th century. 4. Latin America—Foreign relations.
I. Title. II. Title: 2nd century. III. Series.
F1418.G4873   2000
327.7308'09—dc21   99-20921
                                                                                    CIP

∞ The paper used in this publication meets the minimum requirements
of the American National Standard for permanence of paper for printed
library materials, Z39.48, 1984.

To Nancy, for many reasons

About the Author

Mark T. Gilderhus, a specialist in U.S. military and diplomatic history and a former president of the Society for Historians of American Foreign Relations, is the Lyndon Baines Johnson Chair at Texas Christian University in Fort Worth. He holds academic degrees from Gustavus Adolphus College and the University of Nebraska. Professor Gilderhus taught for twenty-nine years at Colorado State University before moving to his present position. His publications include *Diplomacy and Revolution: U.S.-Mexican Relations under Wilson and Carranza* (1977); *Pan American Visions: Woodrow Wilson in the Western Hemisphere* (1986); and *History and Historians: A Historiographical Introduction* (3d ed., 1996). He is married to Nancy, and they have two daughters, Kirsten and Lesley.

Acknowledgments

WHILE PURSUING THIS PROJECT, I accumulated more debts to friends and colleagues than I can possibly acknowledge. I owe special thanks to Richard M. Hopper, vice president and general manager of Scholarly Resources, for his patience and enthusiasm. Also I am grateful for the friendship, good counsel, and hilarity of William H. Beezley of the University of Arizona and Judith Ewell of the College of William and Mary, the series editors. We go back many years. Don Coerver, former History Department chair, and Michael McCracken, dean of the College of Arts and Sciences at my new base, Texas Christian University, allowed me the time and opportunity to complete this book. Most significant, my wife, Nancy, urged me in times of lethargy "to get the damn thing done" and accepted some wrenching but happy changes in our personal lives during the final stages. Of course, I alone have responsibility for errors and misconceptions.

CONTENTS

INTRODUCTION

THE SECOND CENTURY is about U.S. relations with Latin America during a period bounded by the advent of the New Diplomacy late in the nineteenth century and the end of the Cold War about one hundred years later. The main themes center on the political and economic aspects of the relationship, taking two approaches. The first explores U.S. goals and tactics, that is, the nature of hegemony in the Western Hemisphere. The second examines Latin American responses, often nationalistic reactions to unwanted dependencies upon the Colossus of the North. To mitigate any tendency toward national self-centeredness, this work looks at reciprocal interactions between the two regions, each with distinctive purposes, outlooks, interests, and cultures. It also suggests the place of U.S.-Latin American relations within the larger context of global politics and economics.

Most historians accept the view that international behavior is determined by shifting combinations of security needs, economic interests, domestic politics, pressure groups, ideological and cultural commitments, bureaucratic configurations, personality structures, and psychological states. Some argue that international relations form a system with incentives and deterrents all its own. Yet scholars disagree upon the points of emphasis and the overall effects. The ambiguities of historical evidence are often subject to multiple interpretations, compelling historians to regard their discipline as consisting of ongoing debates over the meaning of human experience.[1]

For an earlier generation, Arthur P. Whitaker's conception of "the Western Hemisphere idea" obtained a large measure of interpretive power. Whitaker described a distinctive community of nations characterized by similar political values and aspirations, all shaped by common experiences. For him, the republican rebellions in the New World

against the monarchies of the Old during "the age of dem(
revolutions" assumed a special importance.[2] This view, implyii
the countries of the Western Hemisphere acted on the basis of (
uniform beliefs and practices, took on particular poignancy (
the Second World War, when, in a sense, such a community (
tions actually existed. In more recent times, notions of hemisp
solidarity have impressed scholarly authorities as harder to su;
Instead, scholars have underscored the significance of an unequa;
tribution of wealth, power, and influence, sometimes depicted
consequence of the capitalist proclivities and hegemonic purpos(
the United States.

As a point of reference in this debate, Samuel Flagg Bemis's cl;
work, *The Latin American Policy of the United States*, still holds imp
tance. First published in 1943, it incorporates traditional views from
time of the Second World War and presents the kind of interpretatic
usually characterized as "nationalist." More often than not, this account endorses the legitimacy and good intentions of U.S. goals and
purposes and presumes common interests with other Western Hemisphere countries. For Bemis, such international compatibilities came
about when Latin Americans practiced deference by following the U.S.
lead in the defense of regional security and republican ideology. Otherwise, Latin American behavior typically impresses him as misguided,
perverse, or malevolent. Although he acknowledges the reality of U.S.
imperialism around the turn of the twentieth century, Bemis regards it
as a mistake, a "great aberration," and downgrades its significance over
the long term. He also argues against economic interpretations, claiming that interventionist practices in the Caribbean region served mainly
as strategic defenses of Latin America against European threats and
functioned as a form of "protective imperialism." He sees Franklin
Roosevelt's Good Neighbor policy as having accomplished good
purposes by eliminating the Caribbean and Central American protectorates and, in a culminating moment during the Second World
War, allowing for the development of high levels of inter-American
cooperation against the Axis powers.[3]

Although forceful and erudite, Bemis's work aroused criticism because of its strong opinions and self-congratulatory judgments. In 1974,
for example, Gordon Connell-Smith, a British historian, anticipated
contemporary historiographical tendencies. In *The United States and
Latin America* he charges that Bemis projected ethnocentric and nationalistic biases into his writings. More specifically, in Connell-Smith's
view, Bemis attributed unwarranted benevolence to the United

States and presumed the existence of strong political and ideological bonds with Latin America when in actuality few existed. Seeking to set the record straight, Connell-Smith proposes to depict more faithfully the techniques of U.S. domination, control, manipulation, and exploitation.[4]

The issue retains importance. A variety of more recently published syntheses, although distinct in approach and conception, illustrate the point by emphasizing the effects of competition, inequality, and strife. For example, Lester D. Langley's provocatively personalistic *America and the Americas* employs a version of the idealist/realist distinction, arguing that diplomatic relations in the Western Hemisphere have featured an ongoing contest between the particularistic interests of the United States (America) and the more idealistic concerns within the collectivity (the Americas). Langley hopes for transcendence over national self-centeredness through a triumph of the larger good.[5] Less optimistic in outlook, Robert Freeman Smith's "Latin America, the United States, and the European Powers, 1830–1930" situates regional diplomacy within the context of Great-Power political and economic rivalry. Stressing the clash of divergent aims and purposes, he underscores the unlikelihood that rhetorical devices will ever overcome "basic conflicts of interest" through ritualistic "professions of Pan American harmony."[6] Another recent account, a polemic by Frank Neiss, a German Marxist, appears in *A Hemisphere to Itself*. This book develops an unsubtle economic interpretation by highlighting the capitalist insatiabilities of the United States for markets and resources.[7] By contrast, in *Talons of the Eagle*, political scientist Peter H. Smith draws on international relations theory by arguing that "the inter-American relationship" is "a sub-system" within the larger, global system, subject to distinctive "tacit codes of behavior." According to Smith, compatibilities of interest among the nations of Latin America and the United States may or may not come about, depending upon incentives emanating from the global system.[8] Finally, Lars Schoultz, another political scientist, finds no reason for assuming that common endeavors are possible. In *Beneath the United States,* he argues that "a pervasive belief that Latin Americans constitute an inferior branch of the human species" constitutes "the essential core" of U.S. policy toward Latin America and "determines the precise steps" taken by the United States to protect its interests.[9]

This work explores U.S. efforts to manage affairs within the Western Hemisphere, often by seeking to arrange for order and predictability. To such ends, U.S. policymakers have sometimes resorted to Pan American enticements, inviting Latin Americans to take part in a regional system for settling disputes, expanding trade, and rolling back European influences. In this way, according to the governing assumptions, the participants could advance the vital interests common to all of them by obtaining conditions of peace, prosperity, and security. Consequently, my approach describes U.S. initiatives but does not construe Latin American diplomacy as passive or inert. On the contrary, Latin Americans reacted, resisted, and pursued their own aims. Often they perceived a kind of reality different from that assumed by their northern neighbor. Indeed, the skeptics among them typically denounced the Pan American elaborations of the United States as dangerous snares and deceptions, presumably designed as a subtle means of establishing political and economic controls over Latin America.[10]

In my usage the term "Latin America" refers to a group of independent countries south of the Rio Grande in which many of the inhabitants speak languages derived from Latin, that is, Spanish, Portuguese, and French. These countries include the ten republics of South America, the six republics of Central America, and also Mexico, Cuba, Haiti, and the Dominican Republic. In eighteen of the twenty, Spanish is the dominant language; in Brazil, Portuguese; in Haiti, a French-based *kréyol* (creole). In Mexico, Guatemala, Ecuador, Peru, Bolivia, Paraguay, and Brazil, various native peoples still use their traditional languages. Latin American countries feature Spanish and Portuguese institutional legacies from colonial times, emphasizing hierarchy and authority, and also the economic developmental patterns of the nineteenth century. These patterns stressed the export of raw materials and foodstuffs to the industrializing European countries and to the United States. The consequences have shaped relations with the outside world in significant ways.

I have tried to avoid the use of the term "Americans" as a designation for the inhabitants of the United States. Obviously, all people who dwell in the Americas are Americans. The term "North American" is equally imprecise, since a literal application would have to include Mexicans and Canadians, and the Spanish *estadounidense* allows for no effective translation into English. Although it may be possible to make too much of this issue, I have attempted to deal with it by using terms such as "U.S. citizens."

The rise of the New Diplomacy in the United States late in the nineteenth century and its consequences for the rest of the Western Hemisphere is the focus of Chapter 1. The following chapter offers a description of revolution and war during Woodrow Wilson's presidency and its aftermath in the 1920s. Chapter 3 examines the era of the Great Depression and the Second World War, focusing on U.S. efforts to enlist Latin Americans in collaborative undertakings. Next is a look at the onset of the Cold War and the implications for Latin America. The fifth chapter observes the impact of the Cuban Revolution on U.S. policy during the 1960s and 1970s. Finally, Chapter 6 explores Central American involvements after 1979 and concludes with a brief résumé of ramifications when the Cold War ended between 1989 and 1991. On this matter, I follow Peter H. Smith's lead, seeking a suggestive but not a comprehensive account.

NOTES

1. See Michael J. Hogan and Thomas G. Paterson, *Explaining the History of American Foreign Relations* (New York: Cambridge University Press, 1991); Peter H. Smith, *Talons of the Eagle: Dynamics of U.S.-Latin American Relations* (New York: Oxford University Press, 1996); Mark T. Gilderhus, *History and Historians: A Historiographical Introduction*, 3d ed. (Englewood Cliffs, NJ: Prentice-Hall, 1996).

2. Arthur P. Whitaker, *The Western Hemisphere Idea: Its Rise and Decline* (Ithaca, NY: Cornell University Press, 1954).

3. Samuel Flagg Bemis, *The Latin American Policy of the United States: An Historical Interpretation* (1943; reprint ed., New York: W. W. Norton, 1967), chaps. 8, 20; idem, *A Diplomatic History of the United States*, 5th ed. (New York: Holt, Rinehart and Winston, 1965), chaps. 26, 38, 39; Jerald A. Combs, *American Diplomatic History: Two Centuries of Changing Interpretations* (Berkeley: University of California Press, 1983), 156–62, 248, 272–74, 289–90; Gaddis Smith, "The Two Worlds of Samuel Flagg Bemis," *Diplomatic History* 9 (Fall 1985): 295–302; Mark T. Gilderhus, "Founding Father: Samuel Flagg Bemis and the Study of U.S.-Latin American Relations," ibid., 21 (Winter 1997): 1–14.

4. Gordon Connell-Smith, *The United States and Latin America: An Historical Analysis of Inter-American Relations* (New York: John Wiley and Sons, 1974), ix–xviii.

5. Lester D. Langley, *America and the Americas: The United States in the Western Hemisphere* (Athens: University of Georgia Press, 1989).

6. Robert Freeman Smith, "Latin America, the United States, and the European Powers, 1830–1930," in *The Cambridge History of Latin America*, vol. 4, *c. 1870–1930*, ed. Leslie Bethell (New York: Cambridge University Press, 1986), 91.

7. Frank Neiss, *A Hemisphere to Itself: A History of U.S.-Latin American Relations*, trans. Harry Drost (London: Zed Books, 1990).

8. Smith, *Talons of the Eagle*, 5, 7.

9. Lars Schoultz, *Beneath the United States: A History of U.S. Policy toward Latin America* (Cambridge, MA: Harvard University Press, 1998), xv.

10. See Mark T. Gilderhus, *Pan American Visions: Woodrow Wilson in the Western Hemisphere, 1913–1921* (Tucson: University of Arizona Press, 1986).

CHAPTER ONE

EXPANSION, EMPIRE, AND INTERVENTION

1889–1913

THE MODERN AGE in relations between the United States and the countries of Latin America began in 1889 at the First International American Conference. During the opening ceremonies on 2 October in Washington, DC, Secretary of State James G. Blaine established a central theme by affirming high purposes and common interests. According to his hyperbolic formulation, "no conference of nations" ever before had assembled "to contemplate the possibilities of a future so great and so imposing." Blaine wanted to advance "a close acquaintance" with Latin Americans through peace and trade and to establish what he called "that common confidence on which all international friendship must rest." He also placed his country's wealth and power on display. On the following day most of the seventy-three delegates embarked on a 5,000-mile, 42-day railroad journey through New York, New England, and the industrial heartland into the Midwest, at the conclusion of which the diplomatic work got under way in the nation's capital.[1]

Blaine presented an assortment of proposals. He called for the creation of a formal arbitration system to settle disputes and a customs union to increase trade. He also recommended the adoption of convertible silver currencies and other improvements in customs regulations, steamship travel, copyright laws, and extradition arrangements. Although well intended in his own view, Blaine's initiatives produced controversy because Latin Americans mistrusted his motives and disliked the implications. As a consequence, the larger parts of his plan never materialized. At the end of the conference on 19 April 1890 only the creation of the International Union of American Republics had obtained approval. Later called the Pan American Union, this body functioned as a promotional agency for the distribution of commercial information to business leaders seeking trade.[2]

Although something of a disappointment for Blaine, this first modern Pan American conference nevertheless anticipated future directions in U.S. foreign policy by signaling a transition from the "Old" to the "New Diplomacy." Benjamin Harrison's administration from 1889 to 1893 played an important role in this process. Harrison, a modernizer in foreign policy, was "the first president in the post-Civil War era who attempted to coordinate the strategic, diplomatic, and economic factors of United States foreign policy." Beginning in the late 1880s the United States entered "a more aggressive and expansion-ist phase" and "reached out into the world in an increasingly deter-mined and deliberate fashion." To explain the change, historian Robert L. Beisner invokes Thomas S. Kuhn's conception of a para-digm shift. Defined as a "constellation" of beliefs, values, and percep-tions, a paradigm constitutes a way of seeing the world. In this instance the change altered "the manner of thinking about and executing American foreign policy." Among other things, it moved diplomatic practice away from the reactive, improvisational style so characteristic of the immediate post-Civil War era and toward a more systematic, ex-pansive approach.[3]

LEGACIES AND TRADITIONS

During the era of the New Diplomacy, Latin America became more important to the United States than ever before. In previous times the policymakers had taken only a limited, sporadic, and inci-dental diplomatic interest in the southern regions beyond Mexico, Cuba, and Central America. To be sure, groups of merchants, ship-pers, and political leaders periodically discerned opportunities for ex-panding overseas trade, but such ambitions had difficulty overcoming the distances imposed by geography, language, and culture. During colonial times the inhabitants of the two Americas displayed scant knowledge and awareness of each other. Among English settlers the Spanish and Portuguese colonies were essentially *terrae incognitae*.

The gap narrowed for a time during the independence era. As the first people to break free from colonial control, U.S. citizens perceived themselves as a republican vanguard, a model and an inspiration for others; they regarded the Spanish American rebellions against the mother country as emulations of their own example. Such ethnocen-tric responses somewhat misconstrued complex mixes of motive and purpose. In fact, the Latin American insurrections in 1808 began as defenses of monarchical legitimacy—indeed, as reactions against

Napoleon's removal of Ferdinand VII from the Spanish throne and installation of his brother, Joseph Bonaparte. Later, when Latin American rebels broadened their aims to include national independence, patriotic enthusiasts in the United States looked upon the goal as further evidence of shared commitments to the principles of republicanism and free trade. The result, a utopian expectation, anticipated the advent of "an entire hemisphere peopled by republicans, their political systems and moral virtues modeled on the United States, and, like the United States, aloof from Europe."[4]

Conceptions of realpolitik more than ideology guided official U.S. responses during the wars of the French Revolution and later those of Napoleon. Under President James Madison the U.S. government occasionally expressed sympathy for the independence movements but otherwise assumed a neutral stance. Mainly, Madison wanted to avoid provocative displays toward Spain at a time of dangerous European complexities. Relations with France and Great Britain took priority before the War of 1812. Impatient advocates of Latin America, such as Congressman Henry Clay of Kentucky, called for diplomatic recognition to win over the new regimes, sustain republican solidarity, and advance commercial opportunity, but U.S. policymakers concentrated on European concerns. After the War of 1812, Secretary of State John Quincy Adams successfully resolved outstanding difficulties with Britain and Spain through complicated negotiations over boundaries along the northern and southern frontiers. Meanwhile, triumphant Latin American revolutionaries achieved independence and invited formal diplomatic ties. Insisting upon proper guarantees of order and responsibility, the United States under President James Monroe responded by extending diplomatic recognition to Mexico in 1822, the first country to do so. Recognition followed for Brazil and the Central American Confederation in 1824 and for most of the other countries during the next few years. Haiti, an exception, had to wait until 1862. As an independent nation created through revolution by the descendants of enslaved Africans, Haiti for reasons of race experienced isolation in a world dominated by white authority.[5]

Monroe's famous message to Congress on 2 December 1823 proclaimed support for Latin American independence. Known to posterity as the Monroe Doctrine, the terms established sharp distinctions between the policies and practices of the monarchies of the Old World and the republics of the New. Monroe specifically warned against interference by the former in the affairs of the latter. He also placed a prohibition on European expansion beyond "existing colonies or dependencies" and disallowed all the other regions from serving "as subjects for future colonization." In his words, "any attempt" by the Europeans to extend "their system to any portion of this hemisphere" would appear as "an unfriendly disposition," endangering the "peace and safety" of the United States.[6]

Although assuredly a bold statement, the Monroe Doctrine entailed very few risks. As understood by President Monroe, Secretary of State Adams, and other advisers, British interests ran parallel with those of the United States and militated against European interventions for regaining territory. The British also wanted free, trading states in the Western Hemisphere. As John J. Johnson notes, the Monroe Doctrine implied no "binding commitment" to do much of anything except to uphold the basic interests of the country. Similarly, Walter LaFeber argues that the Monroe Doctrine established "the ground rules for the great game of empire . . . in the New World." Essentially, it sought the "containment" of European presences while reserving for the future the extension of U.S. influence in the region.[7]

Except for Mexico, Cuba, and Central America, Latin America subsequently passed out of vogue as a compelling U.S. interest. Geographically distant and culturally remote, South American countries presented neither dangers to nor opportunities for the United States. Meanwhile, Latin American leaders cultivated European ties as balances against their northern neighbor, which was embarking upon the great surge westward. Driven by land hunger, commercial ambition, and a constellation of ideological convictions known as Manifest Destiny, territorial expansion resulted shortly in the conquest of the continent. Mexico, a principal loser as a consequence of military defeat, suffered some of the effects in 1848 when the Treaty of Guadalupe Hidalgo transferred half of the country's territory to the United States. In the 1850s, Cuba and parts of Central America also took on allure as worthy prizes; for southern slaveowners, Cuba, a slave-owning society until 1871, became a target; for northern commerce, Central American routes became desirable as a means of transit to Asia across the Pacific.

The westward march overwhelmed Spanish, Mexican, British, and Native American presences and ultimately exacted a price. Ironically, the acquisitions of the 1840s transformed the territorial status of slavery into an insoluble issue. The consequence of this political breakdown, the American Civil War, cost 620,000 lives and altered the future forever. By abolishing slavery and modifying states' rights, the North's victory sanctioned the use of federal authority and the rise of business and industrial leaders who put faith in the transformative powers of capitalist enterprise. For the rest of the century and beyond, such men controlled U.S. destiny at home and abroad.[8]

THE NEW DIPLOMACY

According to most historians the New Diplomacy originated in larger, more pervasive patterns of change during the second half of the nineteenth century. Usually perceived as the result of shifting economic, strategic, political, and psychological conditions, the advent of overseas expansion requires an explanation of the nature, causes, and consequences of U.S. imperialism. In 1963 the publication of Walter LaFeber's *The New Empire* initiated the debate among modern scholars. Setting forth a nuanced economic analysis, this book generated controversy by arguing a neo-Marxist case. According to LaFeber the Industrial Revolution in the United States and the ensuing quest for markets and resources functioned as fundamental determinants: "It was not accidental that Americans built their new empire at the same time their industrial complex matured."[9] Indeed, the correlation between economics and expansion in both territorial and commercial forms signified a continuity in U.S. history since colonial times.

In response, critics developed discrete commentaries, cautioning against undue reliance upon economic interpretations, historical continuities, and neo-Marxist models. Seeking to capture the different dimensions of a complex, multifaceted reality, they insisted upon the need for balanced, inclusive explanations to account for the effects of domestic and international politics, strategy, culture, psychology, and economics. Without multiple levels of understanding, they warned, historians could run the risk of misrepresenting the past.

For LaFeber, the antecedents of the New Empire came about soon after the Civil War. Although preoccupied with internal affairs such as Reconstruction, the conquest of the West, and the Industrial Revolution, the leaders of the United States retained an interest in the outside world but with a shifting emphasis. Less concerned than previously with territorial acquisitions, they attached more importance to commercial expansion, hoping by this means to moderate the instabilities of the Industrial Age.

This argument stresses the impact of technology on manufacturing and transportation. Through the development of factories and railroads the United States acquired not only immense productive capability but also the capacity to supply far-flung markets. Economically, it

assumed the rank of a Great Power. At the same time, cyclical boom-
and–bust tendencies brought about unpredictability and wild fluctuations. Beginning with the Panic of 1873 the United States embarked
upon twenty-five years of recurrent depression, occasioned in the
popular understanding by overproduction and underconsumption.
Ironically, high production drove prices down by turning out more
goods than consumers could buy. When market glut resulted, the ensuing hard times meant reduced production and high unemployment.
Meanwhile, strikes, riots, and other manifestations of class conflict
suggested incipient revolution.

1873-98

In a classic response, national leaders tried to dissipate the adverse
effects of depression at home by increasing sales in the markets of Europe, Asia, and Latin America. According to LaFeber, a remarkable
continuity of purpose linked the efforts of Secretary of State William
Henry Seward in the 1860s, James G. Blaine in the 1880s, and their successors in the following years. For such men, visions of commercial
empire and expanding trade formed the core of national aspiration.[10]

LaFeber's critics sometimes conceded an important point, acknowledging that foreign markets counted for something. Yet overall,
they characterized the economic approach as too simplistic and misleading to tell the whole story. For example, Robert Beisner advised
against exaggerating the effects of continuity. In his view, after the
Civil War the practitioners of the Old Diplomacy never possessed the
ability "knowingly" and "skillfully" to execute "a farsighted economic
diplomacy." Indeed, until the 1890s "most U.S. officials were amateur-
ish and maladroit in their diplomacy, ignorant of other societies and
their affairs, and more likely to react to outside events in habitual ways
than to come up with fresh policies." During these "awkward years"
improvisational responses, operating without much planning and coordination, typified U.S. behavior.

challenge LaF

Beisner's study and others sought to expand the focus beyond
commercial questions through the inclusion of a more comprehensive
range of considerations. As Beisner explains, "Most Americans
merged economics into a broader vision" and viewed trade "not just as
a source of profits, but also a wellspring of social enlightenment, moral
improvement, and international peace." The role of economics in foreign policy was "undeniable," also "subtle and complex."[11] Within the
context of the times, it functioned as both an end and a means, inter-
secting always with cultural and ideological concerns.

In addressing this complicated issue, historians have underscored the impact of fundamental assumptions and inclinations. For example, Michael H. Hunt's *Ideology and U.S. Foreign Policy* points to the existence of three "core ideas," each of which had important effects upon public perceptions of foreign affairs. The first, a conception of mission, defined the American experience as "an active quest for national greatness closely coupled to the promotion of liberty." According to this significant and ethnocentric formulation, the advancement of U.S. ideals and interests simultaneously served the well-being of other peoples by expanding the areas of freedom and enterprise. The second, a manifestation of color consciousness, affirmed attitudes toward other peoples within the context of "a racial hierarchy." In this rating scheme white skin connoted higher forms of human quality and worth—indeed, the whiter, the better. Among white people, attitudes of fear, condescension, and paternalism sometimes suggested a need for imposing civilizing discipline upon persons of color in order to redeem them from their own racial handicaps. The third, a set of conservative political attitudes based on conceptions of constraint and propriety, placed limits on the acceptability of revolutionary change. The people of the United States revered their own revolution but mistrusted others, especially those infused with more radical tendencies: for example, the twentieth-century upheavals in Mexico, Russia, China, and Cuba. In modern times each of those three core ideas shaped stereotypes of Latin Americans, often seen in the United States as politically tyrannized and racially mongrelized but nevertheless capable of violent and fanatical outbursts.[12]

The paradigm shift in foreign policy took place when anomalies and inconsistencies debilitated the traditional ways of doing things and rendered them inadequate; the Old Diplomacy could not respond to new realities coherently and effectively. According to Beisner, a series of "sudden and severe shocks" triggered the diplomatic revolution. The first, "a widespread social malaise" during the late 1880s and early 1890s, accentuated "a state of anxiety and gloom" in the United States. The great historian Richard Hofstadter called it "a psychic crisis" whose effects brought into question the viability of American beliefs and institutions. The second, the economic depression of the mid-1890s, intensified bad times and instilled a sense of urgency. The third, intense economic competition manifested by European colonial expansion into Asia and Africa, posed additional threats by closing off foreign markets and restricting exports; its consequences magnified the impact of the other two. In combination, this sequence of "abrupt dislocations" brought about "a reevaluation of diplomatic axioms" and a movement toward the New Diplomacy.[13] Henceforth, U.S. policymakers affirmed their own nation's interests with greater calculation in contests among the Great Powers.

 The advocates of the New Diplomacy favored peace and trade without European entanglements but on occasion accepted such risks as unavoidable. They also developed larger aims in Asia and Latin America. In each region the United States preferred informal and indirect means of expansion in contrast with European methods. In India and Africa, for example, the Europeans created formal colonial empires, relying on overt and direct systems of political and economic control. U.S. leaders wanted commercial access but without too many political costs. In Asia the Open Door policy marked an effort by the United States at the turn of the century to prevent the partition of China into spheres of influence. By committing the Great Powers to the principle of "equal commercial opportunity," U.S. leaders hoped to preserve Chinese self-determination and their own prerogative to employ their great economic power "in a fair field with no favor." The United States would rank as the first among equals.[14] Similarly, in Latin America, citizens of the United States intended to compete more actively by establishing new ties of their own.

The extent to which U.S. practices constituted imperialism is an important question. Part of the problem resides in definitions. For Europeans in the nineteenth century, imperialism was colonialism, that is, a formal apparatus of institutional control. In the twentieth century less direct and costly techniques came into vogue and with them new forms of understanding. In the Marxist-Leninist interpretation, imperialism appeared as a stage in the development of capitalism. Though capable of different guises in diverse circumstances, it always served the same set of purposes and interests. According to V. G. Kiernan, imperialism has existed in "protean forms . . . throughout history" but obtained "special new forms" as a consequence of modern capitalism. Regarded as "inherently expansionist," capitalist systems demanded ever greater access to overseas regions for trade and resources and devised new ways of achieving it. The Europeans traditionally founded empires by "annexing and occupying and subjecting peoples to direct rule." The United States, in contrast, became "the chief exponent" of "neo-colonialism," that is, a more subtle approach using informal means to achieve identical ends. In each case the tactics featured "coercion . . . to extort profits above what simple commercial exchange can produce." Expressing a similar view in his famous and influential book *The Tragedy of American Diplomacy*, historian William Appleman Williams described the techniques of "imperial anticolonialism," by which the United States performed as a great imperial power but without the formal instruments of empire.[15] How best to understand this aspect of the U.S. experience remains a vital issue.

THE NEW DIPLOMACY IN ACTION

In the Western Hemisphere the New Diplomacy encouraged repeated affirmations of U.S. power, prestige, and prerogative. In the 1890s such displays produced a series of confrontations, culminating in 1898 with war against Spain. This brief conflict, only four months in duration, had large repercussions. For one thing, it confirmed the standing of the United States among the Great Powers as a presence in the western Pacific and as the hegemon of the New World. It also bequeathed new problems of management and control of territories within the U.S. sphere of influence. During the early years of the twentieth century these problems occasioned the use of protectorates and other interventionist practices.

As an intimation of change the Harrison administration's sponsorship of the First International American Conference in 1889 had broad implications. To an extent, Blaine's plan for peace and trade was sanctioned by past experience. Simón Bolívar, the Liberator of South America from Spanish rule, had tried to advance international cooperation by suggesting "an august Congress" of American states in 1815. Though abortive in the first instance, the idea did prompt a series of meetings under Latin American auspices at Panama in 1826, Lima in 1847, Santiago in 1856, and Lima again in 1864. None of them accomplished much. Now, with Blaine in charge, the United States instigated another such endeavor.[16]

Blaine first issued invitations to a Pan American conference during his short stint as secretary of state in 1881, but the assassination of President James A. Garfield ruined the plan. When Vice President Chester A. Arthur took over as president, he replaced Blaine with Frederick T. Freylinghuysen, a practitioner of the Old Diplomacy, who wanted no new entanglements and canceled the proposed meeting. The idea nevertheless retained validity among commercial expansionists and other enthusiasts, and so in 1888 the U.S. Congress authorized President

Grover Cleveland to try it again. But then, in another twist, Cleveland, a Democrat, lost the presidency that year to Harrison, a Republican, and Blaine returned as secretary of state in time to act as the host.[17]

Fundamentally a ceremonial occasion, the First International American Conference in Washington, DC, much like its predecessors, fell short in tangible accomplishment. Indeed, an assortment of rivalries and cross-purposes created impediments and manifested high levels of mistrust of the United States and its ambitions. The Chileans, for example, objected to Blaine's proposed arbitration treaty out of concern for their stake in Tacna and Arica, the nitrate-rich provinces they had recently taken from Peru in the War of the Pacific. The Argentines, similarly, opposed a customs union on grounds of economic self-interest. As a trading partner they preferred Great Britain, the traditional supplier of capital, markets, and goods, and regarded the United States as a rival whose agricultural and extractive exports competed with their own. Thus, they saw no advantage in closer affiliation, since for them Great Britain served as a counter against the growing power of the United States.[18]

Unable to obtain his larger goals, Blaine settled for a recommendation in support of commercial reciprocity. This strategy, though less comprehensive than a customs union, suggested another method for expanding trade. The U.S. Congress in 1890 created incentives by removing import duties on sugar, molasses, coffee, tea, and hides in the hope that other countries would reciprocate with exemptions for U.S. exports. Subsequent agreements, though endorsed by eight nations—Spain, Great Britain, the Dominican Republic, Brazil, Guatemala, Nicaragua, Honduras, and El Salvador—yielded mixed results, showing few actual increases in trade.[19]

Weakened by illness and personal loss—the deaths of a brother, a son, and a daughter—Blaine resigned as secretary of state in 1892 and died the following year. Harrison, assuming the conduct of foreign policy, affirmed strong positions. In Latin America his pugnacity produced a war scare with Chile. Though possibly encouraged by the proximity of the 1892 presidential election, as some historians have argued, Harrison more basically displayed his commitment to the New Diplomacy with readiness to uphold a broad conception of national interest and honor. Moreover, the program of naval arms construction initiated early in the 1880s allowed him to coordinate his actions with credible threats of seagoing force. During the Chilean episode he had seven new naval cruisers at his disposal and several more on the way.

The showdown with Chile that put the New Diplomacy into action developed as a kind of culmination after a period of rising tension created by Chile's victory over Peru and Bolivia in the War of the Pacific during 1879–1882.[20] Seeking to maintain a regional balance of power, Secretary of State Blaine had offended Chilean leaders by appearing to support their military adversaries. He then compounded the problem during the Chilean civil war in 1891, again by seeming to back the loser—in this case, the ousted president, José Manuel Balmaceda.

Consequently, anti-U.S. sentiment was running high when Captain Winfield Scott Schley of the USS *Baltimore* permitted his crew to take shore leave in Valparaiso on 16 October 1891. A group of sailors at the True Blue Saloon became embroiled in a violent incident in which two were killed and others were injured and arrested. The Chilean government denied responsibility, blaming the sailors for riotous, drunken behavior. The Harrison administration, however, held the government accountable, demanded an apology and reparations, and forced Chile's capitulation early in 1892 with a threat of war.

Joyce S. Goldberg's careful study places the *Baltimore* affair within the larger international context and explains the process of escalation leading to "extraordinary" effects far out of proportion to the causes. Acute rivalries among the Great Powers at the end of the nineteenth century intensified the impact. Both Chile and the United States "were struggling to develop a dominant position in the Western Hemisphere" and acted according to "their understanding of themselves, the manner in which the rest of the world saw them, and their desire to alter or maintain the images other nations had of them."[21] In other words, perceptions and self-impressions counted for a great deal. Chilean miscalculations in the early stages suggested a dismissive attitude toward the United States and elicited bellicose reactions. In the end the "historical significance" of the episode underscored the extent to which the Harrison administration would assert its presumed prerogatives as a Great Power in the Western Hemisphere.

Another such affirmation took place in 1895, during President Grover Cleveland's second term. On this occasion, Secretary of State Richard Olney proclaimed his corollary to the Monroe Doctrine, declaring in unsubtle terms that "today the United States is practically sovereign on this continent, and its fiat is law upon the subjects to which it confines its interposition." Olney affirmed this statement during a controversy with Great Britain over a disputed territory between British Guiana and Venezuela. A problem of long standing, the issue became significant in the 1890s because of the discovery of gold in the region. When, as a consequence, Great Britain and Venezuela broke diplomatic relations, the Cleveland administration claimed the right to invoke its authority, using the Monroe Doctrine as the rationale. To defend the national "safety and welfare" of the United States against a threat of British expansion in South America, the Cleveland administration insisted upon a settlement by means of arbitration.

The British Foreign Office subsequently suggested calculated disdain for the United States, first by withholding a response for five months, and again by denying the applicability of the Monroe Doctrine. Refusing to back down, President Cleveland raised the stakes by publicly supporting Olney in a message to the Congress on 17 December 1895. A compromise settlement then came about. British leaders, distracted by other matters in Asia and Africa, had no wish to force a crisis in the New World if face-saving devices could avoid one at endurable cost. They accepted arbitration, conditioned on the exclusion of territory occupied by the British for more than fifty years. The terms upheld the essential parts of the status quo; Venezuela also retained control of its traditional claims. In the larger context the controversy speeded a change in relations between the United States and Great Britain. This "great rapprochement" manifested a long-term tendency by which the British more readily acknowledged the preeminence of the United States in the Western Hemisphere. Though economic competition persisted, the two countries accepted an arrangement by which the United States assumed the main political responsibility for maintaining the common interest in order and peace.

Historians usually cite a blend of politics, strategy, and economics as the reasons for Cleveland's opposition to Great Britain. Some have described the administration's behavior as a maneuver to build popularity before the election in 1896 or as a bid to strengthen U.S. authority against European rivals. Others have identified commercial incentives, such as a need to prevent British control of the Orinoco River, the main route of access to interior markets. In a balanced synthesis, Richard E. Welch Jr. also shows the impact of the president's personality upon policy. He argues that Cleveland resented "presumed slights against the national honor" and feared "the expansion of British economic and strategic power in the New World," where he equated "U.S. national security" with "U.S. hemispheric predominance." Yet Welch denies the existence of explicit and aggressive programs of economic expansion. Instead, he depicts U.S. diplomacy under Cleveland as a product of uneven and improvisational attitudes and practices, characterized "by inconsistencies, sporadic personal attention, and an uneasy mixture of anti-imperialism, moralism, and belligerent nationalism."[22]

Similar interpretive difficulties intrude upon studies of the war with Spain. This debate centers on the nature, causes, and consequences of the unfolding imperial policy of the United States. Neo-Marxist historians have affirmed the existence of direct connections between overseas expansion and economic drives for markets and resources; other scholars have insisted upon the multifarious effects of politics, strategy, and psychological states. Yet they all recognize the magnitude of change brought about by the dramatic extension of U.S. influence in the Caribbean and Pacific. Whether these developments occurred because of contingency or by design is a central question.

The Cuban revolt against Spanish authority began in 1868 during the Ten Years' War. Though initially forced into submission, the insurgents rose again in 1895 in a nationalist rebellion against misgovernment, maladministration, and an assortment of social and economic ills. Ranking high among the latter, the U.S. increase in tariff rates on Cuban sugar in 1894 sharply reduced sales, precipitating hardships for Cubans. In defining their goals the rebels drew directly upon the thinking of José Martí, a revolutionary leader whose nationalistic conception of *Cuba libre* required not only emancipation from Spain but also the avoidance of subsequent dependencies on the United States.[23] In addition, Martí called for the creation of an egalitarian society in Cuba through the elimination of poverty and injustice. Since many poor Cubans had experienced plenty of each, masses of people responded with favor.

The anticolonial revolt took on the attributes of racial and class struggle. Among the 1.6 million inhabitants of Cuba, about one-third were descended from African ancestors and had not been emancipated from slavery until 1871. Large numbers, both black and poor, joined the insurgents, with unsettling effects upon the privileged elites, who feared a caste war. A guerrilla army of thirty thousand under leaders such as General Máximo Gómez waged a fierce fight, employing the classic hit-and-run, terror, and scorched-earth tactics. By laying waste, the guerrillas hoped to force the Spanish out of Cuba.

The Spanish responded with regular military forces and a pacification program built on *reconcentrado*. As practiced by General Valeriano Weyler y Nicolau, this technique attempted to isolate the rebels by concentrating thousands of Cubans in relocation camps, where they died in droves. The brutality shocked observers in the United States

and came under scrutiny in such newspapers as William Randolph
Hearst's *New York Journal* and Joseph Pulitzer's *New York World*.
(Though historians once rated sensational journalism as a cause of the
war, scholars today see it as a reflection of public opinion more than as
an actual incitement.) Meanwhile, Cuban factions maneuvered for advantage in the United States. In New York, revolutionary groups
sought political support, money, and arms from sympathizers and
enthusiasts, while Cuban conservatives asked for intercession by
President Cleveland. Unlike José Martí, the conservatives accepted
dependency upon the United States as the price for aid in establishing peace and order.

The Cuban issue also caused political divisions in the United
States. According to one view, the United States possessed both legitimate interests of long standing in Cuba—including investments estimated at $50 million—and also a strategic stake. Only ninety miles
away, Cuba commanded Caribbean sea-lanes and presumably could
function as a strategic base for hostile powers. Cleveland, worried
about European intervention, favored a restoration of Spanish authority, with provision for home rule and other reforms to win over the
rebels. Cuban independence, he feared, would result in chaos over differences of color and class. In contrast with Cleveland's position, U.S.
advocates of a free Cuba saw ideological affinities with their own War
of Independence and thus championed support for the rebels.

Among the Cubans, Cleveland's peace plan had the exceptional
effect of offending both sides. Cuban loyalists wanted no dilution of
Spanish authority and rejected home rule; the rebels demanded full
sovereignty and no compromise. Among Cleveland's deficiencies "an
anti-Cuban bias" suggested "little sympathy for the insurrectionists
and little faith in their political intelligence." Indeed, Cleveland's incomprehension of Cuban nationalism became "a major weakness" and
a principal source of failure.[24]

His Republican successor, William McKinley, also compiled a
controversial record. According to traditional accounts, McKinley
displayed weakness and indecision when faced with political pressures at home after his election in 1896. In Theodore Roosevelt's de-
licious phrase, he showed "no more backbone than a chocolate
éclair!" Elaborating upon the same point, a contemporary cartoon
showed "Willie" McKinley attired in a dress, holding a broom, seeking
ineffectually to drive back huge waves called "Congress" and "The
People." The caption read, "Another Old Woman Tries to Sweep

Back the Sea." This image depicted the president as "cowardly, bumbling, and politically opportunistic." Unable to establish a steady course, he was supposedly "overwhelmed by public opinion and forced into an unnecessary war." This interpretation established a dominant theme in historical writing until the 1960s, when revisionists mounted a challenge. They regarded McKinley as "more courageous and capable than previously portrayed." Also, they described his decision in favor of war as a logical continuation of his own policies more than as a surrender before public and congressional insistence. The effect has been "a substantial redemption of McKinley's historical reputation."[25]

Revisionists have depicted McKinley as a shrewd trade expansionist who understood relationships between means and ends. In actuality a strong leader, he hoped to avoid war in his quest for overseas markets, but in the end he desired "what only a war could provide," that is, "the disappearance of the terrible uncertainty in American political and economic life, and a solid basis from which to resume the building of the new American commercial empire." Throughout the preliminaries before the war, McKinley affirmed the standards of the New Diplomacy and implied the possibility of using force finally as a last resort.[26]

Much of the recent writing incorporates revisionist thinking but without the economic emphasis. In fairness to McKinley, according to Lewis L. Gould, historians must acknowledge his capabilities by accurately representing "the complexity of the diplomatic problems" and the extent of his efforts "to discover a way out of the impasse." McKinley's diplomacy was "tenacious," "coherent," "courageous," and "principled." Indeed, "what is significant is not that war came" but that McKinley postponed it "for as long as he did." By so doing, he retained control of "the terms on which the United States commenced hostilities." Indeed, his strong use of the executive power established him as "the first modern president."[27]

Late twentieth-century scholarship describes the unfolding of McKinley's diplomacy through various stages. The president first aspired to a negotiated solution with Spain, seeking a peaceful separation for Cuba and, perhaps, purchase by the United States. The effort failed. McKinley then reluctantly considered war but accepted it only when convinced that Spain would not acquiesce in other alternatives. Affirming his aversion to an endless, inhumane conflict, he announced soon after his inauguration his insistence upon respect for "the military codes of civilization." Spain never accepted this position. Nevertheless, McKinley's expectation of limits on the conduct of war became a tenet of U.S. policy.

As president, McKinley needed to appoint a new minister to the U.S. legation in Madrid. His first choices included such notables as John W. Foster, Henry White, Whitelaw Reid, and Elihu Root, all first-rate, experienced public figures. They turned him down. The president then picked Stewart L. Woodford for this important post. A lawyer, former Civil War general, and New York state politician, Woodford was "loyal" and "conscientious" but uncomfortable with "the subtleties of international diplomacy." As an amateur in the diplomatic arts, he resembled many other practitioners and policymakers in the McKinley administration.

Eager for improved Spanish relations before Congress assembled in December 1897, McKinley hoped for good results from a political change in Spain. Following the assassination of Prime Minister Antonio Canovas del Castillo in August 1897, an interim Conservative government failed to make any progress in the Cuban difficulty and relinquished power two months later. A new Liberal government under Praxedes Mateo Sagasta then signaled the possibility of a negotiated settlement by recalling General Weyler and accepting home rule in principle. Designed to rally political moderates in Spain, these concessions also sought U.S. support with shows of reasonability. Meanwhile, Minister Woodford presented his diplomatic credentials in Madrid. In a statement of expectations delivered at the same time, he emphasized that unless peace returned quickly to Cuba, the Spanish government must anticipate some action from the McKinley administration. He also inquired when Spain would "put a stop to this destructive war" by offering "proposals of settlement honorable to herself and just to her Cuban colony and to mankind."

Though McKinley never said so, he probably believed that Spain truly lacked the capacity to suppress the revolt and eventually would have to let Cuba go. At the same time, he understood the futility of an ultimatum. No Spanish government would accept independence outright. For that reason, McKinley maintained the pressure, seeking concessions while moving toward a negotiated outcome. In the fall the Liberal government in a show of good faith suspended the policy of *reconcentrado*, bestowed amnesty on political prisoners, and announced an autonomy plan. Though supposedly a step toward Cuban home rule, this approach retained Spanish sovereignty over Cuban military and foreign affairs. McKinley grasped the shortcoming. Probably, he

Fall 1897

hoped for additional concessions. In his annual message to the Congress on 6 December, he commended Spain for the reforms but warned of further action by the United States unless "a righteous peace" ensued in the "near future."

Such determination resulted in part from apprehension over the possibility of European intervention in the Western Hemisphere. As a consequence of imperial competition the Great Powers had partitioned Africa and similarly threatened China. The McKinley administration wanted no such activities in the Caribbean. A supposed German threat, largely illusionary, caused special concern. Definitions of economic interest also functioned as incentives. Business and government leaders perceived the Cuban violence as an obstacle to recovery from the 1890s depression. Some also anticipated the acquisition of new markets and resources through aggressive programs of overseas expansion. Specifically, they wanted dominance in the Caribbean regions and a projection of U.S. influence into the Pacific toward China. Finally, domestic politics also contributed a controlling influence. Ferociously partisan, the struggles between Republicans and Democrats over Cuba reflected deep divisions. Each party hoped to obtain advantage by using the issue against the other. For political reasons, McKinley needed a Cuban settlement on his terms to counter Democrats, many of whom wanted to recognize Cuban independence as "an act of justice to an American nation struggling for liberty against foreign oppression." According to Democrats, the president's autonomy plan was a sham, and the Republican position on Cuba was pro-Spanish.[28]

Climactic events early in 1898 created a crisis atmosphere conducive to war. First, Enrique Dupuy de Lôme, the Spanish minister in Washington, precipitated a public furor. In a letter to a friend he unflatteringly described President McKinley as "weak," "a bidder for the admiration of the crowd," and "a would-be politician who tries to leave a door open behind himself while keeping on good terms with the jingoes of his party." Cuban rebels intercepted the missive and forced de Lôme's recall by publishing it in the *New York Journal* on 9 February 1898. The effects damaged Spanish credibility in the United States. A much greater calamity then compounded the difficulty. Late in 1897 the McKinley administration had demonstrated its resolve by sending the battleship USS *Maine* to Havana. During the night of 15 February 1898 an explosion sank the vessel in the harbor and killed 266 sailors. The cause was unknown but in the ensuing investigation a U.S. Naval Court of Inquiry attributed the disaster to an external blast, possibly a torpedo or submarine mine. Such findings fed suspicions of Spanish treachery. More plausibly, modern scholars place the blame on spontaneous combustion in the bituminous coal bins near the powder magazine.[29]

To avert a war, McKinley needed concessions from Spain. Otherwise, he could not satisfy pro-Cuban contingents in the United States. Stepping up the pressure, he set forth terms on 26 March 1898, stipulating an end to *reconcentrado* and also "full self-government, with reasonable indemnity" for Cuba. Further, the United States should play a role as mediator, if necessary, to obtain a settlement between Spain and Cuba. When U.S. Minister Woodford asked for clarification as to whether "full self-government" meant "actual recognition of independence" or "nominal Spanish sovereignty over Cuba," the State Department told him to insist upon "Cuban independence." Woodford's instructions included these specifics: immediate termination of *reconcentrado,* an armistice as a move toward peace, and acceptance of the "friendly offices" of the United States. Otherwise, the McKinley administration would act as "the final arbiter."

Spain tried to buy time. On 30 March the Sagasta ministry abolished *reconcentrado* but yielded nothing else. Spanish leaders, fearing the possibility of a military revolt at home if they accepted either U.S. mediation or Cuban independence, launched other initiatives. On 10 April they suggested a Cuban cease-fire. Though in some ways consistent with U.S. demands for an armistice, the concession fell short because of omissions and loopholes. Notably, it withheld recognition of Cuban independence and allowed for a subsequent resumption of warmaking. Historian John L. Offner regards the proposal as a Spanish ploy, intended to mobilize European support against the United States. The tactic failed. None of the Great Powers wanted to risk much on Spain's behalf. The Cuban crisis then entered the final stage.

Offner's provocative assessment depicts the Spanish-American War as "inevitable" because of "the irreconcilable political positions dividing the Cuban, Spanish, and American people." In his view no grounds existed for a compromise. The Spanish refused to relinquish royal authority; the Cubans demanded independence; and the United States had no means of breaking the deadlock. At last convinced of these realities, McKinley, in a message to the Congress on 11 April 1898, insisted upon two primary goals: "the instant pacification of Cuba" and "the cessation of the misery that afflicts the island." He also called for the use of armed force to attain them. As justifications he explained the necessity of acting "in the name of humanity, in the name of civilization," and, less exaltedly, "in behalf of endangered American interests." Significantly, he advised against diplomatic recognition of the rebels.[30]

In the ensuing debate the issue of whether to recognize Cuban independence became a central question. Most Democrats and many Republicans initially favored recognition, in opposition to the president, but then came around in McKinley's support. According to some historians, the subsequent denial of diplomatic recognition served legitimate U.S. aims by leaving open the possibility of political accommodation with Spain, serving notice of Cuban accountability for offenses against U.S. citizens and property, and assuring the independence of U.S. forces from Cuban control. Other historians regard the decision as evidence of imperial design. Among them, Louis A. Pérez Jr. describes McKinley's policy as the fulfillment of the long-term expansionist ambitions so graphically expressed by John Quincy Adams in 1823. Positing "laws of political as well as physical gravitation," Adams had reasoned metaphorically that just as an apple from a tree "cannot choose but fall to the ground," so also Cuba, "forcibly disjoined from its own unnatural connection with Spain, and incapable of self-support, can gravitate only toward the North American Union." This "same law of nature" required that the United States "cannot cast her off from its bosom." In Pérez's view the Cuban revolt in the 1890s threatened not only "the propriety of colonial rule" but also "the U.S. expectation of colonial succession." U.S. imperialists regarded the acquisition of Cuba "as an act of colonial continuity" by which to take sovereignty "over a territory presumed incapable of separate nationhood." McKinley's intervention, "ostensibly" against Spain but "in fact" against Cuba, had the effect of transforming "a Cuban war of liberation into a U.S. war of conquest."[31]

This indictment rings true or not, depending on interpretations of the Teller amendment to the declaration of war. Introduced by Senator Henry M. Teller, a Republican from Colorado, this congressional enactment of 16 April 1898 contained a self-denying pledge against the annexation of Cuba by the United States and is subject to various explanations. The question of intent is critical. Was it an affirmation of good faith, an anticipation of eventual Cuban independence, or, more subtly, a recognition of the need for developing indirect means of control? The initial effects of the Teller amendment served several immediate purposes by rallying support for the Cuban intervention among various groups, including the principled advocates of Cuban independence, the skeptics who doubted McKinley's sincerity of purpose, and the Colorado sugar beet growers who wanted no Cuban competition. Three days later, on 19 April, a congressional joint resolution provided authorization for the United States to use force. The president affixed his signature the following day. A U.S. naval blockade took effect on 22 April; Spain issued a declaration of war against the United States on 24 April; and Congress replied a day later that such a condition already existed. What Secretary of State John Hay later called "a splendid little war" was under way.[32]

THE WAR WITH SPAIN AND AFTER

The war with Spain had many consequences. Most important, it consolidated the U.S. position in the New World, projected national interests into Asia, and introduced new problems of management and control. Barred from annexing Cuba by the Teller amendment, the policymakers subsequently experimented with other devices. Cuba, the first among what were called protectorates, became the model, suggesting forms of applicability in other places. For advocates of the New Diplomacy, the war against Spain represented a kind of culmination.

Combat operations began on 1 May 1898 with the destruction of the Spanish Pacific Squadron at Manila Bay in the Philippines. Though conventionally attributed to the bellicose conniving of Assistant Secretary of the Navy Theodore Roosevelt, champion of a "Large Policy" in Asia, the undertaking actually had the approval of President McKinley and other war planners. These leaders wanted to inflict injury by attacking Spain at a vulnerable point and to eliminate a potential threat against the Pacific coast. The victory also established "alluring possibilities," such as "expanding America's economic and political influence in Asia" and asserting its role as "a genuine world power."[33]

In the Western Hemisphere the process of military mobilization produced an array of baffling confusions. Indeed, so many foul-ups took place that some historical accounts have depicted the war as partaking of comic opera.[34] For example, the army lacked sufficient summer-weight material for uniforms and sent the soldiers off to Cuba in outfits more suitable for a winter campaign in Montana. The single railroad line leading into Tampa, Florida, the main embarkation point, produced massive traffic jams; a shortage of transport vessels impeded the movement of troops to their destinations; and an absence of appropriate landing craft meant that animals and men had to leap into the surf to get ashore. Unprepared to conduct large-scale operations anywhere, the War Department had difficulty putting properly trained and equipped ground forces into Cuba, resulting in large-scale congressional investigations after the war. Nevertheless, once landed, regular and volunteer contingents performed creditably in hard fighting around Santiago de Cuba in the south and won additional victories for the United States. The Cuban campaign ended with the eradication of another Spanish naval squadron in the Caribbean, and the loss of Guam and Puerto Rico deprived the Spanish of all hope. An armistice followed, ending the fighting on 12 August.

The peace negotiations confirmed Spain's defeat. Under the Treaty of Paris on 10 December 1898, Spain relinquished sovereignty over Cuba and ceded Puerto Rico, Guam, and the Philippines to the United States in return for $20 million. The fate of the Philippines especially engendered controversy over the question of expansion into the Pacific. In this instance, no self-denying equivalent of the Teller amendment constricted options, and administration leaders could argue in favor of annexation on the basis of obligation to the inhabitants. Any alternative would supposedly lead to chaos and catastrophe among the Filipinos—often described in racial terms as untutored, un-Christian, and uncivilized—and invite Great-Power intervention. Moreover, trade expansionists regarded the Philippines as an East Asian base from which to move into the fabled, if largely mythical, China market. Critics of annexation, the so-called anti-imperialists, objected for various reasons. Mainly Democrats and free traders who preferred other means, they saw no commercial advantage in possessing formal colonies. They also worried about unwanted effects. What if the United States became involved in dangerous international rivalries? Could the United States maintain the principle of self-determination at home while violating it abroad? What of the incorporation of nonwhite peoples? Such arguments failed to stop annexation during the Senate debate in 1899. The opponents then projected the issue into the presidential campaign of the following year and lost again. McKinley's reelection in 1900 assured the outcome. Meanwhile, the U.S. Army fought a pacification campaign against Filipino guerrillas to make good on the claim.[35]

In contrast, in the Caribbean the United States established protectorates instead of colonies. Following the requirements of the Teller amendment, the McKinley administration devised the essential means in Cuba. Later adaptations appeared in Panama, Nicaragua, Haiti, and the Dominican Republic. Under these arrangements the United States allowed for limited self-determination, relying upon indigenous elites to run the countries but retaining the right of intervention as a form of international police power within their sphere of influence.

At the end of the war with Spain the U.S. military assumed direct control of Cuban governmental functions and placed stringent limits on Cuban participation. According to Louis A. Pérez Jr., a strong critic, the occupation authorities had many reasons, some of them based on racial prejudice, for thinking that Cubans had no capacity for self-government. Perceived as childlike, barbarous, and untrustworthy, the *insurrectos*, especially those of African descent, supposedly lacked the proper requisites. To compensate, U.S. supervisors cultivated the better classes—that is, the members of the old colonial elite—supporting them against the advocates of independence. Nevertheless, some *independentistas* won election to municipal office and to the Constituent Assembly, the body charged with responsibility for writing a Cuban constitution. Once installed in such positions, critics of the U.S. presence called for military withdrawal. Ironically, U.S. officials regarded this outcome as a confirmation of their own misgivings. If irresponsible Cubans rejected pro-U.S. candidates, how could the United States trust them to elect the best government?

A reinterpretation of the Teller amendment provided additional justification for staying in Cuba. A key provision disclaimed "any disposition or intention to exercise sovereignty, jurisdiction, or control over said island except for pacification thereof." But as expediency required, the meaning of the word "pacification" expanded to include "stability" and the capacity to protect life, liberty, and property, that is, the very conditions upon which the United States staked any decision to leave. According to Pérez, "The inability of the old colonial elites to win political control" required the United States "to seek alternative means of hegemony." Though "prepared, even anxious, to end the occupation" by the early part of 1901, the United States would not pull out "without first securing guarantees necessary to U.S. interests."

Secretary of War Elihu Root played a special role in defining the terms, including two provisions. First, the United States must retain "the right of intervention for the preservation of Cuban independence and the maintenance of a stable Government adequately protecting life, property and individual liberty." Second, no Cuban government could enter "into any treaty or engagement with any foreign power" that might "tend to impair or interfere with the independence of Cuba." The term "foreign" in this context meant European. Taken together, these requirements transformed Cuba into a U.S. protectorate and established the essential parts of the Platt amendment to an army appropriations bill in February 1901. Named for the sponsor, Senator Orville H. Platt of Connecticut, this legislation obtained for the United States "an adequate if imperfect substitute for annexation" by diluting Cuban sovereignty through incorporation into the "U.S. national system." It also produced a set of devices suitable for adaptation in other countries.

The explanation of these actions resides in various considerations, many of them well established among the precepts of the New Diplomacy. First, Cuba always possessed a special attraction for U.S. expansionists. To an extent, the Platt amendment marked the fulfillment of old ambitions to secure control of the island. Moreover, the context of the times created a sense of urgency. U.S. leaders believed in the existence of legitimate strategic and economic interests in Cuba and worried that continued violence and disorder would invite European intrusions, most likely by Germany, whereas a restoration of peace and order under their direction would head off the danger. Finally, Cuba took on additional importance in connection with plans to build a Central American canal. To safeguard the Caribbean approaches, the U.S. Navy acquired a Cuban base at Guantánamo Bay.

When Cuban nationalists denounced the Platt amendment as an infringement of state sovereignty, Secretary of War Root gave them an option: either accept those provisions or put up with an ongoing military occupation. The U.S. Army would not go home until the amendment took effect. Without much choice, then, early in June 1901 the Cuban Constituent Assembly endorsed limited sovereignty as the best course available, writing the Platt amendment into the new constitution as an appendix. The occupation forces withdrew about a year later, leaving behind, in Pérez's devastating assessment, a "stunted Cuban republic fashioned by the U.S. proconsuls," the organization and institutions of which had "little relevance to Cuban social reality."[36]

Meanwhile, a significant change had taken place in the United States. On 6 September 1901 an assassin twice shot William McKinley at a reception in Buffalo, New York. McKinley lingered for eight days before dying, and then Theodore Roosevelt became the president. Conservative reformer, nationalist, and exponent of the vigorous life, the former vice president assumed the conduct of foreign relations at a critical time, the aftermath of the war with Spain. As president, he

reveled in the responsibilities of his office and brought the New Diplomacy to a kind of fulfillment. Above all, he wanted his country to
function as "a force for stability in the world" and saw "no escape
from the exercise of American influence." Among his fundamental
aims, Roosevelt sought a balance of power in Europe, an Open Door
policy in Asia, and U.S. hegemony in the Western Hemisphere. His

outspoken views and bellicose rhetoric always produced high levels of
controversy. Critics sometimes characterized him as an imperialist
and a militarist. As a young man, according to historian Richard
Hofstadter, "it had always been his instinct to fight, to shoot things
out with someone or something—imaginary lovers of his fiancée,
Western Indians, Mexicans, the British navy, Spanish soldiers,
American workers, Populists." By the time he became president,
however, Roosevelt had acquired self-control and discharged "his
penchant for violence . . . on a purely verbal level."[37] The recent
scholarship plays down his propensity for war. Though typically
ready to use force if necessary, according to Lewis L. Gould, he "sent
no troops into action, and no Americans died in armed combat while
he was in office" except in the Philippines, where the fighting had
started before he assumed the presidency.[38]

Roosevelt scholar Richard H. Collin insists that historians have
too often misrepresented and misunderstood the president by failing to
take into account the appropriate "contexts." Collin particularly dis-
likes present-minded, neo-Marxist accounts because they are more
concerned with "the Cold War or America's role as a superpower than
with Kaiser Wilhelm II's Germany." This misplaced emphasis has obscured the principal point that "Roosevelt's main purpose" in the New
World was "not the subjugation of Latin America" but "the exclusion
of Europe" from the Western Hemisphere. Europe was "central" for
Roosevelt. Moreover, his concern about German intrusions was legitimate, "not because Germany could conquer substantial parts of
Latin America" but "because the introduction of European national
rivalries into the New World, combined with the growing instability
of Central America—Latin America's Balkans—would destabilize
the entire region." Roosevelt valued order. He also encouraged capitalist enterprise, not so much for purposes of moneygrubbing as for
tactical reasons: He hoped thereby to promote material progress,
peace, and stability.[39]

Roosevelt earned much of his reputation for bravado and bluster in
Latin America, where his spheres-of-influence policies in the Caribbean region stirred incessant controversy. Though probably geared in

his own thinking to the defense of strategic purposes and the Monroe Doctrine, his actions served U.S. economic interests as well. Secretary of State Elihu Root acknowledged as much in 1906, when he remarked upon the importance of Latin American markets for the United States. He also looked upon the region as an outlet for "a surplus of capital beyond the requirements of internal development." During this time the total overseas investments of the United States grew impressively from $0.7 billion in 1897 to $2.5 billion in 1908 to $3.5 billion in 1914. About half went into Latin America.[40]

Roosevelt's actions during the Venezuela crisis in 1902–03 illustrated his strategic concerns. Germany, already a source of mistrust, posed the problem. The difficulty developed when Cipriano Castro, the Venezuelan president and strongman, defaulted on European loans and disregarded an ultimatum demanding payment from Germany, Italy, and Great Britain. Germany then instituted a naval blockade, sank some Venezuelan ships, landed troops, and shelled the forts along the coastline. Though initially acquiescent, Roosevelt later became alarmed. He would not allow the collection of international debts to serve as a pretext for the establishment of a European base in the Western Hemisphere. Among other things, his plans for a trans-Isthmian canal ruled out European obstructions.

In this instance, Roosevelt's own historical account has generated a controversy. Thirteen years later, when the United States was struggling to maintain neutrality in the First World War, the former chief executive suggested in an interview that he knew better than President Woodrow Wilson how to deal with the Germans. Indeed, Roosevelt claimed that during the Venezuela crisis he had obtained good effects behind the scenes by employing coercion with threats of force, warning of war unless the Germans accepted arbitration as the means of settlement. In this way, by his own account, Roosevelt applied the adage "speak softly and carry a big stick." For historians the difficulty resides in assessing the credibility of the claim. Since no corroborating evidence exists in the archives of the United States, Great Britain, or Germany, some scholars regard Roosevelt's version as an exaggeration or a fabrication, perhaps the product of fading memory or mounting personal disgust with Woodrow Wilson's efforts to stay out of the war. Other historians credit Roosevelt with truthfulness, citing earlier renditions of the story in his correspondence and even the possibility of a cover-up, that is, the removal of documents from governmental archives to avoid political embarrassment.[41] Whatever the case, German leaders in the end terminated the crisis by consenting to arbitration, thus presumably giving way when faced with Roosevelt's resolve.

Panama   Roosevelt's efforts to build a canal in Panama also displayed a robust readiness to act. This complicated and contentious affair raised difficult questions about the propriety of his means in promoting Panamanian independence to secure the route. Panama, a province of the South American country of Colombia, had possessed strategic significance since colonial times as "a crossroads of global trade" and "the keystone of the Great Spanish Empire." For U.S. entrepreneurs the region became particularly important as a consequence of "their quest for continental and commercial empire." As early as 1825, New York interests had laid plans for the construction of a canal to link the Atlantic and Pacific Oceans. The British had similar aims. To head off competition the United States and Great Britain negotiated the Clayton-Bulwer Treaty of 1850, in which they promised to make any such project a joint venture. The construction of a railroad by New York financiers in 1855 established U.S. influence as dominant.

The French posed a challenge in 1878, when Ferdinand de Lesseps, the builder of the Suez Canal in Egypt, announced plans for the construction of a sea-level waterway across Panama. This project went forward for a decade, despite U.S. opposition, and then failed because of insuperable obstacles, including varieties of poisonous snakes, mud and rock slides, and tropical diseases such as malaria and yellow fever. Unimpressed by the French collapse, U.S. leaders during the economic depression of the 1890s retained a strong interest in reviving the project. Indeed, as McKinley noted in his annual message to the Congress in December 1898, "The prospective expansion of our influence and commerce in the Pacific" provided a strong incentive for building a canal. This commercial justification ran parallel with and reenforced the recommendations of another vocal pressure group, the advocates of sea power in the U.S. Navy and elsewhere, for whom Captain Alfred Thayer Mahan of the U.S. Naval War College in Newport, Rhode Island, functioned as a leading publicist and theorist. Mahan argued from the British example that battle fleets always had sustained national power, commerce, and greatness. According to him, the construction of a canal formed an essential part of a grandiose design to advance U.S. interests around the world.[42] For such champions the voyage of the USS *Oregon* during the war with Spain illustrated the obvious point: The 14,000-mile voyage from San Francisco around the southern tip of South America to Cuba took sixty-eight days. A canal would make it much shorter.

One problem was whether to construct the passageway in Nicaragua or Panama. In 1901 the Walker Commission, a group of engineers named by McKinley to study the issue, recommended Nicaragua, mainly because of difficulties with the French-owned New Panama Canal Company over the purchase of equipment and assets. The asking price ran to $109 million, an excess valuation of $69 million, according to the Walker Commission. Panama in other respects displayed advantages, chief among them cheaper construction and maintenance costs and a shorter distance from sea to sea. Roosevelt knew of these benefits, but before choosing Panama he had to deal with other complications.

Lobbyists pressed hard on Panama's behalf. As advocates of the New Panama Canal Company, William Nelson Cromwell, the head of a prestigious New York City law firm, and Philippe Bunau-Varilla, a French engineer formerly employed by de Lesseps, sought to rig a deal by which the United States would designate Panama as the choice and pay for the privilege. Cromwell cultivated support among Republican leaders with arguments and campaign contributions and also reduced the purchase price to $40 million. The Walker Commission responded by issuing a new report in favor of Panama. Meanwhile, Bunau-Varilla pushed for acceptance of a proposal suggested by Republican Senator John C. Spooner of Wisconsin. Once adopted into law, the Spooner amendment authorized President Roosevelt to buy the assets of the New Panama Canal Company for $40 million and to employ Panama as the site—provided, of course, that he could obtain the treaty rights.

The diplomatic solution consisted of two parts. First, U.S. leaders wanted to break free from the Clayton-Bulwer Treaty of 1850 in order to exercise exclusive control and fortification rights. Discussions between Secretary of State John Hay and British Minister Julian Pauncefote produced an agreement in November 1901. Second, the United States devised a treaty with Colombia to obtain a long-term lease on a swath of land six miles wide across Panama. In return, the United States would pay Colombia $10 million and an annual rental fee of $250,000. The stockholders of the New Panama Canal Company also would benefit from the sale of assets to the United States.

John Hay's treaty, worked out with the Colombian diplomat Tomás Herrán, obtained ratification in the United States but was rejected by the Colombian Senate in August 1903. Colombians wanted more money for sacrificing sovereignty in Panama. Only recently their country had emerged from a disastrous civil war. By stalling until 1904, when the charter of the New Panama Canal Company ran out, Colombian leaders conceivably could rake in a $40-million profit, additional resources for their devastated nation. Moreover, President José Marroquín, a provincial and reactionary ideologue, would not support the work of his own government's more cosmopolitan diplomats by endorsing the treaty with the United States. His unyielding stance based on conservative Catholic views "confounded" Roosevelt by ruling out the transfer of land in Panama to a Yankee, Protestant nation. Viewed from another angle, Marroquín possessed "as little understanding of the commercial aspects of Panama canal diplomacy as Theodore Roosevelt had for Colombia's religious politics."[43]

Furious, Roosevelt denounced the Colombians for bad faith. He told the secretary of state, "I do not think the Bogotá lot of jack rabbits should be allowed permanently to bar one of the future highways of civilization." Conscious of the consequences "not merely decades, but centuries hence," Roosevelt wanted to take "the right step." A convergence of purposes with Panamanian separatists seeking independence from Colombia provided the solution. Remote and isolated by mountains and jungle, Panama had produced fierce nationalism and a series of revolts in the nineteenth century. New efforts got under way in the fall of 1903, when Philippe Bunau-Varilla assumed the role of intermediary between Panamanian dissidents and U.S. officials. The latter included President Roosevelt, who conveyed a clear impression that he would not permit the failure of a new bid for independence. Coordinating plans with Dr. Manuel Amador Guerrero, the head of a revolutionary junta, Bunau-Varilla brought about an uprising on 3 November. The Panamanian rebels swiftly seized control of strategic points, and the arrival of the USS *Nashville* on the following day prevented Colombia from striking back. The revolution cost hardly any bloodshed.

Seeking to salvage something, the Colombian government attempted to revive the previously rejected treaty, this time at a lower price. Not much interested, the Roosevelt administration concentrated its attention on negotiations with the dexterous and omnipresent Bunau-Varilla, who now represented the interests of both newly independent Panama and the New Panama Canal Company. Because of the administration's political concerns, Roosevelt needed favorable terms to assure Senate ratification and got them in the Hay-Bunau-Varilla Treaty of 18 November 1903. This document provided for a perpetual grant of land ten miles wide within which the United States possessed "all rights, power, and authority" as "if it were the sovereign of the territory." In return, the United States agreed to protect

Panama's independence, pay $10 million down and after nine years re-
mit an annual fee of $250,000. For the sale of its assets the New Panama
Canal Company received $40 million. The prime loser, Colombia,
received nothing until 1921, when, under the terms of the Thomson-
Urrutia Treaty, the government accepted the loss of Panama and also
an indemnity of $25 million from the United States.[44]

Negotiated hastily without benefit of Panamanian representation,
the Hay–Bunau–Varilla Treaty distressed officials in the new country's
government. They protested "the manifest renunciation of sovereignty" over the Canal Zone, a central issue during the ensuing years,
but could not change the provisions. A rejection at this point could
have precipitated even worse outcomes. The United States might have
seized a canal route without payment or moved the site to Nicaragua,
leaving Panama without protection against Colombia. The Panamanians really had no choice. Although the U.S. Senate ratified the treaty
by a large margin on 23 February 1904, the acquisition of Panama as a
second protectorate in the Caribbean region left a legacy of bitterness
and ill will. Colombian leaders objected to the U.S. role in bringing
about the loss of the rebellious province. Panamanian nationalists disliked the loss of sovereignty. In each instance, the issue created difficulties for the future.

In the annual message to Congress in December 1904, Roosevelt
enunciated his most comprehensive statement of policy toward Latin
America. As an expression of preferred assumptions and favorite techniques, his corollary to the Monroe Doctrine uncompromisingly affirmed U.S. responsibility to stand against European intervention in
the Western Hemisphere and also to take corrective action when Latin
Americans reneged on international debts. Roosevelt advised preven-
tive intervention by which the United States would step in and set
things right. Such measures inverted the original intent of the Monroe
Doctrine. Initially a prohibition on European intrusion into the New
World, it now became a sanction for U.S. intervention when, in T.R.'s
words, "chronic wrongdoing" or "impotence" caused a breakdown of
"the ties of civilized society" and forced intercession "by some civilized nation." In the Western Hemisphere the United States, "however reluctantly, in flagrant cases" should assume the responsibility by
carrying out "the exercise of an international police power." As
Roosevelt explained to Secretary of State Elihu Root, a decision "to
say 'Hands off' to the powers of Europe" meant that "sooner or later
we must keep order ourselves."[45]

A test occurred soon afterward: An international debt exceeding $32 million threatened the Dominican Republic with bankruptcy and the possibility of European intervention. When Dominican leaders asked the United States for help, Roosevelt first hesitated and then, after his reelection in 1904, accepted a commitment. An agreement in January 1905 engaged the United States to manage the foreign debt in such a way as to "restore the credit, preserve the order, increase the efficiency of the civil administration and advance [the] material progress and welfare of the Republic." Senate opponents, mainly Democrats, delayed ratification until February 1907, but Roosevelt characteristically worked around the problem by obtaining authority through an executive agreement. It enabled U.S. officials to take over the collection of Dominican customs receipts, the principal source of revenue, and also to arrange for a new schedule of payments.[46]

Roosevelt employed strong measures in Cuba as well. Following a presidential election denounced by critics as coercive, corrupt, and fraudulent, Liberal party opponents of President Tomás Estrada Palma rebelled in 1906, hoping thereby to provoke U.S. intervention on their behalf. As required by the Platt amendment, Roosevelt responded to the breakdown of public order by sending in occupation troops. This time they stayed until 1909, retiring finally after U.S. authorities supervised another election resulting in a Liberal party victory. As Louis Pérez notes, "That the United States intervened . . . to displace a government held in disfavor by the opposition . . . suggested that there was more than one way to redress grievances and obtain political ascendancy" in Cuba. The United States became a mediator of local disputes, in this instance "with almost unlimited entrée into Cuban internal affairs."[47]

Such affirmations of power and prerogative established the principal attributes of U.S. hegemony in the Western Hemisphere. Though Roosevelt annexed no new territory and, indeed, denied any interest in doing so, he upheld his definition of U.S. interest by vigorous means. Through the exercise of a self-proclaimed international police authority, supposedly sanctioned by the Monroe Doctrine, Roosevelt created not colonies but protectorates, using intervention as a major instrument of control. For him, such methods probably suggested paternalism rather than outright imperialism. Yet for many Latin Americans the prospect of domination—political, commercial, and cultural—seemed threateningly real. Among intellectuals especially, suspicion of the United States ran deep and appeared in expressions of Yankeephobia. In 1900, for example, José Enrique Rodó, a Uruguayan, published *Ariel,* a book in which he defended Latin American spirituality against North American materialism, for him a prime distinction between the two cultures. In 1904, similarly, Rubén Darío, a Nicaraguan, incorporated anti-imperial themes into his poem "To Roosevelt," which represented the president as a symbol of arrogant condescension toward Latin America.[48]

Although historians generally have depicted negative reactions to Roosevelt among Latin Americans, Frederick W. Marks III has argued to the contrary that "American prestige south of the border was exceptionally high under Roosevelt." If correct, this assessment probably pertains to ruling elites who appreciated the U.S. president's techniques as a defense against forcible European debt collections. But Latin American resentment of U.S. intervention appeared at a succession of Pan American conferences: at Mexico City in 1901, Rio de Janeiro in 1906, and Buenos Aires in 1910. Even though these were mainly ceremonial occasions to celebrate appearances of hemispheric unity, the rituals could not disguise the differences. The Argentines especially pressed for formal endorsements of the Calvo and Drago doctrines, both favorite projects. Carlos Calvo, an Argentine expert on international law, upheld the inviolability of national sovereignty, opposed the Roosevelt corollary, and insisted on the principle of nonintervention on grounds that no state should intervene in the affairs of another for any reason. Luis María Drago, an Argentine diplomat, similarly argued against the use of force in collecting international debts.[49]

Roosevelt's handpicked successor, William Howard Taft, shifted the bases of policy somewhat during his single term in the White House. He too ascribed importance to the Caribbean region but for different reasons. A lawyer by training, Taft had scant understanding of Roosevelt's power politics and grand strategy. He thought of diplomacy as an extension of the law. Arbitration treaties impressed him as a means of maintaining peace. He also defined diplomatic aims in more explicitly economic terms. Much like other contemporaries, he accepted overproduction and underconsumption as explanations for economic instability and regarded economic expansion into Asia and Latin America as an appropriate response.

For such reasons, the Taft administration encouraged innovation. Secretary of State Philander C. Knox tried to court Latin Americans as prospective customers, even though he disliked them on racial grounds. He also experimented with more effective forms of bureaucratic organization. During his tenure, State Department specialization brought into existence the Division of Latin American Affairs. This change created some measure of professionalization, although political patronage remained the principal means of filling diplomatic appointments until the 1920s. Similarly, the creation of the Bureau of Foreign and Domestic Commerce within the Commerce Department in 1912 aimed at the promotion of trade.[50]

In Latin America the Taft administration employed the techniques of "dollar diplomacy," modeled on what the leaders regarded as a successful experience in the Dominican Republic. Much like Roosevelt, Taft and Knox worried about disorder in the Caribbean and tried to mitigate bad effects through the application of expert administration. When troubles occurred, they put U.S. officials in charge of running the customs houses, seeking honesty, efficiency, solvency, and reform. Moreover, they encouraged private loans from U.S. banks as supplemental revenues. Through the application of dollar diplomacy, defined as the substitution of dollars for bullets, they sought incentives for responsible behavior, attempting to move Latin Americans into modern times.[51]

Aided by the advantage of hindsight, historians have assessed such policies as failures. Efforts to apply them in the Dominican Republic, Nicaragua, Honduras, and Guatemala encountered ornate complexities, almost never susceptible to easy solution. As U.S. experts discovered, the causes of instability and turmoil were more difficult to address than anticipated. Indeed, the effects of economic expansion often compounded those conditions by destabilizing other kinds of customary relationships.[52] In traditional societies all over the world, capitalist infusions showed remarkable capacity to precipitate dramatic change sometimes tending toward revolution. Moreover, displays of U.S. paternalistic condescension had the counterproductive consequence of arousing nationalist responses. Latin Americans disliked efforts "to make them over in the North American image."[53]

As a result of the New Diplomacy the United States created protectorates, practiced intervention in the Caribbean region, and established, if not an empire, something very much like one. Within this sphere of influence, successive administrations affirmed a need for stability and invoked the authority of a self-proclaimed international police power. This practice, a form of hegemony, required the subordination of Latin American sensibilities to U.S. preferences, sometimes justified on grounds of serving lesser peoples. U.S. policies aimed at peace, order, and predictability but could not sustain such conditions. During the second decade of the twentieth century the violent disorder of revolution and war assailed U.S. interests all around the world.

NOTES

1. A. Curtis Wilgus, "James G. Blaine and the Pan American Movement," *Hispanic American Historical Review* 5 (November 1922): 695–97.
2. Homer E. Socolofsky and Allan B. Spetter, *The Presidency of Benjamin Harrison* (Lawrence: University Press of Kansas, 1987), chap. 7; Clifford B. Casey, "The Creation and Development of the Pan American Union," *Hispanic American Historical Review* 13 (November 1933): 437–56.
3. Socolofsky and Spetter, *Presidency of Benjamin Harrison*, 112; Robert L. Beisner, *From the Old Diplomacy to the New, 1865–1900,* 2d ed. (Arlington Heights, IL: Harlan Davidson, 1986), 2, 34; David M. Pletcher, *The Diplomacy of Trade and Investment: American Economic Expansion in the Hemisphere, 1865–1900* (Columbia: University of Missouri Press, 1998), chap. 8.
4. John J. Johnson, *A Hemisphere Apart: The Foundations of United States Policy toward Latin America* (Baltimore: Johns Hopkins University Press, 1990), 80–8L.
5. Johnson, *Hemisphere Apart*, 83, 85; Brenda Gayle Plummer, *Haiti and the United States: The Psychological Moment* (Athens: University of Georgia Press, 1992), chaps. 1–3.
6. James W. Gantenbein, ed., *The Evolution of Our Latin-American Policy: A Documentary Record* (New York: Octagon Books, 1981), 323–25; Dexter Perkins, *A History of the Monroe Doctrine* (1941; reprint ed., Boston: Little, Brown, 1963).
7. Johnson, *Hemisphere Apart*, 86; Walter LaFeber, *The American Age: United States Foreign Policy at Home and Abroad since 1750* (New York: W. W. Norton, 1989), 81, 85.
8. LaFeber, *American Age*, chaps. 3–5.
9. Walter LaFeber, *The New Empire: An Interpretation of American Expansion, 1860–1898* (Ithaca, NY: Cornell University Press, 1963), 61.
10. LaFeber, *New Empire*, chaps. 1, 4; LaFeber, *American Age*, chap. 6; Charles S. Campbell, *The Transformation of American Foreign Relations* (New York: Harper and Row, 1976).
11. Beisner, *From the Old Diplomacy to the New*, 19, 21, 24; David M. Pletcher, *The Awkward Years: American Foreign Relations under Garfield and Arthur* (Columbia: University of Missouri Press, 1962). In *Diplomacy of Trade and Investment,* Pletcher also warns against overstating the coherency of U.S. goals and methods. For a commentary, see James A. Field Jr., "American Imperialism: The Worst Chapter in Almost Any Book," *American Historical Review* 83 (June 1978): 644–83.

12. Michael H. Hunt, *Ideology and U.S. Foreign Policy* (New Haven: Yale University Press, 1987), 18, 58–68; Emily S. Rosenberg, *Spreading the American Dream: American Economic and Cultural Expansion, 1890–1945* (New York: Hill and Wang, 1982); Lars Schoultz, *Beneath the United States: A History of U.S. Policy toward Latin America* (Cambridge, MA: Harvard University Press, 1998).

13. Beisner, *From the Old Diplomacy to the New*, 74, 77–78; Richard Hofstadter, "Cuba, the Philippines, and Manifest Destiny," in *The Paranoid Style in American Politics and Other Essays*, ed. Richard Hofstadter (New York: Vintage Books, 1967), 145–87.

14. Thomas J. McCormick, *China Market: America's Quest for Informal Empire, 1893–1901* (Chicago: Quadrangle Books, 1967).

15. V. G. Kiernan, *America: The New Imperialism, from White Settlement to World Hegemony* (London: Zed Press, 1978), 1, 120; William Appleman Williams, *The Tragedy of American Diplomacy*, rev. ed. (New York: Delta, 1962), chap. 1.

16. Wilgus, "Blaine and the Pan American Movement," 662–67; Graham H. Stuart and James L. Tigner, *Latin America and the United States*, 6th ed. (Englewood Cliffs, NJ: Prentice-Hall, 1975), chap. 2.

17. Russell H. Bastert, "A New Approach to the Origins of Blaine's Pan American Policy," *Hispanic American Historical Review* 39 (May 1959): 375–412; Socolofsky and Spetter, *Presidency of Benjamin Harrison*, chaps. 7–8.

18. William F. Sater, *Chile and the United States: Empires in Conflict* (Athens: University of Georgia Press, 1990), chap. 3; Thomas F. McGann, *Argentina, the United States and the Inter-American System, 1889–1914* (Cambridge, MA: Harvard University Press, 1961), chaps. 1–2; J. Lloyd Mecham, *The United States and Inter-American Security, 1889–1960* (Austin: University of Texas Press, 1967), chap. 3; Joseph S. Tulchin, *Argentina and the United States: A Conflicted Relationship* (Boston: Twayne, 1990), chap. 2.

19. Socolofsky and Spetter, *Presidency of Benjamin Harrison*, 119; LaFeber, *New Empire*, 119.

20. Socolofsky and Spetter, *Presidency of Benjamin Harrison*, chap. 8; William F. Sater, *Chile and the War of the Pacific* (Lincoln: University of Nebraska Press, 1986); idem, *Chile and the United States*, chap. 3.

21. Joyce S. Goldberg, *The "Baltimore" Affair* (Lincoln: University of Nebraska Press, 1986), ix–x.

22. Gantenbein, *Evolution of Our Latin-American Policy*, 348, 355–58; Richard E. Welch Jr., *The Presidencies of Grover Cleveland* (Lawrence: University Press of Kansas, 1988), 157, 182–89; Bradford Perkins, *The Great Rapprochement: England and the United States, 1895–1914* (New York: Atheneum, 1968), chaps. 7–8.

23. Louis A. Pérez, *Cuba and the United States: Ties of Singular Intimacy* (Athens: University of Georgia Press, 1990), chap. 3.

24. John L. Offner, *An Unwanted War: The Diplomacy of the United States and Spain over Cuba, 1895–1898* (Chapel Hill: University of North Carolina

Press, 1992), 4, chap. 2; Louis L. Gould, *The Presidency of William McKinley* (Lawrence: University Press of Kansas, 1980), 62–63; Pérez, *Cuba and the United States*, 83–84; Welch, *Presidencies of Grover Cleveland*, 194–95.

25. Thomas A. Bailey, *A Diplomatic History of the American People,* 9th ed. (Englewood Cliffs, NJ: Prentice-Hall, 1974), 460; Joseph A. Fry, "William McKinley and the Coming of the Spanish-American War: A Study of the Besmirching and Redemption of an Historical Image," *Diplomatic History* 3 (Winter 1979): 77–98.

26. LaFeber, *New Empire*, 400.

27. Gould, *Presidency of William McKinley*, viii, 59–60; H. Wayne Morgan, *America's Road to Empire: The War with Spain and Overseas Expansion* (New York: John Wiley and Sons, 1965); David F. Trask, *The War with Spain in 1898* (New York: Macmillan, 1981).

28. Gould, *Presidency of McKinley*, vii–viii, 64–70; Offner, *Unwanted War*, chaps. 3, 4.

29. Offner, *Unwanted War*, chap. 7.

30. Gould, *Presidency of William McKinley*, 79–90; Offner, *Unwanted War*, 174–82, 225; Gantenbein, *Evolution of Our Latin-American Policy*, 465–78.

31. Pérez, *Cuba and the United States*, 94, 96; Gantenbein, *Evolution of Our Latin-American Policy*, 426.

32. Gould, *Presidency of William McKinley*, 88.

33. Ibid., 96; Trask, *War with Spain*, the most thorough military account.

34. Frank Freidel, *The Splendid Little War* (New York: Dell, 1958).

35. John Dobson, *Reticent Expansionism: The Foreign Policy of William McKinley* (Pittsburgh: Duquesne University Press, 1988), 115–16; Robert L. Beisner, *Twelve against Empire: The Anti-Imperialists, 1898–1900* (1968; reprint ed., New York: McGraw-Hill, 1971).

36. Pérez, *Cuba and the United States*, 102–13.

37. Lewis L. Gould, *The Presidency of Theodore Roosevelt* (Lawrence: University Press of Kansas, 1991), 14; Richard Hofstadter, *The American Political Tradition* (New York: Alfred A. Knopf, 1948), 228.

38. Gould, *Presidency of Theodore Roosevelt*, 14; Frederick W. Marks III, *Velvet on Iron: The Diplomacy of Theodore Roosevelt* (Lincoln: University of Nebraska Press, 1979); Richard H. Collin, *Theodore Roosevelt, Culture, Diplomacy, and Expansion: A New View of American Imperialism* (Baton Rouge: Louisiana State University Press, 1985); idem, *Theodore Roosevelt's Caribbean: The Panama Canal, the Monroe Doctrine, and the Latin American Context* (Baton Rouge: Louisiana State University Press, 1990).

39. Collin, *Roosevelt's Caribbean*, xiii–xiv; idem, *Roosevelt, Culture, Diplomacy, and Expansion*.

40. LaFeber, *American Age*, 221, 244.

41. Gould, *Presidency of Theodore Roosevelt*, 77–78; Marks, *Velvet on Iron*, chap. 2.

42. Walter LaFeber, *The Panama Canal: The Crisis in Historical Perspective*, rev. ed. (New York: Oxford University Press, 1979), 3, 8–9, 17; David G. McCullough, *The Path between the Seas: The Creation of the Panama Canal,*

1870–1914 (New York: Simon and Schuster, 1977); Collin, *Roosevelt's Caribbean*, pt. 2; Ronald H. Spector, *Professors of War: The Naval War College and the Development of the Naval Profession* (Newport, RI: Naval War College Press, 1977).

43. Collin, *Roosevelt's Caribbean*, 167, 169, 242–43; Gould, *Presidency of Theodore Roosevelt*, chap. 7.

44. Collin, *Roosevelt's Caribbean*, 239, 281; Gould, *Presidency of Theodore Roosevelt*, 97; Richard L. Lael, *Arrogant Diplomacy: U.S. Policy toward Colombia, 1903–1922* (Wilmington, DE: Scholarly Resources, 1987), chaps. 4–6; Stephen J. Randall, *Colombia and the United States: Hegemony and Interdependence* (Athens: University of Georgia Press, 1992), chap. 7.

45. LaFeber, *The Panama Canal*, 38; Lael, *Arrogant Diplomacy*, chap. 6, epilogue; Randall, *Colombia and the United States*, chap. 3; Gantenbein, *Evolution of Our Latin-American Policy*, 361–62; Gould, *Presidency of Theodore Roosevelt*, 175.

46. Gould, *Presidency of Theodore Roosevelt*, 176; Collin, *Roosevelt's Caribbean*, chap. 17; Lester D. Langley, *The Banana Wars: An Inner History of American Empire, 1900–1934* (Lexington: University Press of Kentucky, 1983), chaps. 3–4.

47. Pérez, *Cuba and the United States*, 155.

48. Collin, *Roosevelt's Caribbean*, 26–33; Charles A. Hale, "Political and Social Ideas in Latin America, 1870–1930," in *The Cambridge History of Latin America*, vol. 4, c. *1870–1930*, ed. Leslie Bethell (New York: Cambridge University Press, 1986); Gerald Martin, "The Literature, Music and Art of Latin America, 1870–1930," in *The Cambridge History of Latin America*, vol. 4, c. *1870–1930*, ed. Leslie Bethell (New York: Cambridge University Press, 1986), 414–17, 460–62.

49. Marks, *Velvet on Iron*, 180; Stuart and Tigner, *Latin America and the United States*, chap. 2; Mecham, *United States and Inter-American Security*, chap. 3.

50. Walter V. Scholes and Marie V. Scholes, *The Foreign Policies of the Taft Administration* (Columbia: University of Missouri Press, 1970), 12, 24–34.

51. Ibid., 35–39; Dana G. Munro, *Intervention and Dollar Diplomacy in the Caribbean, 1900–1921* (Princeton: Princeton University Press, 1964); David Healy, *Drive to Hegemony: The United States in the Caribbean, 1898–1917* (Madison: University of Wisconsin Press, 1988).

52. Walter LaFeber, *The American Search for Opportunity, 1865–1913*, vol. 2 in *The Cambridge History of American Foreign Relations* (New York: Cambridge University Press, 1993), preface.

53. Scholes and Scholes, *Foreign Policies of the Taft Administration*, 105–6; Paolo E. Coletta, *The Presidency of William Howard Taft* (Lawrence: University Press of Kansas, 1973), 190–91.

CHAPTER TWO

REVOLUTION, WAR, AND EXPANSION

1913–1929

FRANCISCO I. MADERO'S REVOLT in 1910 against President Porfirio Díaz in Mexico signaled the onset of a tumultuous age. During the second decade of the twentieth century, great revolutions in Mexico, China, and Russia overturned established orders, the consequences of which paralleled those of the First World War. In each instance the effects challenged prevailing beliefs and institutions. In response, President Woodrow Wilson articulated an ambitious vision of a new world system, the workability of which entailed two stipulations: The Great Powers must cooperate in defense of stability and peace, and the United States should accept a larger role in international affairs than ever before. For Latin America, meanwhile, an assortment of significant changes altered traditional relations with the outside world. As a consequence of the Great War the United States displaced the European powers as the dominant economic presence. Seeking to consolidate the advantage in the 1920s, Republican administrations under Presidents Warren Harding, Calvin Coolidge, and Herbert Hoover experimented with new stratagems in Latin America, anticipating a shift away from interventionist methods and toward the more subtle techniques of the Good Neighbor policy.

LATIN AMERICA AND THE OUTSIDE WORLD

For fifty years after independence in the 1820s, Latin American countries failed to count for much in the international arena. Largely self-contained and self-absorbed, they experienced the disorganizing effects of political turmoil, economic stagnation, and complex diplomatic quarrels over boundaries and territories. Such conditions became less pervasive during the latter third of the nineteenth century, following the establishment of more stable, oligarchical, and usually authoritarian regimes in many countries. During the 1870s and after, such governments endorsed an export-led model of economic development. Seeking trade and investment, government leaders opened their countries to foreign goods and capital and embraced the Europeans in a kind of a neocolonial economic relationship. Unlike the colonized regions of Asia and Africa, Latin America required no formal devices of imperial subjugation. Instead, an informal system came into existence, characterized by specialization of functions. Performing much like colonials, Latin Americans produced raw materials and agricultural commodities for the industrializing Europeans in return for capital and finished goods, thereby experiencing integration into the world market system.[1]

Among the largest countries, Argentina featured livestock and cereal products for export, especially wheat, maize, frozen and chilled beef, wool, hides, and linseed. Between 1875 and 1914, Argentine exports expanded impressively at an estimated rate of 5 percent per year. By 1914 the 7.8 million Argentines relied more heavily on overseas sales than any other group of Latin Americans and enjoyed the highest living standards. Their capital, Buenos Aires, stood out as a testimony. Affluent, cosmopolitan, and European in style and taste, the city symbolized Argentina as the embodiment of wealth, culture, and promise for the future.

Exports similarly served Brazil. A functioning monarchy until 1889–90, then a republic after a virtually bloodless revolution, Brazil relied upon coffee as the mainstay of profit. Indeed, in the years before the First World War, coffee often accounted for more than half of its overseas sales and made the economy vulnerable to cyclical tendencies within the world market. Periodic, often abrupt contractions in demand led to oversupply and low prices. In response, Brazilians experimented with "valorization" plans to restore higher prices by holding coffee off the market. Brazil, a nation of twenty-five million people in 1914, also sold tobacco and cotton in foreign markets and for a time experienced a rubber boom in the Amazon. Overall, the export trade affected different parts of this vast country unevenly, most of the benefits accruing to the coastal regions and the capital city, Rio de Janeiro.

Chile, inhabited by three million people in 1914, relied on copper exports. At the same time, the country avoided some of the dangers of monoculture—undue dependence on one product—by promoting the sale of wheat, wool, and nitrates. The last, especially important in balancing shifting demands for copper, counted heavily in trade with

Europe and the United States. During the early twentieth century the proceeds from nitrate sales totaled around 14 percent of the gross national product and provided the central government in Santiago with more than 50 percent of its operating revenues.[2]

In Mexico too, a country of twelve million people in 1910, economic dependencies characterized the links with the outside world. During the so-called Porfiriato, the era dominated by President Porfirio Díaz from 1876 to 1910, foreign investments centered on such crucial sectors as transportation, mining, and petroleum. Meanwhile, growth patterns typified Mexican overseas sales of silver, gold, rubber, hides, coffee, minerals, cattle, vegetables, and petroleum. The oil industry, controlled by British and U.S. companies, assumed special significance during the first decade of the twentieth century. In Mexico as elsewhere, bad effects occurred when declining demand within the world economy reduced export prices and income from exports.[3]

In the other countries of Central and South America, export economies typically featured monocultures. Colombia depended upon coffee, as did Venezuela until the petroleum boom beginning in the 1920s. In Central America and the Caribbean the pursuit of tropical agriculture produced bananas, coffee, sugar, and tobacco. Everywhere in Latin America the export trade rendered the participants susceptible to downward shifts in demand and price, underscoring unmistakably the risks of involvement in an unstable international economic environment.[4]

Financial relations, another form of dependency, also entailed a mixture of advantages and risks. In the view of many historians, "the era of high capitalism" before the First World War constituted "a golden age for foreign investment in Latin America." Great Britain was the largest investor, followed by Germany and France. Until the 1890s, small-scale U.S. investments centered on rails and mines in Mexico, sugar plantations in Cuba, and a few railroads and landed estates in Central America. During the early years of the twentieth century, U.S. investors also acquired a stake in Chilean and Peruvian mining. By 1914 some 87 percent of the direct, U.S. overseas investments were concentrated in Mexico, Cuba, Chile, and Peru. From around $300 million in 1897 the total increased to almost $1.6 billion in 1914, including direct investments of nearly $1.3 billion.

European investments, estimated at $7 billion in 1914, differed in some respects. More dispersed, they affected every country. In addition, a larger portion appeared in the construction of infrastructure, such as railways, ports, power companies, and utilities. Also, about a third went into government bonds. British investments of nearly $5 billion touched every country but had the greatest significance in Argentina, where they amounted to a third of the total foreign investments; in Brazil, they accounted for about a quarter; in Mexico, about a fifth. French and German investors favored the same three countries. These estimates suggest orders of magnitude and degrees of integration into the world system. The transfer of investment capital into regions without financial resources advanced the European interest in gaining access to Latin American markets and raw materials. The process also enabled Latin Americans to respond to overseas demands with the construction of necessary facilities—railroads, shipping services, and communication systems—without which Latin American producers could not have supplied the consumers. Consequently, more efficient, modern technologies came into existence in the export sectors, including mining, ranching, farming, and milling, and also complex networks of economic dependency. Throughout Latin America, foreign-owned mercantile houses were crucial in organizing the export and import trade, and foreign-owned banks provided the financial means.[5]

Some modern scholars, especially proponents of dependency theory, depict these arrangements as economically debilitating, more attuned to foreign needs than to Latin American interests, actually a form of exploitation. Not all contemporaries would have agreed with this assessment. According to the historian William Glade, most members of the Latin American elites at the end of the nineteenth century exhibited enthusiasm for "the benefits of what they perceived to be modernization" through engagement with the world economy.[6] There were exceptions, however. In Mexico, for instance, revolutionary leaders erected barriers to safeguard themselves against the influence of foreign economic power.

MEXICO AND OTHER MATTERS

The role of foreign interests in Mexico assumed critical importance during the revolutionary era. Indeed, according to one view, the integration of Mexico into the world economy contributed to political destabilization in 1910 by making the country more vulnerable to cyclical tendencies and economic downturns.[7] The revolution, sometimes understood in present-day historiography more as a struggle among rival elites than as a popular uprising, successfully ousted the dictator, Porfirio Díaz, in 1911 and then assumed many implications. During the ensuing factional strife, foreign interests, economic and other, came under threat both from the ongoing violence and the processes of reconstruction. The constitution of 1917 specifically introduced new dangers by incorporating the principles of nationalization and expropriation, thereby providing Mexican leaders with new instruments of control over the resources of their nation.[8]

Based on a political call for free elections and no boss rule, the revolt against Díaz in 1910 mobilized a broad but unstable constituency, incapable subsequently of sustaining President Francisco I. Madero's reformist regime. A series of uprisings culminated in a military takeover on 19 February 1913 in the course of which Madero was assassinated. General Victoriano Huerta, the army chief of staff and a principal instigator, then sought to impose order by authoritarian means and provoked an insurrection among dissidents in the northern states. Led by Venustiano Carranza, the governor of Coahuila, the so-called Constitutionalists denounced Huerta as a usurper and demanded his removal from power.[9]

Shocked by such events, Woodrow Wilson, the new president of the United States, reacted with committed determination. A former university professor with a Ph.D. in political science, Wilson had served as the president of Princeton University and also as a one-term, reform-minded governor in New Jersey. As a scholar and a devout Presbyterian—indeed, the son of a clergyman—Wilson preferred the high moral ground, prized the constraints of constitutional provision, and regarded Huerta's seizure of power as illegitimate and unacceptable. Unlike the leaders of Great Britain and the other European powers, Wilson withheld diplomatic recognition from Huerta's regime and tried to encourage mediation as the means to establish a legal government.[10] He wanted Huerta to stand aside. Huerta's refusal led to an intervention.

Meanwhile, Secretary of State William Jennings Bryan, a Democrat from Nebraska and a three-time failure as a presidential candidate, launched his own initiatives. Though lacking experience in foreign affairs, Bryan had high ambitions, some of them a bit unconventional. As a peace advocate, he urged the negotiation of "cooling off" treaties with every country in the world. These conciliation agreements required a nonpartisan investigation into the causes of a dispute before a resort to war. Latin American governments consented, except Mexico, still unrecognized under Huerta, and Colombia, still aggrieved over Panama. Bryan also envisioned a reduction of Latin American financial dependence on European bankers. He reasoned that cheap loans from the

U.S. government would permit "our country" to acquire "such an increased influence . . . that we could prevent revolutions, promote education, and advance stable and just governments."[11] Bryan's projects stirred some interest within the administration, but Wilson, unpersuaded, preferred to rely on conventional means and private bankers.

Another pressing concern for the new administration was the practice of unilateral intervention by the United States in Latin America. A variety of critics denounced the exercise of an international police power. Some lambasted Roosevelt's corollary as a hegemonic pretension, an inversion of the Monroe Doctrine's original intent to safeguard the Western Hemisphere against outside intervention. Others wanted to apply a multilateral definition so that joint measures with other nations could, if necessary, provide the means of safeguarding peace and order. A leader among them, Professor Hiram Bingham of Yale University, the discoverer of the Inca ruins at Machu Picchu in Peru, described the Monroe Doctrine as "an obsolete shibboleth." For him, it typified paternalistic condescension toward Latin Americans. As a better approach, he proposed some kind of collective action. In the event of trouble, the United States should call together "a family gathering" among the Western Hemisphere nations and "see what if anything needs to be done."[12]

Such advocacy won support from Progressive era reformers and radicals, including leaders in the peace movement, the labor unions, the churches, the universities, and the guild of international lawyers. For many, the development of a collective security system ranked high as a guarantee of national sovereignty. Similarly, Woodrow Wilson, a committed reformer with messianic instincts, favored exalted purposes among nations, seeking to advance mutual interests. Sometimes described as "a liberal-capitalist internationalist," Wilson aspired to the creation of a world system based on a League of Nations to defend representative democracy and economic capitalism. Presuming universal applicability, Wilson intended to serve humankind by extending U.S. values and models throughout the world.[13]

Sometimes flawed by arrogance and delusion, Wilson's emerging vision of international order drew inspiration from experiences with Latin America. On 11 March 1913, his first statement on foreign affairs set forth basic principles and expectations, central among them his belief in international harmony achieved through mutual respect for rights and obligations. To such ends, he invited "the friendship and . . . the confidence of our sister republics" and "the most cordial understanding and cooperation" in relations with them. With General Huerta presumably in mind, Wilson also insisted upon the rule of law. Accordingly, he opposed "those who seek to seize the power of government to advance their own personal interests or ambition" and favored "those who act in the interest of peace and honor, who protect private rights, and respect the restraint of constitutional provision."

In Mexico, Wilson's positions resulted in confusion and contradiction. On 10 October 1913, Huerta dashed the U.S. hope for mediation by dissolving the Chamber of Deputies and declaring himself a candidate for the presidency. On the following day, Sir Lionel Carden, the new British minister, presented his credentials in Mexico City. His arrival impressed U.S. leaders as a deliberate British affront; to them, Huerta now appeared as both an illicit tyrant and a creature of British imperialism.

Wilson discussed this issue on 27 October 1913 in his celebrated address before the Southern Commercial Congress at Mobile, Alabama. Stating his concern over European economic domination in Latin America, he warned that foreign concessions and special privileges threatened self-determination; Mexico, in his view, already had fallen victim. Nevertheless, Wilson promised "emancipation" if Latin Americans would assist in the promotion of "true constitutional liberty" throughout the world. As a pledge of good faith, he affirmed, the United States "never again" would seek "one additional foot of territory by conquest."

Sometimes regarded as a promise of nonintervention, the Mobile address actually anticipated broader involvement in Latin American affairs. In what verged on a declaration of economic war, Wilson wanted Latin American support in rolling back European presences. Colonel Edward M. House, a trusted friend and adviser, understood the intent. For him, Wilson's speech established "a new interpretation of the Monroe Doctrine": For almost a century the United States had tried "to keep Europe from securing political control of any state in the Western Hemisphere"; now, the Wilson administration had taken a position that it is "just as reprehensible to permit foreign states to secure financial control of those weak unfortunate republics." Similarly, John Lind, a special diplomatic emissary to Mexico, expressed his belief that Huerta's continuation in power would make the country "a European annex, industrially, financially, politically."

Mounting suspicions had the effect of producing a chill in U.S. relations with Great Britain. Although British leaders disparaged Wilson's claim as a consequence of bewildered hypocrisy, historian Friedrich Katz credits the president with a correct understanding of

British aims. As Katz shows, the British government consistently opposed revolutionary factions and supported counterrevolutionary
groups. Such positions, in his view, accurately reflected British concerns for economic stakes and petroleum interests.[14]

The Wilson administration, meanwhile, adopted other ambitious
plans. To advance various forms of political and economic integration,
the leaders focused attention on Argentina, Brazil, and Chile. As the
most populous and influential nations in South America, the so-called
ABC countries also contained prospective customers. Close relations
already existed in dealings with Brazil. As a matter of conscious design,
Brazilians had forged an "unwritten alliance" with the United States
early in the twentieth century through the policies of Foreign Minister
José Maria da Silva Paranhos, also known as the Baron de Rio Branco,
who wanted to enlist the United States as a trading partner and a
counterweight against Argentina. For the United States, Brazil's diplomatic status also ranked high. Before Wilson, only Brazil had qualified for an ambassadorial appointment; the other South American
republics received ministers, a designation of lesser rank. Seeking
more cordial ties during the summer of 1914, the Wilson administration established diplomatic parity by exchanging ambassadors also
with Argentina and Chile.[15]

Troubled by trade deficits in South America, the Wilson administration also promoted commercial expansion. The Panama Canal,
scheduled for completion soon, amplified high expectations. U.S. leaders intended to take advantage by renovating the merchant marine
and developing regular steamship routes to South America. The Federal Reserve Act of December 1913 rectified another shortcoming by
authorizing national banks of the United States to establish branches
in foreign countries. The establishment in Latin America of such facilities would free U.S. commerce from dependencies on British banking institutions.[16] But then new difficulties with Mexico produced an
obstruction.

An incident at Tampico, a Mexican port city on the Caribbean
coast, set the trouble in motion. On 9 April 1914, General Huerta's
troops arrested some U.S. sailors who had wandered into a restricted
zone. In response, U.S. Admiral Henry T. Mayo wanted a formal apology. So did Woodrow Wilson. At the same time, another problem impended. The Ypiranga, a German commercial vessel carrying weapons
for Huerta, soon would arrive at Veracruz, the principal eastern port.
Abjuring diplomacy, Wilson obtained authorization from the Congress

to force a showdown. On 21 April 1914, he seized Veracruz by sending in U.S. Marines. In this way, he intended to block the arms shipment, cut off customs revenues to Huerta, and avoid damaging the petroleum installations around Tampico. He erred by anticipating only light resistance: The Veracruz defenders lost over two hundred soldiers, and war threatened. Not only Huerta but also his enemies, the Constitutionalists, condemned the invasion as an unacceptable violation of Mexican sovereignty.

At the very least, the episode revealed limitations in Wilson's understanding of harmony among nations. Paradoxically, he conceived of the intervention as a defense of Mexican self-determination against an illegitimate tyranny backed by British imperialists, but in so doing he underestimated Mexican nationalist reactions. Fortunately, his courtship of Argentina, Brazil, and Chile paid off when their mediation offer enabled him to avoid an unwanted conflict. An international conference at Niagara Falls, Canada, facilitated face-saving devices, achieved cosmetic effects, and provided a way out of war. In Mexico, meanwhile, General Alvaro Obregón's Constitutionalist Army advanced on Mexico City during the summer of 1914 and forced General Huerta into exile.[17]

The leaders in the Wilson administration rejoiced that multilateral measures had assisted in keeping the peace. Colonel House indulged in high praise, comparing the actions of the ABC countries with the efforts of friends and neighbors who in times of crisis banded together to fight house fires. Similarly, Robert Lansing, the counselor of the State Department, called for efforts to build on that achievement. In a June 1914 memorandum, "The Present Nature and Extent of the Monroe Doctrine and Its Need for Restatement," he presented a case against unilateral intervention by the United States and in favor of multilateral approaches to advance "fraternal responsibility" with Latin Americans.

Much like Bryan earlier, Lansing also worried about European encroachments in the Western Hemisphere by means of loans and investments. Specifically, he warned against the "European acquisition of political control through the agency of financial control over an American republic." Similarly concerned, Colonel House addressed this same issue during a European visit in July 1914. In conversations with British, French, and German leaders, House inquired whether they would join with the United States in an agreement to reduce the costs of international borrowing. In his private diary, however, House expressed misgivings, accusing the Europeans of subverting weak, debt-ridden Latin American states through demands for "concessions" and "usurious interest." He wanted to find a better way—but his timing was all wrong. During the summer of 1914 the Great Powers of Europe embarked upon world war.[18]

PAN AMERICAN INITIATIVES

The consequences of the Great War extended into all inhabited regions. In the Western Hemisphere the initial impact injured Latin American economies by obstructing the flow of capital and goods. In response, the United States assumed a larger role as the prime purchaser of raw materials and the main supplier of finished products. During the three years from 1 July 1914 to 30 June 1917, trade between the United States and Latin America increased by more than 100 percent. In contrast, ambitious U.S. political initiatives accomplished much less. For the Wilson administration, the war occasioned both opportunities and rebuffs.

Remaining neutral until the spring of 1917, the United States responded to the war by attempting to insulate the Western Hemisphere against it. As part of this endeavor, it also courted Latin American governments, seeking more intimate political and economic ties. The opening of the Panama Canal in August 1914 served as a powerful symbol. This grand event, knitting the Western Hemisphere more closely together, reduced the distance from Colón on the Atlantic to Balboa on the Pacific from 10,500 nautical miles, the distance around South America, to 45, the actual length of the new passage. The Western Hemisphere had become a smaller place.[19]

The prospect of commercial opportunity encouraged a variety of promotional activities sponsored by leaders in the Wilson administration. On 10 September 1914 a Latin American Trade Conference assembled in Washington, DC, at the behest of Secretary of State William Jennings Bryan and Secretary of Commerce William C. Redfield. Delegates representing the U.S. Chamber of Commerce, the Southern Commercial Congress, and the National Foreign Trade Council enthusiastically called for improved transportation and banking facilities and also for more effective sales techniques, conforming more closely to Latin American tastes and preferences. Elsewhere across the United States the prospect of commercial expansion into Latin America stimulated similar growing interest among local chambers of commerce, boards of trade, and business associations. Even President Wilson became a booster. In his annual message to the Congress on 8 December 1914, he urged the United States "as never before, to serve itself and to serve mankind; ready with its resources, its forces of production, and its means of distribution."

Wilson also experimented with peacekeeping devices. Inspired mainly by Colonel House, these efforts eventuated in a proposed Pan American treaty that among other things called for a regional collective security system, featuring compulsory arbitration, and a multilateral definition of the Monroe Doctrine. House initiated the discussions late in November 1914 by urging Wilson to pay "greater attention" to issues in foreign affairs. Specifically, he wanted the president to devise "a constructive international policy" demonstrating "that friendship, justice, and kindliness were more potent than the mailed fist." House criticized the legacies of unilateral intervention. By "wielding the 'big stick' and dominating the two Continents," he averred, the United States had "lost the friendship and commerce of South and Central America and the European countries had profited by it." A better approach could have more desirable consequences by bringing "North and South America together in a closer union" and "welding together . . . the two western continents."

Three weeks later, in December 1914, House again raised the issue, this time exhorting Wilson "to play a great and beneficent part in the European tragedy." Declaring that "there was one thing [Wilson] could do at once," establish a "model" for peace based on "a policy that would weld the western hemisphere together," he sketched out a draft proposal for collective security arrangements to guarantee territorial integrity, political independence, and republican forms of government. Much impressed, Wilson authorized House to engage the ambassadors of Argentina, Brazil, and Chile in conversations.

The ensuing discussions elicited favorable responses from Rómulo S. Naón of Argentina and Domicio da Gama of Brazil but not from Eduardo Suárez Mújica, the Chilean ambassador. For him, the implementation of such arrangements suggested the possibility of embarrassment over Tacna and Arica, the nitrate-rich provinces taken from Peru in the War of the Pacific. According to the Treaty of Ancón in 1884, a plebiscite should decide the question of ownership of these regions, but none ever had taken place. Chileans also described the proposed commitment in defense of republican institutions as a limitation on national sovereignty and possibly an invitation for U.S. intervention. Undeterred, House pressed on, including in later drafts other requirements for arbitration of territorial and boundary disputes and endorsing Bryan's "cooling off" formula.[20]

Meanwhile, a new civil war was ravaging Mexico. After defeating Huerta the victorious Constitutionalist coalition dissolved into feuding factions, pitting Carranza and his ally Obregón against Francisco Villa and Emiliano Zapata. Wilson again sought peace through reconciliation but without much positive effect. House espoused joint action with the ABC countries as the best means of solution. He also rejoiced when Secretary of State Bryan resigned his position in June 1915 as a protest over the handling of the *Lusitania* crisis. In House's view, Bryan was a fool and a bungler who had obstructed the pursuit of wise and workable policies, whereas his successor, Robert Lansing, the former State Department counselor, shared some of House's convictions and appeared more manageable. Lansing too believed that Germans were "utterly hostile to all nations with democratic institutions" and were hatching plots in Mexico, Haiti, Santo Domingo, and "probably in other Latin American republics." As a counter, he favored "a Pan American doctrine" and the maintenance of "friendly relations with Mexico." In his view, the latter required the diplomatic recognition of Carranza, now regarded as "the stronger."

Beginning in August 1915, Secretary of State Lansing orchestrated moves in conjunction with six countries. Together with representatives from Argentina, Brazil, Chile, Bolivia, Guatemala, and Uruguay, Lansing exhorted the contending Mexican factions to settle their differences. In response, Villa and Zapata took conciliatory positions, supposedly ready for a compromise. But Carranza, an intransigent, would not bend; he insisted that only his government possessed the attributes of sovereignty. Ultimately, Lansing and the other diplomats arrived at the same conclusion. On 9 October 1915, they extended diplomatic recognition on a de facto basis, accepting the existence of Carranza's regime as stable and functioning.

Wilson construed the decision as a triumph for his adherence to high principle. For him, Mexico's right to self-determination had survived the test; in a report to the Congress on 7 December 1915, he claimed, "Her fortunes are in her own hands." He also applauded the good effects of his Pan American policy, choosing to interpret the outcome as a vindication of international cooperation, "a full and honorable association as of partners." To build on this achievement, he publicly endorsed the proposed Pan American Treaty on 6 January 1916 at the Second Pan American Scientific Conference in Washington, DC. By such means, he asserted, the nations of the Western Hemisphere could uphold "the principles of absolute political equality among the states" and "the solid, eternal foundations of justice and humanity."[21]

This pledge notwithstanding, Wilson's policies in the Western Hemisphere never really achieved much coherence. Instead, they manifested inconsistencies and contradictions, as subsequent interventions in Caribbean countries confirmed. In a phrase, Wilson had extreme difficulty reconciling his presumed commitment to self-determination with other U.S. interests in upholding peace, order, and security. In 1915, political turmoil caused violence and disorder in Haiti. Similarly in 1916, instabilities threatened the Dominican Republic. In each instance, the Wilson administration responded by sending in military forces. U.S. leaders justified such measures on grounds of wartime exigency, claiming that threats of German subversion and defense of the Panama Canal required them. In each instance, derogatory racial stereotypes and cultural assumptions provided additional incentives by disparaging the alleged inability of the inhabitants, especially those of African descent, to govern themselves. Once the marines had moved in, U.S. occupation authorities managed government functions and finances. In response, Dominican and Haitian resistance movements precipitated hard-fought guerrilla struggles. Called the "banana wars" by the historian Lester D. Langley, they featured small-scale but brutal violence in which native contingents waged something like "wars of national liberation" against the soldiers of the United States.[22]

Meanwhile, the Wilson administration launched other kinds of programs to win over Latin Americans. On 24 May 1915 the first Pan American Financial Conference assembled in Washington, DC, featuring delegates in attendance from eighteen Latin American countries. The main organizer, Secretary of the Treasury William Gibbs McAdoo, intended to focus on trade and finance. Specifically, he called for consideration of the principal economic problems emanating from the Great War. McAdoo anticipated that the United States would have to step in, replacing the Europeans as the main supplier of goods and capital. To coordinate the pursuit of practical solutions, the conference brought into existence a body known as the International High Commission. It consisted of finance ministers and other specialists from each country who in future years would meet periodically to issue recommendations and advisements—most of which, as things turned out, eluded implementation.

For leaders in the Wilson administration, commercial statistics bolstered high spirits. Between August 1914 and August 1915, U.S. exports totaled $3 billion, at that time the largest amount ever in a single year. Indeed, the United States surpassed Great Britain as the world leader. In South America, U.S. exports rose from $38.7 million during the first six months of 1914 to $60.6 billion during the first six months of 1915, while South American sales in the United States expanded from $105.5 to $153 million. Although these figures marked an undesirable deficit in the balance of payments, they failed to dissipate the optimism over long-term expectations: The National City Bank of New York created branches in Montevideo, Buenos Aires, Rio de Janeiro, Santos, São Paulo, and Havana; the Caribbean and Southern Steamship Company initiated regular voyages from the United States to Argentina and Brazil; and President Wilson accepted a commitment to build a modern merchant marine, fully capable of carrying increased trade.

Though encouraged by such gains in Latin America, U.S. leaders still worried about resumed European competition after the war. They expected that Great Britain and France especially would not submit readily to a permanently weakened economic position in the New World. Indeed, British and French behavior at the Paris Economic Conference in June 1916 intensified such concerns, when the Allies established plans to punish their enemies, mainly the Germans, through the adoption of a mercantilist, state-directed system. The main features included a variety of restrictive devices such as trade preferences, state subsidies, government protection of foreign markets, pooling agreements, and cooperative purchases of raw materials. In 1915 the Central Powers had devised their own *Mitteleuropa* plan, intended to promote economic consolidation through the exclusion of the British, the French, and the Russians. To officials in the Wilson administration, all this portended ill, and they anticipated the possibility of drastic measures. Secretary of State Lansing, for example, reasoned that "the best way to fight combination is by combination." He wanted "some definite plan to meet the proposed measures of the allies" in conjunction with Latin Americans. Similarly, Henry P. Fletcher, then U.S. ambassador to Chile and later to Mexico, advised collective arrangements with the ABC countries to hold "our market position in South America." Somewhat fantastically, he also suggested the establishment of "an American Economic League for mutual protection."[23]

Meanwhile, mounting political difficulties destroyed the negotiations over Wilson's proposed Pan American treaty. At first, Chilean opposition accounted for delays. Later, the U.S. punitive expedition into Mexico in 1916 ruined the plan completely by calling Woodrow Wilson's good faith into question. Francisco Villa precipitated the crisis on 9 March 1916 by attacking the border town of Columbus, New Mexico, probably in an effort to demonstrate Carranza's incapacity to

Punitive Expedition

safeguard the international frontier. In response, the Wilson administration sent in military forces commanded by General John J. Pershing. By insisting upon a right of "hot pursuit," the president created an impasse. Carranza for his own political reasons could not sanction Pershing's presence and wanted him out of Mexico as soon as possible; Wilson insisted upon guarantees against future border violations. Subsequent armed clashes between Mexican and U.S. troops in the northern towns of Parral and Carrizal caused more trouble, even a likelihood of war. Argentina's offer of mediation presented the Wilson administration with a dilemma bearing directly on the President's credibility in the rest of Latin America. Robert Lansing understood the issue and dreaded the prospect of a full-scale intervention in Mexico. Any such action would have "a very bad effect on our Pan-American program"; indeed, "all Latin America" would regard it as "extremely distasteful." Yet border security also had importance, especially in 1916, a presidential election year. Even suggestions of weakness along the border could demolish Wilson as a viable candidate.[24]

Thus constrained by political imperatives, U.S. leaders spurned the Argentine offer and kept the punitive expedition in Mexico; at the same time, they sought direct negotiations. In this way, the Wilson administration retained a free hand but simultaneously wrecked the Pan American pact. During the summer and fall of 1916, while the United States maintained the pressure by refusing to withdraw and insisting upon Carranza's responsibility for border defense, a joint Mexican-American commission sought solutions. The United States also tried to broaden the scope by including discussions of foreign property rights in Mexico, an issue that assumed ever greater importance during the latter part of 1916 during the proceedings of the Mexican Constitutional Convention.

This assembly promulgated the Mexican constitution of 1917 on 5 February and sanctioned the inclusion of radical provisions. From the U.S. viewpoint, Article 27 was an object of special concern: It allowed for the expropriation of privately owned property and for the nationalization of mineral resources. To Mexican leaders, these claims affirmed the prerogatives of national sovereignty and permitted no complaint from other countries through the agencies of international diplomacy. Among outraged U.S. critics, such expressions of hyperinflated nationalism aroused fears over the sanctity of foreign property rights in Mexico; U.S. property holders demanded protection from their government. Unable to reconcile competing interests, Wilson simply withdrew the

art 27

punitive force on 5 February 1917—coincidentally the same day the constitution took effect. Soon afterward, the United States became a participant in the First World War.[25]

WAGING WAR, MAKING PEACE

In 1917–18 the Wilson administration entered the First World War, cultivated cordial connections with Latin Americans, and envisioned an independent role in shaping the postwar world. As a safeguard against subsequent European competition, U.S. leaders still advocated Pan American solidarity but elicited centrifugal tendencies. Notably, Mexico and Argentina espoused Pan Hispanic alternatives, calling for Latin American unity against the United States, while Brazil remained the centerpiece of Wilson's policy in South America.

The German resumption of unrestricted submarine warfare on 1 February 1917 precipitated the U.S. entry into the war. Seeking a quick decision through decisive boldness, German leaders revoked the *Sussex* pledge of May 1916, making Allied merchant ships and passenger liners once again the objects of attack and endangering neutral vessels in the war zone around the British Isles. For the Germans, loans from private U.S. banks to the Allies already had created an informal alliance, but they gambled on a British collapse before U.S. participation could make much difference. Hoping to force a reconsideration by the Germans, Wilson severed diplomatic relations on 3 February 1917.

The German U-boat offensive compelled Latin American governments to decide whether to follow the U.S. lead. The first reactions predictably affirmed support from Cuba, Panama, Haiti, Nicaragua, and Brazil. Chile, in contrast, wanted no trouble with any of the belligerents; Mexico remained aloof; and Argentina pursued an independent course. Indeed, under President Hipólito Yrigoyen, the Argentines endorsed a call for ending the war through neutral mediation. The Wilson administration responded with suspicions of German intrigue in each country.

Though probably inflated, U.S. apprehensions over German activities in Latin America had some basis in fact. In the summer of 1915, German agents supported General Victoriano Huerta's abortive bid to regain power in Mexico. Though frustrated by U.S. Department of Justice agents who arrested the deposed dictator as he moved toward the border, the scheme implied a German interest in diverting the United States from Europe by provoking trouble with Mexico. For similar reasons, Francisco Villa's raid on Columbus, New Mexico, encouraged unproven but much discussed allegations of German incitement. For Germany, Foreign Minister Arthur Zimmermann's clandestine courtship of Carranza's government resulted in a disaster. The details appear most fully and accurately in Friedrich Katz's *The Secret War in Mexico*. In broad outline, Zimmermann sent coded messages to Heinrich von Eckhardt, the German minister in Mexico City, on 15 January 1917, informing him of plans to resume unrestricted submarine warfare. Zimmermann also proposed the possibility of an alliance with Carranza. Under its terms the two countries would make war and peace together, and Mexico as a reward would recover its lost provinces of Texas, New Mexico, and Arizona. The plan went awry when British intelligence intercepted the transmissions and then, after appropriate deceptions, turned the information over to the United States. When published in the newspapers on 1 March 1917, the Zimmermann telegram appeared proof positive of German duplicity. Meanwhile, the German refusal to rescind the U-boat decision moved Wilson closer to war. Convinced that only his vision of harmony among nations contained the mechanism of peace for the future, Wilson paradoxically asked the Congress for a declaration of war on 2 April 1917, believing that only by taking part in the war could he later have a voice in establishing peace.

The U.S. entry into the conflict elicited sympathetic but diverse responses in Latin America. Most governments applauded the U.S. defense of neutral rights but otherwise reacted according to their own interests. Within two weeks, ten countries affirmed neutrality: Argentina, Chile, Colombia, Costa Rica, Mexico, Paraguay, Peru, El Salvador, Uruguay, and Venezuela. Seven others broke relations: Bolivia, Brazil, the Dominican Republic, Ecuador, Guatemala, Haiti, and Honduras. Two declared war: Cuba and Panama. Later in 1917, Brazil, Costa Rica, Guatemala, Haiti, Honduras, and Nicaragua also followed with war declarations. These countries went along with the United States in part because of expected rewards. Cut off from European markets and capital, Brazil supported the United States with a war declaration in October 1917 after a series of torpedo attacks on Brazilian ships; its actual participation consisted of naval deployments in the South Atlantic. The others played no part at all. As neutrals, Mexico and Argentina caused worry by urging mediation to stop the fighting. Such efforts failed but encouraged U.S. leaders to look for other signs of pro-German sympathies. In Mexico the already-suspect Carranza produced more irritation by upholding antiforeign provisions in the constitution of 1917. In Argentina, Yrigoyen similarly aroused mistrust because of his allegedly pro-German nationalism. Nicknamed "El Peludo" after "a hairy kind of subterranean armadillo," also secretive and reclusive, Yrigoyen pugnaciously pursued his own course, independent of the United States.[26]

While preparing for war, the Wilson administration also got ready for peace. To establish a planning agency, early in September 1917 the president created the Inquiry. Consisting of experts, mainly professors and journalists, the members formulated peace terms based upon their understanding of history, geography, economics, and ethnography. In regard to Latin America the recommendations typically incorporated hegemonic and paternalistic assumptions. One report, for example, assigned to the United States "a dominating influence in peace discussions so far as the Americas and Mexico are concerned." The reason was obvious: a simple acknowledgment of the U.S. "historical position" and "special relation to all the nations of the western hemisphere."[27]

After the fighting the planners expected a resumption of "economic warfare." Consequently, the Wilson administration perceived the British mission to South America in the spring of 1918 as an alarming portent. Headed by Maurice de Bunsen, a special ambassador, the delegates had instructions to promote British commerce and goodwill for the future. U.S. observers viewed such initiatives as dangers. To counter them, Colonel House called for international commitments in support of free trade, nonaggression, and representative democracy. In other words, he wanted to adopt a set of rules favorable to the United States.

The Mexican constitution of 1917 remained a source of ongoing difficulty. On 6 June 1918, addressing a group of visiting Mexican journalists, President Wilson ill-advisedly told them of his "sincere friendship" for their country, and compounded the error by recalling the provisions of the failed Pan American treaty. According to him, the proposed agreement had placed a laudable emphasis on multilateral endeavors so that "if any one of us . . . violates the political independence or the territorial integrity of any of the others, all the others will jump on her." Mexican critics immediately spotted the inconsistency, and newspaper editorials in Mexico City attacked U.S. opposition to Article 27 of the new constitution. On 2 April 1918 the State Department had filed an official protest, warning against the infringement of U.S. property rights. Mexican officials regarded the act as a threat of intervention and devised an ideological defense under the terms

of the so-called Carranza Doctrine. Consistent with the nationalist requirements of the Mexican Revolution, Carranza depicted Article 27
as an affirmation of Mexican sovereignty, taking precedence over foreign conceptions of property rights. He also invoked nonintervention
as an absolute principle and exhorted the rest of Latin America to join
with him in repudiating the Monroe Doctrine.

These responses unsettled U.S. officials. The ambassador to
Mexico, Henry P. Fletcher, warned of dire consequences. In his alarmist view, Carranza wanted to eliminate "the financial, economic, and
political influence of the United States in Mexico" and "to isolate the
United States and destroy its influence in this hemisphere." Fletcher
warned, "Under the shibboleth of this Carranza Doctrine," Mexico
would "enforce Article 27 . . . and justify its disregard of the elemental
principles of justice and fair dealings in treatment of foreigners."[28] Big
trouble was brewing. However overblown, Fletcher's perceptions expressed the fears of oil men and politicians who opposed the Mexican
constitution and were spoiling for a showdown at the end of the First
World War.

At the Paris Peace Conference, Woodrow Wilson assumed the
statesman's role. In pursuit of peace, he called for a purge to rid the
European system of autocracy, imperialism, and militarism: that is, those
practices he regarded as causes of the war in the first place. According
to his plan the Central Powers, perceived as the aggressors, unquestion-
ably required an array of changes to bring about reform and rehabilitation. But the same held true for the Allies. Wilson had never identified
very closely with Allied war aims and opposed the division of the spoils
among the victors, as envisioned by the so-called secret treaties. He
preferred "a peace among equals." His Fourteen Points statement of
8 January 1918 established his principal goals. Appropriately described
by some historians as a "liberal-capitalist internationalist," Wilson regarded representative democracy, free trade, and international cooperation as essential parts of a durable peace settlement. Other points
centered on specific territorial issues, emphasizing the right of national
self-determination. The fourteenth point, his most cherished, called
for the creation of a League of Nations.[29]

Wilson's plan for world peace incorporated devices with which he
had already experimented in Latin America. The proposal for defense
of national self-determination through collective security drew upon
many of the same assumptions as the Pan American treaty. Latin American critics immediately identified discrepancies. They described

14 Point
&
Monroe
Doct.

Wilson's hegemonic practices in the Western Hemisphere as contradictions of high-blown principles. How could the Monroe Doctrine coex-
ist with the Fourteen Points? Was not the exercise of a self-proclaimed
hemispheric police power by the United States inconsistent with conceptions of self-determination and international responsibility?

Latin American issues possessed only peripheral importance at the
Paris conference. Dominated by European concerns, the peacemaking
centered on the consequences of the Great War, the collapse of the
Russian, Turkish, and Austro-Hungarian Empires, and the threat of
Communist revolution emanating from the newly created Union of
Soviet Socialist Republics. But Latin Americans wanted to play a part
and eleven nations sent delegations: Bolivia, Brazil, Cuba, Ecuador,
Guatemala, Haiti, Honduras, Nicaragua, Panama, Peru, and Uruguay.
Mexico contributed an unofficial envoy, Alberto J. Pani, who lobbied
against the influence of the big oil companies and the possibility of in-
tervention in his country.

Paris
Conf

The official proceedings began on 12 January 1919. As various committees and commissions exercised authority over routine matters by
conducting investigations, assembling information, and devising recommendations, competition for seats produced high levels of rivalry
among the smaller states. The big decisions came about in other ways.
Wielding primary authority at first, the Supreme Council, or the Council of Ten, comprised the heads of state and the foreign ministers of the
five Great Powers: Great Britain, France, Italy, Japan, and the United
States. Later, the Council of Four functioned as the power center, featuring Prime Minister David Lloyd George of Great Britain, Premier
Georges Clemenceau of France, Premier Vittorio Orlando of Italy, and
President Woodrow Wilson of the United States. The top priority for
the Europeans was the restoration of stable and functioning political
and economic systems in their domains. For them, the threat posed by
the Russian Bolshevik Revolution required immediate attention as did
the definition of German peace terms, the disposition of German colonies, the settlement of territorial issues in Central and Eastern Europe,
and the arrangement of continental security. For Wilson, in contrast, the creation of the League of Nations became the first obligation, transcending all others. Upon completion of the League of
Nations Covenant, he presented the provisions to the assembled delegates
on 14 February 1919, exclaiming, "A living thing is born." For Latin
Americans, Great-Power dominance over the proceedings caused mistrust
and bitterness. Although most favored a League of Nations as a means of

keeping the United States under control in their part of the world, they disliked the insignificance of the roles assigned to them. Their principal concerns, mainly trade issues and border disputes, figured only tangentially in the peacemaking process, and then usually as diversions.

Such was the case with the Monroe Doctrine. At the peace conference, the leaders of the United States insisted upon formal international recognition of what for them had become a hallowed creed. Consequently, under authority of Article 21, the peace treaty endorsed the doctrine by upholding "the validity of international engagements, such as treaties of arbitration or regional understandings . . . for securing the maintenance of peace." Alberto J. Pani, the unofficial Mexican observer, sounded warnings, cautioning that such a stipulation might serve the United States as a justification for military intervention in Mexico. For the same reason, Carranza, an international outsider, repudiated the Monroe Doctrine altogether, calling it a "species of tutelage" unacceptable to Latin Americans.

After the war, during the year 1919, difficulties with Mexico provoked growing criticism in the United States. Ambassador Henry P. Fletcher played a leading role by complaining repeatedly of mistreatment of foreigners and came close to advocating the transformation of Mexico into a U.S. protectorate something like Cuba. In his words, he wanted to issue a "call upon the recognized Government of Mexico to perform its duties as a government" or else "accept disinterested assistance from the United States." This hard-line position obtained support from such powerful interest groups as the Oil Producers Association and the National Association for the Protection of American Rights in Mexico and from many Republicans. Senator Albert Bacon Fall of New Mexico, a border-state politician with long-standing interests in Mexican affairs, abominated Carranza's regime and regarded Wilson's policies toward it as contemptible. To force a change, he proposed measures that included the withdrawal of diplomatic recognition from Carranza, the encouragement of a military revolt against him, and the installation of a new government more friendly to the United States. On 8 August 1919, Fall instigated a Senate investigation into Mexican affairs by means of which he intended to weaken both Wilson and Carranza.

Wilson's foreign policies were in deep trouble after the Paris conference. For reasons of politics and principle, Republicans in the Senate spurned collective security by rejecting the provisions of the Versailles treaty and the responsibilities of the League of Nations. Wilson responded by undertaking an exhausting speaking tour to mobilize public support, in the course of which he suffered a personal catastrophe. On 25 September 1919 he collapsed after a speech in Pueblo, Colorado, and then experienced the effects of a cerebral thrombosis. The illness deprived his pro-League supporters of leadership at a critical time and may have made him more intransigent. He ruled out a compromise with his opponents when votes in the Senate went against him and thereby doomed the larger endeavor: The defeat of the treaty also meant rejection of the League.

The crisis in Mexican affairs took place during a showdown early in December 1919. Using his investigation as a forum, Senator Fall introduced a resolution calling for a break in diplomatic relations with Mexico. From his sickbed in the White House, President Wilson managed to frustrate the plan by stating his absolute opposition to it. He then moved to rebuild his shattered administration by naming a new secretary of state. Robert Lansing resigned early in 1920 after losing the president's confidence, presumably for insubordination; Wilson regarded him as a usurper of presidential prerogatives because of differences over the peace treaty and Mexico. His successor, Bainbridge Colby, a New York lawyer and former Progressive party member, had no diplomatic experience but nevertheless creditably served out the remainder of the term. Among other things, he tried to improve relations with Latin America, mainly by opposing the practice of U.S. intervention. For that reason, he has been characterized as a precursor of the Good Neighbor policy, the less direct, more accommodating approach favored by President Franklin D. Roosevelt in the 1930s. Though probably exaggerated, this view correctly underscores Colby's more discerning appreciation of Latin American affairs. Notably, he questioned the wisdom of sustaining Caribbean protectorates and undertook a goodwill tour into South America in 1920. His voyage was a symbolic gesture signifying the ailing president's ongoing but unfulfilled efforts in the Western Hemisphere. Overall, Wilson's emphasis on Pan American political initiatives had failed.[30]

THE REPUBLICAN RESTORATION

Warren G. Harding's election to the presidency in 1920 restored the Republicans to power after an eight-year absence and initiated a set of alternative approaches in foreign affairs. Republicans embraced a more "independent," or "limited," version of internationalism than Wilson's. For them, the former president's conception of collective security implied unacceptable risks. They too favored peace, order, and liberal capitalism but employed more restricted forms of international engagement. Specifically, they rejected prior military commitments in defense of other countries. Instead, they sought to keep the peace through political accommodations and the application of international law. Employing the former at the Washington conference in 1921–22, they tried to freeze the status quo among the Great Powers in China and to keep naval arms competition under control. Using the latter in 1928, they endorsed the Kellogg-Briand Pact to outlaw war as an instrument of national policy.

Under President Harding's unobtrusive and maladroit style of leadership, Secretary of State Charles Evans Hughes assumed a primary role. An accomplished jurist and a seasoned politician—former Supreme Court justice and New York governor—Hughes had failed in his run for the presidency in 1916. As secretary of state, his background in international law disposed him to favor juridical processes, such as arbitration, and the sanctity of treaties. His successor under President Calvin Coolidge, Frank B. Kellogg, a small-town lawyer and former senator from Rochester, Minnesota, was less cosmopolitan and more temperamental. He reacted with special vehemence to allegations of Bolshevik infiltration in Mexico and Nicaragua.[31]

Secretary of Commerce Herbert C. Hoover also ranked among the influential policymakers of the 1920s. A wealthy and famous mining engineer and humanitarian, he symbolized Republican ideas of individual integrity and responsibility. As Commerce Secretary, he assigned special importance to economic foreign policies. By coordinating endeavors in the public and private sectors, Hoover worked for a close association of government and business interests in promoting investment and trade.[32] His efforts sometimes trespassed on the secretary of state's domain, where, under the Rogers Act of 1924, a new professionalism had boosted salaries, emphasized merit, and combined the functions of the diplomatic and consular corps into the U.S. Foreign Service.

During the 1920s, Republican administrations enjoyed advantageous international circumstances, many of which benefited U.S. interests in Latin America. For one thing, wartime fears of renewed economic competition from Great Britain never materialized; instead, the British decline in trade and finance opened up new opportunities for the United States. For another, the German defeat eliminated all danger of European intrusions into the Western Hemisphere and removed a principal justification for U.S. intervention under the

Roosevelt corollary. At the end of the war the United States possessed greater power and influence than ever before. It was no longer a debtor nation but as a consequence of wartime loans, a creditor nation to which other countries owed large outstanding balances. Moreover, it led the world in trade and industrial production. As the historian Melvyn P. Leffler explains, these changes meant that "economic considerations" had become primary "in the shaping of American foreign policy," in part because of "the absence of strategic apprehensions." Ironically, the Monroe Doctrine remained "the cornerstone" of U.S. policy in the Western Hemisphere but, in the absence of a European threat, had ever less use as "a viable guide to action."[33]

In the postwar period, U.S. trade and investment expanded at British expense. High demand for U.S. machine products, automobiles, farm implements, typewriters, and cash registers created incentives for aggressive selling. In South America, U.S. imports accounted for growing market shares, from 16.2 percent in 1913 to 25.9 percent in 1918 to 26.8 percent in 1927. In Brazil, Chile, Colombia, Ecuador, Paraguay, Peru, and Uruguay, U.S. sales increased impressively. In Mexico, Central America, and the Caribbean, they dominated the market by accounting for 53.2 percent of imports in 1913, 75 percent in 1918, and 62.9 percent in 1927. In contrast, British imports were either stable or in decline, holding smaller parts of the market. Similar patterns appeared with investments. From 1914 through 1919 the total of U.S. foreign investments rose from $3.5 to $6.4 billion, and growth continued in the 1920s. Specifically in Latin America, U.S. investments expanded from $1,641.4 billion in 1914 to $5,369.7 billion in 1929, whereas British investments barely increased at all. As the historian Rosemary Thorp explains, such stagnation resulted from a variety of circumstances, notably British indifference, North American vigor, and U.S. government support for trade and investment.

Thorp illustrates the theme with various examples. Between 1924 and 1928, Latin America absorbed 24 percent of the new U.S. capital issues for foreign accounts and 44 percent of new direct foreign investment. The biggest amounts went into minerals, oil, public utilities, and industrial development in the largest countries. During the 1920s, Chile attracted more U.S. investment in mining than did any other country. By 1926, U.S. national banks were operating more than sixty branches in Latin America, often by contentious means. At one point, U.S. financial houses in Colombia had twenty-nine representatives in competition with one another to peddle loans. Intense rivalry sometimes became unscrupulous when lenders used bribery and sought favors, for example, by paying commissions and retainers to the relatives of government officials.

In a standard work, the historian Victor Bulmer-Thomas depicts the U.S. role as "a mixed blessing for Latin America." To be sure, U.S. investments compensated for "the shrinking capital surplus available from traditional European markets," but "the new borrowing was only achieved at a price." As Bulmer-Thomas notes, "In the smaller republics the new lending was intertwined with U.S. foreign-policy objectives, and many countries found themselves obliged to submit to U.S. control of the customs house or even national railways to ensure prompt debt payment." Nevertheless, the money poured in. In the larger countries "the new lending reached such epidemic proportions that it became known as 'the dance of the millions.'" Consequently, neither the lenders nor the recipients made much effort "to ensure that the funds were invested productively in projects that could guarantee repayment in foreign exchange." In Bulmer-Thomas's view, "the scale of corruption in a few cases reached pharaonic proportions."[34]

Latin American governments welcomed foreign investments and also put up with the economic advisers who came along. One of them, Edwin W. Kemmerer, a Princeton economist known as "the money doctor in the Andes," showed up in Colombia, Chile, Ecuador, Bolivia, and Peru. Working independently of the U.S. government but with its consent, Kemmerer presented himself as a scientific expert. Through the application of precise methods, he sought to produce modernization in South America by creating financial environments more conducive to foreign investment. When a compatibility of interest developed among Latin American elites, private U.S. bankers, and Republican political leaders, the ensuing approach to economic growth resembled what the historian Michael J. Hogan has characterized in another setting as "corporatist." Kemmerer specifically encouraged the reform of monetary institutions and the establishment of central banks patterned on the U.S. Federal Reserve system. When necessary, he also facilitated the negotiation of foreign loans.[35] But to qualify for them, Latin American governments usually had to accept outside supervision. In 1922, U.S. bankers oversaw a Bolivian arrangement in which customs revenues went into payments on a $33 million loan. Similarly, in Peru U.S. officials watched over the customs houses and the central bank. As Thorp remarks, such "typical" examples suggest at the least an "obtrusive" interest in financial control.[36]

The most pressing political issues included the legacies of intervention in the Dominican Republic, Haiti, and Nicaragua. The unintended consequences of such acts aroused dismay among Republicans. The establishment of protectorates in those countries had presumed a purpose of upholding peace and order; instead, the ensuing U.S. military occupations had provoked nationalist resistance and guerrilla war. Republican leaders worried about cost ineffectiveness and public relations: Why encourage Latin American nationalists with interventionist practices when no Europeans posed a threat to U.S. interests? During the 1920 presidential campaign, Republicans subjected Democrats to strong criticism for taking over Haiti and the Dominican Republic during the war, and they urged military withdrawal.[37]

Once in power, Republican administrations succeeded in removing military forces from the Dominican Republic in 1924 but encountered difficulties elsewhere. In Nicaragua a small U.S. Marine legation guard had served since 1911, and for the most part the ruling Nicaraguan elites had not objected. Indeed, they saw the U.S. presence as a way for them to keep their hold on power. In the proposed Bryan-Chamorro Treaty of 1914, for example, Nicaraguan leaders had offered an option on a canal route in return for cash payments and also had indicated their readiness to accept something like the Platt amendment allowing for intervention. Opponents in the U.S. Senate blocked the treaty, and the revised version that passed in 1916 omitted mention of intervention.

For Republicans, military extrication posed a problem. In August 1925 the Coolidge administration removed the marines from Nicaragua and then sent them back in January 1927, following the outbreak of a civil war. This elite struggle over power and patronage pitted Conservatives against Liberals and took on international implications when Mexican President Plutarco Elías Calles supported the Liberals with money and arms. In response, Secretary of State Frank B. Kellogg and Ambassador to Mexico James F. Sheffield issued overwrought warnings of war unless Mexico stopped exporting revolution to Nicaragua. According to Kellogg, Calles intended his Nicaraguan meddling to advance a Bolshevik conspiracy in the Western Hemisphere.

In a show of resolution, the Coolidge administration dispatched two thousand troops to Nicaragua and also a diplomatic emissary, Henry L. Stimson. This Republican stalwart, who had served President Taft as secretary of war, persuaded Conservative and Liberal leaders to accept a truce, followed by an election. But he failed to win over Augusto C. Sandino, the head of a recalcitrant faction. A Nicaraguan by birth, Sandino had imbibed radical nationalism while living as an exile in

Mexico. As an anti-imperialist, he wanted to rid his country of the Yankees. According to historian Thomas M. Leonard, his intransigence was "symptomatic" of a growing nationalist response against the United States.

Sandino's Nicaraguan struggle lasted six years. His army, no more than a thousand soldiers, employed guerrilla tactics to frustrate and wear down government forces and U.S. Marines. In the United States, meanwhile, opposition to the Nicaraguan intervention encouraged President Herbert Hoover to end it. Early in 1931, the administration developed a strategy for removing the troops after sponsoring still another presidential election. When the marines withdrew on 2 January 1932, the State Department proclaimed an end to "the special relationship" with Nicaragua. A year later on 2 February 1933, a Nicaraguan truce ended the Sandinista revolt with promises of amnesty and reform. Sandino himself later was assassinated on 21 February 1934, probably the work of Anastasio Somoza, an emerging strongman whose family would dominate the country for two generations.[38]

Related issues caused trouble with Mexico over the constitution of 1917, regarded by U.S. critics as a dangerously radical precedent. Among other things, it called for land and labor reform and placed limits on foreign property rights. By endorsing expropriation and nationalization supposedly in behalf of the public good, Article 27 overturned the more traditional conceptions of property rights favored by the United States. Carranza's intractability posed problems for the Wilson administration until his death by assassination during a military uprising in the spring of 1920. His elected successor, General Alvaro Obregón, sought normal relations but encountered stiff demands as the price. The Harding administration wanted guarantees in defense of foreign property rights—in effect, the abandonment of Article 27. When Obregón declined, the United States withheld diplomatic recognition.

For Mexican revolutionary leaders, the consequences deepened an already difficult dilemma. Though resentful of economic dependencies on the United States, they needed money to reconstruct their shattered country after a violent decade, but without diplomatic recognition their government could not qualify for loans. When the Harding administration insisted upon a treaty to nullify Article 27, a diplomatic standoff developed.

The big oil companies with properties at risk were well served by the U.S. policy of nonrecognition but other economic interest groups—exporters seeking sales in Mexican markets, U.S. bondholders hoping to collect on previous debts—obtained few benefits. In many ways, diplomatic recognition could advance their interests more effectively. Thomas W. Lamont, a high-level financier with J. P. Morgan and Company and an associate of the International Committee of Bankers on Mexico, previously had negotiated with Mexican officials a new schedule for repaying old debts. On the basis of that experience, he persuaded Harding and Hughes that they could place some trust in Obregón's good faith without risking too much. Subsequently, during the summer of 1923, they sought a negotiated compromise at the so-called Bucareli Conference, named for the location of the Mexican Foreign Ministry at No. 85 Avenida Bucareli in Mexico City. As a consequence of these proceedings, U.S. officials abandoned the demand for a treaty in defense of foreign property rights and accepted instead a ruling by the Mexican Supreme Court. Called "the doctrine of positive acts," this ruling assured foreigners that they would not experience retroactive enforcement of Article 27—that is, the loss of their property—if they had engaged in "positive acts" to develop their holdings before the constitution took effect on 5 February 1917. In addition, a claims convention provided reassurance for foreigners seeking compensation for injuries and losses suffered during the era of revolution. As a seal on the agreement, on 31 August 1923, three weeks after Harding's sudden death, the Coolidge administration extended diplomatic recognition to Obregón's government, seeking thereby to inaugurate a period of more normal relations.[39]

Despite such hopes, new difficulties arose under Obregón's successor, President Plutarco Elías Calles. When he took office in 1924, Calles broke with Obregón's policy and rejected "the doctrine of positive acts." Instead, he threatened to enforce Article 27 retroactively by placing a fifty-year limit on foreign ownership of petroleum lands, followed by nationalization proceedings. For Kellogg and Sheffield, such behavior smacked of Bolshevism. Kellogg wanted to put Mexico on trial before the world. When Thomas Lamont once again stepped in, urging a less belligerent stance, President Coolidge picked a new ambassador, a friend from college days. Dwight Morrow, another financier connected with J. P. Morgan, was a good choice. Indeed, by means of skill and discretion, he moved Calles along toward more moderate views. Specifically, he emphasized the dangers of intransigence, suggesting the likelihood of bad effects and the loss of future loans. When at last Calles came around, he accepted "the doctrine of positive acts" as assurance against outright nationalization.[40]

For Latin Americans the U.S. practice of intervention remained a pressing issue during the 1920s. Unlike their northern neighbor, they joined the League of Nations—in part to devise multilateral constraints against the United States—and also exerted pressure in other ways. At the Sixth International Conference of American States at Havana in 1928, for example, Latin American delegates introduced a resolution calling for adherence to the principle of nonintervention and declaring that "no state has a right to intervene in the internal affairs of another" for any reason.[41] On this occasion the United States succeeded in blocking any action but could not abolish the idea. Nonintervention retained strong appeal for Latin Americans. Somewhat embarrassed by the circumstance, U.S. leaders in the 1920s preferred the use of economic incentives rather than force as the best means of influencing Latin American behavior, but still they regarded intervention as a right authorized by international law. Whenever necessary, they would use it in defense of U.S. citizens and property.

In 1928, Undersecretary of State J. Reuben Clark addressed the issue by establishing important distinctions that overturned the rationale for Theodore Roosevelt's corollary to the Monroe Doctrine. In a State Department memorandum, Clark defended the practice of U.S. intervention in Latin America as legitimate when sanctioned by international law as a means of safeguarding the well-being of U.S. citizens and their property, but he found no similar justification in the Monroe Doctrine. As he described its original meaning, the terms established a prohibition on European intervention in the New World but not a rationale for U.S. intervention. The publication of the Clark memorandum in 1930 marked a shift toward greater subtlety.[42] During the Great Depression, the United States gave up direct interventionist practices in the Western Hemisphere by embracing the policy of the Good Neighbor.

NOTES

1. Victor Bulmer-Thomas, *The Economic History of Latin America since Independence* (New York: Cambridge University Press, 1994), chaps. 1–3; William Glade, "Latin America and the International Economy, 1870–1914," in *The Cambridge History of Latin America*, vol. 4, *c. 1870–1930*, ed. Leslie Bethell (New York: Cambridge University Press, 1986), chap. 1.

2. Glade, "Latin America," 10–16; Bill Albert, *South America and the First World War: The Impact of the War on Brazil, Argentina, Peru, and Chile* (New York: Cambridge University Press, 1988), chap. 1.

3. Friedrich Katz, "Mexico: Restored Republic and Porfiriato, 1867–1910," in *The Cambridge History of Latin America*, vol. 4, *c. 1870–1930*, ed. Leslie Bethell (New York: Cambridge University Press, 1986); Glade, "Latin America," 16–17.

4. Bulmer-Thomas, *Economic History*, chap. 3.

5. Glade, "Latin America," 39–41; Bulmer-Thomas, *Economic History*, 161.

6. Ronald H. Chilcote and Joel C. Edelstein, eds., *Latin America: Capitalist and Socialist Perspectives of Development and Underdevelopment* (Boulder, CO: Westview Press, 1986), provides an introduction to dependency theory; Glade, "Latin America," 47.

7. John Mason Hart, *Revolutionary Mexico: The Coming and Process of the Mexican Revolution* (Berkeley: University of California Press, 1987), chaps. 6–7.

8. Notable works include Hart, *Revolutionary Mexico*; Ramón Eduardo Ruiz, *The Great Rebellion: Mexico, 1905–1924* (New York: W. W. Norton, 1980); Friedrich Katz, *The Secret War in Mexico: Europe, the United States, and the Mexican Revolution* (Chicago: University of Chicago Press, 1981); and Alan Knight, *The Mexican Revolution*, 2 vols. (New York: Cambridge University Press, 1986).

9. Mark T. Gilderhus, "Carranza and the Decision to Revolt, 1913: A Problem in Historical Interpretation," *Americas* 33 (October 1976): 298–310; Kenneth J. Grieb, *The United States and Huerta* (Lincoln: University of Nebraska Press, 1969), chap. 4; Michael C. Meyer, *Huerta: A Political Portrait* (Lincoln: University of Nebraska Press, 1972), chaps. 4–5; Douglas W. Richmond, *Venustiano Carranza's Nationalist Struggle, 1893–1920* (Lincoln: University of Nebraska Press, 1983), chap. 3.

10. Mark T. Gilderhus, *Diplomacy and Revolution: U.S.-Mexican Relations under Wilson and Carranza* (Tucson: University of Arizona Press, 1977), 3.

11. Mark T. Gilderhus, *Pan American Visions: Woodrow Wilson in the Western Hemisphere, 1913–1921* (Tucson: University of Arizona Press, 1986), 14–16.

12. Thomas L. Karnes, "Hiram Bingham and His Obsolete Shibboleth," *Diplomatic History* 3 (Winter 1979): 39–57.

13. N. Gordon Levin Jr., *Woodrow Wilson and World Politics: America's Response to War and Revolution* (New York: Oxford University Press, 1968), chap. 1.

14. Gilderhus, *Pan American Visions*, 7–19; Katz, *Secret War*, chap. 5.

15. Gilderhus, *Pan American Visions*, 28–29; Albert, *South America and the First World War*, chap. 1; E. Bradford Burns, *The Unwritten Alliance: Rio-Branco and Brazilian American Relations* (New York: Columbia University Press, 1966); Joseph Smith, *Unequal Giants: Diplomatic Relations between the United States and Brazil, 1889–1930* (Pittsburgh, PA: University of Pittsburgh Press, 1991), chaps. 2–3.

16. Gilderhus, *Pan American Visions*, 20, 28–29; Burton I. Kaufman, *Expansion and Efficiency: Foreign Trade Organization in the Wilson Administration, 1913–1921* (Westport, CT: Greenwood Press, 1974), chaps. 1–2; Jeffrey J. Safford, *Wilsonian Maritime Diplomacy, 1913–1921* (New Brunswick, NJ: Rutgers University Press, 1978), chaps. 1–2.

17. Gilderhus, *Diplomacy and Revolution*, chap 1; Hart, *Revolutionary Mexico*, chaps. 8–9; Robert E. Quirk, *An Affair of Honor: Woodrow Wilson and the Occupation of Veracruz* (New York: McGraw-Hill, 1964).

18. Gilderhus, *Pan American Visions*, 33–45.

19. Albert, *South America and the First World War*, chap. 2.

20. Gilderhus, *Pan American Visions*, 44–52; William F. Sater, *Chile and the United States: Empires in Conflict* (Athens: University of Georgia Press, 1990), 75.

21. Gilderhus, *Pan American Visions*, 64, 67–70; idem, *Diplomacy and Revolution*, chap. 2.

22. Bruce J. Calder, *The Impact of Intervention: The Dominican Republic during the U.S. Occupation of 1916–1924* (Austin: University of Texas Press, 1984); Hans Schmidt, *The United States Occupation of Haiti, 1914–1934* (New Brunswick, NJ: Rutgers University Press, 1971); Frederick S. Calhoun, *Uses of Force and Wilsonian Foreign Policy* (Kent, OH: Kent State University Press, 1993), chap 4; Brenda Gayle Plummer, *Haiti and the United States: The Psychological Moment* (Athens: University of Georgia Press, 1992), chaps. 5–6; idem, *Haiti and the Great Powers, 1902–1915* (Baton Rouge: Louisiana State University Press, 1988); G. Pope Atkins and Larman C. Wilson, *The Dominican Republic and the United States: From Imperialism to Transnationalism* (Athens: University of Georgia Press, 1998), chap. 2; Lester D. Langley, *The Banana Wars: An Inner History of American Empire, 1900–1934* (Lexington: University Press of Kentucky, 1983).

23. Gilderhus, *Pan American Visions*, 61, 70–74, 77–80; Kaufman, *Expansion and Efficiency*, 165–75; Carl Parrini, *Heir to Empire: United States Economic Diplomacy, 1916–1923* (Pittsburgh, PA: University of Pittsburgh Press, 1969), chap. 2.

24. Gilderhus, *Diplomacy and Revolution*, chap. 3; Linda B. Hall and Don M. Coerver, *Revolution on the Border: The United States and Mexico, 1910–1920* (Albuquerque: University of New Mexico Press, 1988), chap. 5.

25. Gilderhus, *Diplomacy and Revolution*, chap. 3.

26. Ernest R. May, *The World War and American Isolation, 1914–1917* (Cambridge, MA: Harvard University Press, 1959); Gilderhus, *Pan American Vision*, chap. 3; Katz, *Secret War*, chaps. 9–10.

27. Lawrence E. Gelfand, *The Inquiry: American Preparations for Peace, 1917–1919* (New Haven: Yale University Press, 1963).

28. Gilderhus, *Pan American Visions*, 113, 125–27; idem, *Diplomacy and Revolution*, 96.

29. Levin, *Wilson and World Politics*, chaps. 5–7.

30. Gilderhus, *Pan American Visions*, 142–56; idem, *Diplomacy and Revolution*, chap. 6; Dimitri D. Lazo, "Lansing, Wilson, and the Jenkins Incident," *Diplomatic History* 22 (Spring 1998): 177–98; Daniel M. Smith, *Aftermath of*

War: Bainbridge Colby and Wilsonian Diplomacy, 1920–1922 (Philadelphia: American Philosophical Society, 1970), 10–31.

31. Joan Hoff Wilson, *American Business and Foreign Policy, 1920–1933* (Lexington: University Press of Kentucky, 1971); L. Ethan Ellis, *Republican Foreign Policy, 1921–1933* (New Brunswick, NJ: Rutgers University Press, 1968); Warren I. Cohen, *Empire without Tears: America's Foreign Relations, 1921–1933* (Philadelphia: Temple University Press, 1987), esp. chap. 1.

32. Eugene P. Trani and David L. Wilson, *The Presidency of Warren G. Harding* (Lawrence: Regents Press of Kansas, 1977), chap. 5; Joan Hoff Wilson, *Herbert Hoover: Forgotten Progressive* (Boston: Little, Brown, 1975), chap. 4.

33. Melvyn P. Leffler, "Expansionist Impulses and Domestic Constraints, 1921–32," in *Economics and World Power: An Assessment of American Diplomacy since 1789*, ed. William H. Becker and Samuel F. Wells Jr. (New York: Columbia University Press, 1984), 225–26, 242.

34. Rosemary Thorp, "Latin America and the International Economy from the First World War to the World Depression," in *Cambridge History of Latin America*, 4:59–66; Bulmer-Thomas, *Economic History*, 160–61.

35. Paul W. Drake, *The Money Doctor in the Andes: The Kemmerer Missions, 1923–1933* (Durham, NC: Duke University Press, 1989); idem, ed., *Money Doctors, Foreign Debts, and Economic Reforms in Latin America from the 1890s to the Present* (Wilmington, DE: Scholarly Resources, 1994), chaps. 5–7; Michael J. Hogan, "Corporatism," in *Explaining the History of American Foreign Relations*, edited by Michael J. Hogan and Thomas G. Paterson (New York: Cambridge University Press, 1991), chap. 16.

36. Thorp, "Latin America," 72–73.

37. Thomas M. Leonard, *Central America and the United States: The Search for Stability* (Athens: University of Georgia Press, 1991), chap. 5; Plummer, *Haiti and the United States*, chap. 6; Atkins and Wilson, *Dominican Republic*, chap. 2.

38. Calder, *Impact of Intervention*, chaps. 8–9; Leonard, *Central America*, 70–71, 88, 91, 99–100; Neil Macaulay, *The Sandino Affair* (Chicago: Quadrangle Books, 1971); Paul H. Boeker, ed., *Henry L. Stimson's American Policy in Nicaragua: The Lasting Legacy* (New York: Markus Wiener, 1991).

39. Trani and Wilson, *Presidency of Warren G. Harding*, chap. 5; Robert Freeman Smith, *The United States and Revolutionary Nationalism in Mexico, 1916–1932* (Chicago: University of Chicago Press, 1972), chaps. 6–8; Linda B. Hall, *Oil, Banks, and Politics: The United States and Postrevolutionary Mexico, 1917–1924* (Austin: University of Texas Press, 1995), esp. chaps. 5–7; Lorenzo Meyer, *Mexico and the United States in the Oil Controversy, 1917–1942*, trans. Muriel Vasconcellos (Austin: University of Texas Press, 1977), chaps. 4–5.

40. Smith, *The United States and Revolutionary Nationalism*, chap. 9.

41. Walter LaFeber, *The American Age: United States Foreign Policy at Home and Abroad since 1970* (New York: W. W. Norton, 1989), 341; Samuel Flagg Bemis, *The Latin-American Policy of the United States: An Historical Interpretation* (1943; reprint ed., New York: W. W. Norton, 1967), 251.

42. Frank W. Fox, *J. Reuben Clark: The Public Years* (Provo, UT: Brigham Young University Press, 1980), 514–21.

CHAPTER THREE

DEPRESSION, WAR, AND THE GOOD NEIGHBOR

1929–1945

BETWEEN 1929 AND 1945 the United States experienced a global depression and another world war. During this time of grave calamity almost everywhere, economic collapse called forth political instability and nationalist movements. In Europe and Asia the rise of Italian fascism, German nazism, and Japanese militarism intensified economic competition over markets and scarce resources, resulting in conflict and war. In the countries of Latin America the Great Depression led to commercial breakdowns and political difficulties, the consequences of which encouraged the United States to respond in distinctive ways by fashioning a Good Neighbor policy.

The term "good neighbor," a kind of commonplace in diplomatic language, took on actual meaning during the presidencies of Herbert C. Hoover and Franklin D. Roosevelt. For Latin Americans the term signified the end of an era of direct intervention by the United States in Latin American affairs. For the Roosevelt administration the Good Neighbor policy also functioned significantly in other ways: It served as an international counterpart of the New Deal by attacking the economic effects of the Great Depression and later as a means of mobilizing resistance among the nations of the New World against the Axis powers during the Second World War. As the historian Robert Freeman Smith explains, taken together the various components formed "a massive, although ill-defined government effort" under U.S. direction to create "an integrated hemisphere system" characterized by high levels of "political, economic and military cooperation."[1]

Though often as paradoxical and contradictory as the New Deal itself, the Good Neighbor policy introduced important changes. Notably, the United States sacrificed its self-proclaimed international police power for economic reasons and for "hemispheric solidarity" against the Nazis. The main ingredients of Good Neighborliness consisted of nonintervention and other initiatives to promote commercial expansion and regional collaboration. Historians still debate whether the effects constituted a partnership with Latin Americans or a subtle means of imperial domination.

HOOVER AND LATIN AMERICA

Herbert C. Hoover, the former secretary of commerce, won election to the presidency as a Republican in 1928. While claiming, ironically as it turned out, that his party best understood the means of ensuring prosperity for the future, Hoover pledged his support to traditional Republican positions in favor of high tariffs, low taxes, and minimal government spending. During his career as an engineer working in other countries, he had acquired more international experience than any president since John Quincy Adams. During the campaign, he upheld the values of his Quaker ancestors by affirming his preference for peaceful solutions in the conduct of world affairs. He also espoused an interest in Latin America.

A few weeks after his election, Hoover undertook a goodwill tour into Central and South America. As he explained, "Our trip . . . was conceived for the purpose of paying friendly calls upon our neighbors to the south." He saw the venture as "the first step in what was to be a reorientation of policy toward Latin America." After departing from San Pedro, California, on 19 November 1928 aboard the battleship USS *Maryland*, Hoover's ten-week journey took him to Honduras, El Salvador, Nicaragua, Costa Rica, Ecuador, Peru, Chile, Argentina, Uruguay, and Brazil. In a speech at Amapala, Honduras, on 26 November, he declared as his purpose "the friendly visit of one *good neighbor to another*." In other public orations, he emphasized the importance of common welfare, mutual respect, and shared understanding among the nations of the Western Hemisphere. For example, before an audience of skeptical Argentines in Buenos Aires, Hoover criticized the condescension typically built into U.S. policy toward Latin America, especially the stereotype depicting his country as "big brother." He affirmed his belief in the principle of equality among states. Such words, followed by actual deeds, established some claim for Hoover as a founder of the Good Neighbor policy.[2]

Once inaugurated as the president, Hoover reaped the whirlwind. Contrary to Republican expectations the Great Depression descended upon the United States and the rest of the world, causing economic crisis, chaos, and calamity. As a consequence, the international political order as conceived by the Republicans in the 1920s entered into a process of disintegration, signaled initially by Japan's seizure of Manchuria in 1931–32. Herbert Hoover, in some ways a tragic figure, served only one term in the presidency as a result; nevertheless, historians have described his policies in the Western Hemisphere as "highly successful." According to Martin Fausold, Hoover produced positive changes by advocating nonintervention; and according to Robert Freeman Smith, under Hoover "the government came closer to a truly nonintervention policy than at any other time in the 20th century." During this period the United States disengaged militarily from Nicaragua and developed similar plans for Haiti. Moreover, when uprisings and revolts swept Latin America between 1929 and 1933, "the administration refused all requests for armed intervention and constantly admonished diplomats and businessmen to refrain from political meddling." On one occasion, Secretary of State Henry L. Stimson "bawled out" the head of the United Fruit Company in Costa Rica for allowing his subordinates to interfere in politics.[3] Unwilling to wield a big stick like Theodore Roosevelt, neither Hoover nor Stimson intended to use the marines in foreign interventions. They wanted to establish no parallels with Japanese military actions in Asia. As Stimson observed, to land "a single soldier among those South Americans now . . . would undo all the labor of three years" and "would put me in absolutely wrong in China."[4] As peace proponents, Hoover and Stimson also tried—unsuccessfully, as it turned out—to settle border disputes in South America between Paraguay and Bolivia over the Gran Chaco and between Peru and Colombia over Leticia.[5]

The Great Depression, of course, had many bad effects and economic dependence on trade made Latin America particularly vulnerable. Although the larger countries had moved toward industrialization and diversification in the 1920s, heavy reliance on the export sectors remained characteristic. According to the economic historian Victor Bulmer-Thomas, "the composition of exports by the end of the decade was very similar to what it had been on the eve of the First World War." Nearly all export earnings resulted from the sale of primary products, such as coffee, sugar, bananas, tin, and oil. Moreover, almost 70 percent of the foreign trade involved only four countries—the United States, Great Britain, France, and Germany—which meant that Latin America was acutely susceptible to shifts in the world market.

For Latin Americans, economic difficulties began before the Wall Street crash in October 1929. Heavy demand for credit and high interest rates during the boom years in the 1920s had had the effect of "raising the cost of holding inventories" and "reducing demand for many of the primary products exported by Latin America." The crash compounded such problems, further diminishing demand in the world market. The result was that exports fell between 1928 and 1932, in some instances by more than 50 percent. To be sure, import prices for foreign finished goods also fell but, in Latin America, neither as fast nor as far. Bolivia, Chile, Mexico, and Cuba ranked among the hardest hit. Venezuela, protected by oil, suffered somewhat less.[6]

Political changes soon followed. The destabilizing effects of the depression overturned incumbent regimes and installed new parties and personalities in power, sometimes by violent means. In Ecuador, Chile, and Cuba, such political transitions took place after periods of near anarchy; in Peru and El Salvador, they came about through sudden coups. Typically, the new governments moved toward nationalistic, centralized, and authoritarian alternatives. Strongmen such as Getúlio Vargas in Brazil, Rafael Trujillo in the Dominican Republic, and Jorge Ubico in Guatemala stood out. An exception, the Venezuelan dictator Juan Vicente Gómez maintained his regime until his death in 1935. Similarly in Mexico, the ruling Partido Nacional Revolucionario, later called the Partido Revolucionario Institucional, retained its hold on power, featuring behind-the-scenes maneuvers by former president Plutarco Elías Calles.[7]

For Latin Americans, rejuvenation of the export sector encountered formidable obstacles. To safeguard domestic markets against foreign competition the Great Powers resorted to protection, that is, high tariffs and other such barriers. Under Hoover the Republican-controlled Congress enacted the Hawley-Smoot tariff of 1930, the highest in U.S. history. Similarly under the "imperial preference" system the British discriminated against outsiders such as Latin Americans, and under the Nazis the Germans introduced the aski-mark—nonconvertible currency that provided a means of paying foreign sellers for goods and services but could apply only to the purchase of German goods.

Latin Americans had few alternatives. In better times, international borrowing on credit might have gotten them out of trouble but not in this instance; as a consequence of the depression surplus capital dried up in the United States and Europe. The unavailability of additional loans by 1931 forced a cruel choice upon Latin American governments. While export earnings went into decline, the interest payments on existing debts remained the same, placing ever larger demands on shrinking sources of national income. At first, Latin Americans tried to make payments on their debts, hoping to retain access to international money markets. But to reduce growing deficits as the squeeze continued, they reluctantly accepted default on international interest payments as a necessary resort and then stopped making them. When Roosevelt and the New Dealers took office early in 1933, stringent economic conditions existed everywhere.[8]

THE NEW DEAL AND NONINTERVENTION

For Roosevelt and the Democrats the presidential victory in 1932 turned principally on domestic issues. In his comments on foreign relations, Roosevelt suggested his opposition to high tariffs and a personal preference for friendly relations with other countries. His inaugural address underscored a popular theme: "In the field of world policy," he would "dedicate this nation to the policy of the good neighbor—the neighbor who resolutely respects himself and, because he does so, respects the sanctity of his agreements in and with a world of neighbors."[9] This bland formulation implied nothing specific, but in later years the term "good neighbor" acquired very special meanings for Latin Americans.

Cosmopolitan, sophisticated, and well-to-do, Roosevelt engaged in the practice of politics throughout his adult life. He served first as a New York state legislator and then as assistant secretary of the navy under Woodrow Wilson. In 1920, he ran unsuccessfully as the Democratic candidate for the vice presidency and in 1928 won election as governor of New York state. In 1921 he had become ill with infantile paralysis, or polio, a dread affliction that left him dependent upon heavy leg braces and a wheelchair. Many voters never knew the extent of his infirmity.

In foreign affairs, Roosevelt's views initially took shape during the Wilson presidency. During the First World War, he supported Caribbean interventions, worried about German intrusions, and favored order and stability within the U.S. sphere of influence. Later, he shifted his ground as a consequence of misgivings over the Nicaraguan intervention. His 1928 article "Our Foreign Policy" in the journal *Foreign Affairs*, published by the Council on Foreign Relations, contained recommendations reminiscent of Wilson's Pan American treaty. Roosevelt too favored broadly conceived definitions of international police power and preferred cooperative approaches with Latin Americans. Speaking as president before the Pan American Union on 12 April 1933, he called for a multilateral understanding of the Monroe Doctrine, in this way asserting his preference for group action and the avoidance of unilateral enforcement.

In Latin American affairs, Cordell Hull, the secretary of state, and Sumner Welles, the assistant secretary of state, played important roles. Hull, a diplomatic amateur from Tennessee, had served in the Congress, where he possessed a strong political base. A champion of low tariffs and free trade, he had strong ideas about combatting the depression with an expanding commerce. In contrast, Welles had aristocratic antecedents. A diplomatic professional and a Roosevelt family friend, he had joined the Foreign Service in 1915, consciously picking Latin America as his regional specialty. In 1928 he published a two-volume history of the Dominican Republic titled *Naboth's Vineyard*, in which he advised that the United States identify "its interest both political and material, on a basis of absolute equality, with the interests of its sister republics of the continent." Often rivals, Hull and Welles competed for Roosevelt's favor. According to the historian Irwin Gellman, Roosevelt had a preference for Welles because of his "brilliance, penetrating analysis, and quick reactions" but also appreciated Hull because of his "circumspection" and his "patience" while seeking "a complete examination of the issues." Hull also knew how to cultivate support in the Congress.[10]

When the new administration took over, an impending revolution in Cuba caused immediate concern. The first U.S. protectorate in the Caribbean, Cuba also ranked among the first Latin American countries to experience the effects of economic depression. Beginning in the mid-1920s, sugar prices went into eclipse, producing widespread distress among sugar workers, professionals, merchants, and white-collar employees. In response, President Gerardo Machado negotiated loans from international bankers and employed strong-arm techniques to keep order while he sought reelection in 1928. Calamity ensued nevertheless. Because of the Hawley-Smoot tariff, Cuban sugar exporters lost 25 percent of the U.S. market. Consequently, Cuban sugar production dropped by 60 percent, and Cuban exports declined by 80 percent. As businesses failed, wages fell, and unemployment soared, Cuban dissidents in growing numbers came to regard Machado as expendable.

U.S. citizens had invested over a billion dollars in Cuba. They wanted protection, but under Hoover, nonintervention prevailed. The administration justified inaction, supposedly, out of respect for Cuban sovereignty. But in this instance, nonintervention hardly differed from intervention. In the view of most Cubans, Louis A. Pérez suggests, U.S. support sustained Machado's authoritarian regime. Ironically, "political repression" and "economic depression" in combination arrayed "vast sectors of the Cuban population against a government that seemed to be supported only by foreigners."[11]

In the spring of 1933, Roosevelt sent Sumner Welles as a special emissary with instructions to halt the turmoil through "friendly mediation." In the process, Welles came to view Machado as a liability and hoped for a replacement candidate among "responsible leaders" in the opposition parties. At first defiant, Machado resisted the pressure to leave office until other Cuban political and military leaders also withdrew their support. Unwilling to risk another U.S. military intervention, the Cuban army on 12 August 1933 forced Machado into exile. As Pérez explains, Welles's role "set in motion a realignment . . . that released Machado's backers to seek a new arrangement with the United States to guarantee their own survival in post-Machado Cuba."

A provisional government then took office under Carlos Manuel de Céspedes, a friend of Sumner Welles. Representing a tenuous compromise among contending groups, this administration lasted only three weeks. On 3 September 1933, army factions consisting of noncommissioned officers and enlisted men under Sergeant Fulgencio Batista seized control of the headquarters at Camp Columbia in Havana. Calling for better pay and working conditions, the "Sergeants' Revolt" rallied the antigovernment opposition. Together, soldiers and other dissidents proclaimed a Provisional Revolutionary Government headed by Dr. Ramón Grau San Martín, a physician and university professor. *Grau* His government was the first in Cuba to take power since 1898 without official sanction from the United States.

Embracing the slogan "Cuba for Cubans," Grau endorsed ambitious reforms: the eight-hour day, protection for rural workers, women's suffrage, and the abrogation of the Platt amendment. Much alarmed, Sumner Welles warned of communist influences and advocated military intervention. U.S. naval contingents were already positioned in Cuban waters, but the Roosevelt administration refrained from sending in the marines. Instead, the leaders withheld diplomatic recognition, thereby sending signals to Batista, now a colonel and the army chief of staff. Encouraged by Welles, Batista, working behind the scenes, *Batista's 1934 coup* shifted military support to Carlos Mendieta at the end of January 1934 and created a new government more acceptable to the United States. A decision in favor of diplomatic recognition followed only five days later.

In this instance the Roosevelt administration avoided military intervention, in part because of public relations. Late in November 1933 a Pan American conference had assembled at Montevideo, Uruguay. As always, nonintervention became an issue. Headed by Secretary Hull, the U.S. delegation preferred a discussion of peace and trade, whereas the Latin Americans wanted to take up such matters as the cancellation of foreign debts and the Cuban question. When Argentina assumed the lead, U.S. officials reacted negatively to Foreign Minister Carlos Saavedra Lamas—perceived as haughty and condescending in his criticism of the northern colossus—but other Latin Americans joined him in pressing for an endorsement of nonintervention. By insisting that "no state has the right to intervene in the internal or external affairs of another," they forced a tactical change upon U.S. leaders. On this occasion, Secretary Hull accepted the idea in principle; in his words, "no government need fear any intervention on the part of the United States under the Roosevelt administration." At the same time, he employed a kind of diplomatic double-talk by attaching a reservation that could have rendered the commitment meaningless: He retained for the United States a right to intervene militarily if the defense of U.S. citizens and property required it in compliance with treaties or international law.[12]

The qualification notwithstanding, the Roosevelt administration adhered strictly to the pledge. The United States engaged in no more armed interventions and in fact eradicated some of the remnants of previous actions. An executive agreement in August 1933 provided for the withdrawal of U.S. Marines from Haiti but retained financial control until 1941; similar arrangements already existed in relations with the Dominican Republic. A new treaty with Cuba in 1934 eliminated the Platt amendment but preserved for the United States the naval base at Guantánamo Bay. Finally, an agreement with Panama in 1936 produced another modification by affirming joint responsibility for defending the canal.[13]

The United States accepted the principle of nonintervention unconditionally at the Buenos Aires conference in December 1936. Escalating the prestige, Roosevelt himself attended. Mexico introduced the nonintervention resolution, affirming that in the Western Hemisphere the various states regarded as "inadmissible the intervention of any one of them, directly or indirectly, and for whatever reason, in the internal or external affairs of any other."[14] To be sure, the phrase "any one of them" suggested a loophole, leaving open the possibility of collective measures, but the provision conformed with Roosevelt's stated preferences by disallowing unilateral acts.

The principle of nonintervention undergirded the Good Neighbor policy. By embracing it, the Roosevelt administration sanctioned equality among states in the Western Hemisphere and reduced the reasons for Latin American mistrust of the United States. At the same time, nonintervention implied, among other things, readiness to let Latin Americans take charge of their own political destinies. When U.S. military forces subsequently withdrew from the former protectorates, they left behind police contingents, or constabularies, created by U.S. occupation authorities supposedly for purposes of upholding constitutional order. In Nicaragua and the Dominican Republic, such organizations later served the dictators Anastasio Somoza and Rafael Leonidas Trujillo Molina as institutional foundations for authoritarian rule. Whether these corrupt, repressive regimes came into existence because of inadvertence or conscious design on the part of the United States is an important question. In Somoza's case, the historian Paul Coe Clark Jr. absolves the United States of primary responsibility. In his view, Somoza stayed in power not so much because of U.S. support as because of his own ruthless political skills. According to this analysis, acceptance of nonintervention entailed an unintended consequence: The Roosevelt administration would have to put up with Somoza.[15]

ECONOMIC DIPLOMACY

U.S. economic diplomacy in Latin America sought commercial expansion through the negotiation of reciprocal trade agreements. To obtain larger market shares, the Roosevelt administration paid the political price for Latin American cooperation by abandoning obsolete forms of military intervention. Viewed in economic terms, the Good Neighbor policy functioned as part of the New Deal's larger attack on the Great Depression.

In the United States the debate over causes, cures, and consequences pervaded political discourse. Divergent views proposed various alternatives.[16] For economic conservatives and Marxists the explanation for the depression resided in the cyclical boom-and-bust patterns inherent in capitalist economies. Economic conservatives saw no ready solutions; the crisis must run its course and bottom out before prosperity could return. Marxists and other radicals thought some kind of anticapitalist revolution could clear the way. According to Herbert Hoover, the problem originated in Europe and then spread to the rest of the world. For the New Dealers, in contrast, the depression was homegrown, a disastrous manifestation of the traditional imbalance between overproduction and underconsumption, rendered all the worse in this instance by Republican policies in the 1920s. According to this view, high tar-iffs, low taxes, and reduced government spending were to blame. The ensuing maldistribution of income meant that financiers, manufactur-ers, and industrialists, the main beneficiaries of Republican policies, accumulated too much wealth and too much capability to expand pro-duction too rapidly. Lesser folk with smaller incomes—farmers, wage earners, salaried employees—who shared unequally in the wealth were unable to keep up the pace as consumers. Consequently, glutted mar-kets in crucial sectors, notably the construction and automobile in-dustries, generated catastrophic deflation. When producers cut back, slashed wages, and fired workers, they worsened conditions by diminishing purchasing power. Under President Hoover, unem-ployment reached unimaginable levels during the winter of 1932–33. An estimated twelve to fourteen million people—about a quarter of the workforce—had no jobs.

Under Roosevelt the New Deal attacked the depression in various ways through trial and error, employing a scattergun approach. The programs that took shape typically relied heavily on centralized plan-ning, government paternalism, and a host of new federal agencies. One such experiment, the National Recovery Administration (NRA), called for cooperation among producers in basic industries to limit output and cut down on overproduction. The effort failed. Well-intended but clumsy, the NRA resulted in a bureaucratic monstrosity, judged un-constitutional by the Supreme Court in 1935. Another initiative, the Agricultural Adjustment Administration (AAA), withstood the test of the Supreme Court and authorized farm subsidies in return for crop reductions—in effect, paying farmers to grow less. Last, a welfare sys-tem, a vital New Deal component, made relief payments to the poor and the unemployed. Denounced by Republicans as a "dole," the Ci-vilian Conservation Corps (CCC), the Works Progress Administration (WPA), the Public Works Administration (PWA), and other such pro-grams put federal monies into the pockets of destitute people, turning them into low-level consumers.[17]

The New Deal also sought customers in foreign markets but some-times had difficulty reconciling interest groups with competing aims and priorities. Economic nationalists, many of them Republicans, pre-ferred to boost sales in domestic markets through the use of protective tariffs. In contrast, economic internationalists, often Democrats, wanted to promote foreign trade through tariff reductions. Financial and commercial groups also disagreed. The former, including lenders and bondholders, regarded timely payments on international debts as important. The latter, including foreign trade expansionists, preferred to defer debt collection until world economic recovery made repayment possible. Another difficulty was bureaucratic competition within the U.S. government, producing discord and confusion between the State and Treasury Departments. As secretary of state, Cordell Hull often bore the brunt.[18]

During the fall of 1933 the Roosevelt administration initiated a series of steps. On 11 November, the president convened an Executive Committee on Commercial Policy. Consisting of officials from the State and Treasury Departments, the Tariff Commission, and other New Deal agencies, this body advised that Congress allow the downward modification of tariff duties under presidential authority. Subsequently, the Reciprocal Trade Agreements Act of 2 March 1934 addressed the tariff question piecemeal by allowing for the negotiation of tariff reductions with individual countries by as much as 50 percent. Another innovation, the Export-Import Bank, created in the spring of 1934, provided the means for extending government credit to American businesses in foreign counties where commercial banks had closed down or curtailed services. Later, this agency also extended credit to foreign countries.[19]

To U.S. leaders an expanding trade in Latin America became significant for various reasons. For Assistant Secretary of State Francis B. Sayre, Woodrow Wilson's son-in-law and a former law professor from Yale University, the implications went beyond mere commerce. He feared the collapse of political and social systems, making Latin Americans dangerously susceptible to "anti-foreign and nationalistic programs." For U.S. critics the Latin American default on foreign debts appeared as confirmation. In response, financiers asked for help from Presidents Hoover and Roosevelt, both of whom responded cautiously. As Roosevelt explained, the issue was a private matter "between those republics and . . . the bondholders." Consequently, in December 1933 the latter formed a lobby, the Foreign Bondholders Protective Council, seeking to block new loans and other concessions to those countries already in default.

Overall, the Roosevelt administration attached more importance to trade expansion than to debt collection. Nevertheless, bureaucratic competition over priorities and preferences resulted in confusion and inconsistency, impairing the workability of economic diplomacy. In one episode, Treasury officials promised a loan to Brazil for establishing a

central bank and a currency stabilization fund and then encountered
obstruction from the State Department, pending an agreement for paying interest on U.S. loans. Such divisiveness also revealed personal an-
tagonism between the two secretaries, Henry J. Morgenthau Jr. of the
Treasury Department and Cordell Hull of State. According to Gellman,
the "bickering" interfered with otherwise laudable efforts to pursue "a
united approach."

In Latin America, Sumner Welles took charge of reciprocity programs under Cordell Hull's supervision. Described by Gellman as "less
dogmatic than his chief" on trade matters, Welles wanted to construct
"a firm hemispheric alliance" and looked upon improved economic
relations as an appropriate means toward that end. Gellman argues that
reciprocal trade agreements with Latin American nations failed to advance commercial expansion very much but in his view "unquestion-
ably moved the signatories toward greater understanding in other
endeavors." For example, the effects heightened levels of cooperation
during the Second World War.[20]

The first reciprocal trade agreement, signed with Cuba in August
1934, reduced tariff rates and established quotas for Cuban sugar and
tobacco. In effect, it provided a guarantee of access to the U.S. market.
Though advantageous for Cuba in the short term, the long-term consequences have become the object of controversy. For Cuban nationalists, reciprocity inhibited the economic diversification of their country
by perpetuating external economic dependence upon the United States.
As Gellman states, "the agreement . . . bound the island's commercial
activity closer than ever before to American-made decisions over which
Cubans had no control." Other authorities agree, suggesting that the
incorporation of Cuba within the protective system of the United States
in effect replaced the Platt amendment as a means of wielding influence. Henceforth, U.S. officials could administer rewards and punishments by raising or lowering the import quota, with direct effects upon
Cuban well-being.[21]

Brazil, a country more difficult to control, initially engaged in economic maneuvers, playing off one foreign interest against another. In
1930, President Getúlio Vargas, a paternalistic authoritarian, took charge,
supported by the military, and engaged both Germany and the United
States in commercial relationships. A trade agreement with Germany
in 1934 permitted tariff reductions and barter arrangements. A reciprocal trade agreement with the United States in 1935 also reduced tariffs.

State Department officials subsequently objected to Brazilian practices, regarding them as double-dealing. They especially disliked barter arrangements with the Germans, claiming that reciprocity with the United States disallowed them, and suggested a penalty, such as increased duties on Brazilian coffee. But Hull resisted because punishing Brazil might have adverse political consequences: Perhaps the country would side more closely with Germany, Italy, and Japan. Meanwhile, Vargas accepted calculated risks. Something of an opportunist, he sought trade with both Germany and the United States, reasoning correctly that the Roosevelt administration would not jeopardize political relations by resorting to commercial retaliation. The published works of the historians Frank D. McCann and Stanley E. Hilton provide full accounts.[22]

As McCann warns, historians should not interpret this "prewar maneuvering" too exclusively in ideological terms. For him, the competition was not so much a matter of "totalitarianism versus democracy" as "a struggle for raw materials and markets" at a time of global depression. Brazilians acted on the basis of economic imperatives. Following the establishment of the Estado Novo, or New State—a centralized, personalistic, and authoritarian entity created with the support of the Brazilian army in 1937—Vargas for a time became dependent on Germany for various purchases, including weapons. The United States, meanwhile, courted Brazil with offers of assistance in national defense, economic development, and foreign debt. Finally, after the fall of France to the Nazis in 1940, the United States outbid the Germans by making money available for Brazil's construction of the Volta Redonda steel mill. As McCann notes, this most significant agreement "signaled the beginning of Brazil's industrial coming of age" and "marked the end of the period in which Brazil could gain by playing Germany and the United States against each other." Thereafter, Brazil had "no choice but to enter completely the economic sphere of the United States."[23]

Between 1933 and 1945 the United States signed fifteen Latin American reciprocity agreements, eleven of them before 1940, which served the important purpose of drawing Latin Americans toward U.S. policies at a critical time. Sumner Welles regarded them as "the greatest positive achievement of the first Roosevelt Administration in the realm of international co-operation." In Welles's view, they contributed "greatly . . . in establishing a good neighbor policy in the Western Hemisphere."[24] For many Latin American nationalists, however, the reciprocity agreements had the negative consequences of functioning as impediments to economic diversification, providing yet another means of perpetuating economic dependence on the United States.

No Latin American country escaped the effects of the Great Depression. To stimulate recovery the governments employed various devices, including the promotion of foreign exports; the adoption of import-substitution strategies to diversify production in domestic markets; and the use of public works, road building and the like, to bolster demand at home. Such responses encouraged recuperation in eight countries. By 1934, Brazil, Chile, Costa Rica, Cuba, Guatemala, Mexico, Peru, and Venezuela were experiencing economic upswings. Others lagged behind. For most of Latin America, the export sector was critical. As Bulmer-Thomas explains, Latin Americans benefited from a world trade revival after 1932, in part because of U.S. reciprocity. As total foreign sales in U.S. markets grew by 137 percent between 1932 and 1937, Latin Americans obtained a share of the increase. Indeed, their "surprisingly robust" performance followed from traditional commitments to the export sector, viewed in most countries as "the engine of growth in the export-led model."

Germany also presented opportunities for Latin Americans. Based on barter arrangements and the aski-mark, usable only in the purchase of German goods, German trade practices attracted a growing share from Latin America. In 1938, the last year unaffected by the Second World War, Germany absorbed 10.3 percent of Latin America's exports and sold 17.1 percent of the imports. These figures compared favorably with 7.7 percent and 10.9 percent respectively in 1930. To an extent, Latin American sales in Germany expanded because of higher prices, calculated as inducements for accepting the aski-mark. Beneficiaries included Brazil, Colombia, and Costa Rica. Each country found new outlets for coffee sales in Germany but lost them after the outbreak of the war in 1939.[25]

Meanwhile, economic nationalism in Latin America posed other problems for U.S. leaders. First sanctioned in 1917 by Article 27 of the Mexican constitution, the principles of expropriation and nationalization threatened traditional conceptions of private property, especially mineral resources. The danger became acute late in the 1930s when the governments of Bolivia and Mexico actually carried out such procedures. For Latin American reformers and radicals, such forms of economic nationalism implied greater hope for modernization and economic growth than the traditional export-led models. Economic nationalism was also a means of combatting foreign domination through assertions of state sovereignty. In contrast, such doctrines impressed U.S. leaders as examples of predatory lawlessness.

In *The Making of the Good Neighbor Policy*, first published in 1961, the historian Bryce Wood develops a discerning analysis. He sees the leaders in the Roosevelt administration as repeatedly displaying their intention to implement a policy of nonintervention. As they understood the term, it meant a refusal "to employ armed force . . . to secure any policy objectives" in Latin America. They also endorsed a parallel effort to uphold a policy of noninterference, signifying their reluctance "to influence in any way the course of domestic political affairs in Latin American countries." Nevertheless, contrary tendencies sometimes got in the way. Seeking some kind of balance, most officials perceived no need for the United States to give up "all methods of influencing all aspects of the foreign relations of its neighbors," especially in defense of U.S. lives and property.

To obtain the requisite leverage, they accepted various techniques as part of the Good Neighbor policy. These included traditional diplomatic instruments—such as "financial inducements, protests, discriminatory practices of an economic or ceremonial character"—and others "to create positive collaboration among the American states." Wood regards "the idea of reciprocity" as central. In this context, the term refers to something broader than New Deal trade policy, suggesting "a neighborly response to neighborliness." Described as "an essential assumption of the new spirit," reciprocity presumed mutual respect for rights and obligations among states and called for new forms of common understanding. Problems, of course, resided in definitions. What U.S. leaders regarded as a neighborly consideration, that is, a high level of equitable treatment for U.S. citizens and property, sometimes impressed Latin Americans as preferential treatment for foreign interests in their own countries. Diplomatic difficulties arose in dealings with Bolivians and Mexicans who refused to grant the United States unilateral authority to define the term "Good Neighbor"; in their view the United States had to accept "the elimination of what they regarded as an equally offensive interference in their internal affairs" in order to qualify. This position meant abandonment of "that measure of support from Washington" that enabled "certain types of North American business enterprise to maintain the power and status they had secured before 1933."[26]

The Bolivian dispute arose over the holdings of a subsidiary of the Standard Oil Company of New Jersey. For more than a decade the government and the company had squabbled over taxes and royalties.

The problem worsened in the mid-1930s during the Chaco war against Paraguay. To obtain revenues the Bolivians asked for a loan that would be, in effect, an advance payment on future taxes. In refusing this request the company also announced plans to shut down the operation and to leave the country. The Bolivian government responded on 13 March 1937 by annulling Standard Oil's contract and confiscating its holdings. The official explanation alleged various illegalities, including nonpayment of taxes, as justification for denying compensation to the company.

Unprecedented in Latin American relations, this convoluted, drawn-out case took on special importance as a test of the Good Neighbor policy. In response to appeals for help from company officials the State Department first advised reliance on Bolivian legal remedies. In the U.S. view this approach failed when Bolivian judges showed hesitation to rule against the preferences of their own government. The United States then applied discreet pressure by withholding loans and achieved some measure of success. Bolivians wanted simultaneously to deny compensation to Standard Oil and to qualify for U.S. aid and credits.

A settlement finally took place in July 1941 after the failure of an allegedly pro-Nazi plot to overthrow President Enrique Peñaranda del Castillo. To stop German encroachments the United States offered economic and military assistance, signaling a shift in priorities: The European war, regional security, and hemispheric solidarity took precedence over the defense of property rights. A negotiated agreement subsequently provided that Bolivia pay $1.5 million to Standard Oil as compensation and also receive $25 million in U.S. aid. All parties could thus claim some satisfaction. Moreover, the Good Neighbor policy had passed the test. The Roosevelt administration had complied with the requirements of nonintervention, resisted the German threat, and blunted the effects of economic nationalism in Bolivia.[27]

Mexico introduced higher stakes on 18 March 1938 when President Lázaro Cárdenas expropriated the holdings of Dutch, British, and U.S. petroluem companies valued at some $500 million. The U.S. interest amounted to $200 million in land and $60 million in drilling equipment. By taking on foreign-owned oil corporations, Cárdenas accepted exceedingly high risks the consequences of which he could not accurately predict. As Bryce Wood notes, oil company officials, characterized as "influential and uncompromising," might secure "effective support" from their governments.[28] In politically charged Mexico, moreover, a large-scale failure could arouse strong opposition against Cárdenas, possibly even a revolt.

In 1938, Cárdenas occupied a precarious position. Elected to the Mexican presidency in 1934, he was an authentic revolutionary hero and a former state governor of Michoacán. He was also the protégé of the former president, *el jefe máximo* Plutarco Elías Calles. As president, Cárdenas gradually liberated himself from Calles's tutelage, eventually forcing the former president into exile. Once in control of his own regime, Cárdenas presented himself as a committed heir of the revolution of 1910. Among his goals, he championed the redistribution of land to landless campesinos, the country people, by forming agricultural cooperatives known as *ejidos*; he sought better wages and working conditions for the laboring classes by favoring unions, especially the Confederation of Mexican Workers (Confederación de Trabajadores Mexicanos) under Vicente Lombardo Toledano; and he promoted literacy through advances in secular education. But then a resumption of economic crisis in 1937 threatened Mexico with bankruptcy and collapse.

The emergency had many bad effects. Cárdenas resorted to deficit spending to rescue his government but possessed limited resources for reform. Discontent mounted among country people, workers, and the business classes. Moreover, the Spanish civil war beginning in 1936 conjured "a terrifying preview of Mexico's future." What if Mexico should follow Spain's example and disintegrate into mayhem and violence? For enthusiasts among Mexican conservatives and reactionaries, Spanish General Francisco Franco, a leader of the revolt, personified Hispanic traditions of authority and hierarchy. As William H. Beezley explains, Cárdenas embraced programs of economic nationalism "to unite a people deeply splintered by the economic disruption of the Great Depression" and by "the inability of the government to continue the social programs of the revolution."[29]

A labor-management issue ignited the oil controversy. In May 1937, seventeen thousand petroleum workers went on strike, demanding improvements in wages, working conditions, housing, medical care, and education. When an arbitration decision went against the oil companies, the leaders took the case to the courts, where they experienced another setback: The Mexican Supreme Court ruled in favor of the workers, depriving the companies of further legal remedy. Unreconciled, company officials then escalated the issue by rejecting the outcome and challenging the sovereignty of the Mexican government.

Unable to tolerate such defiance, Cárdenas announced expropriation proceedings against the companies in a national radio address on 18 March 1938. As justification, he invoked not Article 27 of the constitution, the restriction on property, but Article 123, the labor provision. In his view, the rights of working people and the jurisdictional integrity of the Mexican Supreme Court allowed room for no compromise: he had to defend them at all costs. Patriotic Mexicans rallied in his support. They applauded Cárdenas for his resolve, in effect, declaring economic independence from foreign control. The oil producers, in contrast, issued protests. They depicted the expropriation as a crime against private property, a despicable act probably inspired by Bolsheviks. To combat it, they gave a strong impression of inviting military intervention.[30]

Put to the test in Mexico, the Good Neighbor policy compelled measured responses. As Bryce Wood describes it, U.S. policy unfolded in four phases. First, within a few weeks the United States accepted the expropriation as legal but expected Mexican compensation to the companies for their losses. Second, for the next two years, until April 1940, negotiations went nowhere, culminating in a Mexican refusal of arbitration. Third, discussions until November 1941 revolved around Mexican counterproposals for a joint commission. Fourth, during the spring of 1942 the joint commissioners at last concluded an agreement, leaving the oil companies no choice except acquiescence.

Wood carefully establishes the key propositions. From the outset a dangerous possibility existed. What if a "peremptory" response by the United States ruled out negotiations by forcing Cárdenas into breaking diplomatic relations? U.S. Ambassador Josephus Daniels played an indispensable role in heading off any such outcome through the exercise of "a remarkable combination of insubordination and suppression of information." A North Carolina reformer who had served as secretary of the navy under Wilson, Daniels had ordered the occupation of Veracruz in 1914 with Franklin Roosevelt as his assistant secretary. Now an advocate of Good Neighborliness, he toned down State Department objections during the early stages and assured Washington of Cárdenas's "sincere intention" to offer compensation. His role established some measure of mutual understanding. Indeed, Daniels in "his unique and unorthodox fashion . . . had imposed on the Department of State his own judgment of the way the United States should deal with Mexico as a Good Neighbor."

Wood also contends that the State Department never seriously considered the use of armed force. Though oil company press releases and propaganda introduced such possibilities, no doubt causing worry in the Cárdenas government, Ambassador Francisco Castillo Nájera of Mexico affirmed his faith in June 1938 in the credibility of the nonintervention commitment. Later, the Roosevelt administration refrained from interjecting the petroleum issue into the Mexican presidential election of 1940. After the victory of the official candidate, General Manuel Avila Camacho, Roosevelt indicated good faith by sending Vice President Henry A. Wallace to the inauguration ceremonies in November 1940.

At the same time, the United States employed economic pressure to encourage prompt settlement. Reduced purchases of Mexican silver inflicted some distress; the oil companies impeded Mexican exports into world markets by denying tankers, pipes, and essential machinery and by discouraging other countries from purchasing Mexican petroleum. Never distinguished by much success, these undertakings also entailed risks: What if Mexico should embrace Germany, Italy, and Japan in bids for overseas markets? The U.S. government also withheld loans from August 1937 until November 1941. But none of these policies ever took the "drastic" form, for example, of denying the legality of the expropriation. The U.S. aim was settlement between the oil companies and Mexico through some kind of compensation.

One possible means of resolution, arbitration proceedings, possessed the sanction of international law. The oil companies and also the governments of Great Britain, the Netherlands, and the United States initially favored this approach. But Mexican leaders regarded arbitration as a function of Great-Power domination, a device more likely to uphold foreign interests than Mexican sovereignty. They preferred to establish a joint commission in which each government would appoint one member and from which no appeal could take place. Once the Roosevelt administration accepted this plan as the best means available to the United States, a settlement followed in the spring of 1942.

U.S. concerns for regional defense and hemispheric solidarity thus assumed priority over property rights, much as in the earlier Bolivian case. Put succinctly, the onset of the Second World War encouraged U.S. officials to perceive "the national interest" as "different from" and "superior to" oil company interests. For example, by the spring of 1941 the War Department urgently wanted access to Mexican air bases as links to Panama. In Wood's word, such considerations became "crucial." Consequently, an agreement on 19 November 1941 approved the use of a joint commission. It also allowed for broad discussion of other issues, including U.S. agrarian property claims against Mexico, the purchase of Mexican silver, the negotiation of a reciprocal trade agreement, and the extension of loans through the Export-Import bank. The terms fixed the compensation for U.S. oil companies at $24 million. Lacking other recourse, the oil companies grudgingly accepted this outcome. At least they got something out of the deal.[31]

The episode had great importance. In the 1930s, Mexico had become a preferred model for Latin American nationalists, and the Cárdenas regime possessed high prestige. As a result, some U.S. leaders worried about the dangers of "socialism," "extreme radicalism," and "communism" in other countries. They also feared Axis influence. In this context, as noted by the historian David Green, oil company "intransigence" had the ironic effect of making Germany, Italy, and Japan potential outlets for Mexican oil exports. To avoid "serious consequences," the United States needed "some kind of rapprochement with Latin American nationalists."

Roosevelt acknowledged as much on 12 January 1940 in a statement before newspaper reporters. In uncharacteristically disarranged syntax, he said, "There is a new approach that I am talking about to these South American things. . . . Give them a share. They think they are just as good as we are, and many of them are." Whatever the degree of condescension, the president's observation signaled a certain readiness to bestow upon Latin Americans "a share of decision-making authority in inter-American economic concerns" and "a share of the wealth being developed from Latin America's vast resources by private and public capital." Otherwise, as Green observes, private firms might risk the loss of everything, since Latin American strategies for economic development required increasingly national control of economic resources.[32]

A similar issue appeared strikingly in relations with Venezuela. In 1935 the death of long-time dictator Juan Vicente Gómez introduced a period of change. Under Gómez, the head of state since 1908, companies such as Standard Oil of New Jersey, Royal Dutch Shell, and Gulf had obtained easy access to Venezuelan resources while enjoying low taxes and high profits.[33] Subsequently, when a new regime headed by

Eleazar López Contreras introduced reforms, including the eight-hour day and collective bargaining, oil company officials worried about the implications. What if Venezuela should follow the Mexican example? By this time the country ranked as the leading petroleum exporter in the world, and U.S. investments in Venezuelan oil in 1940 amounted to $375 million.

For reasons of their own, Venezuelans followed a different model. Less radical in approach, the Venezuelan constitution of 1936 contained no equivalent of Article 27 in the Mexican constitution of 1917. Conducting a kind of cost-benefit analysis, Venezuelan leaders recognized their dependence on petroleum exports and chose to avoid the crippling effects of cutting too heavily into the profits. In Venezuela, then, petroleum resources remained under private control but subject to higher taxes and royalty payments. During the Second World War a policy of collaboration with Latin American governments willing to share their resources became for the United States its best means of assuring access.[34]

FROM NEUTRALITY TO WAR

The Second World War occasioned unprecedented diplomatic cooperation among the nations of the Western Hemisphere. Seeking to coordinate regional responses, the United States first tried to uphold neutrality while providing safeguards against other consequences. The participants at a series of inter-American conferences in Lima, Panama, Havana, and Rio de Janeiro proclaimed "continental solidarity," the existence of a war-free zone, and the applicability of the "no transfer" clause. After Pearl Harbor, all the Latin American nations except Argentina and Chile supported the United States, either by declaring war on the Axis nations or by severing diplomatic relations with them. Among other things, U.S. access to Latin American resources was at stake. In the words of the historian R. A. Humphreys, "In 1939 Latin America was the richest raw material producing area in the world free from the control of any Great Power."[35] At a time of global conflict the prize was well worth having.

Competition over markets and resources had figured prominently in the destabilization of world politics in the 1930s. Economic imperatives drove Japanese expansion in Asia, contributing to the Manchuria crisis in 1931–32 and to "the China incident"—really a full-scale invasion—in 1937. Similarly, German ambitions in Europe, the incorporation of German-speaking peoples into the Third Reich, and the eastward move into the Slavic domains precipitated confrontations in the middle and late 1930s. These encounters culminated in the onset of war over Poland in September 1939. U.S. leaders, meanwhile, espoused neutral policies but increasingly embraced pro-British positions.

Beginning in 1935 the U.S. Congress passed a series of three Neutrality Acts. Based on the experience of 1914–1917, these measures disallowed certain practices. They denied loans and arms sales to warring nations and imposed a cash-and-carry provision to reduce the risk of submarine attacks on U.S. merchants ships: Belligerents had to pay "cash" for U.S. goods and "carry" them away in their own vessels. After the fact, these acts ruled out U.S. participation in the First World War. They also hamstrung President Roosevelt by permitting no aid for the victims and no penalties for the aggressors.

U.S. responses to the Axis threat compelled careful maneuvers. Roosevelt presided over a divided country and could not move too far or too fast. One identifiable group, the "internationalists," functioned as Woodrow Wilson's heirs, championing a conception of world organization and collective security. They favored strong measures by the Western democracies in defense of liberal-capitalist institutions but encountered a classic dilemma: How could they calculate the effects of such measures? Would tough policies deter aggression or precipitate a conflict? The internationalists also faced strong opposition from the so-called isolationists, who resisted commitments in defense of other countries and insisted upon "America First." Some feared the consequences of participating in another European war; for them the U.S. entry into the First World War had accomplished no good purpose and was a mistake that did not bear repeating. The disinclination of others to stand against the Axis powers followed from pro-fascist and anti-Semitic proclivities.

These swirling tides within the two parties and the Congress created immense difficulties for Roosevelt. Increasingly, he saw Axis aggression in Europe and Asia as security threats. He defined the issue less as a danger of invasion than as a menace to fundamental interests and ideals or, put another way, to sets of assumptions and commitments upon which larger purposes depended. In modern historiography, some scholars have used the term "Open Door" as a characterization. Understood symbolically, this phrase conveys an impression of the sort of world preferred by U.S. policymakers in the twentieth century and implies fundamental goals and aims, involving some form of obligation— at least rhetorical—in support of liberal capitalism. The goals included free trade, private ownership of property, national self-determination, and representative democracy. U.S. leaders favored such conventions and usages as affirmations of core values, supposedly appropriate for adoption by other peoples and also the means of serving national objectives, which included high levels of prosperity, safety, and ideological integrity. According to this view, the United States could function best in an open world organized much like itself. Conversely, these objectives called forth resistance to the division of the world into spheres of influence, the creation of exclusive trading blocks, and the depredations of militaristic dictatorships.[36]

Franklin Roosevelt's twists and turns, moving the United States toward a policy of aiding Great Britain by measures short of war, have attracted a great deal of scholarly attention. Many historians have noted that for him the shortest distance between two points was seldom a straight line. According to Robert A. Divine, Roosevelt often "moved two steps forward and one back before he took the giant step ahead." Keeping his own counsel, the president employed devious, secretive methods sometimes verging on outright deception. According to Vice President Henry A. Wallace, he performed as a juggler who "could keep all [the] balls in the air without losing his own." An important book by Warren F. Kimball employs the same metaphor in its title.[37]

Following the outbreak of war over Poland in September 1939, Roosevelt's policies tilted by increments toward the Allies. In response, the Congress in November 1939 changed the Neutrality Acts so that France and Great Britain could purchase arms and supplies in the United States on a cash-and-carry basis. The French defeat in June 1940 and subsequently the Battle of Britain created new concerns, leading to a destroyers-for-bases deal in September 1940. Devised as an executive agreement between Roosevelt and Prime Minister Winston Churchill, it allowed a swap of fifty U.S. destroyers in return for U.S. leases on British bases in the Western Hemisphere. Roosevelt defended this profoundly unneutral act as the means of keeping the United States out of the war and Britain in it. Later, he upheld the Lend-Lease proposal on similar grounds. This measure set off a fierce fight in Congress. Once accepted in March 1941, it permitted the United States to lend or lease instruments and commodities of war to Britain and "any country [such as the Soviet Union] whose defense the President deems vital to the defense of the United States."[38] It also exposed U.S. merchant ships to German submarine attacks. During the fall of 1941 an undeclared naval war got under way against the Germans in the North Atlantic.

Between 1938 and 1941, apprehensive leaders in the New World tried to insulate their region against the worst effects. After the failure of the British and French experiment with appeasing Germany at Munich in September 1938, Assistant Secretary of State Sumner Welles called for vigilance against aggression "from whatever source" and urged the United States "to join with our fellow democracies of the New World in preserving the Western Hemisphere safe from any threat of attack." Considerations of "hemispheric solidarity" figured prominently at the Eighth International Conference of American States at Lima in December 1938, where, happily for U.S. policymakers, the northern colossus no longer looked quite so much like Latin America's natural enemy. Cordell Hull again led the U.S. delegation and stopped along the way in Panama, Colombia, and Ecuador, focusing attention on unity and friendship. In Lima, he encountered dissent from Argentine Foreign Minister José María Cantilo, who cautioned against overreaction. Cantilo recalled Argentina's traditional European ties, especially with Italy and Germany, and opposed a regional alliance against either one. In the end, compromises muted Argentine objections and allowed for the Declaration of Lima on Christmas Eve. This statement affirmed continental solidarity against foreign intervention in the Western Hemisphere but refrained from designating any nation as a specific threat.

It also allowed for conferences of foreign ministers to coordinate future policy. After the outbreak of war in Europe on 1 September 1939 the first Meeting of Consultation of Ministers of Foreign Affairs of the American Republics assembled in Panama on 23 September. This time Sumner Welles headed the U.S. delegation. In a speech on 25 September, he advocated Pan American uniformity in establishing neutral policies. In a sequence of sessions lasting eight days the participants formed committees, discussed common interests, and drafted the Declaration of Panama. This measure—unenforceable, as it turned out—erected a shield against acts of war by establishing a three-hundred-mile security zone around North and South America and instructing the belligerents to keep out. The question was whether the warring countries would abide by the prohibition.

Naval contingents displayed disinclination to do so. In December 1939 the German pocket battleship *Graf Spee* entered the South Atlantic and engaged three British cruisers in battle off the Uruguayan coast. Forced by heavy damage to seek refuge in port at Montevideo, the German captain, Hans Langsdorff, asked for two weeks for repairs; the British stipulated one day, and the Uruguayans settled on seventy-two hours. Faced with an impossibility, Langsdorff scuttled his vessel, arranged for his crew's internment in Argentina, and committed suicide.

How to safeguard the neutrality zone became a source of contention. Diplomatic representations to the Germans and the British had scant effect. Indeed, the United States accepted British "hot pursuit" when German commerce raiders sought safe haven in the zone. Other U.S. practices further bent neutrality in Britain's favor: They allowed the capture of German merchant ships within the zone by the Royal Navy and, in the spring of 1941, aided British operations by providing radio information on German locations. Roosevelt nevertheless kept up a public masquerade, depicting U.S. actions as purely defensive. Ironically, the security zone, initially a function of neutrality and hemispheric solidarity, turned into a cover for aiding the Allies by methods short of war.

Another issue became acute. What if the Germans acquired bases in the Western Hemisphere from conquered countries? Following the French collapse in June 1940 the United States could not rule out such possibilities. To guard against them the State Department formulated a resolution, later endorsed by Congress, based on the "no-transfer" principle. Traditionally associated with the Monroe Doctrine, this tenet withheld U.S. recognition of "any transfer" of "any geographic region of the Western Hemisphere from one non–American power to another non-American power." Though mocked by German officials as delusionary and pretentious, the no-transfer resolution won support from Western Hemisphere diplomats at a conference in Havana on 26 July 1940. In this way, they ruled out the possibility of Germans occupying Dutch, Danish, and French possessions in the New World.[39]

U.S. leaders also worried about Nazi subversion. By 1940 a million German colonists were living in Latin America, most of them in southern South America. Reputedly, the Germans resisted assimilation and affirmed their national identities through schools, newspapers, radio broadcasts, and expatriate organizations. The question of whether they functioned as political affiliates of the Third Reich and promoted Latin American fascism became a source of much discussion. German economic penetration also produced apprehension; for example, the rivalry over Latin American routes between Lufthansa and Pan American Airlines had military implications for air power. Consequently, influential writers such as the journalists Carleton Beals and John Gunther and the historian Samuel Flagg Bemis drew attention to such matters, calling for appropriate safeguards. President Roosevelt, meanwhile, used allegations of aggressive design as justification for British aid. According to his Pan American Day address on 27 May 1941, "Adolf Hitler never considered the domination of Europe as an end in itself"; therefore, "unless the advance of Hitlerism is forcibly checked now, the Western Hemisphere will be within range of the Nazi weapons of destruction." One such disaster scenario imagined German moves from Africa to Brazil to the Caribbean, imperiling the Panama Canal. In another speech on 27 October 1941, Roosevelt claimed to possess a map showing secret Nazi plans for Latin American conquests. When pressed by reporters to display it, he refused, invoking confidentiality to protect his sources. Such statements, unsubstantiated by evidence, underscored his growing pro-British convictions.[40]

Japan's assault on Pearl Harbor brought the United States into the Second World War. Best understood as a desperate act, the attack followed a period of fruitless negotiation in the course of which neither country showed much interest in accommodation. Japanese leaders insisted upon a free hand in what they called a Greater East Asia Co-Prosperity Sphere, described as an equivalent of the Monroe Doctrine. Unconvinced, Secretary Hull defended the sanctity of the Open Door. To the Japanese, this meant either accepting a status of dependency upon the United States or affirming national prerogatives as a Great Power. Taking a big risk, Japan inaugurated hostilities against the United States with a surprise attack. In a war message to Congress the next day, Roosevelt referred to 7 December 1941 in a famous phrase as "a date which will live in infamy." Following the U.S. declaration of war, Germany and Italy honored the Tripartite Pact with Japan four days later by declaring war on the United States. The undeclared conflict in the North Atlantic had turned into a full-scale shooting war on two fronts.[41]

For other Western Hemisphere nations the U.S. declaration of war entailed pressing urgencies. In December 1941, nine Central American and Caribbean republics declared war on Japan, later on Germany and Italy; Colombia, Venezuela, and Mexico severed relations. In response, Adolf Berle, an assistant secretary of state, set forth an assessment later endorsed by many historians: "The heartening thing . . . is the swift and virtually unanimous support from all the republics of this hemisphere. If ever a policy paid dividends, the Good Neighbor policy has. So far, they are sticking with us with scarcely a break."

Following the procedures established at Havana, the Western Hemisphere nations again assembled for consultations, this time at Rio de Janeiro on 15 January 1942. Given the disaster at Pearl Harbor the

delegates had to take into account an act of aggression actually committed against an American state. In preparation, the U.S. State Department sought compliance with Secretary Hull's preferences. The agenda
included a resolution requiring all American republics to sever relations
with the Axis powers but not necessarily to declare war. The distinction was based on an understanding of limited capability. The United
States could not defend the entire Western Hemisphere.

On this occasion, Hull, worn out from the Japanese negotiations,
had allowed Sumner Welles to take over as head of the U.S. delegation. Welles understood Hull's objective but anticipated resistance.
Chile reportedly feared Japanese hit-and-run attacks along the coast,
and Argentina favored neutrality. Welles hoped for support from
Brazil but could not accomplish Hull's goal. Neither Chile nor Argentina would sever relations. On his own authority, Welles accepted
a compromise, recommending but not requiring a break in relations
with the Axis. In a fury, Hull upbraided Welles for sabotaging State
Department policy, but Welles had Roosevelt's support; the recommendation stood. Soon afterward, Peru, Uruguay, Bolivia, Paraguay,
Brazil, and Ecuador broke relations, making the total eighteen. As a
consequence, most historians bestow high marks on the Roosevelt
administration for achieving multilateral cooperation with Latin
America during the Second World War.[42]

WARTIME RELATIONS

Latin American leaders supported the United States during the Second World War for various reasons. Usually, their decisions centered
on questions of political and economic advantage more than on abstract
notions of hemispheric solidarity. Latin American governments feared
for their own security if the Nazis or the Japanese made a move into the
Western Hemisphere, but more significantly, they recognized the U.S.
capacity to reward and punish. By severing ties or declaring war, Latin
Americans might secure the means for coping with inimical circumstances. The Axis powers controlled Europe, and the Allies dominated
the high seas. Taken together, these geopolitical configurations cut off
Latin Americans from the continent and accentuated dependencies
upon the United States. In response, Mexico and Brazil accepted high
risks and declared war, whereas Chile and Argentina for much of the
war stayed neutral for reasons of their own.

Specific judgments varied from country to country. Overall, the
Caribbean and Central American republics fashioned their responses
to please the United States. Among other things, they wanted economic

Caribbean +
CA

outlets and political support against internal dissidents. By declaring war, they advanced each goal. In Cuba, Colonel Fulgencio Batista, formerly the power behind the scenes, won the presidential election in 1940, depending on the army as a base of support. As president, he qualified for U.S. economic and military assistance from the Export-Import Bank and the Lend-Lease Program. In Haiti, President Elíe Lescot's government acted on ideological imperatives by going on record in opposition to Nazi racial doctrines, and in the Dominican Republic, Generalissimo Rafael Leonidas Trujillo Molina somewhat fantastically depicted his dictatorial regime as a bastion of liberty in defense of the Western Hemisphere. In these countries, war declarations meant modest U.S. economic and military aid.[43]

Central American reactions developed similarly. In Costa Rica, President Rafael Calderón Guardia aligned his democratic country with the United States on ideological grounds. Elsewhere, the authoritarian regimes of Presidents Maximiliano Hernández Martínez of El Salvador, Anastasio Somoza of Nicaragua, Tiburcio Carías Andino of Honduras, and Jorge Ubico of Guatemala went along with the United States in anticipation of assistance for their economies and their police forces. The United States especially prized order in regions close by the Panama Canal Zone. In Panama itself, sensitive questions of national sovereignty complicated U.S. efforts to secure air bases and other installations. In return for granting access to them, President Arnulfo Arias required various forms of compensation and also assurances in defense of Panamanian national prerogatives.

When obliged to pick between Germany and the United States, most Latin American leaders opted for the latter. In politically factionalized Mexico after the election of 1940, President Avila Camacho wanted to consolidate his country politically and also to develop more regular relations with the United States. The petroleum issue presented a potential obstacle; nevertheless, a wartime alliance took shape between the two nations. Consequently, Mexico permitted the use of air bases in its territory; the United States purchased Mexican products and strategic materials at high prices; and on 30 May 1942, after German submarine attacks on Mexican tankers, the Mexican government formally entered the war. Later, in March 1945, the Mexican air force participated in attacks against the Japanese in the Philippines and Formosa.

Most South American countries also developed pro-U.S. policies by cutting ties with the Axis. Their reasons included economic advantage and national security. In Venezuela the defense of oil exports compelled such action from President Isaías Medina Angarita. In Colombia, President Eduardo Santos believed that the national interests of his country corresponded with those of the United States. Similar perceptions prevailed in the governments of Carlos Arroyo del Río in Ecuador, Manuel Prado y Ugarteche of Peru, Enrique Peñaranda del Castillo of Bolivia, Higinio Morjínigo of Paraguay, and Alfredo Baldomir of Uruguay. They all broke relations with the Axis powers.

Brazilian leaders actually declared war. Under authority of the Estado Novo, Dr. Getúlio Vargas constructed an "entirely personal" dictatorship. Described by R. A. Humphreys as "a master of the arts of political manipulation and persuasion," Vargas employed "a Machiavellian astuteness" to maintain "a delicate balance" between civilian and military interests. Supposedly standing above partisan strife, he presented himself with some measure of accuracy as "a paternal statesman devoted to his country, the development of its resources, and the welfare of its people."

For Latin Americans during the war, adherence to pro-U.S. policies generally paid some kind of dividends. For Brazil a "steady" economic recovery in 1941 reflected "the great expansion of trade with the United States," regarded by Humphreys as "the prime cause." Various economic devices contributed. For example, the Inter-American Coffee Agreement in April 1941 halted "ruinous competition among the coffee-producing countries" and guaranteed Brazil "a fair share of the North American market at enhanced prices." Other agreements channeled the sale of strategic materials to the United States, increasing Brazilian mineral exports.

The country also possessed geopolitical significance. The great Brazilian "bulge" extending eastward from Natal and Recife made the Atlantic narrows the shortest route to the New World from Africa. Because this largely defenseless region appeared as a potential invitation to German invasion, the United States constructed air bases in Brazil and developed other forms of military and naval cooperation. Though reluctant to admit U.S. troops, Vargas did want military aid through Lend-Lease. Consequently, Brazil broke Axis relations on 28 January 1942 and declared war in August. In 1944, Brazilian army contingents took part in the Italian campaign, the only Latin American military force so engaged in Europe.

Different considerations governed decisions elsewhere. In Argentina, neutrality functioned as the guide. According to Humphreys, pro-Axis sympathies affected the officer corps in the German-trained Argentine army. Moreover, fascist and ultranationalist doctrines appealed, as Humphreys explains, "to arch-conservatives, to upper-class young men-about-town, to right-wing intellectuals and others who sought to rehabilitate the reputation of the greatest and worst of Argentine tyrants": that is, the nineteenth-century strongman Juan Manuel de Rosas. Nevertheless, "the majority of Argentines, if they feared that Britain would lose, hoped that she would win." The "public mind was confused"; the "barometric pressure tended to move up and down according to events in Europe," suggesting a large measure of "uncertainty." British markets absorbed large quantities of Argentine beef and mutton but could not compensate for the loss of continental sales. Mounting surpluses heightened economic insecurity, and the succession of military officers moving in and out of high political offices suggested impending instability. After Pearl Harbor the civilian president, Ramón S. Castillo, officially declared neutrality as "the best and the safest policy." Unlike Vargas, who decided that "he must stand or fall with the United States," neither President Castillo nor the Argentine foreign minister, Dr. Enrique Ruiz-Guiñazú, invested much faith in the credibility of Pan American alignments under U.S. leadership. Moreover, neither one anticipated an Allied victory at the end of the war.

Chile also stayed neutral at first. Beset by "strikes, rising living costs, and administrative incompetence," a Popular Front government dissolved in January 1941, ripped to pieces by the competition among Radical, Conservative, Socialist, and Communist parties. Deeply divided, the country tried to avoid international complications. At the same time, as Humphreys notes, "there was little doubt where the preponderance of Chilean sympathies lay in 1941." Characterized as "hard-headed, cautious and independent," Chileans favored the Allies but feared an outbreak of war in the south Atlantic and the possibility of an Allied defeat. They also worried about Japanese raids along their lengthy, exposed coastline. Chile consequently remained neutral until 20 January 1943, when at last President Juan Antonio Ríos embraced a pro-Allies position by breaking off diplomatic ties with the Axis powers. At this point, he feared the effects of political and economic isolation in the Western Hemisphere more than the Germans and the Japanese.[44]

Although during the Second World War the United States forged closer military, cultural, and economic links with Latin America than ever before, questions of interpretation pose a problem. Some historians argue that the establishment of close ties ranked as a significant form of Pan American achievement, part of a praiseworthy effort to transform "the Western Hemisphere idea" into reality.[45] More skeptical historians depict the wartime Pan American partnership as something of an illusion, perhaps even a deception to obscure hegemonic designs. According to this interpretation, U.S. leaders used the war as a means of consolidating previous gains under the Good Neighbor policy, thereby guaranteeing access to Latin American resources and perpetuating U.S. dominance.[46]

In the years before the war, military collaboration between the United States and Latin America hardly existed at all. Latin American armies typically relied on European professionals and arms suppliers for training and equipment. As late as 1939, German advisers were operating in about half the countries of Latin America. (Brazil, an exception, had hosted small U.S. military and naval missions since the First World War.) During the 1920s and 1930s, U.S. officials displayed little interest in cultivating Latin American military connections. When in support of the Good Neighbor policy Sumner Welles argued in favor of such measures, he encountered mainly indifference and prejudice toward Latin Americans among the U.S. military, naval, and foreign policy elites.

Following the catastrophic French defeat in June 1940, an abrupt change took place in U.S. thinking. The so-called Rainbow strategic war plans anticipated the possibilities of fighting on various fronts and in different combinations in the Atlantic, the Pacific, or both. The planners assumed a vital interest in defending the Western Hemisphere region, especially the Caribbean, and, for such purposes, assigned the primary responsibility to U.S. military and naval forces. Other parts of the plans called for the cultivation of Latin American cooperation to assure access to strategic materials and the acquisition of land, sea, and air bases. U.S. officials showed scant appreciation for Latin American sensitivities over issues of national sovereignty; they wanted long-term leases with full jurisdiction but typically settled for less, since few host governments wanted U.S. troops stationed outright in their countries. As a subterfuge in Brazil, the authorities described them as unarmed technicians who would manage U.S. bases for the duration and get out once the war ended.

The early German successes elicited alarm and pessimism. During the Battle of Britain in 1940, U.S. observers fully expected German attacks in the New World if British forces should suffer a defeat. Although the German invasion of the Soviet Union on 22 June 1941 dissipated the immediacy of that fear, defensive preparations took many forms. The U.S. Navy kept close watch by multiplying the number of seagoing patrols in the Atlantic; the U.S. Army courted military counterparts in Latin America by developing new means of cooperation such as the Inter-American Defense Board created at the Rio conference early in 1942; and the distribution of aid and supplies in conjunction with the Lend-Lease Program proffered an assortment of rewards for compliant Latin Americans. The Panama Canal, vulnerable to either sabotage or air attack, posed special problems in defense. U.S. officials never fully solved them but used air patrols to guard against surprises.[47]

Following Hitler's declaration of war on the United States in December 1941, German submarines inaugurated deadly assaults against merchant ships in the Caribbean. Oil tankers moving precious cargoes from Mexico and Venezuela became favorite targets. The sinkings escalated in number from 24 in February 1942 to 66 in June of the same year. Such attacks concentrated in the sea-lanes around Trinidad, the Panama Canal, the Yucatán Channel, and the Windward Passage between Cuba and Haiti, where a total of 336 ships went down. The worst of the carnage ended early in 1943, once U.S. authorities had learned how to minimize the effects through the proper use of naval convoys, air patrols, and other forms of antisubmarine warfare.[48]

The defeat of the German U-boats extinguished the enemy naval presence in the Western Hemisphere and raised other questions. At a time of fierce fighting around the world, some U.S. leaders, such as Secretary of War Henry Stimson, wondered why Latin American countries that were uninvolved in actual combat should qualify for military assistance under Lend-Lease. In the State Department, Sumner Welles raised the same issue and worried about the effects of an impending Latin American arms race. Also causing criticism was the belief that dictators such as Somoza, Trujillo, and Ubico were using military aid to keep themselves in power. Irwin F. Gellman observes that only small amounts—about 1.1 percent of all Lend-Lease aid—went to Latin America, mainly to Brazil and Mexico. In his view the "hemispheric despots," though admittedly beneficiaries of U.S. miltary aid, relied more heavily on other means to maintain their control. Paul Coe Clark Jr.'s study of the United States and Somoza arrives at a similar conclusion, showing that the dictator's survivability depended more on his own unscrupulous political skills than on U.S. support.[49]

For the United States, military cooperation with Latin American officials paid off in various ways. The Inter-American Defense Board advanced a sense of goodwill and common purpose. As Gellman explains, it functioned something like "a hemispheric war college" in which Latin Americans could acquire instruction in the use of U.S. methods and equipment. Such forms of miltary collaboration also had political significance. Although under the terms of most agreements the United States would lose access to Latin American bases at the end of the war, the War Department intended "to extend inter-American comradeship into the postwar era" through the cultivation of the Latin American officer corps. For proponents of U.S. air power the maintenance of bases in Latin America had particular significance.[50]

The Roosevelt administration also employed cultural diplomacy to combat the Nazis. Wartime propaganda emphasized likenesses and affinities with Latin Americans. Its purpose was to underscore "the mythical ideological unity of the nations of the New World" and draw sharp distinctions between totalitarian powers and the "democratically oriented nations of the Western Hemisphere." A typical State Department memorandum in September 1939 listed the "distinguishing ideals and beliefs which bind us together," including "faith in republican institutions, loyalty to democracy as an ideal, reverence for liberty, acceptance of the dignity of the individual, . . . aversion to the use of force [and] adherence to the principles of equal sovereignty of states and justice under international law." Such formulations played down the prevalence of authoritarian regimes. If necessary for purposes of public relations, U.S. leaders could depict Batista, Somoza, Trujillo, and Ubico as old-fashioned military strongmen who differed in important ways from the European totalitarians.[51]

Negative stereotypes everywhere distorted popular perceptions on all sides. In the United States, pervasive images depicted Latin American males as indolent and licentious. In political cartoons, they took long naps under enormous sombreros during the siesta hour or lustily pursued long-haired, dark-eyed señoritas. Similarly flawed, Latin American renditions depended too heavily on clichéd versions of the Yankee capitalist, notable for his greed and crass materialism. To combat misconceptions and promote goodwill, the Roosevelt administration became "culture conscious." U.S. government officials believed that "economic and political cooperation" would follow from "intellectual and cultural understanding" and consequently emphasized "a sympathetic understanding of tradition, history, literature, and the arts."[52] On 6 August 1940 the Roosevelt administration created the Office of the Coordinator of Inter-American Affairs (OCIAA). Headed by Nelson A. Rockefeller, the talented and ambitious scion of an oil-rich Republican family, this agency assumed the responsibility of promoting a coherent Pan American system, seeking thereby to attain an omnibus purpose "to prevent revolutions in the Americas, fight Axis agents, and increase United States trade." In order to work, the OCIAA had to avoid the impression of "interfering in any way with the internal affairs of those sovereign states." Rockefeller devised "a multifaceted program of ideological, cultural, and financial persuasion." Budgeted initially at $3.5 million from Roosevelt's emergency fund, the OCIAA by 1942 became a $38 million operation, attempting to present the United States to Latin America as "the beneficent, philanthropic, understanding, yet humble sister nation in the hemispheric family of free and equally idealistic republics."

As distribution outlets the agency employed radio broadcasts, newspapers, magazines, and motion pictures, all the while encouraging favorable, upbeat treatment of the United States and Latin America. The office would not sanction criticism of imperfections in the U.S. political system and blocked the distribution of the movie *Mr. Smith Goes to Washington* in Latin America because it reflected negatively on the activities of the U.S. Congress. Similarly, the office compelled changes to eliminate offensive stereotypes in the film *Down Argentine Way*: a smarmy Argentine gigolo who spoke with a Mexican accent and a crooked horse race rigged by elites at the Buenos Aires Jockey Club. In contrast, the Walt Disney Studio in conjunction with OCIAA produced an animated film called *Saludos Amigos*. Properly perky, it featured a peppy little anthropomorphic airplane with human characteristics and a dapper Brazilian parrot, José Carioca, who swapped wisecracks with Donald Duck.[53]

Wartime economics initially played havoc with Latin Americans. Actually the third in a sequence of external shocks to strike them in twenty-five years, the Second World War entailed consequences that "were quantitatively and qualitatively different" from those of the First World War and the Great Depression. The war not only devastated the traditional Latin American export trade by cutting off the markets of continental Europe and diminishing the British demand but hastened "growing disillusionment" with the export-led model of economic growth in Latin America. The result was "a growing sense of nationalism in a number of Latin American republics" and "a greater commitment" to "an inward-looking" approach to economic development and industrialization. Such tendencies, already present in Bolivia and Mexico during the 1930s, accelerated during the war years. According to Bulmer-Thomas, "State intervention in support of industry, particularly in the larger republics, now became direct, with important investments in basic commodities as well as in the infrastructure needed to support a more complex industrial system."

The Roosevelt administration, "more sensitive to Latin American needs than its predecessors," understood "the importance of avoiding economic collapse in the region," if for no other reason than "to secure supplies of raw materials and strategic commodities." Consequently, a system of inter-American economic cooperation took shape after the outbreak of war in September 1939. For example, the Inter-American Development Commission (IADC), established in 1940, sought to stimulate trade between the United States and Latin America, to promote trade among the Latin Americans, and to encourage industrialization. Because access to strategic materials was a priority for the United States, in 1940 the Roosevelt administration originated the Metals Reserve Company and the Rubber Reserve Company to stockpile essential supplies. As it turned out, Latin America became the prime beneficiary. After the Japanese conquered raw materials-producing regions in Asia, the United States relied on its southern neighbors for a vast range of materials such as abaca, antimony, asbestos, cinchona, industrial diamonds, kenaf, mica, quebracho wood, quartz crystals, rubber, and zirconium. Direct U.S. foreign investment in Latin America, much of it in strategic materials, "soared during the war to levels not seen since the late 1920s," and "official U.S. loans through the Export-Import Bank and Lend-Lease—though not restricted to the extraction of strategic materials—became increasingly important." Cooperation developed in other areas as well. Recognizing "the crucial role played by coffee exports in a dozen republics," the United States promoted the Inter-American Coffee Convention (IACC) in 1941. By establishing quotas, higher prices, and guaranteed market access, it became "a lifeline for the smaller republics and a great boon for the larger republics—many of which had become heavily dependent on the German market in the 1930s."

Still, although U.S. purchases of Latin American exports became critically important, they "could not fully compensate for the loss of Japan, continental Europe, and the shrinking British market." Latin Americans increasingly sought trade with one another to sustain the volume of exports. Previously, this kind of commerce had never amounted to much; in 1938 it had accounted for only 6.1 percent of the region's exports. As Bulmer-Thomas notes, "All this changed as a result of both war and the system of inter-American economic cooperation."

Indeed, proliferating bilateral agreements reduced economic barriers and allowed for a significant expansion of interregional trade, amounting to 16.6 percent of the total in 1945. Inter-American cooperation was "the major factor preventing a collapse of exports after 1939."

The war also encouraged industrial growth in the larger republics for three main reasons. First, "the sharp decline in the volume of imports after 1939 allowed domestic manufacturers to expand production even with an unchanged level of real consumption." Consequently, the adoption of an import-substitution plan permitted modest increases in the growth of manufacturing in Argentina, Brazil, Chile, and Mexico. Second, intra-Latin American trade allowed manufacturers to sell their products in neighboring countries. As examples, Brazil increased textile exports; Argentina sold more manufactured goods; and Mexico expanded industrial sales in the United States. Third, "the rise of firms not dependent on consumer demand" also provided a stimulus. They produced capital goods for other productive sectors and the state. For example, the U.S.-financed Brazilian steel mill, Volta Redonda, sold its output to construction and manufacturing enterprises, thereby providing a substitute for previously imported steel. Similarly, in Argentina, Chile, and Mexico, cement works, chemical plants, oil refineries, and operations in plastics, rayons, and machinery relieved existing dependencies upon imports.

Such changes in the industrial sector had links with "the rise of a more interventionist state in Latin America." As Bulmer-Thomas notes, "Even deeply conservative governments could not avoid an increase in state responsibilities during the war years." For one thing, "free markets could not handle the problems posed by dollar inflation, import shortages, and unsold agricultural surpluses." For another, the war effort placed "additional demands on the state through the need for infrastructure and public works." Such developments had huge implications for the immediate postwar period and ran counter to U.S. preferences by moving away from reliance on private capital and free enterprise as the means of economic development. In the short term the Second World War marked a transition from the traditional export-led model of growth toward an alternative, inward-looking approach based on import-substitution industrialization. This change "weakened the link between the external sector and aggregate economic performance," "increased the importance of the nonexport sectors," and "shifted the composition of industrial output toward intermediate and capital goods."[54] In combination, the effects altered important parts of the traditional economic relationship between the United States and the countries of Latin America.

How should historians evaluate the impact of the Good Neighbor policy, the depression, and the war? This large, difficult, and multifaceted question allows for no single answer. Much depends on angles of vision and value systems. In a book published in 1943, Samuel Flagg Bemis praises the wartime partnership with Latin America, claiming that creative changes in the 1930s made it possible. Among more recent works, Irwin F. Gellman's account follows Bemis in looking upon the political achievements of Good Neighbor diplomacy as beneficial. In contrast, David Green underscores the importance of U.S. economic interests and the difficulty of reconciling them with the demands of Latin American nationalism. Too often, according to Green, U.S. leaders displayed arrogance and insensitivity toward legitimate Latin American concerns.[55]

Such differences, based on liberal and radical perspectives, are probably irreconcilable. Michael Grow explicitly addresses the problem in *The Good Neighbor Policy and Authoritarianism in Paraguay*. Using familiar categories, he characterizes the leaders in the Roosevelt administration as "heirs of Woodrow Wilson's 'liberal internationalist' world vision" and explains their behavior on the basis of such convictions. For them, a "world order of capitalist democracies," led by the United States and "linked interdependently through mutually profitable free trade," would constitute "the surest path to international peace and prosperity." From a liberal perspective the expansion of U.S. power and influence during the period might appear as the consequence of "an altruistic and pragmatic campaign to construct a prosperous, stable new hemispheric order mutually beneficial to the United States *and* the nations of Latin America." But for Grow, any such conclusion would be an error. He endorses a more skeptical view, depicting Roosevelt's Latin American policy less as an example of "liberal internationalism" then as a product of "liberal imperialism," that is, "a concerted drive to achieve informal United States hegemony" for reasons of "national economic self-interest."[56]

Frederick B. Pike's recent work, *FDR's Good Neighbor Policy: Sixty Years of Generally Gentle Chaos*, provides a more sympathetic account. Pike begins by asking a fundamental question: Have we been good neighbors? His brutally realistic reply says yes, some of the time, but really "no better . . . than we had to be." For him, "that seems the most one could expect. We might, after all, have been a good deal worse."

That sage point establishes a main theme, emphasizing that whatever its shortcomings, the Good Neighbor policy did rank in some ways as a success. Pike intriguingly and effectively depicts Roosevelt as a "trickster," a kind of political magician who obtained successes through the reconciliation of opposites. In this case, he brought together the defense of vital U.S. interests with some kind of regard for the requirements of Latin American sovereignty. Roosevelt, according to Pike, will always be "an enigma and a source of controversy." Nevertheless, his "enigmatic qualities served him well as a hemispheric statesman." Roosevelt earned respect and admiration from Latin Americans. He was in Pike's account "a gringo in the Latin mold, a man they could understand . . . as a projection of their own political and social style." He was "aristocratic," "patronalistic," "personalistic," and also an affable "populist" who supposedly could intuit the people's will. He was seldom preachy, condescending, or racist in his treatment of Latin Americans and seemed willing to let them count for something by giving them a share. His death on 12 April 1945 deprived the Good Neighbor policy of an essential part. His successor, Harry S. Truman, "an archetypical gringo" in the White House, possessed none of the skills and sensitivities necessary to maintain it.[57]

NOTES

1. Robert Freeman Smith, "The Good Neighbor Policy: The Liberal Paradox in United States Relations with Latin America," in *Watershed of Empire: Essays on New Deal Foreign Policy*, ed. Leonard P. Liggio and James Martin (Colorado Springs, CO: Ralph Myles, 1976), 66–67.

2. Alexander DeConde, *Herbert Hoover's Latin-American Policy* (Palo Alto, CA: Stanford University Press, 1951), 13–15, 18–24; Martin L. Fausold, *The Presidency of Herbert Hoover* (Lawrence: University Press of Kansas, 1985), 32.

3. Fausold, *Presidency of Herbert Hoover*, 183; Smith, "Good Neighbor Policy," 66–67.

4. Bryce Wood, *The Making of the Good Neighbor Policy* (New York: Columbia University Press), 45.

5. Fausold, *Presidency of Herbert Hoover*, 185–86; Bryce Wood, *The United States and Latin American Wars, 1932–1942* (New York: Columbia University Press).

6. Victor Bulmer-Thomas, *The Economic History of Latin America since Independence* (New York: Cambridge University Press, 1994), 194–99.

7. Peter H. Smith and Thomas E. Skidmore, *Modern Latin America*, 2d ed. (New York: Oxford University Press, 1992), chap. 3; Rosemary Thorp, ed., *Latin America in the 1930s: The Role of the Periphery in World Crisis* (New York: St. Martin's Press, 1984).

8. Bulmer-Thomas, *Economic History*, 208–09, 216–17.

9. Irwin F. Gellman, *Good Neighbor Diplomacy: United States Policies in Latin America, 1933–1945* (Baltimore: Johns Hopkins University Press, 1979), 11.

10. Ibid., 14, 17, chap. 2; Irwin F. Gellman, *Secret Affairs: Franklin Roosevelt, Cordell Hull, and Sumner Welles* (Baltimore: Johns Hopkins University Press, 1995), chap. 1.

11. Louis A. Pérez Jr., *Cuba and the United States: Ties of Singular Intimacy* (Athens: University of Georgia Press, 1990), 180, 183, 185.

12. Pérez, *Cuba and the United States*, 186, 191–92, 194, 200–1; Gellman, *Good Neighbor Diplomacy*, 25.

13. Gellman, *Good Neighbor Diplomacy*, 33; Brenda Gayle Plummer, *Haiti and the United States: The Psychological Moment* (Athens: University of Georgia Press, 1992), chaps. 6, 8; G. Pope Atkins, *The Dominican Republic and the United States: From Imperialism to Transnationalism* (Athens: University of Georgia Press, 1998), chap. 2; Michael L. Conniff, *Panama and the United States: The Forced Alliance* (Athens: University of Georgia Press, 1992), chap. 5.

14. Gordon Connell-Smith, *The United States and Latin America: An Historical Analysis of Inter-American Relations* (New York: John Wiley and Sons, 1974), 167.

15. Paul Coe Clark Jr., *The United States and Somoza, 1933–1956: A Revisionist Look* (Westport, CT: Praeger, 1992), esp. chaps. 1, 11.

16. Arthur A. Ekirk, *Ideologies and Utopias: The Impact of the New Deal on American Thought* (Chicago: Quadrangle Books, 1969), chaps. 1–2; William E. Leuchtenberg, *The FDR Years: On Roosevelt and His Legacy* (New York: Columbia University Press, 1995); chaps. 1–2.

17. William E. Leuchtenberg, *Franklin D. Roosevelt and the New Deal* (New York: Harper and Row, 1963), chaps. 3–4.

18. Dick Steward, *Trade and Hemisphere: The Good Neighbor Policy and Reciprocal Trade* (Columbia: University of Missouri Press, 1975), 10; Lloyd C. Gardner, *Economic Aspects of New Deal Diplomacy* (Madison: University of Wisconsin Press, 1964), chaps. 2–3, 6, 10.

19. Frederick C. Adams, *Economic Diplomacy: The Export-Import Bank and American Foreign Relations, 1934–1939* (Columbia: University of Missouri Press, 1976), 65–66, chaps. 5, 7.

20. Gellman, *Good Neighbor Diplomacy*, 40, 43, 47.

21. Ibid., 47–49; Pérez, *Cuba and the United States*, 122–23; David Green, *The Containment of Latin America: A History of the Myths and Realities of the Good Neighbor Policy* (Chicago: Quadrangle Books), 20.

22. Frank D. McCann, *The Brazilian-American Alliance, 1937–1945* (Princeton: Princeton University Press, 1973); Stanley E. Hilton, *Brazil and the Great Powers, 1930–1939: The Politics of Trade Rivalry* (Austin: University of Texas Press, 1975).

23. Frank D. McCann, "Brazil, the United States, and World War II: A Commentary," *Diplomatic History* 3 (Winter 1979): 63–64, 66–67; Gellman, *Good*

Neighbor Diplomacy, 48; R. A. Humphreys, *Latin America and the Second World War*, 2 vols. (London: University of London Athlone Press, 1982), 1:133–46.

24. Gellman, *Good Neighbor Diplomacy*, 48.

25. Bulmer-Thomas, *Economic History*, 201, 212, 217, 219–20, 222–23.

26. Wood, *Making of the Good Neighbor Policy*, 159–60, 162.

27. Gellman, *Good Neighbor Diplomacy*, 49–50; Wood, *Making of the Good Neighbor Policy*, chap. 7.

28. Wood, *Making of the Good Neighbor Policy*, 203.

29. William H. Beezley and Colin M. MacLachlan, *El Gran Pueblo*, 2 vols. (Englewood Cliffs, NJ: Prentice-Hall, 1994), 2:309.

30. Ibid., 309–11, 322–24; Friedrich E. Schuler, *Mexico between Hitler and Roosevelt: Mexican Foreign Relations in the Age of Lázaro Cárdenas, 1934–1940* (Albuquerque: University of New Mexico Press, 1998), chaps. 4–5; E. David Cronon, *Josephus Daniels in Mexico* (Madison: University of Wisconsin Press, 1960), chaps. 1, 7, 8–10; Lorenzo Meyer, *Mexico and the United States in the Oil Controversy, 1917–1942*, trans. Muriel Vasconcellos (Austin: University of Texas Press, 1977), chaps. 8–10.

31. Wood, *Making of the Good Neighbor Policy*, 205–6, 208–9, 213, 222, 233, 249, 253, 258–59; Cronon, *Josephus Daniels*, chaps. 7–8; Schuler, *Mexico between Hitler and Roosevelt*, chaps. 5–6.

32. Green, *Containment of Latin America*, 38.

33. B. S. McBeth, *Juan Vicente Gómez and the Oil Companies in Venezuela* (New York: Cambridge University Press, 1983), chaps. 2–3; Judith Ewell, *Venezuela and the United States: From Monroe's Hemisphere to Petroleum's Empire* (Athens: University of Georgia Press, 1996), chaps. 5–6.

34. Wood, *Making of the Good Neighbor Policy*, 263–65, chap. 10.

35. Humphreys, *Latin America*, 1:1.

36. Thomas G. Paterson, J. Garry Clifford, and Kenneth J. Hagan, *American Foreign Relations: A History*, 2 vols., 4th ed. (Lexington, MA: D. C. Heath, 1995), chaps. 4–6; William Appleman Williams, *The Tragedy of American Diplomacy*, rev. ed. (New York: Delta, 1962), chaps. 4–5; Robert Dallek, *Franklin D. Roosevelt and American Foreign Policy, 1932–1945* (Oxford University Press, 1979), pts. 2, 3; Gardner, *Economic Aspects*, chaps. 7, 8.

37. Robert A. Divine, *Roosevelt and World War II* (Baltimore: Johns Hopkins University Press, 1969), 37; Paterson, Clifford, and Hagan, *American Foreign Relations*, 2:209–10; Warren F. Kimball, *The Juggler: Franklin Roosevelt as Wartime Statesman* (Princeton: Princeton University Press, 1991).

38. Paterson, Clifford, and Hagan, *American Foreign Relations*, 2:213.

39. Gellman, *Good Neighbor Diplomacy*, 74–79, 83–85, 88–92, 95.

40. Ibid., 109–15; Stanley E. Hilton, *Hitler's Secret War in South America, 1939–1945: German Military Espionage and Allied Counterespionage in Brazil* (Baton Rouge: Louisiana State University Press, 1981); Leslie B. Rout Jr. and John F.

Bratzel, *The Shadow War: German Espionage and United States Counterespionage in Latin America during World War II* (Frederick, MD: University Publications of America, 1986); Robert C. Newton, *The "Nazi Menace" in Argentina, 1931–1947* (Palo Alto, CA: Stanford University Press, 1992).

41. Waldo H. Heinrich, *Threshold of War: Franklin D. Roosevelt and American Entry into World War II* (New York: Oxford University Press, 1988).

42. Gellman, *Good Neighbor Diplomacy*, 121, 124–26.

43. Humphreys, *Latin America*, 2:92–96.

44. Ibid., 97–100, 105, 117–19, 136, 138, 143–44, 149–50, 158–59.

45. Samuel Flagg Bemis, *The Latin-American Policy of the United States* (1943; reprint ed., New York: W. W. Norton, 1967), chaps. 22–23; Gellman, *Good Neighbor Diplomacy*, chaps. 10–13.

46. Green, *Containment of Latin America*, chaps. 4–5; Gardner, *Economic Aspects*, chap. 10; Adams, *Economic Diplomacy*, chaps. 5, 7; Michael Grow, *The Good Neighbor Policy and Authoritarianism in Paraguay: United States Economic Expansion and Great-Power Rivalry in Latin America during World War II* (Lawrence: University Press of Kansas, 1981), 113–15.

47. Gellman, *Good Neighbor Diplomacy*, 128–29, 134–35, chap. 10; John Major, *Prize Possession: The United States and the Panama Canal, 1903–1979* (New York: Cambridge University Press, 1993), chap. 12.

48. Humphreys, *Latin America*, 2:2–4.

49. Gellman, *Good Neighbor Diplomacy*, 137–38; Clark, *United States and Somoza*, chaps. I, II.

50. Gellman, *Good Neighbor Diplomacy*, 138–39.

51. Gerald K. Haines, "Under the Eagle's Wing: The Franklin Roosevelt Administration Forges an American Hemisphere," *Diplomatic History* I (Fall 1977): 373–74.

52. Ibid., 378–79; Frederick B. Pike, *The United States and Latin America: Myths and Stereotypes of Civilization and Nature* (Austin: University of Texas Press, 1992), chap. 8; John J. Johnson, *Latin America in Caricature* (Austin: University of Texas Press, 1980); J. Manuel Espinosa, *Inter-American Beginnings of U.S. Cultural Diplomacy, 1936–1948* (Washington, DC: U.S. Department of State, 1976), chaps. 3, 9–10.

53. Haines, "Under the Eagle's Wing," 380, 382–83.

54. Bulmer-Thomas, *Economic History*, 239, 241–48.

55. Bemis, *Latin-American Policy*, chap. 22; Gellman, *Good Neighbor Diplomacy*, chaps. 10–13; Green, *Containment of Latin America*, chap. 4.

56. Grow, *Good Neighbor Policy and Authoritarianism*, 113–15; Abraham F. Lowenthal, "United States Policy toward Latin America: 'Liberal,' 'Radical,' and 'Bureaucratic' Perspectives," *Latin American Research Review* 8 (Fall 1973): 3–25.

57. Frederick B. Pike, *FDR's Good Neighbor Policy: Sixty Years of Generally Gentle Chaos* (Austin: University of Texas Press, 1995), xi, 138–62, 350–53.

CHAPTER FOUR

COLD WAR, DEPENDENCY, AND CHANGE

1945–1959

THE ONSET OF THE Cold War transformed the conduct of international relations by establishing a new context. For U.S. policymakers the breakdown in relations with the Soviet Union after the Second World War became the central preoccupation. Seeking to build liberal-capitalist systems in as much of the world as possible, U.S. leaders guarded against presumed threats of Soviet expansion by applying the containment principles first in Western Europe and then in other regions. The consequences shaped U.S. dealings with most other countries. Those nations operating outside of the Soviet sphere became significant or not, depending on larger calculations of gain or loss in the Cold War struggle.

In the Western Hemisphere, U.S. leaders initially took much for granted. While working toward the construction of a regional collective security system, they embraced Latin American governments as political and military allies but otherwise looked upon the region as peripheral in importance. For that reason, they placed no equivalent emphasis on programs of economic modernization and development. Latin Americans, meanwhile, resented the neglect, regarding it as a sign of indifference and condescension. Yet for many of them, economic dependence on the United States had gone so far that breaking loose posed complicated problems.

Under Presidents Truman and Eisenhower the Good Neighbor policy lost viability as a guide. Neither president possessed much understanding of Latin America, and personnel changes in the State Department compounded the difficulty. In August 1943, Sumner Welles resigned as undersecretary after allegations of personal misbehavior. In November 1944, Cordell Hull, his health failing, also went into retirement. His successor was Edward R. Stettinius Jr., a corporate executive

who possessed no diplomatic experience and no special appreciation for
Latin American issues. According to Irwin Gellman, those shifts marked
"the beginning of the disintegration in Pan American solidarity" by removing from authority the policymakers most committed to it.[1]

FASHIONING A REGIONAL SYSTEM

Questions of regional organization in the Western Hemisphere
ranked high as priorities at the end of the Second World War. Drawing
on wartime experiences stressing hemispheric solidarity, government
leaders fashioned a regional system of collective security at a series of
international conferences in Mexico City, San Francisco, Rio de
Janeiro, and Bogotá. The system consisted of two parts, the Rio Pact, a
military alliance, and the Organization of American States (OAS), a
political counterpart. Taken together, these devices perpetuated at least
an appearance of cooperation but otherwise elicited divergent appraisals. For enthusiasts, the creation of a regional system was laudable for
reasons of national security. For critics, the system emanated from U.S.
hegemonic aspirations and functioned essentially as an alliance between
the United States and the established elites of Latin America in defense
of the status quo.[2]

Serious discussions of regional organization for the postwar period
got under way late in the war, prompted mainly by Argentine ambiguities. By remaining neutral, the Argentine government upheld what its
leaders regarded as sovereign prerogatives and drove Secretary of State
Cordell Hull to distraction. He attributed the Argentine position to
pro-Axis preferences. He also feared the destabilization of neighboring
countries by pro-Nazi influences and wanted a cohesive alignment in
support of the Allies. Actually an amalgam of various tendencies, the
Argentine policy of neutrality followed from traditional aversions. Argentine nationalists perceived Pan American formulations as instruments of U.S. domination. Moreover, in a sense pro-Axis, neutrality
showed the impact of German and Italian immigration; indeed, many
Argentines conceived of their country as European. Another consideration was economic. For the most part, the Argentines lacked restrictive dependence on U.S. markets and capital and so possessed some
additional room to maneuver. As producers of primary agricultural
commodities such as beef, wheat, and mutton, they sold mainly in the
British market. The British, for their part, had less concern about Argentine neutrality than about maintaining a reliable food supply.

The Argentine army took over the government in a bloodless coup
in June 1943 by installing General Pedro Ramírez as interim president.

The leaders, mainly high-ranking officers working through a secret society, the so-called Grupo de Oficiales Unidos, embraced some fascist notions about corporate unity and racial purity and also drew on traditional militarist beliefs in nationalism, hierarchy, and authority. For Argentine military officers the Franco and Mussolini regimes in Spain and Italy served as special inspirations. Nevertheless, the Ramírez government did promise to break with the Axis eventually. Indeed, the new foreign minister, Admiral Segundo Storni, naively asked for patience from the United States in a letter to Secretary of State Cordell Hull in which he also urged large-scale military assistance for Argentina through Lend-Lease. To Hull, this request looked like a bribe. In full fury, he excoriated the Argentine government as a pro-fascist presence in South America. Storni had to resign. Replacing him as foreign minister, General Alberto Gilbert engaged in something of a balancing act, seeking to avoid giving offense to either the United States or other high-ranking Argentine officers. Some of them, notably Colonel Juan Domingo Perón, an emerging power, opposed any concession to the United States as an insult to Argentine honor. When as a consequence of complicated political maneuvers General Ramírez withdrew from the presidency early in 1944, Hull withheld diplomatic recognition from the new government, headed by General Edelmiro Farrell. The secretary sought in this way to force a change in favor of the Allies; he also employed economic sanctions to escalate the pressure.[3] The effort failed. Later, Hull himself resigned. Ill and exhausted, he retired from the State Department soon after Roosevelt won the presidential election in November 1944.

Meanwhile, cross-purposes in the State Department contributed to other diplomatic confusions. Hull's successor, Secretary of State Edward Stettinius, functioned mainly as a figurehead. For a time, he upheld Hull's policy of nonrecognition toward Argentina and thus incurred a challenge from Nelson Rockefeller. Young, smart, rich, and ambitious, Rockefeller became the undersecretary of state for Latin American affairs following Sumner Welles's departure. Unlike Hull and Stettinius, Rockefeller regarded nonrecognition as ineffective and counterproductive. He favored a more conciliatory position toward Argentina, a preference shared by most Latin American diplomats. As a means of clarifying its status the Argentine government requested a special inter-American conference. Disinclined to risk public embarrassment, Stettinius wanted no such gathering but hesitated to oppose it outright. To resolve the dilemma, Mexican Foreign Minister Ezequiel Padilla then proposed a conference of foreign ministers in Mexico City. This

approach allowed for international discussions of the Argentine problem without direct Argentine participation: Under the rules, only those
countries that had broken relations with the Axis powers or declared
war upon them would receive invitations.[4]

The Mexico City conference met at Chapultepec Palace from
21 February until 8 March 1945. Headed by Secretary Stettinius, the
U.S. delegation wanted a carefully controlled agenda to avoid controversy over Argentina and to maintain the appearance of hemispheric
solidarity. Other potentially troublesome and divisive issues included
the relationship between the nations of the Western Hemisphere and
the proposed United Nations organization, one of Franklin
Roosevelt's favorite projects. At the Dumbarton Oaks conference
in Washington late in the summer of 1944, the Big Three—the
United States, Great Britain, and the Soviet Union—had accepted
commitments to create a new world organization, conceiving of it as
something like a remodeled League of Nations. The idea was popular
in the United States, especially among Democrats, who looked upon
it as a "second chance": that is, an opportunity to atone for the rejection of the Treaty of Versailles after the First World War. Administration
planners wanted the United States to participate in a postwar system of
collective security based solidly on the expectation of continued cooperation among the Big Three. Yet unanswered questions produced high
levels of uncertainty. What of the impact on existing regional arrangements, such as the Western Hemisphere system? Would this new organization take precedence over them? Could the United Nations
sanction interference from the outside in Western Hemisphere affairs,
possibly even military intervention?

Among officials in the State Department the discussions ranged
around two broad choices. Advocates of the first portrayed the prerogatives of the United Nations as superior to those of regional systems.
These "universalists" included Alger Hiss and Leo Pasvolsky, both attached to the State Department's International Organization Division.
They worried about the emergence of regional spheres of influence
and regarded any such outcome as incompatible with a truly international system. To check such tendencies, they wanted to vest the dominant decision-making authority in the United Nations. Critics saw this
approach as expanding the role of the Great Powers too much at the
expense of the smaller states. Consequently, a group of "regionalists" in the State Department advocated a second option. Led by
Nelson Rockefeller, they called for a self-sustaining, collective-security

system in the Western Hemisphere as protection against outside meddling and the possibility of subjugation to the Great Powers. One of the regionalists, Adolf A. Berle, the U.S. ambassador to Brazil, conjured up dire possibilities. Adoption of the universalist option "would mean that the United States and others could not prevent Argentina from seizing Uruguay without the consent of Britain and Russia—who at the moment might be backing Argentina." In short, the universalist alternative "would introduce European diplomacy into every inter-American dispute."[5]

Latin Americans desired a regional system for their own reasons. They wanted protection against external interference and also against the United States. At the same time, they perceived in such arrangements a means of facilitating the infusion of U.S. economic aid into Latin America. During the war, at the third meeting of foreign ministers in Rio de Janeiro in January 1942, Sumner Welles had encouraged this expectation by promising U.S. support for Latin American economic development. He hoped to raise living standards by means of aid and assistance for industrialization, modernization, and diversification. To Latin Americans, such rewards seemed proper responses, given their magnitude of support for the Allies during the war.[6]

The outcome of the Mexico City conference, the Act of Chapultepec, allowed for multiple approaches toward common goals. The measure endorsed Latin American preferences by recommending in favor of a "regional arrangement" to maintain peace and security in the Western Hemisphere. It also affirmed support for "the purposes and principles" of the United Nations.[7] By combining the one with the other, the delegates maintained their options, seeking to accommodate both the universalist and the regionalist position.

For Latin Americans, economic relations in the postwar period took on special significance. During the war, they had benefited from special arrangements assuring extensive sales in foreign markets at good prices. Now they worried about the impact of falling prices and shrinking sales in contracting markets. As safeguards, some favored protective tariffs to nurture infant industries; others advocated commodity agreements to stabilize prices. Most hoped for U.S. aid, specifically in the form of loans and grants to bolster growth and diversification. As Mexican Foreign Minister Ezequiel Padilla pointed out at Chapultepec, it was "vital for the [Latin] Americans to do more than produce raw materials and live in a state of semi-colonialism." He looked for some form of assistance from the United States.[8]

Instead of assurances, he got statements of high capitalist principle. The speeches by U.S. delegates indicated that prewar suspicions of economic nationalism and state enterprise in Latin America had not gone away. Indeed, according to official U.S. views, restrictive trade and investment practices in the 1930s had contributed to the world crisis by encouraging cutthroat international competition and eventually war. To avoid "shortsighted" policies, Undersecretary of State Dean Acheson affirmed his belief in free trade as the best means of expanding commerce, enhancing prosperity, reducing world tension, and promoting peace. These views were established orthodoxy among U.S. leaders. As assessed by the historian R. A. Humphreys, the implications for Latin America meant some measure of U.S. encouragement for economic development but typically "within the context of an expanding, interdependent and liberalized world economy." Overall, the discussion placed the United States in opposition to Latin American efforts to escape from "economic vassalage to the more industrialized countries."

Finally, the delegates at Chapultepec addressed the question of Argentine neutrality by affirming a resolution of censure. It castigated Argentine leaders for possessing pro-fascist sympathies and maintaining Axis ties. It also proposed the means of rectification. To set things right, Argentina would have to adhere immediately to Allied principles and issue a war declaration. This outcome gratified Secretary of State Stettinius, an heir of Hull's anti-Argentine animosity. He extolled the achievements of the Chapultepec conference, however vague and mixed, as splendid things and hyperbolically characterized the experience as "a culmination of the Good Neighbor Policy." Whatever the fissures and cleavages among them, the Western Hemisphere nations had retained an appearance of hemispheric solidarity.

The United Nations conference got under way in San Francisco on 25 April 1945. Forty-six countries sent delegations, including nineteen from Latin America—but not Argentina. The neutrality question still caused friction. The Farrell government in Argentina received no invitation, even though the leaders had complied with the Act of Chapultepec by declaring war upon Germany and Japan on 27 March 1945. The problem now resided in Great-Power politics. The Soviet Union regarded Argentina as a pro-fascist enemy state, undeserving of participation in the San Francisco conference. Somewhat more forgiving, the other Latin American delegations accepted in better faith the Argentine war declaration, however belated. With the support of the United States, they suggested a workable solution. If the Soviets wanted White

Russia and the Ukraine to have representation at the conference, they could do so, but only if Argentina could take part.[9]

At San Francisco, Latin Americans displayed special interest in the structure of decision-making authority but otherwise exercised scant influence. To head off Great-Power domination, they hoped for a broad allocation of responsibility to the smaller states in the General Assembly and also for a permanent Latin American seat on the Security Council; President Vargas of Brazil thought his country a candidate for such a spot. In these matters, Latin Americans achieved none of their goals. The Security Council fell under the control of the Big Three, each with veto power, and the General Assembly functioned primarily as an international debating society. These outcomes reflected political realities. The United States, Great Britain, and the Soviet Union, having invested the greatest effort in winning the victory over the Axis powers, also wielded the greatest influence when the conflict ended.

Other discussions centered on ways to reconcile regional and universal approaches. For Latin Americans, the Act of Chapultepec remained the guide. They wanted to reconcile the purposes and principles of the inter-American system with those of the world organization, seeking among other things safeguards against outsiders, including the United States. Meanwhile, the U.S. delegation divided into factions. Secretary Stettinius espoused the universalist option while affirming Great-Power prerogatives. In his view, "we must not be pushed around by a lot of small American republics who are dependent on us in many ways—economically, politically, militarily." But different arguments based on other considerations undercut Stettinius's position and prepared the way for a kind of blending process.

The defense of the Monroe Doctrine especially concerned conservative nationalists. They regarded this ancient creed as the embodiment of U.S. tradition and experience and would sanction neither concessions nor compromises, which, they warned, would bring dire consequences. What of the prerogative to guard against European intrusions? What of the political implications? Could a failure to uphold the Monroe Doctrine result in rejection of the United Nations in the U.S. Senate? Or conversely, could acceptance of the United Nations mean repudiation of the Monroe Doctrine? These touchy matters required clarification and of course recalled the debate in 1919 over the Versailles Treaty. Senator Arthur P. Vandenberg, a Republican from Michigan and a U.S. delegate at San Francisco, had described the Monroe Doctrine in 1926 as "the indispensable bulwark of American independence."

As Gaddis Smith explains, his views in 1945 had not changed: "No politician . . . was more steeped emotionally and intellectually in the principles of the Monroe Doctrine."

Under the terms of Article 51, the UN Charter, as written at San Francisco, provided the means of reconciling universalist and regionalist views by allowing for a form of coexistence: It sanctioned the exercise of regional prerogatives within the context of the world organization. More specifically, it recognized for each member "the inherent right of individual and collective self-defense," thereby permitting defensive measures to be taken alone or in cooperation with others, pending action by the Security Council. Humphreys calls Article 51 "the great compromise." Less positively, he also claims that it established "the legal basis of the post-war blocs that marked the Cold War." This long-term implication, not so clear at the time, caused no bother for Senator Vandenberg. In a celebratory mood, he affirmed, "We have preserved the Monroe Doctrine and the Inter-American system. . . . We have retained a complete veto—exclusive in our own hands—over any decisions involving external activities."[10]

Meanwhile, the disintegration of the wartime alliance between the United States and the Soviet Union initiated a Cold War, resulting in mounting levels of acrimony, mistrust, and confrontation. During the early stages, as Walter LaFeber has explained, the rivalry centered on the shape and structure of the postwar world, symbolized for him by the terms "Open Doors" and "Iron Curtains." For U.S. leaders the essential parts of Woodrow Wilson's liberal-capitalist internationalism retained fundamental validity. They wanted an open world based on free trade, liberal democracy, and collective security. For Soviet leaders, however, the Open Door approach had no appeal. To restore their war-ravaged country, they preferred an emphasis on spheres of influence, notably an extension of the Soviet system into the countries of Eastern Europe. An immense historiographical controversy surrounds the causes of the Cold War. In accounting for Soviet behavior and the split with the United States, modern scholars debate among themselves the relative importance of economic and security considerations, Joseph Stalin's distinctive personality, and the impact of Marxist ideology. For a combination of reasons, Stalin chose to seclude the Soviet domains after the war through the creation of a "closed system" sealed off, in Churchill's phrase, by an Iron Curtain.[11]

In response to mounting difficulties around the world, the Truman administration took alarm over the possibility of Soviet expansion into other regions and endorsed the necessity of containing the communist threat. At the same time, U.S. leaders pursued their own spheres-of-influence policies in the New World. Unbothered by the inconsistency, they denied any sort of parallel. Only Secretary of Commerce Henry A. Wallace perceived an incongruity, noting that the Russians "might feel about the Balkan states in somewhat the same way as we feel about Latin America." In a famous speech in March 1946 at Madison Square Garden in New York City, he stated his conviction that "we should recognize that we have no more business in the political affairs of eastern Europe than Russia has in the political affairs of Latin America." For enunciating such heresy, Truman fired him soon thereafter.[12]

Caught up in a contradiction, the leaders in the Truman administration wanted the Open Door in other regions but regarded Latin America as closed because of special ties with the United States. But then in the famous speech setting forth the Truman Doctrine before the Congress on 12 March 1947, the president found a way of bridging the gap. This speech, the first component in what became the containment policy against Soviet communism, called for extraordinary measures in response to a civil war in Greece. Truman wanted an allocation of $400 million from the Congress to sustain programs of economic and military aid and assistance in the eastern Mediterranean region. In justification, he stressed "the gravity of the situation." In his view, the ideological struggle between democrats and communists in Greece also had geopolitical implications. A communist victory in Greece could threaten Turkey and the rest of the Middle East with Soviet subversion and aggression. To ward off this dread possibility, Truman argued, "it must be the policy of the United States to support free peoples who are resisting attempted subjugation by armed minorities and outside pressures." For good measure, he insisted, "We must assist free peoples to work out their own destinies in their own way."[13]

Through this formulation, as Gaddis Smith explains, "Truman resolved the problem" with Latin America. By extending "to the entire world the definition of American interest in protecting small nations from external coercion," the Truman Doctrine in effect transformed the Monroe Doctrine into a global policy. A contemporary journalist, James Reston of the *New York Times*, drew the same inference. He described Truman's address as the most important statement in U.S. foreign policy since 1823. In Reston's words, "Like the Monroe Doctrine," the Truman Doctrine "warned that the United States would resist efforts to impose a political system or foreign domination on areas vital to our security." For this reason, the Soviets had better keep hands off or risk the consequences.[14]

Meanwhile, Latin American diplomats initiated a process for creating an inter-American collective security system through the implementation of Article 51 of the UN Charter. In August 1945, Brazil offered to host a meeting of American republics in Rio de Janeiro to devise a treaty. At first the United States resisted, again because of Argentina. The Truman administration was reluctant to sign a treaty with President Juan Domingo Perón's government. Indeed, U.S. leaders regarded Perón as an unreconstructed pro-fascist and mounted a determined campaign against him.

The anti-Perón movement, eventually a kind of fiasco, followed from wartime suspicions and Spruille Braden's obsessions. A professional diplomat with experience in Latin America, Braden went to Buenos Aires as U.S. ambassador in May 1945 and developed an intense dislike for Perón, then the vice president, because of his pro-fascist reputation and a reportedly anti-U.S. attitude that Braden characterized as "neurotic nationalism."[15] When Braden later adopted the practice of criticizing Perón in public, presumably seeking to bring him down, he went too far. Perón turned the tables, depicting Braden as persona non grata because of his undiplomatic partisanship.

To avoid trouble, the Truman administration recalled Braden to Washington in September 1945, assigning to him responsibilities as assistant secretary of state for American republic affairs. Now, unwisely and ineffectively, he pursued a long distance vendetta. For example, he allowed himself to became identified with a loosely conceived proposal floating about to destroy Perón by means of a joint international intervention. Braden also meddled in Argentine politics. Perón had become the front-running candidate in the presidential campaign. Seeking to block him, Braden instigated the publication of a State Department Blue Book in February 1946, a short while before the election; it consisted of a compilation of documents, reiterating the charge that Argentina had pursued pro-fascist policies during the war. Without much plausibility, U.S. officials denied any political intent. Unpersuaded, the historian Roger Trask explains that "the Blue Book was an effort to influence Argentine votes against Perón," and it failed. Indeed, it enabled Perón to mobilize Argentine nationalism against the United States by brandishing the slogan "Perón or Braden." Given the choice, Argentines voted for Perón. An embarrassing failure on all counts, Braden's obsession with Perón not only demonstrated an incapacity to influence Argentine elections but also aroused concern among Latin Americans elsewhere over resurgent threats of U.S. intervention. The debacle further diminished the legacies of the Good Neighbor policy.

Braden's successor in Argentina, George S. Messersmith, formerly the ambassador to Mexico, favored a more conciliatory approach. This preference ran parallel with those of his superiors in the State Department who wanted to place relations with Argentina on a more regular basis. They also wanted to move ahead with the negotiation of an inter-American defense treaty. From his post in Buenos Aires, Messersmith defended his position by writing long letters to President Truman, Secretary of State James F. Byrnes, and Undersecretary of State Dean Acheson in which he attacked Spruille Braden for an assortment of misdeeds and misconceptions. At the same time, Messersmith developed an argument based on Cold War assumptions and perceptions for supporting Perón as a strong anticommunist. Seeking support on exactly those grounds, Perón subsequently switched tactics to cultivate leaders in the Truman administration. Now a proponent of diplomatic accommodation, he claimed to foresee an impending war with the Soviet Union, in which case, he vowed, Argentina would side with the United States.

From the Argentine viewpoint, these policy adjustments had good effects by edging the two countries toward the establishment of more normal relations. They also opened the way for the negotiation of an inter-American collective defense treaty at a conference in Rio de Janeiro, beginning on 15 August 1947. Headed by General George C. Marshall, the new secretary of state, the U.S. delegation included Senator Arthur P. Vandenberg, the new chairman of the Senate Foreign Relations Committee, who occupied the position as a consequence of Republican victory in the off-year elections of 1946; for the first time since 1928, they controlled the Congress. Also in attendance, Truman arrived ceremoniously aboard the USS *Missouri*, the great battleship on whose decks the Japanese had surrendered in Tokyo Bay two years earlier.[16]

Formally known as the Inter-American Conference for the Maintenance of Continental Peace and Security, this assembly resulted in the negotiation of a mutual defense treaty among nations within the region. In the Inter-American Treaty of Reciprocal Assistance, also called the Rio Pact, the participants accepted three vital provisions. In the first, they promised to seek peaceful settlements in disputes among themselves before appealing to the United Nations. In the second, they embraced the essential feature of collective security by vowing to look upon an attack against any one of them as an attack against all of them. In the third, they agreed that any resort to collective action would depend upon a two-thirds majority vote and that no state ever would have to use force against its will. Senator Vandenberg, a leading player, waxed eloquent in his request for Senate ratification: "We have sealed a New World pact of peace which possesses teeth. We have translated Pan-American solidarity from an ideal into a reality. . . . This is sunlight in a dark world." The Senate then passed favorably on the treaty by a vote of 72 to 1. As Gaddis Smith notes, "For Vandenberg the Monroe Doctrine had never been so alive and well."[17]

Among Latin Americans too the pact aroused enthusiasm, although, as Roger Trask observes, "the motives of the various American republics varied to a considerable extent." Some took the affirmations of anti-communist purpose seriously. The Argentines, for example, expressed their desire for "a completely united front against extra-hemisphere aggressions, particularly against Russia." For others, economic needs assumed importance. As Trask notes, "One gets the impression that the mutual defense treaty was a secondary concern, perhaps looked upon as something to trade to the United States in return for economic assistance." Mexican Foreign Minister Jaime Torres Bodet candidly remarked that economic development was "the one way to provide [the] only sound basis for hemisphere peace." Brazilian Foreign Minister Raúl Fernandes urged that the United States instigate a large-scale program of aid and assistance to bring about economic change in the Western Hemisphere. To the extent that such words represented Latin American expectations, Truman effectively squelched them in his address before the assembled delegates. While claiming that he understood "the economic problems common to the nations of North and South America," he stated, "We have been obliged . . . to differentiate between the urgent need for rehabilitation of war-shattered areas and the problems of development elsewhere." To underscore the point, he said, "The problems of countries in this Hemisphere are different in nature and cannot be relieved by the same means and the same approaches which are in contemplation for Europe." Although acknowledging a need "for long-term economic collaboration," Truman assigned "a much greater role . . . to private citizens and groups than is the case in a program designed to aid European countries to recover from the destruction of war."[18] In other words, he envisioned no equivalent of the Marshall Plan for Latin America.

First proposed by the secretary of state in a commencement address at Harvard University in June 1947, the Marshall Plan was the second component in the containment policy, after the Truman Doctrine. It called for the use of large-scale aid and assistance, ultimately $12.4 million, to promote the economic reconstruction of Western Europe. For the citizens of the United States, it became a subject of "almost limitless self-congratulation . . . then and since." For Latin Americans, it became a cause of resentment and ill will, a "sorry proof of American priorities." When asked at a press conference about a Marshall Plan for Latin America, Truman replied: "Well, I think there has always been a Marshall Plan in effect for the Western Hemisphere. The foreign policy of the United States in that direction has been set for one hundred years, known as the Monroe Doctrine." As Gaddis Smith observes, "It is difficult to say whether that comment demonstrated more confusion about the Marshall Plan or about the Monroe Doctrine."[19]

Meanwhile, the concluding step in bringing about an inter-American collective security system took place at the ninth International Conference of American States, in Bogotá, Colombia. This gathering lasted from 30 March to 2 May 1948, resulting in the transformation of the old Pan American Union into the Organization of American States. Again led by Secretary Marshall, the U.S. delegation embraced a plan to sidestep the issue of economic assistance by mobilizing resistance against what they perceived as an escalating communist menace. During the preliminaries, U.S. planning documents placed great importance on the development of anticommunist measures for implementation within the inter-American system. They described communism in the Western Hemisphere in alarming terms, characterizing it as a "potential danger," a "tool of the Kremlin," "a direct and major threat to the national security of the United States, and to that of all the other American Republics." Marshall himself underscored the issue by warning of "foreign-inspired subversive activities directed against [the] institutions and peace and security of American Republics."[20]

With apprehension running high, U.S. diplomats anticipated trouble at Bogotá. The ambassador, Willard S. Beaulac, cautioned against possible disruptions by "Communists and left wing Liberals." As if in fulfillment of his forecast, on 9 April an assassin killed Dr. Jorge Eliécer Gaitán, a Colombian politician and reformer in the Liberal Party. Subsequently, a mob lynched the suspected murderer, Juan Roa Sierra, and put the corpse on display in front of the presidential palace. The ensuing violence, known in Colombian history as the *Bogotazo*, featured several days of killing, rioting, and looting in the course of which the conference site, the Capitolio, came under attack. State Department officials urged General Marshall to come home at once, but Marshall refused. In his view, fleeing would encourage revolutionary movements elsewhere. Marshall attributed the outbreak to communist provocations. Historians with the advantage of hindsight are less categorical.

According to Roger Trask, "The riots were essentially an emotional response to the death of a charismatic leader and communist participation was incidental"; Stephen J. Randall points out that CIA observers at the time attributed Gaitán's assassination to an act of personal vengeance. Whatever the cause, the rioting had important consequences. For one thing, it intensified the conflict between Liberals and Conservatives in Colombia and brought about "the virtual collapse" of the political system. For another, it encouraged Latin American support at the conference for an anticommunist resolution favored by the United States. Formally titled "The Preservation and Defense of Democracy in America," the resolution affirmed "that by its antidemocratic nature and its interventionist tendency, the political activity of international communism or any totalitarian doctrine is incompatible with the concept of American freedom." As a safeguard, each nation should adopt "measures necessary to eradicate and prevent activities directed, assisted, or instigated by foreign governments, organizations, or individuals."[21]

Most significantly, the Bogotá conference brought into existence the Organization of American States, which, according to Trask, "provided an institutional framework for the inter-American system and machinery for implementation of the Rio pact."[22] The OAS charter endorsed as goals the pursuit of "peace and justice"; the advancement of "collaboration" and "solidarity" among the states; and the defense of national "sovereignty," "territorial integrity," and "independence." As a fundamental principle, the document affirmed equality among the states; decision making would depend on simple majority rule, whether carried out during inter-American conferences or during meetings of foreign ministers. Unlike the UN Security Council, the OAS gave no government a veto power. Finally, Article 15 formally embraced an absolute version of the principle of nonintervention: "No State or group of States has the right to intervene, directly or indirectly, for any reason whatever, in the internal or external affairs of any other State." It also excluded the use of armed force and "any other form of interference or attempted threat" against the state and "its political, economic and cultural elements."[23] Whether such terms actually could constrain the United States remained an issue for decision in the future.

ORDER, STABILITY, AND ANTICOMMUNISM

The legacies of Franklin Roosevelt's Good Neighbor policy faded away during the early Cold War, providing ever less guidance for diplomatic conduct in the Western Hemisphere. Under Presidents Truman and Eisenhower anticommunism dominated official thinking. The consequences encouraged order and stability as the primary goals and afforded conservative elites in Latin America with incentives to counteract recent political losses. According to the historians Leslie Bethell and Ian Roxborough, the "conjuncture" at the end of the Second World War had important ramifications, among them, a halt in the growth of democratization and a restoration of more traditional forms of authoritarian rule.[24]

This thesis appears more fully in Bethell and Roxborough's *Latin America between the Second World War and the Cold War*. Presented as a series of case studies on a country-by-country basis, the essays argue that from 1944 to 1948 each Latin American republic fashioned "its own history" yet displayed "striking similarities." As the editors explain, late in the war and immediately after, "three distinct but interrelated phenomena" threatened to undermine the political status quo. These consisted of, first, more extensive popular participation in government, second, a shift to the political left and, third, a growing militancy within the labor movement. Seeking to thwart such challenges, conservative elites marshaled resistance, blunted the effects, and reasserted their traditional prerogatives.[25]

Popular parties with mass followings toward the end of the Second World War expanded democratic bases by insisting upon free elections. In some countries the existence of rudimentary democratic forms already existed. In others, authoritarian traditions presented formidable obstacles. In most of Latin America, "reformist" and "progressive" parties became identified with urban interests, including middle- and working-class elements. At the same time, radical groups, often Marxist in orientation, scored political gains, usually in conjunction with the mobilization of labor unions. In some countries, "the incorporation of organized labor into democratic politics" took place for the first time.

Soon after the war the traditional, conservative elites in Latin America struck back, often by repressive means. They targeted for special attention political activists, agitators, union organizers, radicals, communists, and others they looked upon as dangerous. The outcome, a "historic defeat" for the popular parties, marked a lost opportunity "for significant political and social change." Two developments account for the setback: "The shifting balance of domestic political forces in each country" and "the complex interaction between domestic and international politics as the Second World War came to an end." In the latter case, the U.S. role in Latin America took on special importance.

Convincing evidence of increased democratization exists for the mid-1940s. At the beginning of 1944, only Uruguay, Chile, Costa Rica, and Colombia could claim with much veracity to possess functioning democracies: that is, elected civilian governments operating under the rule of law, while respecting civil liberties such as freedom of speech, association, and assembly. Mexico, a special case, conducted regular elections under the tight control of the ruling party, the Partido Revolucionario Mexicano (PRM). Elsewhere, authoritarian governments prevailed. They were "narrowly oligarchical and often repressive regimes," typically "military or military-backed dictatorships, some benevolent, some brutal, and most personalistic."

Democratization took place in Ecuador, Cuba, Panama, Peru, Venezuela, and Mexico, when popular pressure from the masses of people compelled freer electoral procedures and forced transitions away from military or military-backed dictatorships. In Guatemala in July 1944, for example, a popular, urban-based uprising brought down the dictator Jorge Ubico. In Brazil early in 1945, Getúlio Vargas in effect dismantled the Estado Novo by making plans for presidential and congressional elections. In the same year, massive street demonstrations in Buenos Aires set in motion a sequence of events leading to democratic Argentine elections in February 1946. And in Bolivia during the summer of 1946 a liberal-left coalition overturned a military government. In the estimation of one contemporary observer, the great historian Arthur P. Whitaker, these occurrences taken together signified "more democratic changes in more Latin American countries" than at any time since the wars of independence. Notable exceptions, of course, existed in Paraguay, El Salvador, Honduras, Nicaragua, and the Dominican Republic, but even those dictatorial governments had to make "token gestures toward political liberalization."

The Allied victory over the fascist powers functioned as "the principal factor" underlying these changes. To be sure, urban-based, democratic groups, from both the middle and working classes, drew on "a strong liberal tradition" in Latin America while demanding a more open form of politics. At the same time, the triumphant democracies of the United States and Great Britain compelled the "dominant groups in Latin America, including the military . . . to make some political and ideological adjustments and concessions." During the war "an extraordinary outpouring of wartime propaganda" favored "U.S. political institutions, the U.S. economic model, and the American way of (and standard of) life." Democracy emerged as "a central symbol with almost universal resonance," in part because of the role played by the United States.

The democratization process also featured the inclusion of "progressive" parties of the center and the left. Important examples were the Acción Democrática in Venezuela, the Alianza Popular Revolucionaria Americana in Peru, and the Partido Revolucionario Cubano-Auténtico in Cuba. Highly personalist and populist in orientation, these parties secured support from the urban middle classes, the working classes, and in some instances the peasants. Among other things, they offered "an extension of democracy, social reform, and national economic development." Marxists too, especially communists, made gains, in part because of the Soviet Union's role in the Allied coalition. After years of "weakness, isolation, and for the most part illegality . . . the Latin American Communist parties achieved for a brief period a degree of popularity, power, and influence—which would never be recaptured, except in Cuba after 1959 and (briefly) in Chile in the early seventies."

Communist parties became legal in most Latin American countries during the war years. The total membership, less than 100,000 in 1939, increased to about 500,000 in 1947. The parties claimed 180,000 members in Brazil, 30,000 in Argentina, 50,000 in Chile, 35,000 in Peru, 20,000 in Venezuela, 55,000 in Cuba, 11,000 in Mexico, 10,000 in Colombia, and 15,000 in Uruguay. Though probably exaggerated, these figures indicate "an important presence of Communist parties in the major countries." For a time, they enjoyed a measure of electoral success, especially in coalitions with other parties of the center and the left. The explanation resides "primarily in the war itself and its outcome." Following the German invasion of the Soviet Union in June 1941, Latin American communists advocated a political truce with the pro-Allied governments in power, no matter how authoritarian or reactionary. They also played down conceptions of class conflict and encouraged notions of national unity. At the same time, Latin American governments relaxed their earlier strictures against communists. In the short run, communist parties ranked among "the beneficiaries" of victory and democratization.

Organized labor also benefited, especially in Mexico, Argentina, and Brazil. Mainly because of industrialization, import-substitution strategies, rapid population growth, and mass migrations from rural into urban areas, the working classes grew in numbers, especially in the service and transportation sectors, in mining and light manufacturing, and in textiles and food processing. "For the first time, something approaching a recognizably modern proletariat was coming into existence." Similarly, expanded union membership by 1946 reached 3.5 to 4 million workers. The Confederación de Trabajadores de América Latina (Confederation of Latin American Workers), founded in 1938 and headed by a Mexican Marxist, Vicente Lombardo Toledano, reportedly represented some 3.3 million members in sixteen countries. Moreover, since union membership clustered in key industrial and transportation sectors, labor militancy, strikes, and agitation could exercise the greatest clout in vulnerable areas. Although, as Bethell and Roxborough remark, "democrats, leftists, and labor militants were not always and everywhere on the same side," their efforts—"for the most part linked and mutually reinforcing"—nevertheless, constituted "a serious challenge to the established order, at least in the perceptions of the governments of the time." That challenge, whether real or perceived, also elicited countermeasures from traditional elites.

In the immediate postwar period, conservative shifts effectively curbed democratizing tendencies almost everywhere. More closely policed, labor unions fell under state control, often muzzled by antistrike legislation. Purges removed radical leaders from positions of influence, and communist affiliations again became illegal. Taken together, these actions represented "a marked tendency to restrict or curtail political competition and participation, to contain or repress popular mobilization, and to frustrate reformist aspirations." Within a decade, as a consequence, outright dictatorships existed in eleven Latin American countries: Guatemala, El Salvador, Honduras, Nicaragua, Panama, Cuba, the Dominican Republic, Venezuela, Colombia, Peru, and Paraguay.

Bethell and Roxborough explain these reversals by underscoring "the continuing strength of the dominant classes." Unlike those in other parts of the world, the traditional elites in Latin America, including the military, "had not been weakened, much less destroyed by the Second World War." Instead, they had assumed a defensive posture, intending subsequently "to restore the political and social control that was threatened by the political mobilization of 'the dangerous classes.'" The "most progressive parties" also displayed debilitating, internal weaknesses. Often they lacked such vital prerequisites for success as "deep roots" in society, internal cohesion, and "a vocation for power." Overall, they possessed insufficient means to maintain their gains when traditional oligarchs reasserted their authority and privilege.

Bethell and Roxborough also emphasize the importance of "the international environment" at the beginning of the Cold War. According to them, "the international stance" of the United States "reinforced domestic attitudes and tendencies," providing for "an ideological justification for the shift to the right" and for "the counteroffensive" against labor and the left. In many cases, in the official versions set forth by Latin American governments, "popular political mobilization and strike activity, whether or not Communist-led, suddenly became Communist-inspired, Moscow-dictated, and therefore 'subversive.'" Such ploys catered to U.S. preferences and prejudices.

In addition, "the new international economic order and Latin America's place in it" influenced elite perceptions. During the early Cold War the U.S. refusal of economic aid and assistance in favor of private capital conveyed important messages. To attract foreign investors, Latin American governments had to provide "an appropriate climate for direct investment." This requirement meant "various guarantees and assurances, both symbolic and real," including commitment to "liberal, capitalist development and to an 'ideology of production.'" The necessary conditions allowed for no more "Mexican stunts," to use financier Bernard Baruch's term for the oil expropriation in 1938. For such reasons the elites moved against radicals, communists, and labor leaders. Bethell and Roxborough conclude, "Above all, political stability was essential if foreign capital were to be invested in Latin American industry." The observation highlights the importance of external constraints. "Thus, just as the United States *indirectly* promoted political and social change in Latin America at the end of the Second World War, it *indirectly* imposed limits on change in the postwar years."

During the early Cold War the Soviet Union posed no threat of outright aggression against Latin America or any other place in the Western Hemisphere—Soviet leaders possessed neither the means nor, for that matter, the intent—but U.S. leaders worried about communist subversion and penetration by political and ideological methods. Consequently, the intelligence operations initially set up to monitor Nazi activity shifted attention to the communists. In U.S. embassies the legal attachés (usually FBI agents), the military, naval, and labor attachés, and the CIA operatives who made up the apparatus found scant evidence of a threat. A CIA review of Soviet aims in Latin America in November 1947 denied any possibility of a communist takeover anywhere in the region. But such findings ran counter to official U.S. preferences. At the Bogotá conference the delegates described the mere existence of communist parties as a menace to regional security.

U.S. leaders worried especially about communism in Latin American labor unions. Presumably, such influence could endanger U.S. interests in vital enterprises, such as petroleum in Mexico and Venezuela, copper in Chile, sugar in Cuba, and industry and transportation everywhere. Moreover, militant unions, whether or not controlled by communists, appeared as destabilizing elements, fundamentally at odds with the requirements of postwar capitalist development. In most countries the United States had no need to intervene, even by clandestine means, to secure action against communists and labor militants. The ruling elites correctly understood U.S. preferences and responded to U.S. political and economic pressures. As the leaders in the Truman administration saw it, the removal of communists strengthened democracy by expunging alien and hostile presences.[26]

Overall, the Cold War diverted U.S. attention away from Latin America. The containment policy initially manifested a Europe-first orientation that culminated in 1949 with the North Atlantic Treaty Organization (NATO), a formal military alliance and collective security system. It rounded out a sequence of impressive victories for the United States. But then, a turnabout ostensibly situated the advantage with the other side. In August 1949, only four years after Hiroshima and Nagasaki, the Soviet Union broke the U.S. atomic monopoly by setting off a nuclear device. In October 1949, another hammer blow fell: Communist forces under Mao Zedong triumphed in the Chinese civil war, and in the following year the People's Republic of China negotiated a mutual defense pact and military alliance with the Soviet Union. Even worse, the onset of a war in Korea in June 1950 threatened to ignite a global conflict.

As viewed from Washington, these calamitous events indicated a shift in the distribution of world power favoring the Soviet Union, and U.S. responses incorporated frightening, perhaps distorted, assessments of Soviet aims and capabilities. One such appraisal by the National Security Council known as NSC-68 took shape early in 1950. A powerful endorsement of prevailing assumptions among U.S. officials, the text remained classified until 1975. Alarmist and hyperbolic in content, it presumed the existence of a grave crisis and a mortal threat. As the historian Walter LaFeber observes, it established "the American blueprint for waging the Cold War during the next twenty years."[27]

NSC-68 began by describing a profound change in the world balance of power. As a consequence of the Second World War the two

Great Powers, the United States and the Soviet Union, dominated the globe. The document then spelled out the implications: "What is new, what makes the continuing crisis, is the polarization of power which inescapably confronts the slave society with the free." As LaFeber notes, "It was us against them." NSC-68 attributed the threat of Soviet aggression largely to Marxist ideology. Much in vogue at the time, this analysis claimed that the Soviet Union was "animated by a new fanatic faith, antithetical to our own," which sought "to impose its absolute authority over the rest of the world." The ensuing struggle, "endemic" and "momentous," entailed high stakes. The Soviets presumably would use "violent or non-violent methods in accordance with the dictates of expediency." By setting forth a "design" seeking total victory, their ambitions called into question "the fulfillment or destruction not only of this Republic but of civilization itself." The Soviets wanted "the complete subversion or forcible destruction of the machinery of government and structure of society in the countries of the non-Soviet world and their replacement by an apparatus and structure subservient to and controlled from the Kremlin." No compromise was possible.

Most historians in the present day probably would tone down these assessments of Soviet motives and goals. Nevertheless, for many contemporaries the prospect of terrible consequences seemed real enough. How could they avert them? Predictably, NSC-68 called upon the United States to take the lead "in building a successful functioning political and economic system in the free world" to deter "an attack upon us" so that "our free society can flourish." It advised against premature negotiations with the Soviet Union, favoring instead the construction of positions of strength based on a buildup of U.S. military forces, both conventional and nuclear. It also affirmed a need for calculated measures to ensure "unity" and "consensus" at home and to maintain strong alliance systems with other anticommunist nations.[28]

Such expansive definitions of the communist menace encouraged U.S. leaders to think of Latin America almost exclusively in a Cold War context. The region ceased to have much significance in its own right; instead, it became an arena of Cold War competition in which the United States and the Soviet Union would play out a contest for power, resources, prestige, and influence. Typically, U.S. leaders looked upon Latin Americans as minor players who should subordinate their wishes, interests, and aspirations to Cold War imperatives as defined by the United States. Indeed, their countries took on importance not because of anything intrinsic to them but because of connections with the larger struggle. U.S. officials tended to regard Latin

America mainly as a place in which to turn back communist intrusions for reasons of high policy.

Ignorance of the region compounded the tendency. Those in charge—presidents, secretaries of state, secretaries of defense, national security advisers, CIA directors, and the other inhabitants of the U.S. foreign policy apparatus—never possessed much knowledge and understanding of Latin America. Secretary of State Dean Acheson confessed early in 1950 that he was "rather vague" about its people, unsure "whether they were richer or poorer, going Communist, Fascist or what." President Truman made comparisons based on ethnic stereotypes, claiming that Latin Americans reminded him of the Jews and the Irish: They were "very emotional" and hard to manage. Later, Secretary of State John Foster Dulles claimed to know what to do: "You have to pat them a little bit and make them think you are fond of them." President Eisenhower acknowledged that he had a fondness for the Argentines because they are "the same kind of people we are." This kind of condescension at least hinted of racism.

A remarkable memorandum by George F. Kennan revealed something of official perceptions. A senior Foreign Service officer and State Department counselor, Kennan obtained renown as "the father of containment" for his "Mr. X" article, "The Sources of Soviet Conduct," in *Foreign Affairs* in July 1947. Early in 1950, he undertook his first journey into Latin America. His subsequent report, "Latin America as a Problem in United States Foreign Policy," contained his observations. As Gaddis Smith explains, this report had no direct bearing on the formulation of foreign policy but nevertheless qualified as "a seminal document" because it set forth the "Kennan corollary," following in the tradition of the Richard Olney and Theodore Roosevelt corollaries to Monroe's original message to Congress and the J. Reuben Clark memorandum. As "an unvarnished statement of widely held attitudes," it affirmed a rationale for supporting repressive dictatorships when compelled to do so by the requirements of anticommunism.[29]

Kennan left Washington, DC, by train on 18 February 1950 on his way to Mexico City and then traveled by plane to Caracas, Rio de Janeiro, São Paulo, Montevideo, Buenos Aires, Lima, and Panama City. What he saw and experienced along the way dismayed and distressed him. In Mexico City, he disliked the altitude and the disturbed, sultry, and menacing sounds of "nocturnal activity." In Caracas, he reacted against a "feverish economy debauched by oil money." In Rio, the "noisy, wildly competitive" traffic and "the unbelievable contrasts between luxury and poverty" repelled him. In Lima, he became "depressed" while reflecting "that it had not rained . . . for twenty-nine years." Overall, his memorandum conveyed an impression of distaste for the people, the leaders, and their countries. In Kennan's words, "It seemed unlikely that there could be any other region of the earth in which nature and human behavior could have combined to produce a more unhappy and hopeless background for the conduct of human life than in Latin America." Placing heavy responsibility on the legacies of miscegenation, he wrote, "The handicaps to progress are written in human blood and in the tracings of geography; and in neither case are they readily susceptible of obliteration. They lie heavily across the path of human progress."[30]

Kennan nevertheless attached geopolitical importance to Latin America. In a war against the Soviet Union, he feared catastrophic consequences if "a considerable portion of Latin American society were to throw its weight morally into the opposite camp." Such an association "might well turn the market of international confidence against us and leave us fighting not only communist military power, but a wave of defeatism among our friends and spiteful elation among our detractors elsewhere in the world." For him, communism in Latin America posed a real threat. "Here, as elsewhere, the inner core of the communist leadership is fanatical, disciplined, industrious, and armed with a series of organizational techniques which are absolutely first rate."

How could the United States turn back the danger? Kennan found the answer in the Monroe Doctrine: Soviet efforts to make "pawns" of Latin American countries from "beyond the limits of this continent" clearly ran against Monroe's historic prohibition. The United States needed support from Latin American governments. To enlist it, positive incentives—possibly economic and military aid—could encourage anticommunist measures such as crackdowns on radical agitation. Otherwise, coercion, perhaps diplomatic penalties, could dissuade Latin American governments from engaging in "excessive toleration of anti-American activities." As Gaddis Smith explains, Kennan saw in Latin America "a political culture too weak and selfish to support a democracy strong enough to resist the superior determination and skill of the Communist enemy."

The Kennan corollary articulated a basic premise: "We cannot be too dogmatic about the methods by which local communists can be dealt with." In Kennan's view, everything depended upon "the vigor and efficacy of local concepts and traditions of self-government." If these were as sound and reliable "as in our own country," then "the body politic may be capable of bearing the virus of communism without permitting it to expand to dangerous proportions." He regarded this approach as "undoubtedly the best solution of the communist problem, wherever the prerequisites exist." But lacking them, if "the concepts and traditions of popular government are too weak to absorb successfully the intensity of the communist attack," then "we must concede that harsh governmental measures of repression may be the only answer." He went on to explain "that these measures may have to proceed from regimes whose origins and methods would not stand the test of American concepts of democratic procedures; and that such regimes and such methods may be preferable alternatives, and indeed the only alternatives to further communist success." In short, relying on right-wing military dictators as anticommunist bastions was preferable to risk communist advances. Gaddis Smith remarks that Kennan's position on this matter "is inconsistent with much of his subsequent thought" and attributes it to "the culture shock of a Europeanist who had never visited Latin America before." During his trip, he experienced "an uncharacteristic susceptibility to the views of the American ambassadors with whom he talked" and to "the near-hysterical sense of a worldwide Communist menace in that year 1950." His own preference for "realism" over "moralistic rhetoric" also contributed. Nevertheless, and this is the important point, Kennan's assumptions and observations typified official thinking and undergirded important parts of U.S. policy toward Latin America during the next forty years.[31]

The Korean conflict intensified apprehension over communist expansion and the possibility of a third world war. The causes, much discussed in historical literature, appeared straightforward to U.S. leaders at the time. In their view, the North Korean invasion of South Korea on 25 June 1950 came about because the Soviet Union had willed it, establishing another case in which totalitarian aggression threatened the freedom of peace-loving nations. Recalling Nazi behavior in the late 1930s, Truman acted upon a set of analogies derived mainly from the Munich conference in 1938. Constituting for him and others of his generation the primary lesson of the Second World War, the Munich analogy set forth a simple proposition: Appeasement in the face of totalitarian aggression never works. Indeed, shows of weakness and irresolution merely invite further aggression. Therefore, democratic nations must stand their ground or subsequently run the risk of bigger wars. Scholars have since questioned Truman's analysis, asking whether the Munich analogy holds in this instance. Some recent works depict the conflict less as Stalin's creation than as a consequence of a Korean civil war. North Korean leader Kim Il Sung probably took the initiative on his own to unify the country, and Stalin, for his own reasons, went along. Indeed, some scholars now wonder whether U.S. intervention improved the situation or made it worse.[32]

Taking the lead, the Truman administration resisted Soviet aggression while working through the Security Council of the United Nations. The United States obtained a resolution urging a cease-fire, the withdrawal of North Korean forces, and the restoration of the status quo ante bellum. When North Korea failed to comply, a second UN resolution called upon members to respond with military support for South Korea. During the next three years, until the armistice on 27 July 1953, the United States supplied most of the ground, air, and naval forces from the outside. Other contingents came from the United Kingdom, Turkey, Greece, the Philippines, and Thailand.[33]

The countries of Latin America, whose twenty votes constituted two-fifths of those in the General Assembly in 1950, initially backed the United Nations. Moreover, the Organization of American States went on record on 28 June 1950, declaring its "firm adherence to the decisions of the competent organs of the United Nations" and reaffirming "the pledges of continental solidarity which unite the American States."[34] Latin American republics displayed no equivalent readiness to take part in the fighting, however. Only Colombia sent a token force, an infantry battalion, primarily because the dictator, Laureano Gómez, anticipated payoffs from the United States in return.[35] U.S. leaders tried to recruit the participation of other Latin American ground forces as a sign of commitment, especially after the Chinese intervention late in 1950. These attempts centered on Bolivia, Chile, Uruguay, Mexico, Peru, and Brazil and failed in each instance. At first, Brazil and Peru indicated some interest but only in return for military and economic subsidies. Most Latin American governments claimed that public opinion in their countries would not accept troop commitments.

The historian William Stueck attributes such "meager results" partly to the fact that Latin America, "a grievously poor region," lacked "any tradition of direct involvement" in overseas conflicts. Only Mexico and Brazil had sent military contingents abroad during the Second World War. In addition, Latin Americans perceived no communist threat to themselves and resented what they understood as U.S. neglect, specifically the absence of a Marshall Plan. In Stueck's phrase,

"Tired of being taken for granted by their big brother in the north . . . the Latin republics hedged when asked to provide cannon fodder for a U.S. crusade in a remote land."[36]

Latin American recalcitrance became apparent at the fourth Meeting of Consultation of Ministers of Foreign Affairs of the American Republics in Washington from 26 March to 7 April 1951. Summoned by the Truman administration "to consider problems of an urgent nature and of common interest to American States," and sponsored by the OAS, the conference revealed deep divisions over questions of hemispheric security and economic development. Latin American delegations denied the existence of a communist threat in the Western Hemisphere and argued that in any case, improved living standards sustained by U.S. aid would provide the best means of defense.[37]

Resisting this appeal, the United States emphasized the military requirements of collective self-defense. Later on in 1951, the U.S. Congress implemented a program under the Mutual Security Act, which authorized the negotiation of "mutual defense assistance agreements" with Latin American countries. Beginning with Ecuador in January 1952, twelve such pacts eventually came into existence. Under the terms first established with Ecuador, the United States agreed to make available "equipment, materials, services, and other military assistance designed to promote the defense and maintain the peace of the Western Hemisphere." In return, Ecuador would utilize the aid to strengthen its military defenses and, significantly, "to facilitate the production and transfer . . . of . . . strategic materials required by the United States." From the U.S. standpoint, these provisions contained strong incentives for pact partners to provide adequate supplies of raw materials and to guard against radical subversion. Subsequent military programs also emphasized the training of Latin American officers in "counterinsurgency" techniques, proposing to use them as anticommunist bulwarks.[38]

In the end, the Korean War destroyed the Truman presidency. Weakened politically by the military inconclusiveness of the conflict, his firing of General Douglas MacArthur, and the spurious Republican allegations of softness on communism, Truman lacked the grounds to present himself in 1952 as a candidate for a second full term. Instead, the Democratic nomination fell to Adlai Stevenson, a former Illinois governor. The Republicans, seeking to gain the presidency for the first time since 1932, took full advantage. Particularly, they assailed the Democrats for perpetuating big government at home and incompetency

US Domestic policies [handwritten annotation]

in foreign policy. Korea supposedly stood as a case in point. While characterizing the Democratic policy of containment as "defensive, negative, futile, and immoral," the Republicans suggested a more dynamic approach by which to seize the initiative, roll back the communist tide, and win victories in the Cold War.[39] Their efforts to advance such goals during Dwight D. Eisenhower's presidency had many implications for Latin America.

ANTICOMMUNISM UNDER IKE: TRADE, AID, AND INTERVENTION

During the 1950s, Cold War issues preoccupied the leaders of the Eisenhower administration in Latin America. Anticommunism, the hallmark of U.S. policy, required order, stability, and constant vigilance against radical subversion. At the same time, Latin American nationalists, reformers, and homegrown revolutionaries blurred distinctions by insisting upon state activity to instigate economic development. For the United States, how to sort them out from Soviet-style communists posed a real problem. Other issues also caused difficulties. A critical one centered on trade, or aid, as the best means of moving Latin America toward modernization. Another concerned the utility of intervention by the United States. A clandestine operation in Guatemala in 1954 toppled a popularly elected government that was perceived in Washington as communist-dominated. This short-term success led later to similar efforts against Fidel Castro in Cuba. Looked upon by the United States as a dangerous precedent, Castro's revolutionary triumph symbolized a repudiation of U.S. tutelage and suggested to the remainder of Latin America the option of following Cuba's lead.

As depicted by Eisenhower during the 1952 campaign, Truman's policies in Latin America had gone dangerously wrong. According to Ike, the U.S. had "frantically wooed Latin America" during the Second World War but then "proceeded to forget these countries just as fast" after the peace. Consequently, a "terrible disillusionment set in," and "Communist agents" who were standing ready "skillfully exploited" economic distress and political unrest for their own purposes. "Through drift and neglect," the Truman administration had embraced what Ike called "a poor neighbor policy," now very much in need of a change.[40]

Ike's PR. 1952 [handwritten annotation]

In an important book on the Eisenhower administration and Latin America, the historian Stephen G. Rabe takes a revisionist stance by arguing that the president "decisively" established and oversaw the policies of his administration. Unlike the earlier body of writing that depicted Eisenhower as a kind of figurehead, the more recent scholarship portrays him as a chief executive truly in charge. According to the political scientist Fred I. Greenstein, Eisenhower often misled observers by employing indirect and obscure methods in a "hidden hand" style of leadership. Operating unobtrusively behind the scenes, he exercised command while allowing subordinates to indulge in appearances.[41]

In the case of Latin America, Eisenhower moved quickly to institute corrective actions. Within two months of taking office, he approved a statement formulated by the National Security Council, "United States Objectives and Courses of Action with Respect to Latin America." This document emphasized the necessity of "hemispheric solidarity" against international communism and called for the enlistment of Latin American support in the struggle against the Soviet Union, especially the threat of internal communist subversion. Recalling the requirements of the Kennan corollary, this approach encouraged the administration to embrace anticommunist leaders in Latin America—including repressive dictators—as allies.

Before becoming president, Eisenhower had had modest experience with Latin America. After graduating from the U.S. Military Academy in 1915, while serving at Fort Sam Houston in San Antonio, Texas, he went on hunting trips into Mexico and acquired a "romantic" if somewhat "patronizing attitude" toward Mexicans. In Panama in the early 1920s, he developed a dislike for the tropics and for the blatant forms of discrimination experienced by Panamanians in the Canal Zone. Early in the Second World War, he worked with Lend–Lease programs for Latin America and later paid official visits to Mexico, Panama, and Brazil. In the main, he thought that military aid to Latin America well served U.S. interests in national security.

Eisenhower's secretary of state, John Foster Dulles, had a reputation as the Republican expert on foreign affairs. As a young man, he had attended the Paris Peace Conference in 1919 in a minor capacity. He built his professional career with the Wall Street law firm of Cromwell and Sullivan, often working out of its Berlin and Paris offices on matters of international investment and finance. In Latin America, he represented U.S. corporations such as the United Fruit Company. Outspoken, acerbic, and assertive, Secretary Dulles played an influential role but never dominated Eisenhower. The "hidden-hand" president allowed subordinates to take credit or blame, depending on his needs, but always kept his own prerogatives intact.

Eisenhower also relied heavily on his youngest brother, Dr. Milton Eisenhower, as a source of information on Latin American affairs.

Regarded by Ike as "the most knowledgeable and widely informed of all the people with whom I deal," Milton Eisenhower possessed no particular Latin American expertise but a broad understanding based on a variety of career experiences, including stints as a former Foreign Service officer and an Agriculture Department official. He had also served as the president of Kansas State University, Pennsylvania State University, and Johns Hopkins University. Ike corresponded with his brother regularly and often spent weekends in his company. On two occasions, he sent Milton as a special ambassador on fact-finding missions to Latin America.[42]

Top Eisenhower leaders were united in the conviction that communism posed a worldwide danger. During his confirmation hearings before the Senate Foreign Relations Committee, Dulles described the "threat" as "the gravest . . . that ever faced the United States," indeed, "the gravest . . . that has ever faced what we call western civilization, or . . . any civilization which was dominated by a spiritual faith." In Latin America, in Dulles's view, communists had penetrated every country. Animated by "hatred of the Yankee," they sought "to destroy the influence of the so-called Colossus of the North in Central and South America." Distressed by what he regarded as a disturbing parallel, he claimed that "conditions in Latin America are somewhat comparable to conditions as they were in China in the mid-thirties when the Communist movement was getting started." Therefore, "the time to deal with this rising menace in South America is now."

Such rhetoric aptly reflected the administration's apprehensions. Sometimes Eisenhower and his aides used this kind of language for political effect to rally anticommunists in the Republican party, but in the Latin American case "the private discussions and classified policy statements of administration officials differed little from their public positions." For example, the president worried about the consequences of surging nationalism in the Third World, identifying it as a cause of instability and a potential vehicle of communist expansion. For Ike, nationalism "on the move" required special wariness. In his diary, attempting to describe "actually what is going on," he wrote that "communists are hoping to take advantage of the confusion resulting from the destruction of existing relationships and uncertainties of disrupted trade, security, and understanding." He feared that communists would capitalize on nationalist agitation "to further the aims of world revolution and the Kremlin's domination of all people."[43]

Ike's critics have suggested that such anxieties, however overdrawn, should have elicited more imaginative reactions. Specifically, the

Eisenhower administration should have tried to neutralize communist appeals by mobilizing pro-U.S. nationalist elements with positive incentives. As it turned out, the leaders never attained such creative levels. Their error resided in apprehending third-world nationalism so exclusively in Cold War terms. As a consequence, the historian Robert J. McMahon argues, the Eisenhower administration "grievously misunderstood and underestimated the most significant historical development of the mid-twentieth century."[44]

How to distinguish third-world nationalism from Soviet communism remained a principal problem for U.S. policymakers in Latin America throughout the Cold War. Among his primary goals, Eisenhower wanted to secure "the allegiance of these republics in our camp in the cold war." But he could not tell whether policies to accommodate Latin American nationalists would win them over or open the way to communist advances. In other words, he was unsure how to calculate the effects of meaningful reforms: Would they undercut communist appeals or encourage revolution by disrupting traditional relationships? Dulles, a pessimist in these matters, feared that "the Communists are trying to extend their form of despotism in this hemisphere." Underscoring what he regarded as the true nature of the threat, he defined communism as "an internationalist conspiracy, not an indigenous movement." "In the old days," Dulles claimed, "we used to be able to let South America go through the wringer of bad times . . . but the trouble is now, when you put it through the wringer, it comes out red."

The National Security Council initiated discussions of these matters in February 1953. Stating the theme, the CIA director Allen Dulles, brother of the secretary of state, spoke of "deteriorating" relations with Latin America, marked by a "Communist infection" in Guatemala, and warned of "an approaching crisis." A month later, on 18 March 1953, the National Security Council established essential aims in a policy document known as NSC-144/1. As Stephen G. Rabe notes, the planners "interpreted inter-American affairs solely within the context of the global struggle with the Soviet Union." Essentially, the Eisenhower administration wanted four things from Latin America: support in the United Nations, eradication of "internal Communist or other anti-U.S. subversion," access to strategic raw materials, and military cooperation in defending the hemisphere. Yet the document demonstrated scant faith in the reliability of Latin American leaders and their capacity to comprehend the international danger. NSC-144/1 disparaged as "immature and impractical idealists" such influential figures as Lázaro Cárdenas in Mexico, Juan José Arévalo in Guatemala, José Figueres in Costa Rica, Rómulo Betancourt in Venezuela, Víctor Haya de la Torre in Peru, and Getúlio Vargas in Brazil. It asserted that these men were "inadequately trained to conduct government business efficiently," lacked "the disposition to combat extremists within their ranks, including communists," and displayed a Latin American penchant for "irresponsible acts." Much like the Kennan corollary, NSC-144/1 invoked "overriding security interests" as a justification for U.S. intervention. Whenever necessary, the United States should employ unilateral measures, even if they might violate "our treaty commitments, . . . endanger the Organization of American States . . . and . . . probably intensify anti-U.S. attitudes in many Latin American countries."

The anticommunist campaign in Latin America also employed political propaganda and military aid. According to Rabe, the U.S. Information Agency spent $5.2 million a year in such efforts to get out the message as, for example, the production and distribution of comic books, cartoon strips, and movie shorts. Intended for mass consumption, these devices warned of totalitarian threats menacing the freedom and property of individuals. Sometimes they elicited faulty inferences; in Mexico, some audiences reportedly thought the danger emanated from their own government. Anticommunist initiatives placed special importance on Latin American trade unions. The military establishments also received special treatment. Viewed by U.S. leaders as anticommunist bulwarks, Latin American armies became the recipients of increased military aid. Rabe questions whether "the strategic benefits of inter-American military cooperation" really amounted to much. At the same time, he acknowledges that "the political advantages of military aid" were "significant," especially when training and assistance programs gave access to the dominant military caste. Military officers wielded power in so many of the countries that U.S. leaders regarded shows of support for them as essential. In dealings with Juan Perón's Argentine government, for example, Cold War considerations ultimately overcame earlier suspicions of his pro-fascism.

As staunch anticommunists, Eisenhower officials displayed no equivalent devotion to democracy and human rights. Some thought the defense of such values might violate the nonintervention principle or, worse, incite radicalism and subversion. Others shared Milton Eisenhower's misimpression. After a trip to South America in the fall of 1953 the president's brother reported with stunning inaccuracy that

"most American nations which still have degrees of feudalism and dictatorship are moving gradually toward democratic concepts and practices." As Rabe observes, military dictators at the time controlled
thirteen Latin American republics and enjoyed many favors from the
Eisenhower administration. Indeed, two military strongmen, Manuel
Odría of Peru and Marcos Pérez Jiménez of Venezuela, received from
the United States a special award for foreign leaders called the Legion of
Merit citation. After all, as Rabe notes, "Communists, not dictators,
were the enemies of the United States."[45]

The Guatemalan intervention in 1954 destroyed whatever remained
of the Good Neighbor policy. In conformance with the Kennan corollary, Eisenhower officials aided in the overthrow of a government
perceived as procommunist. Whether they overreacted or not has
occasioned some debate. Most historians have taken a critical stance.
Some have emphasized the importance of confusion and misperception:
Typically, Eisenhower and his advisers had trouble distinguishing between nationalist reform and communist subversion. Others have
perceived a conscious design: To safeguard capitalist interests against
radical threats, the United States reverted to interventionist techniques.[46]

Among the Western Hemisphere nations, Guatemala ranked high
in misery and hopelessness. The masses of people, descended from the
native Mayas, suffered oppression, poverty, and illiteracy; the effects
included disease, malnutrition, high infant mortality, and low life expectancy. In contrast, a small, landed elite monopolized political power
and economic advantage, usually with the support of army officers and
foreign corporations. The United Fruit Company, owned by U.S. investors, was the biggest property holder and employer in the country. It
also dominated transportation and communications. Traditionally, military strongmen, or *caudillos*, upheld order and authority on behalf of
elite interests. From 1931 until 1944, the dictator Jorge Ubico y
Castañeda governed with repressive efficiency. Under his criminal code,
death was the penalty for union organizers. Laws supposedly intended
to curb vagrancy compelled the rural poor to labor in public works
projects in circumstances close to slavery. Ubico, a self-styled Napoleon figure, displayed an exhibitionist need for regal uniforms and public displays. A riding accident had rendered him impotent when he was
a young man. Nevertheless, in later shows of prowess, he went into the
cages at the Guatemala City zoo to roar at the lions.[47]

Ubico fled the country late in 1944 following an urban-based uprising among middle-class elements: disenchanted schoolteachers,

shopkeepers, students, lawyers, and junior military officers. Inspired by Allied ideals during the Second World War and the Mexican example under Lázaro Cárdenas, they joined in marches, demonstrations, and strikes to demand democracy and modernization. An honest election in 1945, probably the first in the country's history, resulted in the victory of Juan José Arévalo, who won 85 percent of the votes cast by literate adult males. A professor of literature and philosophy and a long-time enemy of Ubico, Arévalo had fled into exile in Argentina in 1935. Back in Guatemala after a decade, he found appalling conditions. The majority of people, mainly agricultural workers, earned less than $100 a year; 2 percent of the population owned 70 percent of the land. Backwardness pervaded the rural regions. Hardly any industry existed at all. More than half of the people were illiterate, including almost all the native peoples.

During a six-year term in office, Arévalo fashioned for Guatemala a reformist program reminiscent of the New Deal in the United States. Among other things, it extended voting rights to all adults, abolished forced labor, instituted minimum wages and collective bargaining for workers, redistributed small amounts of land confiscated from Germans during the war, established a social security agency, and launched a literacy campaign. Predictably, members of the privileged elite opposed these changes. In the course of his presidency, Arévalo survived more than twenty attempts to overthrow him.

Nevertheless, a legal election produced a peaceful transition in March 1951, when Jacobo Arbenz Guzmán took over as president. A professional soldier, a graduate of the Guatemalan military academy, and the secretary of defense under Arévalo, Arbenz Guzmán "accelerated the pace of change in Guatemala." In his inaugural address, he promised to build an independent, modern, capitalist state. Later, his efforts to improve the economic infrastructure through the construction of ports and highways trespassed upon the United Fruit Company's control of such facilities. Similarly, he offended elite interests by supporting an income tax and land reform. Described as "the centerpiece of his program," Arbenz's agrarian reform bill sought to advance progress and modernization by redistributing land more equitably to rural workers. One controversial provision authorized the expropriation of uncultivated portions of large estates, in many instances as much as 75 percent of the land controlled by these plantations. Between 1952 and 1954 the Arbenz government disbursed 1.5 million acres to 100,000 families. As Rabe notes, this reform operated well within "the boundaries set by twentieth-century reform movements in the West." Neverthe-less, "the process and pattern of change in Guatemala" collided with the interests of the United Fruit Company.

Based in Boston, United Fruit had operated in Guatemala since the late nineteenth century. Tight linkages connected the company with the traditional ruling elites. Under Ubico the company supported the regime and received tax concessions and vast tracts of land. It owned 550,000 acres, about 85 percent uncultivated, supposedly for reasons of crop rotation and soil conservation. When the Arbenz government initiated expropriation proceedings, offering compen-sation at three dollars an acre in government bonds, company offi-cials rejected the terms. Instead, they appealed to the Eisenhower administration, claiming that communists had taken over in Guate-mala and threatened the Western Hemisphere.[48]

Much as expected, Eisenhower officials responded sympatheti-cally. Indeed, similar suspicions had percolated through the State De-partment for some time. In 1949, the Assistant Secretary of State for Inter-American Affairs, Edward G. Miller Jr., had warned of bad ef-fects if Guatemala threatened the properties of United Fruit. In the same year, U.S. Ambassador to Guatemala Richard Patterson pledged his personal opposition to the "cancerous doctrine" of the commu-nists. With "undivided attention," he would protect "American inter-ests." He also advised company leaders to employ "an all-out barrage" to win support in the U.S. Senate. Gaddis Smith describes Patterson as a "hysterical, paranoic anti-Communist." Guatemalan officials regarded his undiplomatic behavior in their country as a form of intervention. In response, Patterson quit his job in the spring of 1950, claiming that com-munists planned to kill him.

Relations deteriorated further after Arbenz's inauguration in March 1951. The U.S. government expressed displeasure by means of economic pressure, cuts in foreign aid, and attempts to block the Guatemalan pur-chase of European military and industrial goods. The United Fruit Company encouraged direct action. In February 1952, company offi-cials characterized "communist infiltration in Guatemala" as "a mod-ern day violation of the Monroe Doctrine." Guatemalans, however, professed bewilderment. As Foreign Minister Guillermo Toriello told Secretary of State Dean Acheson in the fall of 1952, his government merely wanted "to remove the evils" that had allowed communist sym-pathies to develop in the first place.

Covert military action was one way of dealing with Arbenz. The Truman administration considered it but held back. According to

Gaddis Smith, Truman and Acheson adhered somewhat more literally than their successors to the nonintervention principle as "one of the very keystones of the Inter-American system."[49] Such inhibitions counted for less in the Eisenhower administration. As Supreme Allied Commander in Europe during the Second World War, Ike had become enamored of clandestine operations, particularly the exploits of "Wild Bill" Donovan and the Office of Strategic Services (OSS). Moreover, his administration could point to an actual success. In 1953 the CIA carried out a covert action in Iran: It ousted Mohammed Mossadegh's nationalist government for expropriating the holdings of U.S. and British oil companies and returned to power a more pliable figure, the Shah Reza Pahlavi.[50]

The Iranian venture reinforced fundamental assumptions within the administration. In the Guatemalan case, Ike and Dulles invested more faith in the workability of the Kennan corollary than in the principle of nonintervention. Republican leaders also regarded the Democratic version of the containment policy as too passive. During the 1952 campaign the Republicans supported a "New Look" in foreign affairs, advocating a more active approach. By seizing the initiative, they would roll back the communist tide and win victories in the Cold War. Otherwise, Dulles feared, "we might well wake up ten years from now to find that our friends in Latin America had become our enemies."

Covert action in this instance brought about the overthrow of the Arbenz regime and the establishment of the kind of government anticipated by Kennan: harsh, repressive, and undemocratic. As Gaddis Smith explains, this undertaking, "one of the most minutely studied in the history of U.S.-Latin American relations," followed three tracks: economic pressure, collective action through the Organization of American States, and a clandestine operation using anti-Arbenz rebels organized by the CIA in Honduras. Historians' interpretations have established different points of emphasis: a determination to defend U.S. corporate interests, the influence of anticommunism, the role of misperception, and the presumed necessity of standing strong in the Cold War struggle. But all agree on the effects. The Guatemalan intervention in 1954 closed down Franklin Roosevelt's Good Neighbor policy for keeps.[51]

At the tenth Inter-American Conference at Caracas, Venezuela, in March 1954, Dulles hoped to obtain multilateral support for measures against Guatemala but failed to get it. Latin Americans again differed with the United States over priorities and preferences. They wanted open discussions of economic issues focused on trade, aid, and the like, whereas the U.S. delegates insisted on the primacy of security matters and pushed for an anticommunist resolution. It declared that "the domination or control of the political institutions of any American state by the international communist movement . . . would constitute a threat" to regional security, therefore necessitating "appropriate action in accordance with existing treaties." This statement, a reference to the Rio Pact of 1947, specifically Article 6, had procedural implications. It meant that a two-thirds majority among the OAS members would have to agree to take action against "an aggression which was not an armed attack," either by means of economic sanctions or a joint intervention. In conformance with the Kennan corollary, Dulles really wanted to extend "the Monroe Doctrine to include the concept of outlawing foreign ideologies in the American Republics."

The leaders in the Eisenhower administration wanted a demonstration for Latin Americans to illustrate the incompatibility of communism with nationalism. In the U.S. view, no conceivable mix was possible; therefore, communism in Guatemala constituted subversion, not reform. To counter it, the leaders contemplated drastic measures. A State Department memorandum circulating among U.S. diplomats in Latin America suggested the feasibility of a unilateral intervention. If Latin Americans refused to accept their responsibility to police the Western Hemisphere against communist incursions, so the reasoning went, then the United States would have no choice except to reassess "the soundness of the OAS relationship," perhaps by taking action alone.

At Caracas, Dulles pressed the anticommunist case during two weeks of debate. In the course of it, he urged immediate action and fought off fifty amendments proposed by Latin Americans. In the end, he got a resolution but not the one he wanted. Passed by a vote of 17 to 1 (Guatemala opposed), with Mexico and Argentina abstaining, the measure in Dulles's view lacked "vitality." Instead of calling for immediate action against the communist threat in Guatemala, the OAS advised in favor of future deliberations to consider the means of upholding treaty obligations. As Rabe notes, by employing the ancient tactics of procrastination and delay, "the Latin Americans rejected the administration's contention that communism in Latin America constituted external aggression."[52] At no point during the ensuing Guatemalan intervention could the United States count unambiguously on Latin American support.

Nevertheless, the plan for covert action got under way. In the middle of May a Swedish vessel, the *Alfhelm*, arrived in Guatemala with a cargo of arms from communist Czechoslovakia. Presented as proof of communist complicity with Guatemalan officials, this event enabled Secretary Dulles to issue another indictment of "Communist penetration" of the Western Hemisphere. Soon thereafter a clandestine operation supported by the United States successfully eliminated the offending Arbenz regime from power. A small rebel army of two hundred began the invasion of Guatemala on 18 June 1954 by moving across the Honduran border. Recruited and trained by the CIA, this force, commanded by Lieutenant Colonel Carlos Castillo Armas, was incapable of waging war against the much larger Guatemalan army; instead, it utilized indirect methods. As Allen Dulles reported to President Eisenhower, the success of the venture depended more on "psychological impact" than on "actual military strength." Nevertheless, Dulles wanted to create "the *impression* of very substantial military strength" through the use of deception and disinformation. Fake radio reports of large-scale fighting instilled panic and demoralization, and a real but small-scale bombing raid against Guatemala City produced hysteria.

The effects unhinged President Arbenz. Unsure of the reliability of his own army, he feared the possibility of U.S. military action. Reportedly influenced by strong drink, he resigned on 27 June and fled into exile, leaving the government to a military junta. For a week, army officers jockeyed for position. Then on 2 July, under U.S. pressure, they settled on Colonel Castillo Armas, also the CIA's favorite choice. As head of state, Castillo Armas instituted a series of anticommunist measures, nullified the reforms, and restored the old regime. The consequences were political polarization and civil war. During the next four decades, more than 100,000 Guatemalans died in the ongoing violence. Carlos Castillo Armas was one of them; assassins gunned him down in 1957. Around Latin America, the reactions were mixed. In the countries where dictators had control, official responses suggested at least a readiness to acquiesce in the U.S. intervention. But critics and protesters in Argentina, Bolivia, Chile, Cuba, Ecuador, Mexico, and Uruguay condemned the United States for what they called aggression against Guatemala, indicating at the very least their displeasure with the application of the Kennan corollary in their part of the world.[53] The supposed geopolitical imperatives of the Cold War held less importance for them than questions of economic growth and modernization.

As Stephen G. Rabe shows, Latin American leaders in the 1950s typically looked upon the inter-American system less as an anticommunist alliance than as "a mechanism for economic cooperation."[54] They wanted programs of economic assistance from the United

States and ultimately compelled the Eisenhower administration to grapple with tough questions of trade or aid. During Ike's first term, U.S. officials expressed preferences for trade over aid as the primary engine of economic progress but shifted ground grudgingly during his second term, thereby allowing for a possibility of discussing both.

Ike's economic views conformed with convention by regarding free trade and private investment as the main requisites for peace and prosperity. Eisenhower regarded mass poverty, hunger, and insecurity as threats, that is, as incitements to the spread of communism. He believed that free enterprise could best advance the collective well-being: It would "allow backward people to make a decent living—even if only a minimum one measured by American standards," and the United States would also benefit. In his diary, he underscored the importance of ready access to raw materials—tin, cobalt, uranium, manganese, crude oil—and noted that "unless the areas in which these materials are found are under the control of people who are friendly to us and who want to trade with us, then . . . we are bound in the long run to suffer the most disastrous and doleful consequences."

As a self-styled fiscal conservative, Eisenhower fretted over the excesses of government spending, yet between 1953 and 1961 his administration granted or lent nearly $50 billion in military and economic aid to other countries. But for him, such programs had limited applicability; as he told his brother Milton, they pertained only to those regions directly imperiled by "the Communist menace." Consequently, Latin America ranked low in priority. On 18 March 1953 the National Security Council in NSC-144/1 confirmed this view with a statement of expectations. Latin American governments would have to learn that if private enterprise could best supply "the capital required for their economic development," then "their own self-interest requires the creation of a climate which will attract private investment." The same admonitions appeared in November 1953 in Milton Eisenhower's report of his fact-finding tour to South America. Subsequently regarded as orthodox and unimaginative even by the author, it expressed views that unsurprisingly favored fiscal responsibility, "honest money," and balanced budgets over other approaches featuring economic nationalism, "industrialization for its own sake," and "creeping expropriation." For their own good, Milton Eisenhower exhorted Latin Americans to uphold the principle of free trade and the sanctity of foreign investments and to understand that private monies "must be *attracted* by the nation desiring the capital." Such banalities amused Brazilian diplomats, who wondered why Milton Eisenhower had to make a trip to Latin America to arrive at these conclusions.

In the State Department, Assistant Secretary John Moors Cabot developed doubts about them. He had accompanied Milton Eisenhower on the tour and drew some bleaker inferences. In much of Latin America, he reported, per capita income was about one-eighth that of the United States. In the poorest countries—Bolivia, Ecuador, and Haiti—the situation was even worse. Yet the United States sent only about 1 percent of its economic development assistance to Latin America, and Cabot warned, "We cannot indefinitely continue the present discrimination against our sister republics in this hemisphere without gravely prejudicing our relations with them." Moreover, he placed scant faith in the capacity of private investment to solve the problem. In his view, a variety of impediments obstructed economic advancement, including inadequate transportation and communication systems, multitudes of impoverished people who lacked educational and technical skills, and vast disparities of wealth and power with the upper classes exercising "an almost feudal control." For all these reasons, he concluded, "trickle-down" economics would neither produce great bursts of economic growth nor nullify communist appeals.

As a place to begin, Cabot suggested modest increases in developmental loans, relying primarily on the Export-Import Bank to support the improvement of infrastructure. In response, Secretary of the Treasury George Humphrey, an ideologue, took offense at the heresy. Devoutly combative in his fiscal conservatism, Humphrey demanded that Latin Americans conform with history and tradition by adhering to the developmental model of the United States. For him, this approach meant reliance on private foreign capital. Secretary of State Dulles supported Cabot's ideas but not Cabot. Convinced that boom-and-bust cycles increased Latin American vulnerability to communist insinuation, Dulles secured the president's consent for the use of the Export-Import Bank in support of "sound development projects." He also agreed to take part in a long-deferred Latin American economic conference. Nevertheless, he punished Cabot for pushing too hard. The assistant secretary lost his job and went off to Stockholm as the ambassador to Sweden.

More bureaucratic wrangling occurred as plans developed for the economic conference, scheduled to begin in Rio de Janeiro late in November 1954. As head of the U.S. delegation, Secretary of the Treasury George Humphrey predictably favored trade, not aid, but on this occasion the president differed with him. Ike, as it turned out, had agreed to expand the operations of the Export-Import Bank in Latin America and to increase its overall lending capacity by $500 million. This move ranked as "the only significant initiative" by the United States at the conference. It also conformed with the administration's understanding of Cold War imperatives. As Ike explained to Humphrey, U.S. policy in Latin America was "chiefly designed to play a part in the cold war against our enemies." Extraordinary measures had become necessary because the "United States was not merely doing 'business' in Latin America, but was fighting a war there against Communism."

Latin Americans had hoped for more. According to the Brazilian ambassador, João Carlos Muniz, government leaders had believed ever since the Second World War that "the vast resources of the United States were going to be brought to bear on wide and rapid economic change in Latin America." But delay and inaction has caused "an intense pro-cess of disillusionment." Brazilians could not understand why the United States used large-scale programs of economic aid and assistance in the fight against communism in Asia and Europe but depended upon "politico-police" methods in the Western Hemisphere.[55]

Evolving Latin American economic theories dissented from the established orthodoxies in the United States. Latin Americans de-picted free markets and private investments as failures in their part of the Western Hemisphere. Such practices simply had not worked. In-stead of diffusing growth, progress, and modernization throughout the region, free trade and private investment had locked Latin America into conditions of economic dependency and underdevelopment. In other words, they perpetuated an inequitable economic system based on neocolonial relationships.

For Latin Americans, integration into the world capitalist system meant dependence on market fluctuations in Europe and the United States, entailing extreme vulnerability in times of economic downswing. Their experience during the two world wars and the Great Depression appeared as cases in point. Moreover, Latin Americans operated at a disadvantage because of the terms of exchange. As producers of pri-mary commodities, they provided the industrialized world with low-cost agricultural products and mineral resources and purchased in return high-cost manufactured goods. The very structure of the transaction placed them at a disadvantage and enabled foreign inter-ests to exercise control over their economic destinies. Indeed, as de-scribed by the Argentine economist Raúl Prebisch, the situation was getting worse. The cost of manufactured products had increased steadily in comparison with the prices obtained for raw materials and agricultural goods. For a decade after 1952 the combined price index of commodities sold by Latin Americans—coffee, wheat, corn, tin, cotton, sisal, lead, zinc, nitrates, sugar—declined in every year except one.[56]

For many Latin Americans, the impact of traditional trade and investment practices helped account for the poor performance of their economies. The statistics were disheartening. In the early 1950s, annual per capita income in Latin America amounted to $250; life expectancy was forty-three years; and an expanding population eroded whatever gains might come about in productivity. Structural considerations contributing to the difficulties included unresponsive and unstable political systems, a maldistribution of wealth and land, insufficient economic infrastructure, inadequate educational systems, and indifference among the ruling elites.

The dimensions of the problem became clearer in a series of studies by the Economic Commission for Latin America (ECLA), a UN agency headed by Prebisch. These reports described shortages of investment capital for economic development as the chief deficiency and accounted for them by tracking the flow of money in and out of Latin America. According to Prebisch, the economic outlays in Latin America—that is, interest payments and profit remittances on public loans and private investments—exceeded the inputs. In other words, the advanced countries took more money out than they put in. As a consequence, economic growth was calculated at 1 percent a year. To enhance it, ECLA economists estimated that Latin America needed $1 billion a year for ten years, most of which would have to come from international lending institutions and the United States.

U.S. traders and investors already played an enormous role in Latin American economies. By the early 1950s, their investments in Latin America ran to $6 billion, about 40 percent of direct U.S. investments in the world. Most of the money went into extractive industries such as Chilean copper and Venezuelan oil. Annual trade between the United States and Latin America amounted to $7 billion, the overall balance slightly favoring the United States. Latin America accounted for 25 percent of U.S. international trade.

In these circumstances, Latin Americans still looked to the United States for assistance. In anticipation of the Rio economic conference from 22 November to 2 December 1954, Ambassador Muniz expressed his hope for "great things." Specifically, he wanted an Eisenhower Plan for Latin America, presumably something like the Marshall Plan for Western Europe. But his hopes failed to materialize. U.S. leaders rejected any such approach as inconsistent with established policies, priorities, and preferences; they favored free trade and private investment. During the conference the U.S. delegation made a small concession by agreeing to expand the lending authority of the Export-Import Bank but otherwise provided no satisfaction for Latin Americans. As Rabe remarks, "By intervening in Guatemala and by ignoring Latin America's economic needs," the Eisenhower administration appeared to endorse the "attitudes and practices" of an earlier time.[57]

After the Korean armistice on 27 July 1953, the United States enjoyed a period of peace and prosperity. Eisenhower won reelection in 1956, following a campaign in which Latin America figured hardly at all. The main policy tenets—anticommunism, free trade, and private investment—persisted into the second term, as did the practice of supporting military dictators. Though privately a bit ambivalent about the matter, Eisenhower usually evaded questions concerned with civil liberties and human rights. In all likelihood the president would have preferred the existence of more democratic regimes and on occasion may have maneuvered behind the scenes to curb abuses. When Juan Perón fell from power in 1955, Ike expressed his approval. At the same time, he embraced military strongmen as necessary allies in the anticommunist struggle. By the mid-1950s, military aid in Latin America was one of the costliest budget items in the region. Ike understood that Latin American forces possessed scant fighting ability. Yet he wanted not only "to preserve . . . the good will of the Latin American Republics" but also "to assure their internal security, without which their good will would be useless to us." As Rabe concludes, "The transfer of arms and the training of Latin American officers and soldiers continued, because the administration wanted powerful, anti-Communist friends in Latin America."

Also in the mid-1950s, changes in the Soviet Union caused mounting concern. Following Stalin's death in March 1953 the aspiring heirs engaged in a complex power struggle in which foreign policy played a role. An early claimant to Stalin's position, Nikolai Bulganin, offered in January 1956 to expand diplomatic, economic, and cultural relations with Latin America, especially through trade and technical assistance. As part of a larger Soviet effort in the Third World, Bulganin's initiatives anticipated more effective forms of peaceful competition. But in Latin America, they accomplished almost nothing. As consumers, Latin

Americans regarded Soviet merchandise as shoddy and unattractive. Moreover, they disliked the brutal Soviet suppression of the Hungarian uprising during the fall of 1956. Consequently, Secretary Dulles arrived at the comforting conclusion in 1957 that "we see no likelihood at the present time of communism getting into control of the political institutions of any of the American Republics."

Anticommunist apprehensions escalated in 1958 following Vice President Richard M. Nixon's disastrous visit to South America, which produced protests, riots, and a life-threatening mob scene. First conceived by Roy Richard Rubottom, then serving as the assistant secretary of state for Latin American affairs, the plan envisioned the trip as a goodwill gesture, conveying to Latin Americans some new readiness to address economic issues. Rubottom had worried late in 1957 that "the economic situation in the whole area has deteriorated" and that communists would take advantage. He suggested that Dulles lead the delegation, but the secretary begged off, claiming other responsibilities. Eisenhower then sent Nixon.

Unenthusiastic about his assignment, Nixon went to Latin America grudgingly late in April 1958. The schedule called for a stop in Argentina to attend the inauguration of President Arturo Frondizi and for others in Uruguay, Peru, and Venezuela. In Montevideo and Lima, Nixon encountered hecklers, and in Caracas, even worse. Earlier that year, Venezuelans had ousted Marcos Pérez Jiménez, a dictator formerly cultivated by the United States. Now they vented their rage against Nixon with menacing demonstrations. As he moved through the streets, they even threatened his life directly by attacking his car before the driver sped away to safety. Nixon later described this event as one of the six crises shaping his political character.

These incidents elicited a new round of debate among Eisenhower officials. Nixon blamed communist agitators, but others had different views. CIA Director Allen Dulles found no evidence of linkages with Moscow and reasoned "there would be trouble in Latin America [even] if there were no Communists."[58] Nevertheless, both houses of the U.S. Congress launched inquiries, and Eisenhower sent his brother Milton on a second fact-finding tour, this time to Central America. Such concerns, as Rabe explains, "merged into a wider debate in 1958 about the United States' position in the world and the quality of President Eisenhower's leadership." One source of high anxiety was the Russian *Sputnik,* a satellite placed in orbit around the earth late in 1957, which immediately took on military and strategic implications. A Soviet missile capable of such a feat also presumably could hit targets in the United States. Other Cold War crises in Lebanon, in Berlin, and in Asia (over the islands of Quemoy and Matsu) kept tensions high. Finally, a crowning blow, the U.S. economy went into recession. Unemployment rose, production fell, and so did Eisenhower's popularity. Later, Ike described the year 1958 as one of the worst of his life.[59]

These events produced modest changes in Latin American policy. Notably, while retaining the emphasis on military assistance, the administration displayed somewhat more readiness to support political democracy and human rights. To an extent, this shift made a virtue of necessity. Between 1956 and 1960, ten military dictatorships in Latin America tumbled from power. Corrupt and incompetent, they had provided neither political stability nor economic growth. Tad Szulc, a journalist, referred to the process as "the twilight of the tyrants." Eisenhower leaders, although they responded with more enthusiastic defenses of representative government, still regarded military establishments as valuable anticommunist allies. In 1959–60, assistance programs in Latin America expanded, providing more than $160 million in military aid.[60]

The administration also accepted modest changes in economic policy. In part because of Nixon's misadventure, in-house critics became more persuasive, especially those who feared that collapsing dictatorships might precipitate revolutions. Such critics included the president's brother Milton and State Department officials Rubottom, Thomas Mann, and C. Douglas Dillon. Among the Latin American leaders, Juscelino Kubitschek, a former state governor of Minas Gerais and president of Brazil from 1956 until 1961, pressed especially hard. Embracing the slogan "Fifty years of progress in five" and seeking dramatic results, he intended to stimulate economic growth by the unorthodox means of government action based on deficit spending. He also instituted a national development program for building infrastructure, roads and railroads, and created new state enterprises such as an automobile industry. Most spectacularly, he built a new capital city, opening up the interior and symbolizing the advance of progress. Brasília, a showplace, attracted world attention because of its advanced architectural conceptions. But the high costs of such endeavors also had negative consequences, notably, high levels of debilitating inflation.

Two weeks after the anti-Nixon riot in Caracas, Kubitschek called for a "thorough revision" of U.S. programs. Cleverly linking economic development with presumed Cold War imperatives, Kubitschek wanted a solution to "the problem of underdevelopment" so that Latin American nations could "more effectively resist subversion and serve the Western cause." Specifically, he suggested a pledge of $40 billion from the United States to aid Latin America during the next twenty years. Called Operation Pan America, Kubitschek's plan, if accepted, would have established an equivalent of the Marshall Plan.

U.S. officials withheld endorsement from anything so grandiose, but they did display new readiness to take part in commodity agreements to stop falling prices for coffee and other such goods. In addition, in August 1958 they announced U.S. support for a regional development bank in Latin America, resulting in the creation of the Inter-American Development Bank in October 1960. These modifications implied "a moderate shift in the administration's philosophical approach toward Latin America." But many traditional commitments remained firm; as indicated by NSC-5902/1 in February 1959, the administration still sought the expansion of trade and investment, the promotion of capitalism, and the exclusion of economic nationalism. At the same time, the leaders embraced a new objective, endorsing the view that "Latin America is and must be dealt with primarily as an underdeveloped area." To accommodate rising levels of expectation, the United States must encourage free enterprise but with recognition of a need to adapt "to local conditions." Such shifts implied hardly any fundamental change. Administration leaders anticipated only modest expenditures in Latin America through the Inter-American Development Bank. They still believed that progress in Latin America depended upon private enterprise.[61]

There remained deep divisions over basic issues. For U.S. leaders the inter-American system served national security interests as an anti-communist alliance in defense of order, stability, and the Monroe Doctrine. For the Latin Americans the main rationale took other forms. They wanted regional devices to contain U.S. intervention and to facilitate economic aid and assistance. The absence of a Marshall Plan for the Western Hemisphere disenchanted Latin American leaders, widened the political fissures, and undermined the security apparatus. The shifts that developed during Ike's last two years never had much impact, and in the U.S. view the circumstances worsened significantly when Fidel Castro took over in Cuba. This event marked the most significant change in the New World since the Mexican Revolution and established the foremost issues of the next thirty years.

NOTES

1. Irwin F. Gellman, *Good Neighbor Diplomacy: United States Policies in Latin America, 1933–1945* (Baltimore: Johns Hopkins University Press, 1979), 179; idem, *Secret Affairs: Franklin Roosevelt, Cordell Hull, and Sumner Welles* (Baltimore: Johns Hopkins University Press, 1995), chaps. 13–14.

2. Enthusiasts include J. Lloyd Mecham, *The United States and Inter-American Security, 1889–1960* (Austin: University of Texas Press, 1961), chaps. 9–10; Gordon Connell-Smith, *The Inter-American System* (New York: Oxford University Press, 1966), chaps. 6–7; and Robert Freeman Smith, "U.S. Policy-Making for Latin America Under Truman," *Continuity: A Journal of History* 16 (Fall 1992): 87–111. Critics include Lloyd C. Gardner, *Economic Aspects of New Deal Diplomacy* (Madison: University of Wisconsin Press, 1964), chap. 10; and David Green, *The Containment of Latin America: A History of the Myths and Realities of the Good Neighbor Policy* (Chicago: Quadrangle Books, 1971), chaps. 7–9.

3. Gellman, *Good Neighbor Diplomacy*, 191–93; R. A. Humphreys, *Latin America and the Second World War*, 2 vols. (London: University of London Athlone Press, 1982), 2: chap. 6; Randall Bennett Woods, *The Roosevelt Foreign-Policy Establishment and the "Good Neighbor": The United States and Argentina, 1941–1945* (Lawrence: Regents Press of Kansas), chaps. 1–3.

4. Gellman, *Good Neighbor Diplomacy*, 196–97.

5. Ibid., chap. 14; Gaddis Smith, *The Last Years of the Monroe Doctrine, 1945–1993* (New York: Hill and Wang, 1994), 44.

6. Stephen G. Rabe, "The Elusive Conference: United States Economic Relations with Latin America, 1945–1952," *Diplomatic History* 2 (Summer 1978): 279; Humphreys, *Latin America*, 2: chap. 8.

7. Humphreys, *Latin America*, 2:215.

8. Rabe, "Elusive Conference," 281–82.

9. Humphreys, *Latin America*, 2:216–17.

10. Smith, *Last Years*, 43, 48–49, 55; Humphreys, *Latin America*, 2:220–21.

11. Walter LaFeber, *America, Russia, and the Cold War, 1945–1992*, 7th ed. (New York: McGraw-Hill, 1993), chap. 1; Howard Jones and Randall B. Woods, "Origins of the Cold War in Europe and the New East: Recent Historiography and the National Security Imperative," in *America in the World: The Historiography of American Foreign Relations since 1941*, ed. Michael J. Hogan (New York: Cambridge University Press, 1995), chap. 9.

12. Smith, *Last Years*, 56.

13. Thomas G. Paterson and Dennis Merrill, eds., *Major Problems in American Foreign Relations*, 2 vols., 4th ed. (Lexington, MA: D. C. Heath, 1995), 2:259–61.

14. Smith, *Last Years*, 56.

15. Roger R. Trask, "The Impact of the Cold War on United States-Latin American Relations, 1945–1949," *Diplomatic History* 1 (Summer 1977): 277.

16. Trask, "Impact of the Cold War," 274–77; idem, "Spruille Braden versus George Messersmith: World War II, the Cold War, and Argentine Policy, 1945–1947," *Journal of Inter-American Studies and World Affairs* 26 (February 1984): 69–95; Jesse H. Stiller, *George S. Messersmith: Diplomat of Democracy* (Chapel Hill: University of North Carolina Press, 1987), chap. 7.

17. Trask, "Impact of the Cold War," 277–79; Smith, *Last Years*, 58–59.

18. Trask, "Impact of the Cold War," 277–78; Rabe, "Elusive Conference," 285.

19. Smith, *Last Years*, 62.

20. Trask, "Impact of the Cold War," 279–80.

21. Stephen J. Randall, *Colombia and the United States: Hegemony and Interdependence* (Athens: University of Georgia Press, 1992), 192–94; Trask, "Impact of the Cold War," 281–82.

22. Trask, "Impact of the Cold War," 281–82.

23. O. Carlos Stoetzer, *The Organization of American States*, 2d ed. (Westport, CT: Praeger, 1993), 35.

24. Leslie Bethell and Ian Roxborough, "Latin America between the Second World War and the Cold War: Some Reflections on the 1945–8 Conjuncture," *Journal of Latin American Studies* 20 (May 1988): 167–89.

25. Leslie Bethell and Ian Roxborough, eds., *Latin America between the Second World War and the Cold War: Crisis and Containment, 1944–1948* (New York: Cambridge University Press, 1994), 1–2.

26. Ibid., 1–7, 10–20, 22–23, 26–28.

27. LaFeber, *America, Russia, and the Cold War*, 96.

28. Smith, *Last Years*, 66; LaFeber, *America, Russia, and the Cold War*, 96–97; Ernest R. May, ed., *American Cold War Strategy: Interpreting NSC 68* (Boston: St. Martin's Press, 1993).

29. Smith, *Last Years*, 61, 67–68.

30. Roger R. Trask, "George F. Kennan's Report on Latin America (1950)," *Diplomatic History* 2 (Summer 1978): 307–11.

31. Smith, *Last Years*, 69–71.

32. Bruce Cummings, *The Origins of the Korean War*, 2 vols. (Princeton: Princeton University Press, 1981, 1990) states a revisionist case. Burton I. Kaufman, *The Korean War: Challenges in Crisis, Credibility, and Command* (New York: Alfred A. Knopf, 1986); and William W. Stueck, *The Korean War: An International History* (Princeton: Princeton University Press, 1995), take more traditional approaches.

33. Stueck, *Korean War*, 194.

34. Gordon Connell-Smith, *The United States and Latin America: An Historical Analysis of Inter-American Relations* (New York: John Wiley and Sons, 1974).

35. Randall, *Colombia and the United States*, 199.

36. Stueck, *Korean War*, 198.

37. Connell-Smith, *United States and Latin America*, 207.

38. Ibid.; Edwin Lieuwen, *Arms and Politics in Latin America*, rev. ed. (New York: Frederick A. Praeger, 1961), 198–202.

39. LaFeber, *America, Russia, and the Cold War*, 136.

40. Stephen G. Rabe, *Eisenhower and Latin America: The Foreign Policy of Anti-communism* (Chapel Hill: University of North Carolina Press, 1988), 6.

41. Ibid., 1–5, 26; Mary S. McAulliffe, "Commentary: Eisenhower, the President," *Journal of American History* 68 (December 1981): 625–32; Fred I. Greenstein, *The Hidden-Hand Presidency: Eisenhower as Leader* (New York: Basic Books, 1982); Mark T. Gilderhus, "An Emerging Synthesis? U.S.-Latin American Relations since 1945," in Hogan, *America in the World*, 445–50.

42. Rabe, *Eisenhower and Latin America*, 26–29; H. W. Brands Jr., "Milton Eisenhower and the Coming Revolution in Latin America," in idem, *Cold Warriors: Eisenhower's Generation and American Foreign Policy* (New York: Columbia University Press, 1988); Milton S. Eisenhower, *The Wine Is Bitter: The United States and Latin America* (Garden City, NY: Doubleday, 1963), chap. 2.

43. Rabe, *Eisenhower and Latin America*, 29–30.

44. Robert J. McMahon, "Eisenhower and Third World Nationalism: A Critique of the Revisionists," *Political Science Review* 101 (Fall 1986): 457.

45. Rabe, *Eisenhower and Latin America*, 30–36; Chester J. Pach Jr., *Arming the Free World: The Origins of the United States Military Assistance Program, 1945–1950* (Chapel Hill: University of North Carolina Press, 1991), chap. 2; Liewen, *Arms and Politics*, chaps. 8–9.

46. Gilderhus, "An Emerging Synthesis?" 444; Bryce Wood, *The Dismantling of the Good Neighbor Policy* (Austin: University of Texas Press, 1985), chap. 9; Richard H. Immerman, *The CIA in Guatemala: The Foreign Policy of Intervention* (Austin: University of Texas Press, 1982); Piero Gleijeses, *Shattered Hope: The Guatemalan Revolution and the United States, 1944–1954* (Princeton: Princeton University Press, 1991).

47. Kenneth J. Grieb, *Guatemalan Caudillo: The Regime of Jorge Ubico, Guatemala, 1931–1944* (Athens: Ohio University Press, 1979), 18, 21.

48. Rabe, *Eisenhower and Latin America*, 43–47.

49. Smith, *Last Years*, 75–78.

50. Stephen E. Ambrose and Richard H. Immerman, *Ike's Spies: Eisenhower and the Espionage Establishment* (Garden City, NY: Doubleday, 1981); John Prados, *Presidents' Secret Wars: CIA and Pentagon Covert Operations since World War II* (New York: William Morrow, 1986); Rhodri Jeffreys-Jones, *The CIA and American Democracy* (New Haven: Yale Universty Press, 1989); Charles D. Ameringer, *U.S. Foreign Intelligence: The Secret Side of American History* (Lexington, MA: D. C. Heath, 1990).

51. Smith, *Last Years*, 70, 78; Wood, *Dismantling of the Good Neighbor Policy*; Immerman, *CIA in Guatemala*; Gleijeses, *Shattered Hope*.

52. Rabe, *Eisenhower and Latin America*, 49–52.
53. Smith, *Last Years*, 82–86; Rabe, *Eisenhower and Latin America*, 56.
54. Rabe, *Eisenhower and Latin America*, 64; Burton I. Kaufman, *Trade and Aid: Eisenhower's Foreign Economic Policy, 1953–1961* (Baltimore: Johns Hopkins University Press, 1982).
55. Rabe, *Eisenhower and Latin America*, 64–75.
56. Victor Bulmer-Thomas, *The Economic History of Latin America since Independence* (New York: Cambridge University Press, 1994), chaps. 8–9.
57. Rabe, *Eisenhower and Latin America*, 75–77. For consideration of an anomaly, see Kenneth Lehman, "Revolutions and Attributions: Making Sense of Eisenhower Administration Policies in Bolivia and Guatemala," *Diplomatic History* 21 (Spring 1997): 185–213.
58. Rabe, *Eisenhower and Latin America*, 86, 89–90, 92, 102, chap. 6; Richard M. Nixon, *Six Crises* (Garden City, NY: Doubleday, 1962), chap. 4.
59. Rabe, *Eisenhower and Latin America*, 114.
60. Tad Szulc, *Twilight of the Tyrants* (New York: W. W. Holt, 1959); Rabe, *Eisenhower and Latin America*, 107.
61. Rabe, *Eisenhower and Latin America*, 96–97, 110–14.

CHAPTER FIVE

CASTRO, CUBA, AND CONTAINMENT
1959–1979

AFTER 1959 THE Cuban Revolution became the focal point of U.S. policy toward Latin America. Fidel Castro's triumph challenged the traditional relationship while espousing radical alternatives, thereby establishing an unacceptable precedent from Washington's viewpoint. Successive administrations responded with efforts to contain Castro's influence or to destroy it. Perceived as a communist vanguard in the Western Hemisphere, the new regime in Cuba provoked fears of Soviet encroachments in the Caribbean. It also provided an opportunity for asserting the utility of noncommunist models of economic development for the rest of Latin America and a justification for subsequent acts of intervention by the United States in the Dominican Republic, Chile, Central America, and elsewhere. During the ensuing decades, stalwart opposition to radical regimes became the hallmark of U.S. policy toward Latin America.

UNDER IKE

Castro and the rebel forces making up the 26th of July Movement took control of Havana, the capital city, on 1 January 1959. This victory marked the end of a three-year guerrilla struggle against Fulgencio Batista, the Cuban strongman who had dominated the island by one means or another since the 1930s. In 1952, Batista returned as the head of state, following a military coup d'état against President Carlos Prío Socarrás. Castro, the illegitimate son of a well-to-do Spanish immigrant and sugar planter, assumed the role of political activist and professional agitator as a young man. While earning a law degree at the University of Havana, he embraced the martyr of Cuban independence, José Martí, as his national hero. On 26 July 1953, in defiance of Batista, he led a group of students in an abortive attack on the Moncada army barracks in the southeastern city of Santiago. For his crime, he received a fifteen-year jail sentence but had served only two years when Batista proclaimed an amnesty in 1955.

Castro and his brother Raúl then fled to Mexico City, where they planned an uprising against Batista for early December 1956. Following a harrowing, week-long voyage aboard an overcrowded, undersupplied, and unreliable vessel called *Granma*, eighty-one bedraggled, seasick invaders clambered ashore in a mangrove swamp at the southeastern end of the island, only to meet with disaster. Batista's waiting forces killed most of the insurrectionists within a few days. No more than twenty survivors, including Fidel, Raúl, and Ernesto "Che" Guevara, an Argentine expatriate, withdrew into the mountains, the Sierra Maestra. From secret base camps, they attracted new recruits, mounted occasional attacks, and gradually extended the rebellion into the more populated regions. By the end of 1958, even though no clear idea of Castro's intentions had emerged, most of the Cuban people had turned against Batista.[1]

During the insurgency, Castro assumed an eclectic, nondoctrinaire stance. In one statement, the "History Will Absolve Me" speech at the end of his trial in 1953, he invoked José Martí's nationalism as the basis for reform and change. Among other things, he supported the principle of equality before the law, the restoration of constitutional rights, the distribution of land to landless farmers, the adoption of profit sharing for workers, the confiscation of illicit wealth stolen by public officials, and the nationalization of the electric and telephone companies.[2] He gave another example of his eclecticism in a dramatic interview with Herbert Matthews, a *New York Times* correspondent, at a backcountry retreat in February 1957. On this occasion, Castro placed greater emphasis on reform than on radical change. He had not yet given final form to his programs. At this juncture, moreover, he lacked any particular attachment to Marxist-Leninist ideology or to the Soviet Union. Indeed, the Cuban Communist party—one of the largest in Latin America, with 17,000 members—regarded him as a putschist: that is, in Marxist jargon, an adventurer and potential suicidalist engaged in premature revolutionary action.[3]

Nevertheless, Castro's charismatic leadership capitalized on high levels of Cuban discontent. Under Batista, corruption, dissolution, and greed for tourist dollars had turned Havana into a wide-open purveyor of alcohol, narcotics, saloons, brothels, and casinos, promising satisfaction for all manner of tastes. These activities meant big profits for U.S.

mobsters such as Meyer Lansky and Santos Trafficante, who collabo-
rated with Cuban crooks, but the disparities of opportunity, privilege,
power, and wealth rankled other Cubans. Per capita annual income
averaged $400—not so bad by Caribbean standards but very low in
comparison with the United States. As an example, the seasonal sugar
harvest required a large labor force but, once completed, left rural
workers without jobs for the rest of the year. Similarly, slums and
sweatshops had a pervasive presence in the towns, where the burdens
of hardship and exploitation fell most heavily on Cubans of African
descent. These poorest among the poor also endured the effects of
racial discrimination and segregation. For discontented persons among
the middle classes, the primary characteristics of a corrupted Cuban
political system appeared in various forms of repression, tyranny, de-
pravity, brutality, and inefficiency. Consequently, in response to
Castro's revolt, large segments of Cuban society rallied against Batista,
hoping for a change for the better.

As conceived by many Cubans, the traditional U.S. role in their
country accentuated their problems. An object of admiration and envy
for its wealth and power, the northern colossus also seemed a cause of
Cuban failures. According to this view, U.S. political and economic
dominance over the years had retarded the island's maturation by perpetuating conditions of monoculture and dependency. Cuba relied
too much on sugar sales in the U.S. market; Cuban buyers purchased
too many finished goods from U.S. sellers, creating an unfavorable balance of trade. Other indicators underscored the magnitude of economic
presence. Direct U.S. investment in Cuba, calculated at $900 million at
the time, ranked as the second largest in Latin America. U.S. companies controlled 40 percent of Cuba's sugar production, 36 of the 161
sugar mills, 2 of the 3 oil refineries, 90 percent of the public utilities,
and 50 percent of the mines and railroads. For such reasons, many
Cubans looked upon their island as an economic appendage of the
United States.[4]

Until the mid-1950s, U.S. policy under Eisenhower had supported
and sustained Batista for reasons of security and order. Regarded officially as "a good thing from the standpoint of the U.S.," the Batista
regime obtained $16 million in military aid during this period, much
like other Caribbean dictatorships that propagated stability. But then
the administration shifted its ground, seeking to create at least an appearance of even-handedness. Subsequently, diplomats were urged to avoid
unduly partisan displays in Batista's favor. In 1957, the administration

sent a new ambassador. Earl E. T. Smith, a Wall Street financier and a faithful Republican, who had no diplomatic experience and no knowledge of Spanish. Upon his arrival in Havana, he supported Batista, mistrusted Castro, and soon found himself in a difficult bind.

Smith invested scant faith in the reliability of the rebel movement and hoped for an honest presidential election in November 1958 to resolve the problem of the presidential succession. But Batista's manipulations got in the way: The dictator tried to rig the outcome in favor of his preferred candidate, Dr. Andrés Rivero Aguero. Reacting against this ploy, the Eisenhower administration somewhat unrealistically hoped to find a replacement for Batista who could head off Castro while simultaneously maintaining order and the appearance of procedural regularity. The Spanish phrase *Batistianismo sin Batista* affirmed the goal, calling for the preservation of the regime's essential features but without the dictator. To pursue this purpose, the administration sent an emissary, William Pawley, a former ambassador to Brazil and Peru. He urged the dictator to resign in favor of a military junta. But Batista refused, pending a variety of assurances, terms, and conditions. Bowing to necessity, the Eisenhower administration then cut him loose, serving notice on 17 December 1958 that Batista no longer enjoyed the official support of the U.S. government.

Unsure what to expect, U.S. officials also had doubts about the intentions and capabilities of Castro and the 26th of July Movement. At the time, U.S. leaders could find no convincing evidence of communist contaminations, but could the insurrectionists exercise control over Cuba? Would they respect U.S. interests? On 31 December 1958, Batista fled from the island, taking refuge initially in the Dominican Republic under Rafael Trujillo's protection. When Castro took over on 1 January 1959, the United States promptly extended diplomatic recognition and, as an indication of goodwill, also recalled Ambassador Smith, now regarded in Cuba as an undesirable presence. His replacement, Philip Bonsal, a career Foreign Service officer and former ambassador to Bolivia, expressed a more tolerant attitude toward change in Latin America. Indeed, he appraised Cuba's future optimistically, looking upon Batista's fall as evidence of progress toward democracy and justice.

Such expectations diminished quickly in January and February 1959, when Castro allowed the Communist party to operate legally in Cuba, ousted political moderates from positions of authority, disallowed electoral proceedings for a period of two years, and declared himself the premier of the country. He also inaugurated a series of public trials and executions by means of which he eliminated some five hundred former high-level Batista supporters. Nevertheless, when Castro came to the United States in April 1959 for an eleven-day tour arranged by the American Society of Newspaper Editors, he retained some measure of credibility, projecting in Stephen G. Rabe's phrase "a sincere, progressive image."[5] Speaking frankly, Castro explained why conditions in Cuba required improvements and corrections. He included agrarian reform among his aims. He admitted that his plans might cause disagreements with the United States but disclaimed any intention of instituting a communist regime.

During his stay, Castro spent three hours with Vice President Richard M. Nixon as a stand-in for Eisenhower, who refused an audience because of the political trials and executions. Nixon later reported in his memoirs, *Six Crises*, that all along he had favored a policy of getting tough with Castro. At the time, however, he displayed some sympathy and understanding, despite his suspicions of the new Cuban leader's presumed socialist tendencies. Nixon refrained from branding Castro a communist, expressed appreciation for those "indefinable qualities which make him a leader of men," and anticipated that he would function as "a great factor in the development of Cuba and very possibly in Latin American affairs generally." Nixon wanted "to orient him in the right direction"—in favor of the United States.[6]

Castro nevertheless pursued his own course and soon offended U.S. officials. Upon his return home, he promulgated an agrarian reform law that provided for the expropriation of agrarian properties larger than a thousand acres and also for compensation in the form of Cuban bonds. The values would depend on the declarations property owners had made for tax purposes in 1958. Caught in a trap of their own making, sugar growers who had submitted low estimates to justify low taxes had to endure the consequences. To make matters worse, Castro disallowed foreign ownership of agricultural properties and named Antonio Núñez Jiménez, a Cuban communist, as the administrator in charge of the expropriation.

Growing numbers of disenchanted Cubans deserted the island, often seeking safe haven in Miami, Florida, while denouncing Castro as a communist. During the ensuing months, exile groups organized an anti-Castro opposition. Among other things, they flew missions out of Florida to drop propaganda leaflets over Cuba and set fire to sugarcane fields. Castro charged U.S. authorities with responsibility for such

actions and warned Cubans of an impending invasion to restore Batista
to power. In September 1959, in a speech before the United Nations, he
denounced U.S. imperialism as the fundamental cause of Cuba's plight.
In February 1960, he signed a commercial agreement with the Soviet
Union. It provided for the annual purchase of a million tons of Cuban
sugar during the next five years and for a credit of $100 million to fi-
nance the purchase of Soviet equipment and machines. This important
initiative signaled Castro's determination to weaken Cuba's dependence
on the United States and his willingness to move his country toward
the Soviet bloc.[7]

Various accounts of Castro's behavior have stimulated an ongoing
debate. Critics have insisted that Castro always possessed communist
preferences and revealed them at last by embracing the Soviet Union.
Apologists have castigated the United States, holding that Eisenhower's
unreceptive inflexibility drove Castro into a reliance upon the Soviets.
Neither view is correct. For Castro as a young man, the Cuban patriot
José Martí exercised more ideological authority than Marx, Lenin, or
Stalin. Martí's writings upheld as absolute the principles of human
equality and national sovereignty. Castro thought the Cuban Revolution should adhere to the same ideals. These meant the abolition of
inequality based on the distinctions of race and class and also the elimination of U.S. power and privilege. After all, in the 1890s, Martí had
warned of the danger of exchanging one form of subservience to Spain
for another to the United States. At least in its initial stages, then,
Castro's attempts to obtain a Soviet counterweight against the Yankee
colossus had practical purposes and effects, less connected with the
requirements of Marxist-Leninist ideology than with tactical considerations and opportunism.[8]

Anti-Castro sentiments within the Eisenhower administration grew
stronger as the year 1959 advanced. Taking the lead was Christian Herter,
the former undersecretary who became secretary of state when Dulles
died of cancer. He advised Eisenhower on 5 November that U.S. policies should "encourage within Cuba and elsewhere in Latin America
opposition to the extremist, anti-American course of the Castro regime." Convinced that Cuban "policies and attitudes" ran counter to
"minimum United States security requirements," he reported high levels of communist infiltration into the government, apparently with
Castro's sanction. If "emulated by other Latin American countries,"
Herter warned, such practices would have "serious adverse effects on
Free World support of our leadership." Moreover, he cautioned, the

nationalization of property posed a danger to U.S. business interests and menaced the principles of free trade and investment all over Latin America. Herter wanted a set of policies to bring about either "a reformed Castro regime or a successor to it." At the same time, he advised against stirring up nationalistic responses by arousing Latin American fears of U.S. intervention. The problem was how to accomplish such contradictory aims.

The CIA spymaster, Allen Dulles, was among the first to suggest Castro's ouster. On 13 January 1960, he expressed his view that "over the long run" the United States could not "tolerate the Castro regime in Cuba" and might have to use covert action to precipitate his downfall. About the same time, Eisenhower boiled over in a rage in which he characterized Castro as a "mad man" who was "going wild and harming the whole American structure"; Ike imagined various responses, including a naval blockade of Cuba and a buildup of U.S. forces at Guantánamo Bay. Later, he cooled down; nevertheless, a hard-line view had won him over.

On 17 March 1959 the president indicated his approval of a course of possible action suggested by a CIA task force and the NSC. It recalled the Guatemala operation in 1954 and bore the title "A Program of Covert Action against the Castro Regime." The recommendations consisted of four parts: first, the creation of "a responsible and unified Cuban opposition to the Castro regime located outside of Cuba"; second, the instigation of "a powerful propaganda offensive" against Castro inside Cuba; third, the establishment of a "covert action and intelligence organization within Cuba"; and fourth, "the development of a paramilitary force outside of Cuba for future guerilla action." Ike later placed a benign construction on such preparations by drawing a distinction between a "program" or general approach and a "plan" entailing specific acts. He also denied any connection with or responsibility for the subsequent Bay of Pigs invasion in 1961. In Stephen G. Rabe's view, his explanations allow for some believability, since the March 1960 decision "was not an irrevocable commitment to invade Cuba." At the same time, it "ended any possibility of a rapprochement between the Eisenhower administration and Castro." The United States no longer would tolerate mischief from the Cuban upstart.

Other undertakings in 1960 had the intention of curbing Castro's appeal in the rest of Latin America. Leaders in the Eisenhower administration now understood more clearly some of the connections between the wretchedness of social and economic conditions for the poor and the causes of violence and revolution. To alleviate the misery, they accepted the necessity of using higher levels of economic aid and assistance as a means of promoting growth. In the course of a trip to Argentina, Brazil, Chile, and Uruguay in February 1960, Eisenhower had something of an epiphany when he encountered placards among the crowds along the way reading, "We Like Ike; We Like Fidel Too." Such displays underscored the extent to which Castro functioned as a symbol of hope and change in Latin America. In July, the president announced the creation of a new program for Latin America. Mainly the brainchild of Milton Eisenhower, the Social Progress Trust Fund called for $500 million in U.S. loans. Aimed at health, education, housing, and land reform, the project operated through the Inter-American Development Bank, an agency created in 1959 for this purpose. Though small in scope compared with the Marshall Plan, the undertaking established a point of departure for the subsequent Alliance for Progress under Kennedy.[9]

Meanwhile, the administration proceeded with plans to employ covert operations against Castro. Drawing upon the Guatemala experience and relying on some of the same men—such as Allen Dulles, Richard Bissell, and E. Howard Hunt—the leaders of the CIA prepared for the training of a guerrilla force in Guatemala. They also sought to sabotage Castro's regime, to isolate Castro economically and diplomatically, and probably to kill him. According to the November 1975 report of the U.S. Senate Select Committee chaired by Senator Frank Church of Idaho, findings based on "concrete evidence" indicated no less than eight plots to assassinate Castro between 1960 and 1965, none of which succeeded and some of which never advanced beyond "the stage of planning and preparation." The plots involved the enlistment of gangsters and underworld characters such as John Rosselli, Momo Salvatore "Sam" Giancana, and Santos Trafficante as prospective executioners, using "poison pills, poison pens, deadly bacterial powders, and other devices which strain the imagination." One especially exotic scheme, really slapstick, called for the use of thallium salt, a depilatory: Sprinkle the stuff into Castro's shoes and make his body hair fall out. Bald and beardless, according to the plan, he could not hold the political loyalties of macho-minded Cubans.[10]

In 1960, leaders in the Eisenhower administration imposed additional penalties. They prohibited U.S. refineries in Cuba from processing Soviet crude oil, slashed the Cuban sugar quota in the United States by 700,000 tons, and imposed trade restrictions under which only food and medicine could enter Cuba. Caught up in an escalating sequence of moves and countermoves, Castro retaliated by expropriating U.S.

properties in Cuba, including sugar mills, petroleum refineries, public utilities, tire plants, and banks. By the end of October 1960, these measures had wiped out the direct investments of the United States in his country. Eisenhower then broke diplomatic relations with Castro's government on 3 January 1961 as one of his final presidential acts.[11] The unsolved Cuban problem, a kind of diplomatic tiger trap, awaited the untested new administration of President John F. Kennedy.

UNDER JFK

Young, vibrant, handsome, rich, and a former Massachusetts congressman and senator, Kennedy won the presidential election by a close margin in November 1960. (According to popular lore, he might have lost to Vice President Richard M. Nixon if Mayor Richard J. Daley, the old-fashioned boss of Chicago, had not delivered the Democratic votes of dead and missing persons.) During the campaign, few fundamental differences in foreign relations separated the two candidates. Both Kennedy and Nixon endorsed the containment policy, Nixon defending the Eisenhower record, Kennedy subjecting it to hyperbolic attacks. Among other things, Kennedy claimed that the United States had fallen behind the Soviet Union in the Cold War competition, specifically alleging a "missile gap," a drop in U.S. prestige in the Third World, and a significant setback when Cuba went over to the communist side. This indulgence in political tit for tat recalled Republican charges that Democrats had lost Eastern Europe and China to the Reds. As the historian Thomas G. Paterson notes, "Apparently unaware that President Dwight D. Eisenhower had initiated a clandestine CIA program to train Cuban exiles for an invasion of the island, candidate Kennedy bluntly called for just such a project."[12]

Kennedy's appeal mobilized support among members of a younger generation. Many of his top aides and advisers had served in the Second World War, as had Kennedy himself. They looked upon themselves as "the best and the brightest" and regarded the Eisenhower administration, in contrast, as worn out and sclerotic. Through the exercise of youth, energy, and imagination, they proposed to get the country moving again, for example, by winning victories in the Cold War. For them, the omnipresent Communist menace recalled the lessons of Munich in 1938. Appeasement could never stop totalitarian dictators from aggression, only vigilance and strength.[13]

The Kennedy administration embraced the containment policy as a global necessity, especially in response to recent Soviet pronouncements. Two weeks before Kennedy's inauguration on 20 January 1961,

Soviet Premier Nikita Khrushchev had delivered a speech in which he prophesied an ultimate victory for his side as a consequence of communist support for "wars of national liberation." This appeal for the hearts and minds of men, a calculated propaganda ploy, focused on Latin America, Asia, and Africa. Specifically, Khrushchev called for alliances between communists and nationalists in the Third World. By working together, serious radicals presumably could engage in a joint struggle in favor of self-determination and in opposition to the adverse legacies of Western imperialism.

For Kennedy, Soviet initiatives required vigorous responses. Consequently, he inaugurated a military buildup marked by a 15 percent increase in the defense budget to enhance both nuclear deterrence and conventional capabilities. Specifically, he wanted more intercontinental ballistic missiles to close the alleged missile gap, a larger number of combat-ready infantry and armored divisions to expand war-fighting abilities on the ground, and a new emphasis on counterinsurgency techniques. The last called for the development and utilization of special forces capable of employing guerrilla-style tactics against potential insurgents in the Third World. He also displayed a readiness to build upon Eisenhower's policies by instituting larger-scale programs of economic aid and assistance.[14]

Once established in office the Kennedy administration disclosed ambitious plans. One called for a means to undercut Castro through the promotion of economic growth and modernization in Latin America. Called the Alliance for Progress, or La Alianza para el Progreso, this approach followed up on earlier Eisenhower initiatives and entertained grandiose expectations. The White House first announced them at a ceremony on 13 March 1961 before 250 guests, including an assembly of Latin American diplomats. The proposal called for "a vast cooperative effort, unparalleled in magnitude and nobility of purpose, to satisfy the basic needs of the Latin American people for homes, work and land, health and schools—*techo, trabajo y tierra, salud y escuela.*" Among other things, Kennedy sought the eradication of illiteracy, hunger, and disease. Designating the 1960s as "the decade of development," he promised an allocation of $500 million to begin a process of long-term economic planning and integration, scientific and technical cooperation, and an expansion of cultural relations. He also called for political and social reforms to accompany material progress. Democracy, constitutional order, and a reduction of class distinctions were the goals, including the elimination of military despots, antiquated

tax laws, and feudalistic systems of land tenure. Kennedy's vision affirmed the attainability of freedom and progress within the context of
democratic capitalism, a preferred and viable alternative to the Castro
example.

Even higher expectations appeared in August 1961 at an inter-
American conference at Punta del Este in Uruguay. Speaking for the
Kennedy administration but without specific authorization, Secretary
of the Treasury C. Douglas Dillon pledged ongoing U.S. support in
the amount of $20 billion over the next ten years. The funds suppos-
edly would come from public and private sources, including international lending agencies, charitable foundations, and U.S. investors.
Supplemented by an additional $80 billion from Latin American
sources, this expanded level of investment would generate an anticipated economic growth rate of 2.5 percent a year, about twice that of
the 1950s. For good measure, Dillon also predicted the elimination of
illiteracy among Latin American children by 1970.[15]

Such grandiose aims always exceeded capabilities and never
achieved the mark. Under Presidents John F. Kennedy and Lyndon B.
Johnson the United States made good on a large part of its share by
contributing $18 billion in various forms of public and private invest-
ment. Nevertheless, the programs floundered, falling far short of
transforming Latin America in the image envisioned by the U.S. planners. A variety of things went wrong. In the aggregate, Latin American
economies grew slowly during the 1960s, at only 1.5 percent a year. Consequently, already high unemployment increased from 18 to 25 million,
while agricultural production went into decline. In crucial areas such as
health care and education the hope of extending life expectancy and
reducing illiteracy defied fulfillment. And too frequently, the mecha-
nisms for maintaining democratic and constitutional order broke down.
In most countries, the traditional ruling elites remained very much in
charge, typically in cooperation with officers in the army. During the
Kennedy years, military officers ousted popularly elected presidents in
six countries.[16]

Ultimately, as Jerome Levinson and Juan de Onís observe, the Alliance for Progress "lost its way." Most historians accept this appraisal
but differ over the reasons. Some scholars emphasize Latin American
obstacles such as the accumulation of deep-seated inequities over long
expanses of time and the traditional elites entrenched resistance to
change. Other scholars attribute the shortcomings to false expectations
and faulty execution on the part of U.S. officials. Rabe shows that the

interaction of both sets of causes contributed to the creation of formidable barriers.[17]

First, the Kennedy administration embraced inflated expectations. As Rabe explains, the leaders "undoubtedly overestimated their ability to foster change" and "underestimated the daunting nature of Latin America's socioeconomic problems." For example, Teodoro Moscoso, a high-level administrator, typified "naive optimism" in 1962 when he proclaimed that "within a decade the direction and results of centuries of Latin American history are to be changed." This sort of statement verged on hubris and in some countries collided with debilitating realities: 90 percent illiteracy rates, life expectancy of thirty-five years, and 11 percent infant mortality. These daunting figures applied especially to peoples of Amerindian and African descent.

Next, U.S. projections neglected the effects of a population explosion. With an annual growth rate of 3 percent, Latin America's population of 195 million was expanding faster than the economy. (It was cruelly ironic that a reduction in the infant mortality rate would have offset economic gains.) The problem was complicated by religious convictions and cultural mores in favor of large families. Out of expediency, the Kennedy administration sidestepped these issues, in part because of unwillingness to offend Roman Catholic opinion. Secretary Dillon dismissed the matter, affirming his belief that "in Latin America the question of population control is not as serious as it may be in other areas of the world because there are substantial resources, substantial land, substantial availability for a growing, expanding population." According to this view, supply, not demand, would prevail in the end.

Finally, U.S. officials invested too much faith in Latin American receptivity to reform and change. Optimistic assessments presumed the readiness of the elites to accommodate the emerging "middle sectors." U.S. planners counted upon these mainly urban groups, defined as democratic, capitalist, and modern, to exercise a moderating influence and to behave in conformance with the precepts of established social-scientific theory. According to the views of, for example, Walt Rostow, a presidential adviser and the author of *The Stages of Economic Growth: A Non-Communist Manifesto* (1960), the advent of middle-class reform movements in Latin America meant that democratic capitalism could serve as the best means for moving into the future without the costs of a social revolution.

The sources of such anticipations included misleading historical parallels and assumptions. The Marshall Plan served officials as a kind of model but allowed for insufficient appreciation of important distinctions. The processes of economic development in Latin America in the 1960s differed in context from those of economic recovery in Europe in the 1940s and responded to dissimilar incentives, stimuli, and techniques. What succeeded in Europe would not necessarily apply in Latin America. Thomas Mann, a State Department official who mistrusted the whole effort, later attributed its failure to an "illusion of omnipotence" among leaders in the Kennedy administration. Since the Marshall Plan had such good effects in Europe, they reasoned erroneously, "it's going to work in Latin America."

Still another misperception developed from a particular reading of U.S. history. According to this view, enlightened programs of reform and change undertaken by elites at propitious times could ward off revolutionary threats by accommodating political antagonisms and class differences. For Kennedy officials, historical experiences during the Progressive era and the New Deal confirmed the point and implied a kind of universal, at least hemispheric, applicability. In contrast, Latin American elites derived other premises from their own history. To them, reform appeared not so much a way to head off revolution as a first step toward bringing it about; therefore, tinkering with the system was a high-risk option with the potential to weaken traditional conceptions of order and constraint, to unleash pent-up furies and frustrations, and to create situations with unpredictable consequences.

As always, Latin American military organizations functioned to support stability. During the Kennedy years, army officers seized power in six countries: Argentina, Ecuador, Guatemala, Honduras, Peru, and the Dominican Republic. In response, U.S. officials tried uncertainly to balance commitments in favor of constitutional order against concerns over Castro and communism. Consequently, perceptions of the internal communist threat and assessments of the prevailing attitudes toward Cuba influenced administration leaders who determined the policies of diplomatic recognition. Staunchly anticommunist regimes usually obtained it. As explained by Assistant Secretary of State Edwin M. Martin in October 1963, the U.S. government preferred constitutional democracy as a framework for economic development but understood the limitations, because "in most of Latin America there is so little experience with the benefits of political legitimacy." As Martin remarked, the United States lacked the ability to create "effective democracy" by keeping "a man in office . . . when his own people are not willing to fight to defend him."

Support for miliary organizations appeared prominently in Kennedy's efforts to achieve internal security and counterinsurgency. As seen from Washington, "Communist subversion and indirect attack" had become "the principal threat." Administration leaders particularly worried about guerrilla wars, possibly instigated by Fidel Castro in conjunction with "wars of national liberation." As a counter, the Kennedy administration provided $77 million per year in military aid, a 50 percent increase. The emphasis fell on training programs to enhance techniques of riot control, psychological warfare, and counterguerrilla operations. For the enthusiasts within the administration, such efforts were legitimate means of strengthening national security and, more dubiously, democratic institutions. Critics pointed out that the military officers responsible for the political overthrows usually had received training and assistance from the United States. Though unwilling to say so in public, the Kennedy administration used military aid to preserve access to and influence with the military establishments regarded as the arbiters of Latin American political life.[18]

The Cuban difficulty yielded two portentous episodes during the Kennedy presidency. The Bay of Pigs invasion in 1961, a fiasco by most accounts, humiliated administration leaders and signified a damaging setback. Holding larger implications, the Cuban missile crisis in 1962 produced a confrontation between the two Great Powers, the United States and the Soviet Union, and conjured a nightmarish prospect of nuclear war. In each instance, an incapacity to distinguish between Cuban nationalism and Soviet communism deepened the problem.

The Kennedy plan for a clandestine move against Castro took shape during the early part of the new administration. The president-elect, only forty-three years old, learned of the proposed covert action soon after his victory in the course of CIA briefings from Allen Dulles and Richard Bissell. Later, Kennedy consented to it but disallowed direct participation by U.S. forces. The earliest versions called for an invasion by Cuban exiles near Trinidad, a port city on the south Cuban coast near the Escambray Mountains. Subsequently, the site shifted to the Bay of Pigs, a location about forty miles west of Trinidad along the Zapata Peninsula, where the CIA planners hoped to achieve a surprise. Isolated, remote, and removed from the mountains by eighty miles of swamp, the operation's architects anticipated only light opposition and not much need for air cover.

Misgivings within the administration were not strong enough to head off the ensuing debacle. The Joint Chiefs of Staff reacted against the stifling secrecy, wondered about the invaders' fighting proficiency, and warned of insufficient intelligence both about the terrain and Cuban political attitudes. Would the people really rise in revolt against Castro? Dean Rusk, Kennedy's taciturn secretary of state, reportedly questioned such assumptions in private but withheld a full articulation of his views. Other skeptics included J. William Fulbright, an Arkansas senator and the chair of the Senate Foreign Relations Committee; Chester Bowles, undersecretary of state; Arthur Schlesinger Jr., a historian working as a White House adviser; and Dean Acheson, the former secretary of state, who thought the military imbalance favored Castro. Characterizing the idea as potentially "disastrous," Acheson correctly anticipated that some 1,500 Cubans could not cope with Castro's forces, numbering some 225,000 regular troops and militia.[19]

The Kennedy administration nevertheless accepted the risks, only to experience what the historian Trumbull Higgins called "the perfect failure." The calamity at the Bay of Pigs resulted from false assumptions, erroneous expectations, defective planning, bureaucratic malfunctions, poor leadership, and a measure of hubris. According to most authorities, the untried Kennedy administration disregarded an assortment of dangers and warnings. Perhaps unduly awed by the experts and equally unwilling to show doubt or weakness, administration officials unwisely accepted at face value the exaggerated enthusiasms of the CIA. As eager advocates for success, Dulles and Bissell lost the capacity for dispassionate appraisal; Secretary of Defense Robert McNamara and National Security Adviser McGeorge Bundy succumbed to the prevailing views and conveyed to the president a false impression of full confidence. Perhaps intimidated by Eisenhower's reputation as "the greatest military man in America," the hero under whom the plan intially took shape, Kennedy—untested, inexperienced, and in this instance vulnerable—became the victim of "a situation where insufficient bureaucratic safeguards existed, and the excessive security only compounded the problem." The president and his advisers accepted the likelihood of a safe landing and a successful move into the Escambrays—through swamp, eighty miles away—while Dulles and Bissell held to a notion that Kennedy would not allow the invasion to fail.[20]

Viewed in retrospect, the Bay of Pigs invasion appears as a sure failure. By trusting to good luck—his "Midas touch," as enthusiasts described it—Kennedy magnified the invaders' capabilities, exaggerated the likelihood of a Cuban uprising, and failed to calculate Castro's abilities to take countermeasures. The brigade of Cuban exiles, numbering fourteen hundred, lost the element of surprise on 15 April 1961 when a bomber force of eight old B-26s, under exile command, launched an air strike. It destroyed much of Castro's air force but also triggered a military alert. Castro dispersed his remaining planes and rounded up suspects in the anti-Castro underground. Then Kennedy, seeking to avoid direct U.S. involvement, canceled another air attack scheduled in support of the invasion on the morning of 17 April. By so doing, according to critics such as Samuel Flagg Bemis, he sacrificed all chance of success. More likely, the cancellation of the air strike made no difference; the invasion would have failed anyway. Castro's ground and air forces moved in fast, pinned down the invaders on the beach, killed about two hundred, and captured the rest.

Thoroughly shaken, Kennedy wondered out loud how he could have been stupid enough to go ahead. At the same time, he retained his anti-Castro commitments. During the following year the United States persisted in punishing Cuba by tightening the economic blockade, arranging for Cuba's eviction from the Organization of American States, intensifying the propaganda campaign, and conspiring against Castro's life. In addition, Operation Mongoose, another CIA enterprise, encouraged anti-Castro exiles to engage in hit-and-run attacks against Cuban economic targets. From Castro's standpoint, the likelihood of an outright U.S. invasion appeared very high end encouraged him to obtain Soviet military assistance as a safeguard for his regime.

The consequence, a Big-Power confrontation in October 1962, ranked as one of the most dangerous periods of the Cold War. Moreover, the missile crisis originated not in Soviet megalomania but in the high levels of tension in relations between the United States and Cuba. As Thomas G. Paterson explains, if there had been "no exile expedition, no destructive covert activities, and no economic and diplomatic boycott"—in other words, "no concerted United States vendetta to quash the Cuban Revolution"—then "there would not have been an October missile crisis." Indeed, "Nikita Khrushchev would never have had the opportunity to begin his dangerous missile game." U.S. policymakers knew of Cuban fears. A CIA report in September 1962 concluded that "the main purpose of the present military build-up in Cuba is to strengthen the Communist regime there against what the Cubans and Soviets conceive to be a danger that the US may attempt by one means or another to overthrow it." The U.S. threat against Cuba linked Castro and Khrushchev together in a mutual endeavor. Each calculated a vital interest in the installation of medium- and intermediate-range rockets. For Castro, such weapons were a way to discourage a U.S. invasion. For Khrushchev, they underscored Soviet deterrence capability in defense of a new ally.[21]

In an important book entitled *Inside the Kremlin's Cold War: From Stalin to Khrushchev*, the Russian scholars Vladislav Zubok and Constantine Pleshakov provide illuminating insights. According to them, Khrushchev mixed hard-boiled realpolitik with romantic, revolutionary zeal. He had initially regarded Castro and his followers "as anything but Marxists" and "discounted their chances of success." Later, he experienced a change of heart, "embraced" the Cuban Revolution, and acquired an emotional commitment to it. Indeed, he looked upon "the young Cubans as heroes who had revived the promise of the Russian Revolution" and admired them for daring "to do it under the very nose of the most powerful imperialist country on earth." During an encounter in New York City in September 1960, Khrushchev hugged and kissed Castro. According to Zubok and Pleshakov, Khrushchev allowed himself "to get carried away" and subsequently gambled dangerously on Operation *Anadyr*, the Soviet code name for deploying missiles in Cuba.[22]

Zubok and Pleshakov downplay the impact of strategic calculations on Khrushchev's thinking and emphasize instead a commitment in defense of the Cuban Revolution. Khrushchev regarded the nuclear balance as an "important" but "not crucial" consideration in the conduct of Soviet international relations. More significantly, they argue, Khrushchev became "fervently dedicated" to Cuba, seeking to preserve the revolution against a possible U.S. invasion. For him, this aim became a means of upholding "the victorious march of communism around the globe and Soviet hegemony in the Communist camp." To obtain maximum deterrent effect, the Soviets decided early in the summer of 1962 to supply medium-range (MRBM) and intermediate-range (IRBM) ballistic missiles. With surface-to-surface ranges of 1,020 and 2,200 nautical miles, respectively, these missiles could hit targets in the United States. Forty-two MRBMs arrived in Cuba; the IRBMs never made it.

U.S. officials received "hard" evidence of the missile sites in Cuba from photographs taken by a U-2 spy plane on 14 October 1962. When informed of Soviet actions on the 16th, Kennedy, who had cautioned Khrushchev against placing "offensive" missiles in Cuba, snapped, "He can't do that to me!" The president immediately convened a meeting of top advisers. He particularly wanted to know whether the missiles carried nuclear warheads and had the capacity of firing them. As a tentative answer in each instance, intelligence appraisals said probably not but warned that they might have operational capability in a short while. These discussions centered on possible military responses—specifically, whether to use an air strike or an invasion as the most expeditious method of eliminating the threat. In either case, Soviet technicians and soldiers probably would die.

In a second meeting on the same day, diplomatic considerations became more prominent. Secretary of State Rusk favored "a direct message to Castro" instead of an air attack. Sharply divided, participants such as General Maxwell Taylor, Secretary of Defense McNamara, and Secretary of the Treasury Dillon contemplated the effects on "the strategic balance." Did the missiles in Cuba provide Moscow with an advantage or at least the appearance thereof? The advisers also wondered whether Khrushchev's move had any bearing on Berlin, a city divided by the Cold War, or perhaps on Turkey, where the United States had based Jupiter missiles with targets in the Soviet Union.[23]

During the next several days an advisory group called the Executive Committee, or Ex Comm, met in exhausting, secret sessions under high pressure. The participants included National Security Adviser Bundy, Secretary of State Rusk, Secretary of Defense McNamara, Attorney General Robert Kennedy, Vice President Lyndon Johnson, CIA Director John McCone, Secretary of the Treasury Dillon, Chief Presidential Counsel Theodore Sorensen, Undersecretary of State George Ball, Deputy Undersecretary of State U. Alexis Johnson, Chairman of the Joint Chiefs Maxwell Taylor, Assistant Secretary of State for Latin America Edwin M. Martin, former ambassador to the USSR Llewellyn Thompson, Deputy Secretary of Defense Roswell Gilpatrick, and Assistant Secretary of Defense Paul Nitze. Sometimes, UN Ambassador Adlai Stevenson and former Secretary of State Dean Acheson also joined in.[24]

The exchanges occasioned heated disagreements. As General Taylor later summarized them, the policy options, boiled down, consisted of three choices: "talk them out," "squeeze them out," or "shoot them out." The majority finally settled on a middle course: a quarantine, a semantical evasion meaning but not saying naval blockade; an actual blockade under international law could not exist except in time of war. McNamara functioned as an advocate in opposition to Taylor, McCone, and Acheson, all of whom favored an air strike. Robert Kennedy, the president's brother, also recommended against risky military responses, warning of a Pearl Harbor effect in reverse, possibly leading to an atomic war.

President Kennedy, meanwhile, arrived at two decisions. First, he ordered the deployment of U.S. warships around Cuba to prevent the arrival of more missiles and to display his resolve. If subsequently challenged, he could move on to more drastic measures. Second, he chose to announce his action by means of a television address. By going public instead of relying on diplomatic channels, Kennedy presumably intended to rally opinion in the United States and to convey his seriousness of purpose to the Soviets. Unlike secret diplomacy, this gambit allowed for almost no space to maneuver. Once having stated his position to the nation, the president could not easily back down.

The president's address on the evening of 22 October placed the responsibility for the crisis squarely on Soviet leaders. Kennedy reviewed the special relationship of the United States with other Western Hemisphere nations, recalled the lessons of Munich and the Second World War, and defined as imperative the need to resist manifestations of totalitarian aggression. He also called upon the Soviets to reverse their "deliberately provocative" behavior by dismantling their "strategic" missiles in Cuba. The quarantine constituted an "initial" step. Unless the Soviets acquiesced, other measures—unspecified—could follow. Moreover, the president warned, a missile launched from Cuba would precipitate instant retaliation against the Soviet Union. Over the facilities of the U.S. Information Agency, his words went around the world in thirty-seven languages, including Spanish. For the Cubans, Kennedy emphasized that Castro and his minions had become "puppets" of an "international conspiracy" led by the Soviet Union.

As Paterson describes the ensuing events, the missile crisis now became "an international war of nerves." More than sixty U.S. naval vessels assumed the responsibility of patrolling Cuban waters; the Strategic Air Command went on nuclear alert, meaning that B-52 bombers with atomic weapons stood ready; military forces in the southeastern United States prepared for a possible invasion. U.S. diplomats, accordingly, informed the NATO allies of these steps; the OAS voted to endorse the Kennedy policy; and the United Nations Security Council embarked upon a debate. The Soviets, meanwhile, neither mobilized their forces nor tested the quarantine. Instead, their vessels turned around and went back home, leaving U.S. officials to wonder, what next? If the Soviets stalled on the removal of the missiles from Cuba, a military strike still

could occur. Without investing too much faith in the effort, Kennedy
also allowed Brazilian diplomats to act as intermediaries, urging Castro
to sever ties with the Soviets.[25]

A means of resolution then appeared from an unlikely source. On
the afternoon of 26 October a Soviet embassy officer, Aleksander
Fomin—actually the KGB chief in Washington—arranged for a meeting with John Scali, an ABC news correspondent, in the course of which
he presented a proposal for transmission to the State Department. According to its terms, a straight-across deal, the Soviet Union would take
out the missiles if the United States would promise not to invade Cuba.
In response, Rusk sent an indication of interest. Meanwhile, a letter
from Khrushchev arrived for Kennedy, conveying the same offer and a
reminder that this trouble had come about because of the threatening
U.S. attitude toward Cuba.

A crisis atmosphere resumed on the following day, the 27th, when
a second letter from Khrushchev amplified the stakes. Possibly influenced by hard-line pressure at home, he now offered on this occasion
to remove the Soviet missiles in Cuba if the Americans similarly agreed
to remove theirs in Turkey. This stipulation made a larger strategic connection explicit for the first time. In anger and frustration, President
Kennedy spelled out the dilemma: "We are now in a position of risking
war in Cuba . . . over missiles in Turkey which are of little military
value." Indeed, he already had considered the possibility of phasing them
out but was unwilling to appear to be caving in before nuclear black-
mail; he wanted to accept no such public obligation while confronted
with Soviet pressure.

The difficulty deepened during the afternoon when a surface-to-
air missile (SAM) shot down a U-2 plane over Cuba. Regarding the
event as a dangerous escalation, Robert McNamara expressed his concern that "invasion had become almost inevitable." But President
Kennedy resisted the temptation, still seeking a peaceful resolution.
Following his brother Robert's advice, the president took a gamble by
accepting the terms not in Khrushchev's second letter but in the first.
He also sent Robert Kennedy on a mission to the Soviet ambassador,
Anatoly Dobrynin, to say that if the Soviets had not begun to take out
the missiles within forty-eight hours, then "we would remove them."
At the same time, he offered a concession. When Dobrynin inquired
about the Jupiter missiles in Turkey, Robert Kennedy promised to get
rid of them but emphasized the need for secrecy; if word leaked out,
the United States would not feel bound by the offer.

Thoroughly panicked at this point by the consequences of his own rash acts, Khrushchev refrained from seeking advantage, accepted the settlement as outlined, and concluded the crisis short of the nuclear brink. An unwritten agreement called for the elimination of the MRBMs under UN supervision and a U.S. pledge against launching an invasion. In this way, each Great Power could claim the fulfillment of one of its goals. Later, in April 1963, the removal of Jupiter missiles in Turkey completed the remaining obligation. Castro, meanwhile, brooded and fussed. Unconsulted by his Soviet ally during the final stages, he felt betrayed and demeaned.[26]

Kennedy's handling of the missile crisis has elicited divergent assessments. Enthusiasts, among them, administration memoirists, depicted his performance as a model, indeed, a masterpiece of crisis management effectively combining toughness with restraint. In this view the president, characteristically cool under pressure, acted rationally, retained control, and skillfully manipulated rewards and punishments as incentives. His strong stand, moderated by appropriate concessions at propitious times, allowed for a peaceful denouement at acceptable cost.[27] Consequently, he emerged as a kind of victor, his defense of the Western Hemisphere and the Monroe Doctrine supposedly vindicated.

Less laudatory appraisals portray the outcome as "a near miss." Thomas G. Paterson's account, for example, raises questions about "a mythology of grandeur," contending that "illusion" and "embellishment" have "obscured" important facets. As John Kenneth Galbraith observed, "We were in luck, but success in a lottery is no argument for lotteries." Paterson emphasizes the uncertainties and contingencies. What if Cuban exile groups had conducted raids or tried to kill Castro? What if Soviet vessels had challenged the blockade or merely blundered across the line? What if naval vessels or submarines had started shooting out of fear or miscalculation? What if caution and prudence had lapsed among the top leaders? Any one of these possibilities could have escalated the crisis and resulted in deeper difficulties. The tension and stress among the Ex Comm members approached the intolerable, depriving them of sleep and clearheadedness. Presumably, similar processes took place in the Kremlin. Whether Kennedy could have deactivated the crisis earlier by accepting a diplomatic option remains a source of sharp contention.[28]

In the aftermath of the Cuban missile crisis the leaders in Washington and Moscow installed a teletype hot line to place them in ready communication. The war scare in 1962 also encouraged the two Great

Powers to accept the Limited Test Ban Treaty on 25 July 1963. A partial effort, disallowing nuclear explosions in the atmosphere but permitting them underground, it had only a small effect on the arms race. Indeed, the Soviets emerged from the Cuban encounter with their nuclear inferiority exposed and a strong determination to catch up. They also maintained large-scale subsidies for the Cuban economy. Still in power, Castro elicited animosity from his Cuban enemies. For them, the Cuban Revolution still constituted a source of communist contagion in the Western Hemisphere. It remained the defining issue in the New World.

UNDER LBJ

President John F. Kennedy died on 22 November 1963 in Dallas, Texas, the victim of an assassin. His successor, Vice President Lyndon B. Johnson, a Texan, had served in the Congress since 1938, first in the House of Representatives and later in the Senate, where he was the Democratic majority leader during Eisenhower's second term. A sure-handed consensus builder and deal maker, Johnson practiced domestic politics as the art of constructing working majorities but lacked any equivalent experience or expertise in foreign relations. This shortcoming, a kind of tragic flaw, destroyed his administration after his reelection in 1964 and later drove him out of office. Under Johnson the escalation of the Vietnam War became the nation's preoccupation, transforming a small-scale insurgency in a far-off place into a large-scale conflict that engaged 535,000 U.S. troops.

Among the ramifications of Kennedy's demise were changes in priority and perception. Latin Americans regarded President Kennedy with special appreciation. They liked his reputation for eloquence and idealism, his beautiful, Spanish-speaking wife, Jacqueline, and his advocacy of the Alliance for Progress. His death touched them emotionally. Johnson, in contrast, appeared more provincial and less sympathetic. Although he claimed on occasion to understand Mexicans on the basis of his dealings with them as a young man in Texas, he never persuaded Latin Americans that he knew or cared very much about them or their countries.[29]

Typical of his generation, Johnson embraced the lessons of Munich and the Second World War as the crucial guides. For him, the communist menace recalled the Nazi threat and required constant vigilance. Collective security, alliance systems, and military supremacy ranked high as international priorities. The prospect of "wars of national liberation"

in third-world regions still caused some worry. When political opposition forced the Soviet leader Nikita Khrushchev into retirement in 1964, his successors, Leonid Brezhnev and Alexei Kosygin, inspired no more confidence in the Johnson administration. To counter Soviet activity in other countries, Johnson proposed in a literal-minded sort of way to uphold the containment principle wherever necessary. He also sought legitimation by claiming continuities of policy and purpose with the Kennedy administration and retained foreign policy advisers such as William and McGeorge Bundy, Walt Rostow, Robert McNamara, and Dean Rusk. One of the best books on Lyndon Johnson, Paul Conkin's *Big Daddy from the Pedernales*, provides an insightful account.[30]

As a tribute to President Kennedy, Johnson pledged an ongoing commitment to the Alliance for Progress at his first White House ceremony on 27 November 1963, where his audience included the Latin American ambassadors. Subsequently, Johnson's priorities centered on political stability and economic growth more than on democracy and reform. To an extent, this emphasis showed the influence of Thomas Mann, appointed by Johnson as undersecretary of state for Latin American affairs. Another Texan, a career Foreign Service officer, and a former ambassador to Mexico, Mann possessed a reputation for hard-boiled practicality. He regarded the Cuban Revolution with special aversion, describing it as a "cancer" that could be remedied only by heavy doses of free enterprise and private investment. In taking over the coordination of Latin American policy, Mann encountered a variety of bureaucratic obstacles. As Joseph S. Tulchin explains, no matter what the investment of time and energy, the Johnson administration engaged primarily in improvisational responses. Tulchin characterizes them as "spasmodic reactions" to "an overpowering fear that instability would lead to 'another Cuba' in the hemisphere." Unwilling to tolerate any such outcome, Johnson assumed a defensive stance toward Castro at a time when the Vietnam War functioned as a powerful diversion.[31]

Johnson encountered his first difficulties with Latin America over the Panama Canal. A source of contention since the Hay–Bunau–Varilla treaty of 1903, U.S. sovereign rights in the Canal Zone affronted Panamanian nationalists for many reasons. They objected to the imperialist implications, the division of their country into two parts, and other manifestations of inequality such as racial discrimination and low wages. As rectification, they wanted to assert Panamanian sovereigny over the Canal Zone and to share more fully in the management and the profits.

An episode on Panamanian Independence Day, 3 November 1959, had showed the magnitude of tension. A volatile circumstance turned ugly when student demonstrators carrying Panamanian flags marched into the Canal Zone, and ensuing encounters with police and military forces precipitated riots lasting several days. President Eisenhower, while professing puzzlement, attributed the responsibility to "extremists."[32]

Panamanian officials then invited diplomatic discussions as a means of resolving the difficulties and hoped to do so on their terms. In 1962, President Roberto Chiari asked for the negotiation of a new treaty. In response, the Kennedy administration stalled, claiming a need for feasibility studies of alternate canal routes, and then permitted a modest concession: It allowed Panamanians to fly their flag at sixteen designated points in the Canal Zone. Seeking in this way to circumvent theoretical debates over the "formalisms of sovereignty," the United States also tried to uphold its prerogatives for reasons of military defense. But the issue would not go away.

In Januuary 1964, a series of confrontations between Panamanian nationals and Canal Zone authorities over flag-flying privileges led to more violence, killing over twenty people. As an indication of the seriousness, U.S. officials, anticipating a showdown with "left wing agitators," evacuated the embassy staff and destroyed classified documents and code machines. Meanwhile, President Chiari suspended diplomatic relations, pending a response to his demand for the negotiation of a new treaty. When Johnson would not budge under pressure, Chiari broke diplomatic relations.

The Johnson administration ruled out large concessions. As White House adviser McGeorge Bundy explained, expediency permitted flexibility but not "retreat." He would stand strong "on gut issues," especially those concerned with the perpetual-rights clause and "our own ultimate responsibility for the security and effectiveness of the Canal." Senator Mike Mansfield of Montana, the president's friend, warned against any misunderstanding and emphasized the historical context. The Panama difficulty, he explained, "comes mainly from the inside." In his words, "Don't credit Castro for the problems; they existed before Castro and will continue to exist as long as the canal is there."

Meanwhile, presidential politics in each country constricted opportunities for an early resolution. For Johnson, seeking election in 1964, any concessions on Panama could serve Republican opponents as a campaign issue. Taking an unbending stance, he urged his counterpart, the Panamanian presidential candidate, Marco Robles, to appreciate the practicalities: Since economic advantages had more importance to his country than abstract notions of sovereignty, he should focus on questions of aid and assistance, profit sharing, and the like, all of which depended upon a cooperative attitude on other issues.

The election victories of Johnson and Robles subsequently allowed for diplomatic engagement. The drafts of three treaties at the end of June 1967 produced an uneven compromise, favoring the northern neighbor. Under its terms the United States could expand the Panama Canal or build a new one. In either case the right to defend the neutrality and security of the existing canal resided with the United States. Meanwhile, Panama obtained sovereignty over the Canal Zone but in a limited way. U.S. control of canal operations and military bases continued under extended leases. Regarded by Panamanian nationalists as unacceptable, these provisions became divisive issues provoking protest and turmoil. Consequently, treaty ratification became impossible in Panama, allowing for no settlement during the next decade.

Leaders in the Johnson administration struggled to bring coherence and focus to Latin American policy. On 18 March 1964, Undersecretary Thomas Mann announced a statement of purpose and intent. Known as the Mann Doctrine, this formulation displayed insistent apprehension over possibilities of communist subversion. To defend against it, Mann favored stability and growth over democratic reform. As Tulchin explains, the latter issue, never completely absent as "a policy objective in the region," became less conspicuous in comparison with the administration's other concerns over Communist sedition.[33]

The implications of the Mann Doctrine acquired special significance in relations with Brazil. During the Cold War the "unwritten alliance" with the United States experienced severe strains, in the Brazilian view, because of unfulfilled promises. During the Second World War, Brazilian leaders had supported the United States in the struggle against the Axis Powers, anticipating a reward consisting of economic aid and assistance. But for Brazilians, satisfactory programs never developed, and the absence of a payoff, a Marshall Plan for Latin America, caused distress and disenchantment. Another contentious point concerned the means of economic development. In the U.S. view, Brazil demonstrated too much susceptibility to nationalistic formulas based on state planning and intervention and too little appreciation for proven capitalist methods, free enterprise, and private investment. In the late 1950s, President Juscelino Kubitschek had produced particular irritation among U.S. officials by pressing for the adoption of "Operation

Pan America," an ambitious but vague proposal involving large-scale U.S. aid, multilateral endeavors, and anticommunism. President Eisenhower reportedly had trouble concealing his personal dislike of Kubitschek.[34]

Brazilian foreign policy then moved in new directions by affirming more independence from the United States. Kubitschek broke loose from traditional Cold War constraints with initiatives seeking broader international connections. In the United Nations, his government supported disarmament programs and third-world interests; it also invited more extensive diplomatic and economic relations with the communist world. In the Western Hemisphere, Brazil still functioned as a mediator between the United States and the rest of Latin America but "with an unusual twist." Abandoning traditional efforts "to soften Latin American hostility to U.S. proposals," Kubitschek's government functioned as "the advocate" of Latin America, attempting thereby to bring U.S. positions into line with Brazilian inclinations.

These tendencies persisted under Kubitschek's successor. In the election of 1960, Brazilians voted for Janio Quadros, a former state governor of São Paulo. This choice worried U.S. leaders, who perceived Quadros as a political deviant, insufficiently tough on communists. He favored a more neutral stance in the Cold War, supported Castro's right to maintain his regime, urged the promotion of economic growth by nationalist methods, and promised to lead Brazil toward its destiny as a Great Power. The era of the unwritten alliance was over. Indeed, in 1961 a kind of transposition took place whereby the two countries switched roles, the United States now acting as the ardent suitor. Seeking to have its way, the United States later resorted to covert actions that aided conspiratorial antigovernment groups and facilitated a coup d'état on 31 March 1964. The result was a military dictatorship.

The Kennedy administration tried to court Quadros in conjunction with the Alliance for Progress but obtained ambivalent responses. Quadros wanted loans and assistance to cope with inflation and balance-of-payments problems but condemned intervention, including the Bay of Pigs invasion. At the same time, he opened discussions of trade-and-aid issues with West Germany and Eastern bloc nations, though without much success. Meanwhile, the Kennedy administration suppressed its exasperation while negotiating a $500-million aid-and-assistance package, hoping for good effects but worried about mass poverty and discontent in Brazil's northeastern regions, viewed as potentially "the next Cuba."

Confusion mounted on 25 August 1961 when Quadros suddenly and without explanation resigned his position as president. In a risky political gamble, he may have wanted the Congress and the army to insist upon his reinstatement and to lure him back by bestowing upon him special powers. If so, he lost his bet; instead, his act confirmed impressions of him as mercurial, impulsive, and unreliable. To make matters worse, his presumed successor, Vice President João Goulart, *Goulart* seemed to share such traits, causing a coalition of congressional and military factions to stipulate the terms under which he could take office. In an extraordinary arrangement, they imposed strict controls on presidential prerogatives, resulting for a short while in the creation of a Brazilian parliamentary system. Taken unaware, U.S. leaders regarded Goulart as dangerous and demagogic but had no say in the succession crisis.

For U.S. leaders, Brazil under Goulart became recalcitrant and troublesome. For example, in January 1962, at a foreign ministers meeting at Punta del Este, Uruguay, the Brazilian delegation resisted U.S. efforts to expel Cuba from the Organization of American States. A few weeks later, Goulart's brother-in-law, Leonel Brizola, the state governor of Rio Grande do Sul, expropriated a subsidiary of the International Telephone and Telegraph Company. Though actually the culmination of a dispute going back to the early 1950s, this act appeared to be part of a coordinated campaign against property rights in Brazil, and Kennedy officials feared there was worse to come. With Brazil suffering high inflation, low productivity, food shortages, peasant unrest, and urban tension, Goulart seemed maladroit and indecisive. He could neither command congressional majorities nor articulate a viable course of action. Meanwhile, a process of political polarization dividing the country at the extremes suggested the possibility of civil war. The Kennedy administration, always on guard, reviewed the applicability of counterinsurgency plans and sent Colonel Vernon Walters as a military attaché and troubleshooter. A talented *Col. Walters* linguist, Walters had served with the U.S. Army as a liaison with Brazilian forces in Italy during the Second World War and retained connections with high-ranking members of the officer corps. He now assumed a responsibility for cultivating and consolidating ties with military officials.

Relations deteriorated further in 1963. A plebiscite in January reestablished a presidential system, but Goulart made no headway against the economic crisis. In his view, the fault resided with the Kennedy administration's reluctance to supply him with unconditional large-scale, long-term aid and assistance. As mounting chaos in many places took the form of local protests, strikes, military mutinies, and outbreaks of rural violence, Goulart contemplated the declaration of a state of siege. U.S. Ambassador Lincoln Gordon was similarly alarmed. In August 1963, he saw signs of "substantial imminent danger" of a communist takeover in Brazil.

Following the assassination of President Kennedy in November 1963, the troubles deepened. According to W. Michael Weis, "a majority of Brazilians" anticipated either a communist revolution or a presidential coup. To salvage his position, Goulart tried ineffectively to win over the Johnson administration and to rally popular support, especially among the political left. By so doing, he further alienated the political right, resulting in the military coup of 31 March 1964. As Weis explains, "virtually no one" was willing "to risk anything" to save him. The takeover was quick and easy.

Elated U.S. officials applauded the outcome. The Johnson administration had considered the possibilities of direct action but preferred indirect means. On 16 March, Johnson, Rusk, Mann, and other top officials endorsed stability as the main priority, thereby affirming the central premise of the Mann Doctrine. Two days later, Lincoln Gordon met in Washington with Rusk, Mann, McNamara, and CIA Director John McCone to discuss policy options, including intervention in the event of a coup or a civil war. Meanwhile, conspiratorial efforts in Brazil, probably with U.S. encouragement, coalesced around General Humberto Castello Branco, the army chief of staff. By 27 March the U.S. embassy in Brazil had prepared contingency plans to assist the Brazilian military with arms and supplies, a decision that may have functioned as a green light. Preparing also for more extreme measures, the Johnson administration assembled a U.S. carrier task force. Code-named "Brother Sam," this operation got under way on 31 March. Fortunately for U.S. leaders, Goulart's ouster that day nullified any need for it to proceed. An endorsement of the interim government's legitimacy quickly followed. On 1 April, U.S. officials authorized emergency aid and also characterized the change as constitutional, thereby avoiding the question of diplomatic recognition. Johnson sent "warmest wishes" to the new leaders, commending them for resolving the Brazilian crisis "within a framework of constitutional democracy and without civil strife."[35]

Such euphemistic words served the U.S. interest in order and sustained the Brazilian army in the creation of a dictatorship. On 9 April

1964, the Supreme Revolutionary Command issued the first of a series of "Institutional Acts," the effects of which were to consolidate military control and suspend constitutional privileges. They also allowed for the declaration of a state of siege and the denial of citizenship rights to persons regarded as threats to national security. This latter provision soon took effect against three former presidents (Kubitschek, Quadros, and Goulart), two members of the Supreme Court, six state governors, fifty-five congressmen, and three hundred other political figures. On 11 April, under careful military supervision, the Brazilian Congress elected General Castello Branco as president. He became the first of five military dictators who ruled Brazil until 1985. They functioned as the conservators of internal security and national development, operating under the auspices of political authoritarianism and market capitalism.[36]

Brazil's military rulers

Another such experience became a defining episode for the Johnson administration during the U.S. military intervention in the Dominican Republic in 1965. As Tulchin explains, "crisis management" in the Western Hemisphere became a short-term substitute for the articulation of long-term goals and objectives and the suppression of perceived Communist threats a special preoccupation. Without a crisis to manage, regional specialists had difficulty getting Johnson to pay much attention at all. The Dominican crisis revealed some of the pitfalls of improvization.

DR?

The Dominican Republic, a former protectorate, had experienced U.S. interventions before. In 1905, President Theodore Roosevelt took control of the customs offices to ward off the possibility of European intrusions. As justified by the Roosevelt corollary to the Monroe Doctrine, the president chose to exercise an international police power to ensure civilized behavior. Later, U.S. Marines occupied the country from 1916 until 1924. When they withdrew, a police constabulary, established by U.S. authorities, served as a base for an aspiring dictator, Rafael Leonidas Trujillo Molina. For three decades after he took power in 1930, Trujillo and his family ruled the Dominican Republic as a fiefdom, growing ostentatiously rich over the years. Posing much of the time as a champion of anticommunism, Trujillo operated with U.S. indulgence if not outright support. Yet by the late 1950s, embarrassment over his heavy-handed excesses and murderous ways encouraged the Eisenhower administration to initiate a process of cutting loose from him. This policy persisted under President Kennedy, who demonstrated his unhappiness with Trujillo while courting Latin

American reformers. Trujillo's enemies in the Dominican Republic gunned him down on 31 May 1961—possibly with CIA assistance: Tulchin asserts that "the story of CIA involvement in the assassination . . . told in many versions . . . is no longer disputed."[37]

The ensuing crises over political succession then produced an intervention. Following the dictator's death the United States used various means, including diplomatic influence and the deployment of warships off the coast, to prevent Trujillo's sons and brothers from retaining power. Meanwhile, the Dominican military exercised authority until a presidential election took place in December 1962, the first free exercise of voting rights in thirty years, possibly ever. The victor, Juan Bosch, a prominent reformer and social democrat, identified his political program with the goals and aspirations of the Alliance for Progress but could not contain fractious disputes over land and labor reform and military prerogatives. Conservative opponents among the propertied elites and the military officers undermined his regime. Moreover, because his shows of radicalism appeared to leaders in the Kennedy administration as evidence of a pro-Castro proclivity, they accepted without much complaint his ouster by Dominican military contingents in September 1963.

From exile, Bosch placed the blame for his downfall on the United States and urged support from his loyalists. Subsequently, as Tulchin notes, "jealousies among the military leaders and the absence of any strong civilian alternatives to Bosch made the transition back to civilian rule very complicated."[38] Nevertheless, preparations proceeded for a new election, but before it took place, a military contingent loyal to Bosch attempted a seizure of power on 24 April 1965, seeking to put him back in the presidency. During the next few days, civil war threatened as a consequence of the struggle between pro- and anti-Bosch elements in the Dominican military.

The Johnson administration, in what critics regard as an overreaction, allowed the requirements of crisis management to override the nonintervention provisions of the OAS charter. On 28 April, seeking to protect the rights and interests of U.S. citizens, Johnson ordered five hundred U.S. Marines into the capital city, Santo Domingo. Subsequent reports, probably overstated, indicated high levels of violence and atrocities with a strong likelihood of Communist involvement. Unwilling to permit another Cuba, Johnson then authorized a full-scale military intervention with twenty-three thousand troops, intending to keep Bosch out of office, to eliminate the chances of a communist takeover, and to "avoid another situation like that in Vietnam." Throughout, according to Tulchin, "Johnson exaggerated the danger to U.S. lives" and used the threat of communist subversion mainly as a "gambit" to arouse public support. His main concern was to prevent another Castro, but he lost interest when Bosch faded as a threat. Disgusted by what he saw as the "venality" of Dominican politicians and "the corruption and deceit of the military leaders," Johnson arranged for an OAS "cover," calling upon a multinational peace-keeping force from Nicaragua, Honduras, El Salvador, Costa Rica, and Brazil to enforce the ensuing cease-fire agreements.[39]

Through a difficult sequence of failed efforts and diplomatic breakdowns, U.S. officials subsequently obtained the means of safeguarding order and authority. To facilitate the process, as sardonically noted by the historian Robert Freeman Smith, many of the factional leaders in the Dominican military accepted overseas jobs. An agreement on 31 August 1965, the Act of Dominican Reconciliation, provided for an interim government until elections could take place in 1966. The winner, Dr. Joaquín Balaguer, a politician with Trujillista antecedents, served two consecutive terms, represented elite interests under a democratic facade, and became a fixture in Dominican politics for the next twenty-five years. For U.S. officials, the Dominican intervention as an exercise in crisis management constituted an acceptable outcome, admittedly costly but nevertheless a pointed demonstration of administrative resolve against radical threats. As suggested by the Kennan corollary years earlier, it showed a readiness to act in support of anticommunist stability within the U.S. sphere of influence, no matter what the effects on the OAS charter. To Johnson's growing legion of critics, in contrast, it seemed an unhappy regression to the imperialist practices of Theodore Roosevelt and Woodrow Wilson, part of a larger pattern exemplified by the Vietnam War.[40]

After the Dominican crisis, U.S. policy toward Latin America concentrated on "damage control," that is, "trying to salvage something from the ashes of the dream." Thomas Mann left the government early in 1967. Johnson became even more absorbed with Vietnam. When on occasion he showed concern for Western Hemisphere issues, he focused on "specific, uncontroversial development projects, such as roads." Improvements in physical infrastructure became "his mantra in conversations with visitors from Latin America." Though Cuba remained an obsessional subject, the Alliance for Progress became a lost cause for administration leaders. They blamed the failure on Latin

Americans, whom they regarded as self-centered, irresponsible, and unwilling to engage in "constructive cooperation" with the United States to safeguard the hemisphere against internal and external threats.

Latin Americans likewise became disenchanted with the United States. A mounting sense of alienation disposed many of them against U.S. definitions of multilateral endeavor and hemispheric security.[41] For them, the Cold War fixation entailed neglect and subordination; indeed, it perpetuated ongoing patterns of exploitation and underdevelopment. To counter them, Latin Americans recast the issues on a North-South basis, highlighting the asymmetries between "modern" and "modernizing" nations and the alleged responsibility of the former for conditions of poverty and destitution among the latter. In the versions called "dependency theory," this formulation contrasted starkly with the East-West emphasis, that is, the tendency to understand most international issues as a function of U.S.-Soviet relations.

Dependency theory adapted Marxist analysis to account for the prevalence of poverty and inequality. Among other things, it posited the existence of a world capitalist system by which the very structure of economic relationships enabled the metropolitan centers—London in the nineteenth century and New York in the twentieth—to maintain ascendancy by expropriating the wealth of peripheral regions in the Third World. According to this critique, the terms of exchange operated as a form of neo-imperialism, assuring economic subservience by discriminating against those countries that produced cheap primary materials and in favor of those that turned out more expensive finished goods. Moreover, a central part of this analysis asserted that the system operated in such a way as to perpetuate underdevelopment and dependency in large portions of the world, keeping them in thrall, unless the victimized regions could find viable ways of breaking loose through the adoption of more equitable, conceivably noncapitalist alternatives. In whatever form, the North-South perspective established different categories for understanding the plight of third-world nations in a world dominated by the East-West considerations of the Cold War.[42]

UNDER NIXON AND KISSINGER

The Johnson administration's self-destruction over Vietnam opened the way for a Republican restoration in January 1969. Richard M. Nixon, the new president, had served Eisenhower as vice president during the 1950s and failed in his run for the presidency against Kennedy in 1960. As the Republican candidate in 1968, he unveiled a "new" Nixon, supposedly more mellow and less partisan. Claiming foreign relations as his expertise, he promised a peace with honor in Vietnam. His partner, National Security Adviser and later Secretary of State Henry A. Kissinger, shared the president's proclivities. A professor of political science from Harvard University, previously a minor player in the national security establishment, and a German Jew whose family had fled from Hitler in the 1930s, Kissinger brought with him to the White House an attraction for European frames of reference. Conceptions of realpolitik in his usage allowed for small notice of Latin America.

As conservative geopoliticians, Nixon and Kissinger regarded order and equilibrium among the Great Powers as essential requirements. As political realists, they disliked utopian designs, eschewed idealistic and moralistic abstractions, and favored stability as the road toward peace and predictability in a dangerous world. Their statecraft, seeking détente, or a relaxation of tension, centered on relations with the Soviet Union, Western Europe, Japan, and the People's Republic of China. Premised on the possibility of achieving some measure of consensus and cooperation, this strategy anticipated the establishment of a concert of power among the Great Powers and provided incentives for accepting the essential parts of the international status quo. Once created, a community of common interest might result in the containment of Communist expansion by subtle means and the enlistment of Soviet and Chinese assistance in the termination of the Vietnam War.[43]

In peripheral regions such as Latin America the intricacies of Nixon-Kissinger diplomacy, the balancing and calibration of Great-Power interests, suggested a perception of second-class status. When confronted with such matters, Kissinger sometimes showed impatience. In June 1969, for example, the Chilean foreign minister, Gabriel Valdés, criticized U.S. policy for disregarding economic development in Latin America. Kissinger disparaged his concerns: "Nothing important can come from the South. History has never been produced in the South. The axis of history starts in Moscow, goes to Bonn, crosses over to Washington, and then goes to Tokyo. What happens in the South has no importance." When Valdés responded by suggesting that Kissinger knew nothing of Latin America, the so-called Doctor of Diplomacy replied, "No, and I don't care."[44] On another occasion, Kissinger dismissed Chile on geopolitical grounds, describing the country as "a dagger aimed at the heart of Antarctica."[45] Subsequently, in writing their memoirs, neither Kissinger nor Nixon displayed much interest in Latin American affairs. For them, Latin America functioned primarily as an

annoyance when North-South issues intruded upon the more significant patterns of East-West relations.

For such reasons, Cuba remained a source of irritation following
the missile crisis. Perceived as a Soviet foil, Fidel Castro espoused a brand
of revolutionary romanticism, supposedly a threat to the stable countries of Latin America. Often out-of-sync with more cautious Soviet
renditions of Marxist doctrine and practice, Castro's long, emotional
speeches presented a radical call for heroic struggles against daunting
odds. His rhetoric anticipated the advent of revolution throughout the
Third World, igniting many Vietnams and precipitating a collapse of
world capitalism by means of violent overthrow. Yet the extent to which
 Castro supported his words with acts is subject to debate. On at least
one occasion, in Bolivia, his proposed strategy for exporting the revolution failed dramatically in actual application.

 Headed by Ernesto "Che" Guevara, an Argentine revolutionary
associated with Castro since Mexico City days, the Cuban expedition
into Bolivia late in 1966 obtained a base in the southwestern part of the
country in the Andean foothills. Modeling his efforts on Castro's experience in the Sierra Maestra, Guevara expected to set off uprisings
among peasant masses with subsequent domino effects into Peru, Paraguay, and adjacent regions. But false hopes and defective plans caused
setbacks in an inhospitable environment. Uncooperative and hostile,
the native peoples spoke a dialect of Guaraní, not the Quechua that
Guevara had anticipated, and received the revolutionary message with
incomprehension. Guevara could not adapt. Forlorn and isolated, the
Cuban revolutionaries experienced a sequence of breakdowns culminating in disaster: In October 1967 Guevara was captured by contingents of the Bolivian army and executed before a firing squad soon
thereafter. As the historian Robert Quirk explains, his memory then
passed from history into myth. After death, his reputation for heroism
as a guerrilla fighter, however much embellished, became part of radical iconography around the world.[46]

Allegations of Cuban support for third-world revolution distressed
Richard Nixon. His friend Bebe Rebozo, an anti-Castro Cuban, reinforced his suspicions. Kissinger once suggested that Nixon had "a
neuralgic problem" on the subject. Cubans reciprocated in kind. They
looked upon the new president, an old enemy, as a fascist. To underscore the point, Cuban propaganda employed a distinctive spelling of
his name, replacing the "x" in Nixon with a swastika.[47]

Trouble impended in August 1970, when photographic reconnais-
sance over Cuba discovered an installation under construction in the

USSR
nuclear
subs
in
Cuba

harbor at Cienfuegos. To some intelligence analysts the images looked like a Soviet base for nuclear submarines. Kissinger accepted this appraisal. With Sherlockian powers of deduction, he observed soccer fields in the picture and warned of possible war, explaining, "Cubans play *baseball*. Russians play *soccer*." His inference, though partly wrong— Cubans do play soccer—correctly identified a Soviet submarine facility. In September, Kissinger told Nixon that such a base could mark "a quantum leap in the strategic capability of the Soviet Union against the United States."[48] With no need to return home for service and maintenance, Soviet submarines with nuclear weapons could multiply in number off the Atlantic coast.

Back in the limelight as an East-West issue, Cuban malfeasance aroused Kissinger's indignation. Viewed as a violation of bans on offensive weapons during the missile crisis, Soviet actions as Kissinger portrayed them could have produced another confrontation. But in these circumstances, Nixon for his own reasons chose another course. He wanted no political uproar over Cuba to place his administration on the defensive before the congressional elections in November 1970. Moreover, he attributed higher priority to questions of détente in relations with the Soviets. As described by his biographer, Stephen E. Ambrose, his display of "intelligent and admirable restraint" allowed for quiet diplomacy, enabling the Soviets to save face while accepting retreat. No threat of war developed. As before, Cubans had no say in the resolution.

Cuban revolutionary enthusiasms still nettled administration leaders and warded off suggestions for placing relations with Castro's government on a more regular basis. During Nixon's second term, discussions in the Organization of American States over the possibility of dropping economic and diplomatic sanctions against Cuba went nowhere. Opposition among anti-Castro exiles obstructed any such process, as did questions of compensation for U.S. losses to Cuban nationalization and Castro's leadership efforts in the Third World. Indeed, Castro ruined all hope of rapprochement in the mid-1970s when he sent Cuban troops into a complex civil war in Angola, a former Portuguese colony in Africa. Something of a public relations coup for the Cubans, the intervention highlighted Castro's claim to champion revolutionary nationalism in the Third World. Kissinger railed against Castro's audacity, viewing it as a consequence of Soviet manipulations.

The geopolitical propensities of the administration continued to arouse Latin American misgivings, and Kissinger sometimes responded to them. In October 1972, he attended a luncheon with Latin American delegates to the United Nations. As described by an aide, William J. Jorden, once "warmed by the evident good fellowship in the room," Kissinger waxed eloquent and promised the beginning of "a new dialogue" on hemispheric affairs. Though rhetorical in intent, Kissinger's statement engaged Latin American diplomats, who showed signs of taking it seriously. To an extent, this expectation formed a context for and perhaps moved the administration toward a softer line when a new round of discussions got under way with Panama over the canal and the 1903 treaty.

Panama

These issues ranked among the most conspicuous legacies of U.S. imperialism in the Western Hemisphere. For the Panamanian government, now dominated by the military strongman Omar Torrijos, the renegotiation of terms and provisions retained a vital importance but initially did not for President Nixon; during his first term, he avoided discussions of them. After his reelection he shifted ground. Perhaps in a gesture to mollify third-world opinion, his administration reopened the talks, with Ellsworth Bunker in charge. An experienced diplomat, Bunker encountered a complicated array of competing interests and objectives, including questions of sovereignty and the management and defense of the canal. Unsusceptible to easy resolution, the difficulties remained unsettled when Nixon resigned the presidency because of the Watergate scandal in August 1974. Subsequently, under President Gerald Ford, fundamental differences prevented further progress, in part because leading Republicans such as Ronald Reagan, the former governor of California, vehemently opposed concessions to Panama.[49]

Chile

Another set of issues came about in relations with Chile during the presidency of Dr. Salvador Allende Gossens, a murky episode over which suspicions, allegations, and polemics have abounded. Allende's government fell from power in September 1973 during a military uprising in the course of which Allende died under mysterious circumstances, by either suicide or assassination. Critics attributed complicity to the United States for supposedly orchestrating a campaign against him.

Allende, a physician of bourgeois origins but with Marxist philosophical tastes, had unsuccessfully sought the presidency in 1958 and 1964 before his victory in 1970. As a Socialist party member, he denied communist affiliations but accepted communist support and campaigned on the need for radical changes. His priorities included the redistribution of land and wealth and the nationalization of basic enterprises, including banks, insurance companies, public utilities, and extractive industries. For an assortment of reasons, his presence in La Moneda, the Chilean executive mansion, disconcerted Nixon and Kissinger, who pressed for countermeasures.

Large-scale U.S. political involvements in Chile had accelerated in the 1960s. A tempestuous multiparty democracy inhabited by ten million people, Chile experienced economic distress during the postwar period because of high inflation, maldistribution of income, and heavy reliance on copper exports, especially those of the U.S.-owned corporations Anaconda and Kennecott. The 1964 election of President Eduardo Frei Montalva, a reform-minded Christian Democrat supported by CIA funds, made Chile a centerpiece during the Alliance for Progress. An adherent of democratic capitalism, Frei favored land, labor, and tax reform and a larger share of the profits from the copper companies but failed to achieve his goals. Moreover, his independence in foreign relations offended Richard Nixon, who viewed him as a creature of previous Democratic administrations. By 1970, Nixon was happy for Frei's term to end.[50]

To replace Frei, the presidential campaign of that year featured a three-way race. Allende, a Socialist, ran with communist support against Radomiro Tomic, a Christian Democrat, and Jorge Alessandri, a conservative former president. U.S. officials opposed Allende but had trouble choosing between the other two. Their apprehensions deepened when Allende won a plurality with 36 percent of the vote. Kissinger complained of standing by and letting Chile "go Communist due to the irresponsibility of its own people." He anticipated no more free elections if Allende took office. The geopolitical implications for South America and the effects on U.S. corporations also caused worry. For such reasons, Kissinger and Nixon considered various means of preventing Allende from becoming the president. One possibility entailed political manipulation. Since under law the power of choice fell to the Chilean Congress when no candidate obtained a majority, deals among other parties might head him off. Another option was covert action, possibly leading to a military coup, but this route became impossible when resistance developed among military officers, some of whom took threats of civil war seriously. When anti-Allende conspirators botched an attempted kidnapping in October 1970 and shot to death General

René Schneider, an opponent of military intervention, Chileans closed ranks in support of the constitution and inaugurated Salvador Allende as president in November.[51]

Allende subsequently challenged the status quo. He blamed economic woes on dependency and exploitation, supposedly the consequences of an alliance between foreign capitalists and domestic elites who looted resources and sent them overseas. To retain the wealth for Chile's benefit, he favored nationalization and expropriation. He also identified his positions with third-world radicals such as the Vietcong and underscored the point by establishing diplomatic ties with communist countries: Cuba, the German Democratic Republic, North Korea, North Vietnam, and the People's Republic of China. For him, the apparatus of hemispheric cooperation, including the Organization of American States, functioned as a tool of U.S. dominance. He regarded it as a "servant" of the United States in the Cold War, operating "against the interests of Latin America." Such expressions animated Allende's foreign policy. For Chileans to become free, they required liberation from U.S. hegemony, capitalist exploitation, and economic dependency.

For Allende and his supporters, U.S. corporations in Chile became powerful symbols of an assortment of ills. Anaconda and Kennecott, for example, controlled the country's most important resource, copper, which accounted for most of the state revenue and hard currency. Chileans with otherwise divergent political views agreed on a need to share more fully in the profits. Eduardo Frei had favored a strategy of buying into the companies with stock purchases; Allende wanted to take them over, and soon after assuming office, he introduced nationalization legislation. Under the prescribed proceedings as subsequently enacted into law by the Chilean Congress, compensation was subject to special terms. If foreign companies had earned "excess profits" as calculated by the government, then the totals would shrink by that amount. For Anaconda and Kennecott the calculations permitted no compensation at all, and the companies complained of confiscation. The U.S. State Department objected to Chilean deviations from "accepted standards of international law." As punishment, the Nixon administration arranged for restrictions on international credit through private U.S. banks, the Inter-American Development Bank, and the World Bank, thus reducing Allende's capacity to finance his economic programs. Significantly, no equivalent acts stopped military aid to the Chilean armed forces.[52]

A sequence of domestic crises later engulfed Chile. State-run enterprises functioned inefficiently, and output declined. Consequently,
inflation mounted and also worker discontent. A truckers' strike in
October 1972, an expression of unhappiness among Allende's working-
class constituents, caused special embarrassment. Other difficulties
developed over food shortages, urban protests, and rural violence.
Nevertheless, the government retained power until 11 September 1973,
when the Chilean military executed a coup d'état. The circumstances
of Allende's demise during the fighting around La Moneda remain the
subject of speculation and polemical debate.   *debate*

The same is true of allegations of U.S. responsibility. According
to critics, the Nixon administration engineered the drive against
Allende for geopolitical and economic reasons. Allende's death,
though probably unintended, nevertheless came about as a consequence of U.S. policies, especially the adoption of covert means to
destabilize the regime, engender economic distress, and mobilize the
opposition. By cutting off bank credit while allowing military aid,
the Nixon administration sent unmistakable signals, in effect inviting a move by the military. Other accounts place the blame on Allende
himself. To be sure, U.S. economic coercion caused difficulty but
never as much as Allende's own mismangement. According to this
view, his regime collapsed as a result of its own incompetency and
failure. These divergent accounts test the capacity of scholars to tolerate
high levels of ambiguity, uncertainty, and contradiction. Whether future access to archival materials such as CIA records will clarify such
issues is also problematical.[53]   *Pinochet*

Following the military takeover, a junta under General Augusto
Pinochet Ugarte instituted its authority by repressive means. Although
estimates vary, as many as ten thousand Chileans suspected of pro-
Marxist sympathies may have been killed during the ensuing roundup
and crackdown. Later, many more spent hard time in prison, fled the
country, turned up dead as victims of political murder, or simply disappeared. General Pinochet, sometimes compared in his methods with
Spain's Francisco Franco, became a champion of order and an object of
criticism among human-rights advocates around the world. His government ruthlessly secured Chile for anticommunism and free enterprise. Under his purview, Anaconda and Kennecott obtained payments
in cash and bonds for their mines and equipment, and the country again
became receptive to infusions of foreign investment. Free-market economic doctrines associated with Adam Smith, Milton Friedman, and

the "University of Chicago boys" became the official guides. Subsequently, under Nixon and Ford, U.S. dealings with Chile became more satisfactory. Pinochet's government assured anticommunist stability and a friendly environment for foreign capital—while Chilean political dissidents paid for their opposition with their lives.[54]

UNDER CARTER

In 1976 a political outsider from Plains, Georgia, won the presidency for the Democrats. James Earl Carter, better known as Jimmy, came out of nowhere by capitalizing on public disenchantment with the Vietnam War and the Watergate scandal. The Nixon administration had accomplished an important goal late in January 1973 by disengaging U.S. forces from the fighting and calling the outcome "a peace with honor." In May 1975, North Vietnamese forces won the war by sweeping into Saigon, the South Vietnamese capital, and taking control of the country. Meanwhile, Nixon's presidency had collapsed under high crimes and misdemeanors. When he resigned in August 1974, Vice President Gerald R. Ford became the president and destroyed his chance for election in his own right by pardoning Nixon. U.S. voters wondered how to account for such disasters. The political effects made Carter a winner.

A 1946 U.S. Naval Academy graduate, Carter carried out his service obligation until 1953, when he returned home to Georgia for a career in agriculture, business, and politics. As governor in the early 1970s, he decided to run for the presidency. A devout Baptist, he aspired to make politics conform more closely with his personal standards. His insistence upon ethical integrity, an essential part of his message, later handicapped him by impeding his adjustment to Washington folkways. According to his critics, a puritanical streak and an absence of *savoir faire* reduced his political effectiveness. In a more favorable assessment, Gaddis Smith has characterized his term in office as a creative attempt to reconcile the imperatives of morality and reason with power.[55]

In foreign affairs, Carter possessed strong convictions but no experience. For Gaddis Smith, such traits recall "the ghost of Woodrow Wilson." Nevertheless, Carter sought to enhance his understanding in 1973 by accepting membership in the Trilateral Commission. This elite group based in New York City consisted of business, political, and academic leaders who defined the triangular relationship of the United States, Western Europe, and Japan as critical. However vague and unformed, Carter's views during the campaign suggested his readiness to move away from the geopolitical formulations of Nixon and Kissinger. Espousing more principled approaches, he wanted to slow the arms race, diminish competition with the Soviets, and overcome outdated Cold War notions in East-West relations. At the same time, his absorption with questions of human rights disposed him more readily toward the Third World and North-South issues.

Once in office, Carter had trouble bringing focus to his policies, partly because of his choice of top advisers. Secretary of State Cyrus R. Vance, a Yale-trained lawyer and a pillar of the foreign-policy establishment, operated in the traditions of Elihu Root, Charles Evans Hughes, Henry L. Stimson, and Dean Acheson by moving easily among power elites in the corporate world and the government. Also, the well-connected head of the National Security Council, Zbigniew Brzezinski, a Harvard-educated political scientist and a Columbia professor, resembled other university-based social scientists and policymakers such as McGeorge Bundy, Walt and Eugene Rostow, and Henry Kissinger. In the Carter administration, Vance and Brzezinski, both strong-willed and assertive, produced confusion for outside observers by giving divergent, sometimes contradictory signals. Vance, a proponent of accommodation with the Soviet Union, responded with sympathy to North-South problems. Brzezinski, more inclined toward Cold War orthodoxies, accepted East-West definitions of international relations as the dominant reality.

For the Carter administration, Latin America presented an opportunity to open "a new, happier era of relations." The defense of human rights became an organizing theme. As Gaddis Smith notes, new presidents often engage in "a ritual" of proclaiming a "more sensitive and understanding approach," but in Carter's case the promise assumed some measure of actuality. During the campaign, he vowed to move away from responding with "an attitude of paternalism or punishment or retribution" if Latin Americans did not "yield to our persuasion." This statement implied an aversion to any more invasions or interventions or exercises in destabilization. Vance and Brzezinski shared Carter's view. Early on, Brzezinski noted that in the United States the Monroe Doctrine might appear as "a selfless . . . contribution to hemispheric security," but "to most of our neighbors to the south it was an expression of presumptuous U.S. paternalism." As Gaddis Smith observes, administration speakers never used the term "Monroe Doctrine" in public.

Carter took something of a personal interest in Latin America. He knew some Spanish and with his wife, Rosalyn, had traveled in Mexico and Brazil. He saw the region as an appropriate place to apply what Smith calls his "philosophy of repentance and reform," that is, "admitting past mistakes" and "making the region a showcase for human-rights policy." Moreover, at least in the beginning, he perceived Soviet involvement in the Western Hemisphere as insufficiently large or purposeful to warrant much concern. His priorities included negotiations with Panama to resolve the status of the Canal Zone and efforts to place relations with Castro's Cuba on a more regular basis. Ironically, it was his much criticized reaction to a Latin American issue, the Nicaraguan revolution in 1979, that aided in establishing his reputation for incompetency in foreign affairs. This perception as much as anything made him a one-term president.

Stalled for a dozen years, negotiations over the status of the canal assumed a top priority. Carter wanted a success, hoping to obtain "a positive impact throughout Latin America" and "an auspicious beginning for a new era." But domestic politics got in the way. Conservatives, represented by the former actor Ronald Reagan, then California governor, strongly opposed concessions. For them, a compromise on this matter signified a loss of will, steadfastness, and national greatness. As a candidate for the Republican nomination in 1976, Reagan had made the canal a central issue. His applause line affirmed an unbending position: "We bought it, we paid for it, it's ours and we're going to keep it." For Carter to prevail, a new treaty would have to reconcile somehow an assortment of rival demands and expectations.

Under General Omar Torrijos, a shrewd leader, the Panamanian government had kept the canal issue in the international spotlight. Consequently, in 1974, Secretary of State Henry Kissinger and Panamanian Foreign Minister Juan Antonio Tack had agreed to a set of principles. They called for the eventual abrogation of the 1903 treaty and the negotiation of new terms, providing for a fixed termination of the date and a more generous distribution of revenues for Panama. In addition, Panama at some point in the future would assume full sovereignty over the Canal Zone and responsibility for operating the waterway. At the same time, subsequently a sticking point, Panama would have to grant to the United States the right to protect the canal.[56]

The urgency appeared obvious. In 1976 a U.S. Commission on Latin America headed by Sol Linowitz, a Xerox Corporation executive, described the Panama problem as one of the most pressing in the region.

The Carter administration went into quick action. Soon after the inauguration in early 1977, the leaders endorsed the Kissinger-Tack principles as the basis for diplomatic discussions. As a negotiator, Sol Linowitz teamed with Ellsworth Bunker, a veteran diplomat. U.S. Ambassador William Jorden has described the ensuing processes in detail.

Three principal issues confronted the diplomats. How much money should go to Panama? How long should the United States retain authority over the canal? What words should describe U.S. rights once Panama took control? Through patience and effort, the diplomats found solutions. Wisely, they drafted two treaties. The first set the termination date of U.S. control over the canal for 31 December 1999 and provided for joint responsibility with Panama in the interim; meanwhile, Panama would receive $10 million a year and additional sums out of operating revenues. The second defined U.S. rights to defend the canal thereafter. As described by Brzezinski, these accomplishments represented for Carter "the ideal fusion of morality and politics." They did "something good for peace," responded to "the passionate desires of a small nation," and helped "the long-range U.S. national interest."

Nevertheless, tough fights lay ahead. To put the treaties into effect, both Panamanian voters and two-thirds of the U.S. Senate had to register their approval. For political reasons, Torrijos had to claim the acquisition of full sovereignty and an end forever to the threat of U.S. intervention. Similarly, Carter had to affirm an ongoing prerogative to safeguard access to the canal in all circumstances. Such contradictions elicited intense debate. When Senator Dennis DeConcini, a Democrat from Arizona, proposed an amendment authorizing all necessary measures, including the use of force, to keep the canal open, he nearly stalled the proceedings. Panama would not accept any such amendment. Happily for the Carter administration, DeConcini consented to place his affirmation of U.S. prerogatives in a reservation; as such, it required no Panamanian approval. Nevertheless, the terminology almost provoked General Torrijos into forsaking the effort. As it turned out, the treaties won acceptance by Panamanian voters and the U.S. Senate, where ratification took place in March and April 1978 by identical margins of 68 to 32. A shift of two votes would have resulted in a defeat. Torrijos later said that he would have destroyed the canal if the proceedings had gone the other way. Normally, Gaddis Smith notes, "a President grows stronger by winning a hard political fight." But Carter's narrow victory brought him no credit among the constituents of the conservative right. In fact, the treaties turned into liabilities when

Ronald Reagan, the most likely Republican challenger in 1980, assailed them as signs of weakness. According to Reagan, the Carter administration had given away the Panama Canal, thereby running a risk of making "this nation NUMBER TWO."

A second risky endeavor featured overtures to Fidel Castro, seeking a return of normal diplomatic relations. As Cyrus Vance explained to Carter in October 1976, "The time has come to move away from our past policy of isolation." As reasons, he claimed that "our boycott has proved ineffective, and there has been a decline of Cuba's export of revolution in the region." Moreover, he suggested, Castro might reciprocate with greater restraint in Africa. Though ambivalent during the campaign, Carter subsequently removed restrictions on travel to Cuba and authorized "interest sections" in third-world embassies to facilitate quasi-official communications. Castro responded with caution, indicating that he welcomed better relations and might release some American prisoners from Cuban jails.

Nevertheless, there were insuperable problems. Officials in the Carter administration objected to the presence of Cuban troops already in Angola and to a parallel move into Ethiopia early in 1978. In the U.S. view, such acts in unstable African regions served Soviet interests, not legitimate Cuban concerns. Other difficulties arose with reports of Soviet misbehavior in Cuba. In 1978, Carter's critics alleged the arrival of twenty-three Soviet MiG fighter-bombers, presumably in violation of earlier agreements, and in 1979, a combat brigade. Though unsubstantiated and probably overdrawn, such suspicions effectively ruined all hopes for a Cuban rapprochement during the Carter presidency.

Finally, the Carter administration's advocacy of human rights pertained most directly to the ABC countries. Historically different from the smaller and weaker nations of Central America and the Caribbean, Argentina, Brazil, and Chile on occasion had displayed more capacity to resist pressures from Washington. During the Carter years, they had all operated under authoritarian military rulers who lacked much sensitivity to human rights. Indeed, murderous campaigns against political dissidents had resulted in outrageous violations. Moreover, each regime responded with fierce resentment to criticism from the Carter administration. As Brzezinski noted, the United States consequently ran the risk "of having bad relations simultaneously" with all three.[57]

In Argentina, a military junta under Army Chief of Staff Jorge Rafael Videla took over on 24 March 1976. Seeking order after a period of instability, inflation, and despair, the government cracked down on

dissent, waging "a dirty war" at home with scant recognition of traditional political or civil rights. Armed gangs, operating presumably with
official sanction, attacked suspected subversives. They often vanished
without a trace, becoming known as *desaparecidos*; probably as many as
ten thousand were killed. The ensuing mix of authoritarian politics and
free-market economics constituted an intriguing contradiction.[58]

Such violations ran counter to Carter's human rights policy. To
ignore them would render the policy meaningless. Soon after taking
office, Secretary of State Vance in February 1977 expressed disapproval
by announcing reductions in foreign aid from $32 million to $15 million. Argentine officials responded with denunciations of U.S. interference in their internal affairs. Meanwhile, human rights champions in
the U.S. Congress also demanded cuts in military aid. The Carter administration agreed and arranged, in addition, to block Argentine
loans through the Inter-American Development Bank and the Export-
Import Bank and to impose trade penalties. How to measure the consequences is a problem. In all likelihood the sanctions had more impact
on U.S. companies doing business in Argentina than on the government. Still, President Videla promised in March 1978 to restore civilian
government in another year or so—a promise he did not keep—and he
also released some political prisoners. "On balance," Gaddis Smith explains, "the application of human-rights principles" in relations with
Argentina was a mixed thing, a combination of sticks and carrots, favoring the former. As Smith also suggests, it was "not pure, but it was
good." In response, the junta may have adjusted its practices somewhat.

In relations with Brazil, defined as the most developed country in
the Third World, the era of the "unwritten alliance" had long since
passed away. For the most part the military authoritarians in control
since the mid-1960s had pursued their own course, more or less independent of the United States, unless they found it advantageous to do
otherwise. Carter had offended them during the campaign by characterizing their regime as "a miliary dictatorship" that was in many
instances "highly repressive to political prisoners." Consequently,
early in 1977, when the State Department issued a report on Brazilian human rights violations, President Ernesto Geisel simply canceled a military assistance agreement of twenty-five years' standing.
In this way, he rejected the aid before the Carter administration
could deny it.

Another issue in Brazilian relations concerned nuclear prolifera-
tion. In 1967, Brazil had refused the Treaty of Tlatelolco, banning

nuclear weapons from Latin America. Then, in June 1975, Brazil struck a deal with West German suppliers by which to increase nuclear-generating capability and to acquire the means for reprocessing uranium for weapons production. Distressed by the implications, U.S. officials objected, and the Ford administration tried without much success to mitigate the effects. When Carter, once in office, authorized a protest to Chancellor Helmut Schmidt of West Germany against sales of nuclear materials to Brazil, outraged Brazilian leaders claimed unwarranted and devious interference in their affairs. Seeking then to repair the damage, the Carter administration let up on the pressure over human rights and nuclear issues and, instead, commended Brazil for moving toward a more open political system. For symbolic reasons, the administration also arranged for a series of official visits to Brazil in 1977 and 1978 by Cyrus Vance, Rosalyn Carter, and the president himself. But despite such shows, the United States could not persuade Brazil to join in the grain embargo against the Soviet Union after the invasion of Afghanistan in 1979.

Chile   Relations with Chile also soured during the Carter years. The regime under General Pinochet was friendly toward U.S. corporations but not to Carter, who during the campaign had attacked the Nixon administration's supposed complicity in the overthrow of Salvador Allende. Though the worst excesses had ended by 1977, the State Department remained critical of human rights violations and cut back aid. Pinochet in turn aroused U.S. anger by refusing to extradite three Chileans accused of murdering a Pinochet opponent, Orlando Letelier, in Washington.[59] Poor relations persisted. The record of accomplishment for human rights advocacy remained mixed.

The Carter administration's effort to break loose from traditional Cold War constraints fell short of its aims. The Panama negotiations, despite treaties, entailed damaging political costs because of Republican attacks. The Cuban issue defied settlement, and attempts to uphold human rights in Argentina, Brazil, and Chile had ambivalent consequences. The defense of morality and reason in conjunction with power had side effects, sometimes unforeseen, that almost always precipitated complications in relations with countries defined as friendly. For the Carter administration, everything got worse during the disastrous year of 1979. A resurgence of Cold War tension following the Soviet invasion of Afghanistan altered the international context and enhanced perceptions of Carter as a weak and ineffective president. The triumph of revolutionary movements in Nicaragua and Iran had similar effects, and Carter's critics flayed him for them. In 1980, Ronald Reagan and the Republicans promised to set things right.

NOTES

1. Robert E. Quirk, *Fidel Castro* (New York: W. W. Norton, 1993), chaps. 1–6; Morris H. Morley, *Imperial State and Revolution: The United States and Cuba, 1952–1986* (New York: Cambridge University Press, 1987), chap. 2.

2. Thomas G. Paterson, *Contesting Castro: The United States and the Triumph of the Cuban Revolution* (New York: Oxford University·Press, 1994), 20.

3. Stephen G. Rabe, *Eisenhower and Latin America: The Foreign Policy of Anti-communism* (Chapel Hill: University of North Carolina Press, 1988), 118.

4. Rabe, *Eisenhower and Latin America*, 120; Paterson, *Contesting Castro*, chaps. 1–4; Louis A. Pérez Jr., *Cuba and the United States: Ties of Singular Intimacy* (Athens: University of Georgia Press, 1990), chaps. 8–9.

5. Rabe, *Eisenhower and Latin America*, 120–23.

6. Richard M. Nixon, *Six Crises* (Garden City, NY: Doubleday, 1962), 352; Rabe, *Eisenhower and Latin America*, 124.

7. Rabe, *Eisenhower and Latin America*, 124–25.

8. Richard E. Welch Jr., *Response to Revolution: The United States and the Cuban Revolution* (Chapel Hill: University of North Carolina Press, 1985), 9–26; Pérez, *Cuba and the United States*, chap. 9; Paterson, *Contesting Castro*, chaps. 21–22.

9. Rabe, *Eisenhower and Latin America*, 127–33, 141, 149.

10. Ibid., 137; Thomas G. Paterson and Dennis Merrill, eds., *Major Problems in American Foreign Relations*, 2 vols., 4th ed. (Lexington, MA.: D. C. Heath, 1995), 2:462–67.

11. Rabe, *Eisenhower and Latin America*, 163–73.

12. Thomas G. Paterson, "Fixation with Cuba: The Bay of Pigs, Missile Crisis, and Covert War against Fidel Castro," in *Kennedy's Quest for Victory: American Foreign Policy, 1961–1963*, ed. Thomas G. Paterson (New York: Oxford University Press, 1989), 126.

13. Thomas G. Paterson, "John F. Kennedy's Quest for Victory and Global Crisis," in Paterson, *Kennedy's Quest*, 3–23.

14. James N. Giglio, *The Presidency of John F. Kennedy* (Lawrence: University Press of Kansas, 1991), 45–48.

15. Stephen G. Rabe, "Controlling Revolutions: Latin America, the Alliance for Progress, and the Cold War," in Paterson, *Kennedy's Quest*, 105–22.

16. Ibid., 105–7; Edwin Lieuwen, *Generals vs. Presidents: Neo-Militarism in Latin America* (New York: Frederick A. Praeger, 1964), 10–68.

17. Jerome Levinson and Juan de Onís, *The Alliance That Lost Its Way: A Critical Report on the Alliance for Progress* (Chicago: Quadrangle Books, 1970); Rabe, "Controlling Revolutions," 110–13.

18. Rabe, "Controlling Revolutions," 110–12, 115–19; Edwin McCammon Martin, *Kennedy and Latin America* (Lanham, MD: University Press of America, 1994), chap. 10.

19. Giglio, *Presidency of John F. Kennedy*, 52–55.

20. Trumbull Higgins, *The Perfect Failure: Kennedy, Eisenhower, and the CIA at the Bay of Pigs* (New York: W. W. Norton, 1989); Giglio, *Presidency of John F. Kennedy*, 51, 55, 57.

21. Higgins, *Perfect Failure*, chaps. 7–8; Paterson, "Fixation with Cuba," 132, 136–41.

22. Vladislav Zubok and Constantine Pleshakov, *Inside the Kremlin's Cold War: From Stalin to Khrushchev* (Cambridge, MA: Harvard University Press, 1996), 206–7.

23. Ibid., 260; Paterson, "Fixation with Cuba," 142–43.

24. Giglio, *Presidency of John F. Kennedy*, 193; Michael R. Beschloss, *The Crisis Years: Kennedy and Khruschchev, 1960–1963* (New York: HarperCollins, 1991), 450.

25. Paterson, "Fixation with Cuba," 143–45.

26. Zubok and Pleshakov, *Inside the Kremlin's Cold War*, 262, 266–68; Paterson, "Fixation with Cuba," 145.

27. Roger Hilsman, *To Move a Nation: The Politics of Foreign Policy in the Administration of John F. Kennedy* (New York: Dell, 1964), chaps. 13–16; Arthur M. Schlesinger Jr., *A Thousand Days: John F. Kennedy in the White House* (Greenwich, CT: Fawcett, 1965), chap. 30; Theodore C. Sorensen, *Kennedy* (New York: Harper and Row, 1965), chap. 24.

28. Paterson, "Fixation with Cuba," 148–55; Richard J. Walton, *Cold War and Counter-Revolution: The Foreign Policy of John F. Kennedy* (Baltimore: Penguin Books, 1972), chap. 7.

29. Joseph S. Tulchin, "The Promise of Progress: U.S. Relations with Latin America during the Administration of Lyndon B. Johnson," in *Lyndon Johnson Confronts the World: American Foreign Policy, 1963–1968*, ed. Warren I. Cohen and Nancy Bernkopf Tucker (New York: Cambridge University Press, 1994), 211.

30. Paul K. Conkin, *Big Daddy from the Pedernales: Lyndon Baines Johnson* (Boston: Twayne, 1986), 176–200.

31. Tulchin, "Promise of Progress," 219–20, 227–28.

32. John H. Coatsworth, *Central America and the United States: The Clients and the Colossus* (New York: Twayne, 1994), 96; Michael J. Conniff, *Panama and the United States: The Forced Alliance* (Athens: University of Georgia Press, 1992), 116–25.

33. Tulchin, "Promise of Progress," 228–32; Coatsworth, *Central America and the United States*, 112, 114–16.

34. Gerald K. Haines, *The Americanization of Brazil: A Study of U.S. Cold War Diplomacy in the Third World, 1945–1954* (Wilmington, DE: Scholarly

Resources, 1989), chaps. 4–8; Samuel L. Baily, *The United States and the Development of South America* (New York: Franklin Watts, 1976), chap. 5; W. Michael Weis, *Cold Warriors and Coups d'Etat: Brazilian-American Relations, 1945–1964* (Albuquerque: University of New Mexico Press, 1993), 135; Elizabeth A. Cobbs, *The Rich Neighbor: Rockefeller and Kaiser in Brazil* (New Haven: Yale University Press, 1992).

35. Weis, *Cold Warriors*, 134, 138–39, 141, 143–46, 149–57, 162, 166–67.

36. Ibid., 166–68; William O. Walker III, "Mixing the Sweet with the Sour: Johnson and Latin America," in *The Diplomacy of the Crucial Decade: American Foreign Relations during the 1960s*, ed. Diane B. Kunz (New York: Columbia University Press, 1994), 62.

37. Tulchin, "Promise of Progress," 233–35; Piero Gleijeses, *The Dominican Crisis: The 1965 Constitutionalist Revolt and American Intervention*, trans. Lawrence Lipson (Baltimore: Johns Hopkins University Press, 1978), chaps. 1–3; G. Pope Atkins and Larman C. Wilson, *The Dominican Republic and the United States: From Imperialism to Transnationalism* (Athens: University of Georgia Press, 1998), chaps. 4–5.

38. Tulchin, "Promise of Progress," 235.

39. Robert Freeman Smith, *The Caribbean World and the United States: Mixing Rum and Coca-Cola* (New York: Twayne, 1994), 49; Tulchin, "Promise of Progress," 236.

40. Tulchin, "Promise of Progress," 236–37; Atkins and Wilson, *Dominican Republic and the United States*, chaps. 6–8.

41. Tulchin, "Promise of Progress," 236–37, 241.

42. Introductions to dependency theory appear in André Gunder Frank, *Latin America: Underdevelopment or Revolution: Essays on the Development of Underdevelopment and the Immediate Enemy* (New York: Monthly Review Press, 1969); Ronald H. Chilcote and Joel C. Edelstein, eds., *Latin America: The Struggle with Dependency and Beyond* (New York: John Wiley and Sons, 1974); idem, *Latin America: Capitalist and Socialist Perspectives of Development and Underdevelopment* (Boulder, CO: Westview Press, 1986); and Fernando Henrique Cardoso and Enzo Faletto, *Dependency and Development in Latin America* (Berkeley: University of California Press, 1979). Robert A. Packenham, *The Dependency Movement: Scholarship and Politics in Development Studies* (Cambridge, MA: Harvard University Press, 1992), presents a devastating criticism, seeking to disenroll dependency theory as a form of knowledge.

43. Robert D. Schulzinger, *Henry Kissinger: The Doctor of Diplomacy* (New York: Columbia University Press, 1989).

44. Seymour M. Hersh, *The Price of Power: Kissinger in the White House* (New York: Summit Books, 1983), 263.

45. Paul E. Sigmund, *The United States and Democracy in Chile* (Baltimore: Johns Hopkins University Press, 1993), 91.

46. Quirk, *Fidel Castro*, 567–85; Jorge Domínguez, *To Make a World Safe for Revolution: Cuba's Foreign Policy* (Cambridge, MA: Harvard University Press, 1989), chap. 8.

47. Michael J. Francis, "United States Policy toward Latin America during the Kissinger Years," in *United States Policy in Latin America: A Quarter Century of Crisis and Challenge, 1961–1986*, ed. John D. Martz (Lincoln: University of Nebraska Press, 1988), 35.

48. Stephen E. Ambrose, *Nixon*, 3 vols. (New York: Simon and Schuster, 1989), 2:381.

49. Ibid., 2:382–83; Francis, "Kissinger Years," 39–42; Coniff, *Panama and the United States*, 128–34.

50. William F. Sater, *Chile and the United States: Empires in Conflict* (Athens: University of Georgia Press, 1990), 139–58.

51. Hersh, *Price of Power*, 265, 278; Sater, *Chile and the United States*, 167–71.

52. Sater, *Chile and the United States*, 167–71.

53. Sater, *Chile and the United States*, presents a balanced view. Hersh, *Price of Power*; and James D. Cockcroft, *Latin America: History, Politics, and U.S. Policy*, 2d ed. (Chicago: Nelson-Hall, 1996), chap. 17, are critical of the U.S. role. Mark Falcoff, *Modern Chile, 1970–1989* (New Brunswick, NJ: Transactions, 1989), holds Allende responsible for his own demise.

54. Sater, *Chile and the United States*; Sigmund, *United States and Democracy in Chile*.

55. Gaddis Smith, *Morality, Reason, and Power: American Diplomacy during the Carter Years* (New York: Hill and Wang, 1986), chap. 1.

56. Ibid., 15, 40, 109–13.

57. Ibid., 115, 117, 127; William J. Jorden, *Panama Odyssey* (Austin: University of Texas Press, 1984).

58. Joseph S. Tulchin, *Argentina and the United States: A Conflicted Relationship* (Boston: Twayne, 1990), 141–45.

59. Smith, *Morality, Reason, and Power*, 129–31.

CHAPTER SIX

SINCE 1979
The Limits of Hegemony?

PERCEPTIONS OF FAILURE in foreign relations ruined the Carter presidency in 1979 and 1980. A seeming incapacity to respond effectively to the Soviet invasion of Afghanistan created impressions of incompetence and impotence, and the overthrow of dictatorial but pro-U.S. regimes by revolutionary forces in Iran and Nicaragua reinforced the point. According to the distinction established by Jeane K. Kirkpatrick, the United States possessed a responsibility to support and sustain less than perfect *authoritarian* rulers as bulwarks against more insidious forms of *totalitarian* communism. Under Reagan in the 1980s, the United States sought to correct the failure to do so through the exercise of determination and strength.

CARTER'S LAST DAYS

In Latin America, Carter's attempt to affirm a more valid combination of morality, reason, and power obtained a kind of vindication in the Panama Canal treaties. As Walter LaFeber notes, those agreements actually constituted a "diplomatic triumph" for the United States. By agreeing to give up control of the Canal Zone after a period of twenty-five years, the Carter administration successfully eliminated what had become a constant irritant in Latin American relations and, at the same time, John Coatsworth observes, secured from Panama an agreement to permit unilateral intervention "in perpetuity." Although the United States gave up military bases in Panama, it retained the right for its warships and commercial vessels to have top priority in case of an emergency.[1] Nevertheless, clamorous outrage among political rightists in the United States exacted a political cost. Chief among the critics, Ronald Reagan, a presidential aspirant in 1980, excoriated Carter for giving away the canal.[2]

Other conspicuous difficulties in Central America emanated to an extent from economic conditions. Unlike the 1960s, a time of booming exports for coffee and bananas, the 1970s saw trade contractions that caused instability and political polarization. The rise in oil prices during the shock of 1973 also hit Central America hard. The combined effects increased popular discontent "to levels unprecedented in Central American history." As Coatsworth explains, organizational efforts among workers and peasants seeking amelioration led to protests and demonstrations. In Costa Rica, Honduras, and Panama, conciliation on the part of political leaders headed off full-scale crises, but in Nicaragua, Guatemala, and El Salvador the traditional elites responded with ruthless repression. The result was chronic violence and conflict that reached a peak late in the 1970s.

None of Carter's advisers, who had viewed Central America as a region in which to press for human rights, anticipated the actual extent of the turmoil. In El Salvador, widespread discontent over a fraudulent election in 1977 encouraged the government of General Carlos Humberto Romero to employ terror against the opposition, using government-sanctioned death squads. Such methods ignited a civil war. Similarly, rigged elections in Guatemala brought into power the military governments of General Kjell Laugerud in 1974 and General Romeo Lucas García in 1978. Each used armed force indiscriminately against a growing guerrilla movement in the countryside, wreaking havoc among rural people. Many of the one hundred thousand Guatemalans who lost their lives for political reasons after 1954 did so during the crackdown between 1977 and 1983.[3]

In Nicaragua, by contrast, a broad-based revolutionary movement actually succeeded in taking power by ousting the right-wing regime of Anastasio Somoza. Named for Augusto César Sandino, the revolutionary hero assassinated in 1934, the Frente Sandinista Liberación Nacional (FSLN), or Sandinista National Liberation Front, encompassed a range of political views affirmed through a collective leadership. The group asserted strong nationalism, Marxist convictions, and Christian religious fervor by embracing a form of liberation theology. This shift in Roman Catholic thinking weakened the traditional association between the church hierarchy and the conservative elites of Latin America. Based on Pope John XXIII's encyclicals of 1961 and 1963, liberation theology stressed the importance of human rights and decent living standards for all people. Without these, the pope warned, a floodtide of violence and revolution could engulf the Christian world. At the Second Vatican

Council (1963–1965), he encouraged studies of economic development through the use of the social sciences. One effect was to expose Roman Catholic clergy to dependency theory as a means of explaining the stagnation of Latin American economies and the gap between the rich and the poor.

At the second General Conference of Latin American Bishops at Medellín, Colombia, in 1968, church officials went on record in support of social justice and condemned the prevalence of "institutionalized violence." This term referred to structural inequalities presumably built into political, economic, and social systems, the effects of which were poverty and powerlessness for throngs of people. As a means of alleviating inequities the bishops called upon the masses of poor people to assume greater responsibility for their own well-being by joining in positive action to ensure a fairer distribution of freedom, justice, and opportunity. Seeking to avoid the extremes of capitalism and communism, they hoped to locate a third and independent option. Just where it might reside, no one knew for sure.

Political activists found hope in the idea of working directly with poor people in the fields and slums. As one means of doing so, priests and nuns in various localities established base communities from which to advance the interests of peasants and workers in a kind of grassroots operation. Though usually nonviolent in intent, such forms of engagement and agitation exposed priests, nuns, and other dissidents to retaliation, sometimes in the form of torture and murder. In El Salvador a vigilante group known as the White Warriors circulated pamphlets that exhorted: "Be a patriot! Kill a priest!" In response, some clerics subordinated commitment to nonviolence in favor of direct political action. Consequently, by the time the third Council of Latin American Bishops met at Puebla, Mexico, in 1979, many priests and nuns at the parish level had undergone a process of radicalization that marked a growing political distance between them and their more conservative superiors. At Puebla the bishops struggled with the difficulty of achieving social justice. They condemned both capitalist and communist systems for tending to abuse human beings; at the same time, they opposed the violence perpetrated by guerrilla terrorists and by government thugs. They also criticized the selfishness of multinational corporations, affirmed the irrelevancy for most third-world countries of Walt Rostow's "stages of economic growth" theories, and endorsed broad definitions of human rights for all peoples. Church leaders paid the price; according to one source, about 850 priests, nuns, and other officials in

Latin America during the 1970s experienced intimidation, harassment, torture, or murder. As LaFeber remarks, the Roman Catholic
church had moved onto "the firing line."[4]

The advocates of change in Central America won a significant
victory on 19 July 1979 when the FSLN took over the government in
Nicaragua. Founded in 1961, the movement had been fighting the
Somoza dictatorship for eighteen years. President Anastasio Somoza
Debayle, son of the founder of the dynasty, had withstood Sandinista
guerrilla actions in the 1960s and early 1970s, usually with the aid and
assistance of the United States. But his power had waned significantly
after the earthquake of 23 December 1972. In response to the devasta-
tion in the capital city, Managua, his government's display of corruption and incompetency alienated and offended even former loyalists
in the business community and elsewhere. Consequently, as
Coatsworth explains, "widespread popular discontent" developed
among workers, peasants, and students who reacted to deteriorating
wages and landlessness with demands for democracy and justice.
Meanwhile, strong denunciations of Somoza's rule appeared in the
newspaper La Prensa and among the intellectual and political leaders
of the opposition.

As the country descended into civil war, the FSLN emerged as a
major force among Somoza's enemies. The Sandinistas had tried unsuccessfully to coordinate a major military effort against Somoza in
October 1977, but they benefited politically on 10 January 1978 when
unknown assailants assassinated Pedro Joaquín Chamorro, the anti-
Somoza publisher of La Prensa. This event triggered a series of strikes
lasting three weeks and further unsettled the nation's economy. In 1978
and 1979 the anti-Somoza agitation increased, and the guerrilla movement escalated. To the surprise of many observers, Somoza's military
forces, the National Guard, could not ensure victory against the insurgents, and Somoza as a consequence conceded defeat. On 17 July 1979,
he fled to Paraguay, where later he too was assassinated. John
Coatsworth sums up the outcome with these words: "Support for the
revolution was so widespread among all social classes and political organizations in the country that the survival of the Somoza regime, with or
without Somoza at the helm, could not have been guaranteed without
a foreign occupation."

When the Carter administration took office in January 1977, U.S.
officials displayed a tendency to overestimate Somoza's staying power.
For more than two years, Carter officials followed a consistent strategy,
seeking simultaneously Somoza's departure from office and a takeover

by political moderates instead of the FSLN. Conceivably, free elections could do the trick, but Somoza's term would not end until 1981. U.S. officials therefore indulged in a double game: on the one hand, allowing the FSLN to put pressure on Somoza, and, on the other, looking for a more moderate alternative. They hoped to achieve political transition in which the traditional political parties and the business community could play a major role. Meanwhile, Somoza attempted to save himself through obstruction and delay, seeking to prevent the emergence of a moderate alternative.

Neither strategy had the desired effect. For the United States, no workable means for locating a moderate alternative ever materialized, and Somoza was unable to save his regime. During the spring and summer of 1978 the intensification of the guerrilla war reinforced the view in the Carter administration that Somoza would have to go. The stabilization of the country presumably depended upon it, for a protracted struggle might produce such polarization that moderation could not exist. The efforts of the OAS to mediate a settlement met with failure, largely because of Somoza's resistance, and the idea of holding a national referendum, favored by other Latin Americans, also came to nothing. The United States, meanwhile, chose to wait until military setbacks forced Somoza into negotiations.

By the summer of 1979 the FSLN stood on the verge of a victory unless the United States intervened in some dramatic way to alter the outcome. U.S. leaders at this point wanted to encourage Somoza's resignation but hoped to avoid a full-scale defeat of the National Guard in order to retain some leverage for picking a successor. That aim eluded fulfillment. On 17 June 1979 the opposition established an interim government by creating a Council of National Reconstruction, a process in which the Carter administration had no say. The group consisted of Daniel Ortega, Sergio Ramírez, and Moisés Hassan—all representatives of the FSLN—plus Violeta Chamorro, the widow of the murdered newspaper editor, and Alfonso Robelo, a businessman. This fairly broad-based, collectivity attracted support from all the anti-Somoza organizations in Nicaragua, and U.S. Ambassador Lawrence Pezzullo failed in his efforts to expand the presence of political moderates. Meanwhile, units of Somoza's National Guard disintegrated completely. On 19 July 1979 the Sandinistas announced a victory.[5]

Bitter recriminations quickly followed. When the Sandinistas endorsed Marxist principles and accepted aid and support from communist Cuba, Carter's critics in the United States had a field day. Ranking high among them, Jeane K. Kirkpatrick, a political scientist from

Georgetown University, assailed Carter's shortcomings in the November 1979 issue of *Commentary*, a journal of neoconservative opinion. Her essay "Dictatorships and Double Standards" argued that Carter's "lack of realism" rather than "deep historical forces" had accounted for recent disasters in foreign affairs, typified by the overthrow of Somoza and the Iranian Shah, whom Kirkpatrick described as old friends of the United States. In her view, Carter had erred by failing to appreciate the distinction between authoritarian and totalitarian rulers. To be sure, corrupt authoritarian governments in Latin America, including the defunct regimes of Trujillo and Batista, had committed acts of oppression and thievery against their own people. But their leaders had affirmed friendship for the United States and respect for its interests; moreover, sometimes they had moved toward democracy. For such reasons, they deserved support from the United States. In contrast, totalitarians such as Hitler or Stalin and his successors deserved none because of the immensity of their crimes and atrocities; moreover, they had never moved toward democracy.[6]

Such theoretical formulations established no basis for predicting the collapse of the Soviet Union a decade later but did provide effective grounds for attacking Jimmy Carter. In the Nicaraguan case, Kirkpatrick criticized Carter for selling out a sympathetic and friendly authoritarian whose ouster opened the way for a takeover by supposedly hostile totalitarians. Instead of undercutting Somoza with criticism and pressure, she asserted, the United States should have sustained him against his enemies. Ronald Reagan agreed with this assessment and later, as president, named Kirkpatrick U.S. ambassador to the United Nations. Subsequently, when Reagan left office and a team of ghostwriters assembled his autobiography under the title *An American Life*, the nuances of Kirkpatrick's analysis escaped them completely. Indeed, they reversed the distinction by describing venal Latin American despots as totalitarians and absolute rulers in the Kremlin as authoritarians.[7] So much for political science in high places during the Reagan administration.

The question of whether Carter ever possessed the means to preserve Somoza in power or to prevent a Sandinista victory has inspired a polemical debate. His critics have claimed that wiser policies could have altered the outcome. He should have followed precedents by accepting Somoza on his terms and defending him against his enemies, or he should have headed off a Sandinista victory by getting rid of Somoza earlier, or perhaps he should have stabilized the situation by intervening with U.S. troops.

Coatsworth finds no reason for thinking that any such proposals could have succeeded. Carter officials reduced their own room to maneuver by consistently overrating Somoza's ability to remain in power. Although they hoped for his resignation, they regarded the pressure on him primarily as a means of diverting political unrest into peaceful channels through reform. Moreover, they lacked the means to shut down the anti-Somoza opposition in Nicaragua or to muzzle shows of sympathy and support for the Sandinistas all around the world. Any attempt to displace the dictator at an earlier time in favor of Nicaraguan moderates surely would have failed because of Somoza's intransigence. Finally, a U.S. military intervention would have culminated in disaster. Because of Vietnam, no support for military action existed in the United States; critics everywhere in Latin America would have opposed it; and almost certainly an intervention would have transformed Nicaragua's civil struggle into a war against foreign occupation.

As one way to limit the damage, it seemed imperative to contain the trouble by preventing an expansion of revolutionary turmoil into Guatemala and El Salvador, where rising levels of discontent entailed the possibility of civil war. During the 1970s the military-dominated governments in Guatemala responded with repression and terror, paying scant heed to Carter's emphasis on human rights. In El Salvador, however, the administration located a more effective means of exercising influence by taking advantage of divisions within the dominant military and political elites and playing them off against one another.

Carter officials initially criticized the Salvadoran regime of Carlos Humberto Romero for abusing human rights, hoping to encourage a transition to democratic rule. In 1979, seeking to avoid another Nicaragua, they shifted their ground by placing more importance on maintaining the integrity of the Salvadoran armed forces. For them, this goal required the creation of a pro-U.S. government under civilian control but willing to work with the military in support of pacification. Within the Salvadoran military the officers debated whether to pursue the goal by means of conciliation or suppression. Divisions over this issue ran deep. Meanwhile, violence mounted in rural areas. Mainly the work of right-wing elements, it centered on peasants, agitators, dissidents, and other people suspected of political infractions.

On 15 October 1979, junior officers in favor of reform carried out a takeover. A ruling council, or junta, consisted of two military men and three civilians. They promised free elections, the rule of law, and other changes to improve the agrarian, banking, and tax systems. Subsequently, as the worst forms of repression lifted, discontented groups took advantage by engaging in strikes, demonstrations, and protests. Sometimes these acts were disruptive or violent, but according to Coatsworth, "the vast majority were relatively peaceful expressions of pent-up frustration over falling real wages, declining living conditions, the lack of basic public services, and the abusive treatment of the police and the military." Nevertheless, conservative military elements reacted with "a wave of brutal attacks on popular organizations, including death-squad kidnappings and executions." The junta's orders to stop such murderous outrages proved futile. Early in January 1980 the civilian members resigned their positions, claiming that the military's behavior had destroyed a historic opportunity for a peaceful and democratic solution in El Salvador. At the insistence of the United States the army then asked the Salvadoran Christian Democratic party to represent the civilian sector in a new junta, but the party split over the issue of whether to cooperate with military officers. As an incentive in January 1980 the Carter administration restored programs of aid and assistance and tried to supervise the day-to-day activities of the Salvadoran government. Consequently, the middle-of-the-road Christian Democrats, now regarded as objects of political disdain by both extremes, became dependent on U.S. support to remain in power. Meanwhile, out-of-control security forces operating independently of the government's authority killed more than nine thousand people in 1980, most of them unarmed civilians.

The Christian Democrats cracked under the pressure and divided into factions. Only the most conservative, led by José Napoleón Duarte, agreed to remain in the government. The army instituted a state of siege and developed plans to relocate into strategic hamlets, or concentration camps, the peasant peoples suspected of aiding the guerrillas. On 24 March 1980 a death squad consisting of army officers assassinated Oscar Romero, the outspoken archbishop of El Salvador who had criticized the military. At his funeral, army contingents fired on the mourners, killing fifty and wounding six hundred.

Against high levels of repression the battered opposition parties fought to preserve political viability. On 18 April, they founded the Democratic Revolutionary Front (FDR) as an umbrella organization. It became one of the largest political movements in the nation's history by including liberal and left-wing parties, trade unions, professionals, and Roman Catholic activists. More radical guerrilla groups formed a joint political-military structure called the Farabundo Martí National Liberation Front (FMLN), named for the communist martyr killed during the great massacre of thirty thousand peasants by the government of General Maximiliano Hernández Martínez in 1932. Subsequently, the FDR and the FMLN, though distinct political groups, engaged in cooperative endeavors to advance common causes. The election of President Ronald Reagan encouraged Salvadoran elites to anticipate the abandonment of human rights issues. More murder and mayhem followed in response to the FMLN's planned "final offensive." The rebels wanted this effort to coincide with Reagan's inauguration in January 1981 but failed to accomplish much, lacking the requisite firepower.

When Carter left office, his administration could claim the accomplishment of two of its goals. The Salvadoran army remained a functioning military force, and a pro-U.S. government with a civilian front retained authority in the capital. But the costs of such successes were substantial, taking the form of a full-scale civil war. Tensions also abounded in relations with Nicaragua during the remainder of Carter's tenure. After the Sandinista victory the administration tried to uphold proprieties by maintaining formal relations while encouraging moderates in the governing coalition. By making aid and loans available and avoiding shows of hostility, U.S. leaders hoped to sidestep a confrontation. They wanted no repeat of the experience with Castro's Cuba two decades earlier. Ultimately, they desired some kind of accommodation. In contrast, the Sandinistas intended to consolidate their political authority, to establish sufficient military capability to safeguard their regime, and to keep U.S. influence in Nicaragua at a minimum. While pursuing these goals the collective leadership, increasingly under FSLN control, shifted leftward and announced a postponement of elections until 1985. By the end of 1980, FSLN dominance in the Nicaraguan government was almost complete.

Relations deteriorated further during the acrimonious U.S. presidential campaign of 1980. The agreement with Nicaragua then in effect contained an important provision stipulated by Congress: It required a halt to U.S. aid and assistance if credible evidence showed signs of Sandinista support for guerrilla insurgencies in other countries. Suspicions centered on El Salvador. By January 1981 the U.S. government possessed what it described as proof of arms shipments and other forms of support for Salvadoran guerrillas.[8] But Carter officials refrained from cutting off the aid, leaving that decision for the new administration. Under Reagan, the goals and methods of U.S. foreign policy shifted significantly.

UNDER REAGAN

President Ronald Reagan, a former sportscaster, movie actor, and television announcer, lacked experience in and, according to critics, understanding of foreign relations. His two terms as governor of California in the 1960s provided a grounding in the operations of government, but as president he often displayed a flimsy grasp of the details and implications of public issues. On one occasion, he expressed the erroneous view that intercontinental ballistic missiles could return to base after launch. On another, he was astonished to learn that the U.S. Air Force lacked the means for shooting down incoming Soviet rockets.[9]

No intellectual, Reagan won the hearts of voters and enjoyed two landslide victories in 1980 and 1984 for other reasons. His amiability, his down-to-earth homespun manner, his apparent sincerity of purpose, and his self-deprecating humor all helped to deflect criticism. Representative Patricia Schroeder, a Democrat from Colorado, called the Reagan presidency "Teflon-coated": No matter how big the mess, nothing seemed to stick to it. As Reagan once remarked, "Being a good actor pays off."

Dubbed "the great communicator," Reagan espoused simple, presumably self-evident truths. For him the federal government was the problem, not the solution, and in foreign affairs the Soviet Union was the source of most wrongdoing in the world. To combat it, Reagan assigned to his administration a conscious mission to revive U.S. hegemony. To do so, he would have to shake the country free from the effects of "the Vietnam syndrome," a debilitation supposedly suffered by the Carter administration and manifested in diplomatic impotency. Reagan embarked upon a different course; he promised to rearm the United States and to act with boldness and initiative in defense of vital interests. To confront the "evil empire"—a reference to the movie *Star Wars*, typical of Reagan's style—he mounted the greatest military buildup in the history of the world. It cost over $2 trillion. To overcome "self-doubt," he wanted a "national reawakening" based on traditional religious, patriotic, and capitalist beliefs in God, country, and enterprise. Proclaiming his own election in 1980 a portentous event, he affirmed, "We've closed the door on a long, dark period of failure."

Reagan's policies differed from Jimmy Carter's in many ways. The leaders in the new administration attached less importance to the defense of human rights and to North-South issues than to the East-West collision between the United States and the Soviet Union. For them, the Cold War assumed the highest priority. Moreover, they embraced the Kirkpatrick distinction, seeking to avoid Jimmy Carter's error by sustaining friendly authoritarians and opposing unfriendly totalitarians. In a phrase, they would allow no more Nicaraguas.

In public, administration leaders tried to present a solid phalanx of ideological unity, but behind the scenes, they squabbled in fierce bureaucratic conflicts over questions of power, prerogative, and privilege. The president often seemed aloof and oblivious. His first secretary of state, General Alexander M. Haig Jr., an aggressive professional soldier with a propensity for mixing metaphors and giving offense, conducted a sequence of feuds with officials around him. In a light moment, Reagan joked about it, saying, "Sometimes our right hand doesn't know what our far-right hand is doing." In June 1982, Haig resigned his position, frustrated, he claimed, by the absence of centralized leadership. Indeed, he said the Reagan White House was "as mysterious as a ghost ship; you heard the creak of the rigging and the groan of the timbers and even glimpsed the crew on deck. But which one of the crew was at the helm?" Haig's successor, Secretary of State George P. Shultz, carried on the tradition by dueling bureaucratically over various issues with Secretary of Defense Caspar W. Weinberger. Among other things, Shultz criticized Weinberger, a big military spender presiding over a massive buildup, for his hesitation to employ military force in support of foreign-policy objectives. Nevertheless, as Thomas G. Paterson notes, "Unlike Haig, Shultz accepted his role as the president's servant and team player" and retained Reagan's favor.[10]

In Latin America, the Reagan administration disfavored those regimes defined as hostile to the United States because of reformist or revolutionary enthusiasms and tried to cultivate improved relations with military rulers. The preferred security doctrines attached special importance to Central America and the Caribbean. As UN Ambassador Jeane K. Kirkpatrick explained, those regions have become "the most important place in the world for us," because the ability of the United States to wield global influence and to face down Soviet challenges depended on "not having to devote the lion's share of our attention and our resources to the defense of ourselves in our own hemisphere." Other officials spoke ominously of a "Moscow-Havana" axis as threatening to spread revolution. Reagan warned specifically of enemy plans to choke off the U.S. "lifeline to the outside world" and to promote destabilization by encouraging tides of unassimilable immigrants into the country. He also described Nicaragua under the Sandinistas as a

"Soviet ally on the American mainland." When in an imaginative leap he envisioned an advance guard of Sandinistas driving a convoy of armed pickup trucks to attack the border town of Harlingen, Texas, Garry Trudeau, a political philosopher and satirist, resorted to parody in his comic strip "Doonesbury." Trudeau had a group of "good ole" Texas boys with big hats and hunting rifles going out to repel the invaders.[11]

The Reagan effort to revive U.S. hegemony introduced some significant changes. The president outlined the economic component in an address before the OAS on 24 January 1982. Called the Caribbean Basin Initiative, it invoked free-market models as the best guarantee of economic growth. The program offered modest aid and lower tariffs on exports to the United States as rewards for those Caribbean countries willing to implement free-market economic reforms, but to other Latin American countries featuring pro-U.S. military regimes the president offered no equivalent. Politically, he moved toward a tougher stance. In Nicaragua, U.S. leaders stood strong in opposition to the Sandinistas and eventually tried to overthrow them. In El Salvador, they called for strong U.S. support of the military in order to suppress the guerrillas.

Viewed in retrospect, Reagan's policies in Central America, despite large efforts, failed to achieve the primary goals. When Reagan retired from office early in 1989, deteriorating economic conditions around the Caribbean had produced decreases in trade and investment; the Sandinistas still held power in Nicaragua; and the FMLN still waged guerrilla war in El Salvador. According to observers such as John Coatsworth, the United States had lost some of its hegemonic capability to dominate the politics of the region. Yet, U.S. policies still exerted a huge impact on Central America. During the 1980s a large-scale mobilization of the region's resources took place either for or against U.S. objectives. Estimated military expenditures increased from $140 million to $600 million, and the number of soldiers employed by Central American governments expanded from 48,000 to 207,000. In El Salvador, Guatemala, and Nicaragua at least two hundred thousand people died as a consequence of political violence, and as many as two million became refugees or immigrants to other countries, sometimes the United States. As Coatsworth observes, "The carnage and dislocation had profound effects on Central American society, politics, and culture," effects that might persist well into the future.

The leaders in the new administration established El Salvador as a top priority. Fearing an insurgent victory, they asked for the Pentagon's assistance in preparing a strategy to defeat the guerrillas. U.S. leaders also boosted economic and military aid, mainly in the form of outright grants. From 1980 to 1984 the military share expanded from $5.9 million to $196.6 million. Such increases, favored by the administration, required congressional approval—a potential obstacle, since leaders in the House and the Senate had grown skittish over reports of human-rights violations by the armed forces. Some of them probably wanted to bring about the defeat of the insurgents but also wanted the Salvadoran government to promote reform as a means of attracting popular support. Others preferred some kind of negotiated settlement. The Reagan administration initially responded with allegations of conspiracy, depicting the Salvadoran guerrillas as creatures of a plot engineered by the Soviets, Cubans, and Nicaraguans. To establish the point the administration issued a White Paper on 23 February 1981, supposedly based on FMLN documents, but this move failed to win over the skeptics and doubters. The Congress later sanctioned an aid package for El Salvador but attached an important condition: Every six months the president would have to certify that the Salvadoran government was making progress in defense of human rights; otherwise, the aid would stop.

On 16 July 1981, Thomas Enders, the new assistant secretary of state for inter-American affairs, delivered a speech intended to reassure members of Congress. He promised U.S. support for human rights, democratic procedures, agrarian reform, and a negotiated end to the civil war. At the same time, administration leaders sought a military victory and wanted to provide the Salvadoran army with the means for winning the war. Military advisers encouraged the adoption of smaller-scale, more fluid tactics, in part because they would inflict less collateral damage on innocent civilians than large-scale, more indiscriminate operations.

To advance at least the appearance of political authenticity, the Reagan administration facilitated the election of a constituent assembly in 1982, even though the liberal-left parties associated with the FDR refused to take part. The major players were the Christian Democrats, a party of the political center, and two new parties of the right, both pro-military: the Partido de Conciliación Nacional and the Alianza Republicana Nacional. The new constitution completed in 1983 required a presidential election in the following year. To head off right-wing candidates and to maintain congressional support, the leaders in the Reagan administration championed the candidacy of José Napoleón Duarte, a Christian Socialist. His reputation as an honorable politician with democratic commitments made the policy workable, and the Congress continued the flow of U.S. aid into El Salvador during Reagan's second term. Nevertheless, Duarte's mixed record as president included significant failures. He never succeeded in curbing the excesses of the Salvadoran military, implementing programs of agrarian reform, or negotiating a compromise settlement with the FDR-FMLN. Yet he did manage to pull off a significant accomplishment. Ironically, according to some observers, Duarte's tenure in office resulted in the creation of a complex, hybrid regime, which though certainly not a democracy in any conventional sense, established a set of political arrangements that had the effect of expanding the limits of political activity in the country. Meanwhile, the Salvadoran civil war turned into a stalemate between the army and the guerrillas. By the time President Reagan left office the number of deaths had passed seventy thousand.

In the parallel case of Nicaragua, U.S. policy under Reagan never strayed very far from the basic goal of overthrowing the Sandinista regime by supporting its enemies. At the same time, shifting domestic and international pressures required various forms of accommodation and subterfuge, some of which bordered on illegality. During Reagan's years in office, as Coatsworth explains, U.S. policy toward Nicaragua moved through four phases, in the course of which administration tactics shifted about depending on circumstances. But the main objective remained the same: getting rid of the Sandinistas through limited forms of intervention.

During the first phase, from Reagan's inauguration on 20 January 1981 until early in December 1983, the administration increased the pressure, resulting in a steady escalation of tensions in relations with Nicaragua. More specifically, the leaders employed a variety of military measures against the Sandinistas, including the organization and funding of a counterrevolutionary military group called the *contras*, an abbreviation of the Spanish *contrarrevolucionarios*. Led by former military officers in Somoza's National Guard, they initially mounted raids into Nicaragua out of bases in Honduras and Costa Rica. During this phase, Reagan officials rejected Nicaraguan proposals for negotiations, spurned West European and Latin American calls for mediation, employed CIA agents to mine harbors and attack other targets in Nicaragua, sponsored large-scale and intimidating military exercises from outposts in Honduras, and asked the Pentagon to investigate the workability of direct military intervention. The administration also suspended the economic aid program initiated by Carter, pressured the West Europeans to scale back their assistance, and reduced the Nicaraguan sugar quota in the United States by 90 percent. This phase ended late in 1983 when, as a political choice, the president decided to downplay the Nicaraguan issue in preparation for his bid for reelection.

During the second phase, extending until the presidential election on 6 November 1984, the administration shifted ground, making a show of seeking accommodation. The leaders publicly accepted a congressional ban on aid to the *contras* but secretly attempted to circumvent it. They also claimed readiness to open negotiations with Nicaragua and to support mediation by the so-called Contadora Group, named for Panama's Contadora Island, the location of a meeting among the governments of Colombia, Mexico, Panama, and Venezuela. Unexpectedly, the group's efforts nearly succeeded when the Nicaraguans surprised everyone by agreeing to sign a proposed peace agreement—but not one that the Reagan leadership really wanted. Hoist with its own petard, the administration had a problem based on its own rhetoric, having created a false impression that mediation actually could bring about an acceptable agreement.

During the third phase, lasting until November 1986, Reagan's second administration escalated the conflict with Nicaragua. The leaders suspended negotiations, imposed a full economic embargo, refused to accept the jurisdiction of the International Court of Justice over Central American matters, and persuaded Congress to vote military aid to the *contras* for the first time. Other endeavors sought to isolate Nicaragua from international sources of aid and assistance—activities constituting a form of intervention but stopping short of outright military action. In any case, the latter became unfeasible after 4 November 1984, when the Republicans lost control of the Senate to the Democrats in the midterm elections. Two weeks later, troubles deepened for the Reagan administration because of the Iran-*contra* scandal.

During the fourth phase, from November 1986 until the inauguration of George Bush in January 1989, the Reagan administration displayed less and less capacity to exercise control of events in Central America. As a proposed means of working toward peace the so-called Arias plan generated a great deal of interest, despite administration opposition, by obtaining endorsements from the Contadora Group, other South American countries, and the communist bloc. The U.S. Congress also extended support, significantly, while rejecting appeals for more military aid to the *contras*. By January 1989 the peace process, in full swing, had isolated the *contras* politically and enabled the Nicaraguan government to begin planning for elections. Again according to Coatsworth, "U.S. policy toward Nicaragua had virtually collapsed."[12]

The Reagan administration had opposed the Sandinistas from the beginning, arguing that under them, Nicaragua would become a Marxist-Leninist bastion and an agency for extending Soviet influence—another Cuba in the New World. Academic specialists and journalists called the claim into question. Many doubted the relevance of communist models for Nicaragua. According to Coatsworth, the Sandinistas "never abandoned [their] public commitment to 'pluralist democracy' and a mixed economy," never carried out large-scale programs of nationalization, and never imposed "a single-party monopoly on political power." They, of course, did "consolidate their authority as the country's dominant political party, mobilize domestic support through a diverse array of mass organizations, create a new security apparatus impervious to U.S. influence, and seek closer relations, including economic and military aid, from a wide range of foreign governments"—among them, countries from the Soviet bloc. Nevertheless, Coatsworth speculates that the Sandinista regime, if left to its own devices, might have developed according to "a populist variant of the Mexican model," resulting in "a relatively open political system." Similarly, in economics the regime probably would have embraced "a state-centered development model" in which investors and entrepreneurs would have had to accept high levels of supervision and regulation. At the same time, Nicaragua's dependence on trade would have functioned as a powerful incentive for assigning some autonomy to the private sector.[13]

Sandinista foreign policies favored nonalignment, admittedly with a tilt away from the United States. The leaders preferred caution both in dealings with the United States and in exporting the revolution to other countries. No doubt the regime extended some aid to the Salvadoran FMLN in 1980–81, possibly hoping by such means to deflect the Reagan administration from concentrating too exclusively on Nicaragua. Sandinista leaders never made a secret of their sympathy for the Salvadoran rebels but hesitated to engage in large-scale efforts in their support.

The Reagan administration nevertheless accused the Sandinistas of totalitarian proclivities and shifted U.S. support away from political moderates, mainly businessmen and politicians, in favor of the more extreme right-wing *contras*. In the ensuing diplomatic tug-of-war, Sandinista leaders tried to signal Washington their willingness to lift restriction on civil liberties if, in return, Reagan officials would call off the *contras*. But administration leaders, though engaged in various forms of subterfuge for public-relations purposes, remained committed to the ouster of the FSLN by military means.

During the *contra* war the Sandinistas refrained from systematic repression of the opposition but not from periodic harassment. Their government compiled a mixed record: It censored the main opposition newspaper, *La Prensa*, and also radio broadcasts put on by the Roman Catholic Church, yet opposition parties ran candidates in the 1984 elections and also participated in writing the new constitution. And their wartime restrictions on civil liberties never resulted in the wholesale abuses so common in El Salvador, Guatemala, and formerly in Somoza's Nicaragua.[14]

Soon after the Sandinistas took over, the *contras* initiated raids into Nicaragua from along the Honduran border. Such practices had the sanction of Honduran officials who wanted to contain the revolution in Nicaragua. The *contras* also won support from the Argentines, whose government under General Leopoldo Galtieri provided military training for them as a favor to the Reagan administration. This association, as it turned out, conveyed false impressions to Argentine leaders. Because of delusionary notions about the existence of intimate ties with the United States, the Argentine government in 1982 indulged in the colossal miscalculation of allowing the armed forces to settle an old issue by challenging Great Britain for control of the Falkland Islands (Islas Malvinas). The Argentines premised this undertaking on a mistaken supposition that the United States would stand with them against Great Britain in defense of the Monroe Doctrine. The magnitude of their error became evident in a short war, beginning in April 1982, in which Argentine military and naval forces took a drubbing. Contrary to their expectation the United States provided neither assistance nor solace. On the bright side the defeat discredited the Argentine generals and speeded a process toward democratization, ending the "dirty war" against alleged radicals and subversives.[15]

Reagan officials had advised members of the Senate Intelligence Committee in March 1981 of their intentions to create a paramilitary force of five hundred men, supposedly for the purpose of stopping the flow of military supplies from Nicaragua to the guerrillas in El Salvador; they later committed nearly $20 million in support of the plan. The CIA assisted in the creation of the Nicaraguan Democratic Front to take political charge. The *contra* forces had expanded to about fifteen thousand by the late 1980s, mainly through the recruitment of peasant boys from remote regions. Fighting capabilities depended upon arms and supplies provided by the U.S. government, either directly or through intermediaries. Early on, the funding came from the CIA. In 1983 the U.S. Congress voted in favor of continuing it, but in the following year a series of damaging revelations undermined congressional resolve to support the administration. Reports indicated that CIA operatives had carried out terrorist attacks and mined Nicaraguan harbors; other sources of information attributed corruption, human-rights abuses, and possibly drug trafficking to the *contras*. Consequently, congressional support, especially among Democrats, became sporadic and unreliable.

From the administration's viewpoint, Congress was indulging in obstructionism. In December 1982 the so-called Boland amendment, the first of two named for Representative Edward P. Boland, a Massachusetts Democrat who chaired the House Select Committee on Intelligence, forbade any U.S. expenditure for the purpose of overthrowing the Sandinista regime. The Reagan administration responded with evasion, claiming no intent to force out the Sandinistas but only to interdict the flow of military supplies into El Salvador. Congress reacted by imposing the same restriction a second time but without much effect. In 1984 it passed another Boland amendment, this one flatly banning any aid by U.S. intelligence agencies to the *contras*. The Reagan administration then permitted an elaborate deception under the conduct of Colonel Oliver North, a Marine Corps officer on loan to the National Security Council. Taking the form of clandestine operations, North's illicit activities provided more than $50 million in arms and supplies to the *contras* between 1984 and 1986 and precipitated what came to be known as the Iran-*contra* scandal, a major episode during the second Reagan administration.

The funds came from various sources, including private donors and foreign countries—among them, Costa Rica, El Salvador, Guatemala, Honduras, Israel, Panama, Saudi Arabia, and Taiwan—and moved through complicated networks organized by North and other U.S. military and intelligence officials. The most blatant of these undertakings, the one tying Iran to the ensuing scandal, actually engaged the administration in violations of its own policy banning the sale of weapons to alleged terrorists. Under such terms, Iranian leaders—that is, the Islamic fundamentalists who had taken power in 1979 while denouncing the United States as "the great Satan"—did not qualify. But North's deal provided a loophole: They could buy antitank missiles and weapons parts if, in return, they provided assistance in seeking freedom for a group of U.S. hostages held by other alleged terrorists in Lebanon. The proceeds from the sales may have run as high $30 million. When the news broke during the fall of 1986 amid great public outrage, congressional support for the Reagan administration's policies in Central America simply withered away.

Even with arms and supplies provided by these dubious methods, the *contras* lacked the capacity to throw the Sandinistas out of office. Successes on the battlefield eluded them in confrontations with the Nicaraguan army. In addition, they never developed enough political credibility; too many of Somoza's former National Guard officers occupied positions of authority. Together, military incapacity and political weakness rendered the *contra* stand against the Sandinista revolution a futility.

Meanwhile, the Reagan administration reiterated its willingness to accept a negotiated settlement but never seriously attempted one. In 1981, for example, Assistant Secretary of State Thomas Enders suggested the possibility of improving relations if the Sandinistas would sever ties with the Soviets, stop their aid to the FMLN in El Salvador, and scale back the size of their armed forces. The Sandinistas expressed some interest in the plan but had their own expectations. In particular, the Reagan administration would have to halt its aid to the *contras*. The proposed negotiations went nowhere. The same held true for another such attempt in 1984. No subsequent efforts took place. In a bitter characterization of the U.S. position, Nicaraguan Foreign Minister Miguel D'Escoto complained, "What President Reagan has said is: 'You drop dead or I will kill you.' "

Documents released during the Iran-*contra* investigations show that administration leaders understood the inherent limitations of the *contra* movement. Why then should the United States have embarked upon a course of action bound to fail? The body of literature suggests various interpretations. The journalist Roy Gutman points to bureaucratic politics. According to him, Reagan's uninvolved style of decision making invited competition among the policymakers and resulted in a failure to develop coherent diplomatic objectives. This circumstance supposedly favored hard-line *contra* supporters who exploited the president's deficiencies for their own purposes. Another line of explanation places the responsibility on domestic politics: The administration could not abandon the *contras* without alienating the right wing of the Republican party upon whose votes the leaders depended to sustain them. A third explanation places Nicaraguan policy within a larger context. Though possibly irrational in a narrow sense, William LeoGrande has argued, the pro-*contra* commitment made sense as part of "the longer term goal of breaking the back of the domestic political opposition to Reagan's aggressive use of military force to overthrow the government of Nicaragua." In other words, the long-term intent sought "to create the political support necessary for a direct U.S. military intervention." As Coatsworth remarks, Reagan officials never publicly proposed to employ U.S. military forces to overthrow the Sandinista government. On the other hand, they never ruled out the option. Indeed, by undertaking Operation Urgent Fury in October 1982, a military intervention against a government described as communist on the tiny Caribbean island of Grenada, the Reagan administration may have intended, among other things, to underscore the possible validity of similar measures elsewhere—for example, in Nicaragua.[16]

U.S. policies in Central America elicited a sequence of efforts by other countries to find political solutions. Early attempts by the Contadora Group—Colombia, Mexico, Panama, Venezuela—failed, but a subsequent effort in 1987 did succeed, once the Iran-*contra* scandal had sufficiently weakened faith in the administration's position. The Arias plan—named for its main sponsor, President Oscar Arias of Costa Rica—won support from the Contadora Group, the other countries of Central America, and the Speaker of the House Jim Wright, a Democrat from Texas. Indeed, Wright played a vital role in extracting from the Reagan administration a commitment to abandon its efforts to overthrow the Sandinistas in exchange for specific Nicaraguan concessions.

Fundamentally, the agreement contained these provisions. The Nicaraguan government and the *contras* would initiate a process aimed at a cease-fire, after which the United States would terminate military aid to the *contras*; similarly, the Soviet bloc would cease arms shipments to the Sandinistas. Humanitarian aid, in contrast, could continue in each instance. To round out the arrangements, Nicaragua would move away from the state of emergency, restore civil liberties, create an electoral commission with representation for all parties, and make plans for a national election. Support from many sources helped to clinch the deal, especially from Argentina, Brazil, Peru, and Uruguay (the four new South American democracies), the West European countries, the Soviet bloc, the United Nations, and the Organization of American States. If the Reagan administration counted on Nicaraguan

why FSLN accepted contadora

opposition to defeat the Arias plan, as was probably the case, the Sandinistas served up another surprise by endorsing it, even though acceptance required negotiation with the hated *contras* and subjected Nicaraguan politics to external supervision. According to Coatsworth, "The Sandinista leaders took a calculated risk: they traded sovereignty for peace, with the expectation that internationally supervised elections would, in the end, confirm the FSLN in power." Economic necessity probably compelled it. The *contra* war, U.S. economic sanctions, and the Sandinistas' own miscalculations had placed their country in an economic depression. By the time Reagan left office in January 1989, the Nicaraguans had complied with the peace accord and set a date for national elections on 25 February 1990. They did so in the expectation of winning the contest and then repairing the damage already done to their ravaged economy.[17]

AFTER THE COLD WAR

During the one-term presidency of George Bush, from 1989 to 1993, a sequence of astonishing events transformed the structure of international relations for the entire world: After more than forty years the Cold War suddenly came to an end. To the surprise of most observers, the Soviet Union precipitated the process by allowing the East European nations to declare independence and then itself dissolved and disappeared as the various constituent states of the USSR affirmed their sovereign rights.[18]

For Latin Americans, these world historical events had at least three main consequences. First, the end of the Cold War reduced the levels of rivalry and competition among the Great Powers in the Western Hemisphere. The Soviet Union, a principal player, no longer existed, and others—mainly the West Europeans and the Japanese—shifted their attention toward the new states emerging from the former Soviet Union. For Latin Americans, not all of the implications were positive. For example, what if these changes diverted the international flow of capital away from the south toward the east, thereby enhancing Latin American dependence on the United States? In response, Latin Americans engaged in maneuvers to enlarge political and economic relations with West Europeans and the Japanese and also to structure dealings with the United States to benefit themselves, notably through the negotiation of free-trade agreements.

Second, the presumed security threat posed to the United States in the Western Hemisphere by the Soviet Union and its allies simply ceased to exist. This shift altered the debate in the United States over Central America, specifically by undermining a principal argument in favor of interventionist activities. Seeking to place this matter in a proper context, Coatsworth argues that no significant U.S. security interests ever had been at stake in Central America during the 1980s. Rather, the region had taken on importance for the Reagan administration largely as a function of maintaining U.S. credibility in the East-West struggle. Consequently, when the Cold War ended, Central America ceased to have as much importance.

Third, the Soviet collapse shuffled political priorities in Latin America. Notably, it set back and confused various radical and populist movements traditionally looked upon by the United States as hostile to its interests. At the same time, it also undermined the position of right-wing, pro-military, and anticommunist groups whose status derived at least in part from U.S. support. In other words, the end of the Cold War played down the incentive for the United States to become involved in local politics. It also strengthened a trend toward democratization, the long-term consequences of which might favor social reform.

Bush

The Bush administration responded to these new conditions with diverse policies, some of which suggested continuity and others change. Bush built on the Caribbean Basin Initiative of the Reagan era by adding in 1990 a new Free Enterprise Initiative for the Americas. Its promises included increases in U.S. aid and the negotiation of free-trade agreements as rewards if Latin American countries complied with U.S. policy preferences in economic affairs. On similar grounds, President Bush also encouraged new agreements on debts, allowing Latin Americans to reduce debt service obligations if they would accept austerity programs. Since relations with Mexico also required attention after some deterioration during the Reagan years, in part because of Mexican opposition to U.S. policies in Central America, in 1992 the United States, Mexico, and Canada signed the North American Free Trade Agreement (NAFTA) for the purpose of obtaining closer political and economic ties among the three nations.

As one of their top priorities, the leaders in the Bush administration wanted to eliminate Central America as a political issue and a cause of contention between the White House and the Congress. Acting fast, they dealt with one trouble spot, Panama, by removing from power the head of state, General Manuel Antonio Noriega. Though once a CIA asset in the funneling of aid to the *contras*, he had become a liability as a notorious drug smuggler and a violator of human rights. In disregard of

Panama

the OAS charter, U.S. military forces unilaterally invaded Panama on 23 December 1989, seized Noriega, and installed a new government. The former strongman ended up in a federal detention center in Miami, where in 1992 he was convicted on drug charges and sentenced to a long prison term. In explanation, Coatsworth argues that the Panama invasion "was not undertaken to defend traditional U.S. economic or security interests" but "in response to U.S. domestic political circumstances." Noriega's defiant involvement with drug smuggling threatened the Bush administration by jeopardizing its relations with Congress and its credibility in foreign affairs.

The Bush administration also responded favorably to the outcome of elections in Nicaragua. On 25 February 1990, Violeta Chamorro, the wife of the murdered publisher of *La Prensa* and the candidate backed by a coalition of fourteen opposition parties, won a majority of the votes in an election supervised by international authorities. The defeat of President Daniel Ortega, the Sandinista nominee, came as a surprise to many observers and may have occurred in part because Nicaraguan voters anticipated a positive reaction from the United States, perhaps in the form of economic aid to help revive their sagging economy. Moreover, the intervention in Panama may have persuaded some Nicaraguans that their country might come next.

The conflict in El Salvador finally terminated on 31 December 1991, when the guerrillas and the government signed a peace agreement. According to its terms, the guerrillas had to lay down their arms. In return, the government would scale back the size of the armed forces, eliminate abuses by the military, and guarantee the exercise of political and human rights. In this case the Bush administration, unlike its predecessor, came around to support the negotiation process as a viable means of solving the problem.[19]

For the rest of Latin America the end of the Cold War entailed, at the very least, uncertainty about what new kind of international order might emerge from the wreckage of the old and how it would affect the conduct of relations with the United States and the rest of the world. In *Talons of the Eagle: Dynamics of U.S.-Latin American Relations*, published in 1996, the political scientist Peter H. Smith provides some insight into a new "age of uncertainty." He identifies three fundamental effects. First, the end of the Cold War produced a new "multipolarity" that contrasted markedly with the "bipolar dominance" of the United States and the Soviet Union and meant a more even distribution of power and capability among the nations of the world. Second, it encouraged a process of "democratization," that is, a "transition . . . from authoritarianism toward pluralism," whose effects appeared prominently in East European countries (the former East Germany, Poland, Hungary, and Czechoslovakia) and also in Latin America, notably in Argentina, Brazil, Chile, and Peru. Third, it reduced the blatant competition and hostility associated with the Cold War and offered the possibility of establishing new priorities for defining goals and allocating resources.[20]

Accounting for such momentous change immediately set off a polemical debate in which one side underscored the importance of indigenous causes within the Soviet Union and the other the significance of competitive pressures from the United States. The question of whether the Soviet Union collapsed primarily for internal or for external reasons will probably divide historians forever. According to Thomas G. Paterson, "The Cold War waned because the contest had undermined the power of its two main protagonists." The costs had exceeded the gains in a cyclical process experienced by other Great Powers since the fifteenth century. To maintain themselves, the superpowers required "the restoration of their economic well-being and the preservation of their diminishing global positions." Bringing an end to the Cold War became a matter of enlightened self-interest. To be sure, the Soviet Union took a far greater fall than the United States; nevertheless, "the implications of decline became unmistakable for both: The Cold War they made in the 1940s had to be unmade if the two nations were to remain prominent international superintendents."[21] In the process, the old Soviet Union ceased to exist.

How to measure the impact on U.S. relations with Latin America also poses many problems. According to some observers, the U.S. ability to exercise hegemony over Latin America declined gradually during the Cold War and dropped off even further after 1989. For example, the U.S. share of Latin American exports fell from 45 percent in 1958 to 34 percent in the late 1970s. The U.S. share of direct foreign investments went down—in Brazil's case from over 50 percent in 1965 to 30 percent in 1979—as did weapons sales. All during the 1980s, Central American difficulties functioned as public-relations disasters for the United States in the rest of Latin America. And in 1982 the Reagan administration could not head off an unwanted war over the Falkland Islands. Such outcomes suggested a reduced capacity to dominate the region.[22] Still another argument in support of this claim depicts U.S. interventions in Latin America during the Cold War as manifestations of weakness. According to political scientist Abraham Lowenthal, for example, U.S. efforts to overthrow Salvador Allende in Chile were "anachronistic," since "U.S. preponderance in the Americas was already substantially diminished." Similarly, according to Paterson, U.S. interventions in the 1970s and 1980s "attested not to U.S. strength but to the loosening of its imperial net." This view implies that the survival of Castro's regime in Cuba shows the limits of U.S. hegemonic capability.[23]

In a contradictory assessment, Peter H. Smith argues that "this notion of declining hegemony rests on dubious assumptions," specifically, the erroneous notions that hegemony requires "near total control" over Latin America and that Latin American resistance became a bigger problem for the United States during the 1980s than it was before. Yet even in the 1950s, the refusal of Latin American countries to send troops to Korea, the anti-Nixon riots in Caracas, and the Cuban Revolution all showed the limits of U.S. domination. Nevertheless, the United States in his view has exercised "a strong and continuous degree of hegemony over the Western Hemisphere from the 1950s to the 1990s." If "within this overall pattern, U.S. hegemony suffered a slight decline from the 1960s to the 1980s," it "climbed to an all-time high between the mid-1980s and mid-1990s." In other words, "the general trend has *always* been for the United States to exert a great degree of influence over Latin American countries," even though "the level of this influence revealed some oscillation (up, down, up) from the mid-1950s to the present time."

To substantiate the point, Smith presents an array of data concerning gross domestic product (GDP) and population size. As he argues, "The differences in demographic trajectories are startling." In 1950 the number of people in all the Latin American countries and in the United States was about the same, 150 million. By 1990 the population of Latin America had exceeded that of the United States by a margin of 436 million to 250 million. Yet the U.S. economy consistently outproduced the economies of Latin America. The GDP of the United States was more than seven times as large as Latin America's in 1950, seven times as large in 1970, and five times as large in 1990. In 1950 the U.S. GDP was thirty times Argentina's, thirty-three times Brazil's, and thirty-seven times Mexico's; in 1990, it was fifty-eight times Argentina's, thirteen times Brazil's, and twenty-three times Mexico's. To underscore the implications, he claims, "Within the global arena, the United States lost a good deal of ground in relation to the other major powers between 1950 and 1990; within the Western

Hemisphere, by contrast, the United States managed to retain its position of preponderance."

Smith draws similar conclusions from the data on trade. In spite of gains by the West Europeans and the Japanese, the United States in 1990 ranked as the largest single trading partner for every country in the region. As for investments, from 1990 to 1992 the United States put about $22 billion into Latin America—nearly twice the amount from Western Europe and Japan—suggesting that it "thus asserted and affirmed its hemispheric position of economic supremacy." Though the West Europeans and the Japanese improved their positions, "they did not begin to pose a political challenge to Washington's preeminence in the Americas."

Smith explains the circumstance by holding that "United States predominance resulted in large part from a systematic retreat by extrahemispheric rivals," resulting in "hegemony by default" because "outside powers withdrew from the Americas and directed their attention elsewhere." The West Europeans concentrated on Eastern Europe; the Russians disengaged to deal with matters at home; and the Japanese too had other priorities. Lacking much competition the United States retained its "supremacy," characterized by Smith as "uncontested" and "complete."

What importance should the United States as a Great Power attach to Latin America in the post-Cold War era? The answer in many ways holds more significance for the people of Latin America than for the United States. In purely economic terms, Latin America has declined in significance for the United States. Its share of total U.S. trade worldwide declined from 28–35 percent in 1950 to 12–14 percent in the mid-1970s, where it has remained for the most part ever since. By the 1990s, Mexico accounted for half of the U.S. trade in Latin America, establishing the southern neighbor as the third-ranked trading partner, behind Canada and Japan. Trade elsewhere in the region amounted to less and less for the United States, certainly in comparison with the 1950s.

Patterns of investment reflected a similar decline in relative importance. In 1950, Latin America accounted for over one-third of U.S. direct overseas investments. By 1970, Latin America absorbed about 16 percent and by 1990 less than 10 percent; Western Europe, Canada, and Asia had become much more significant. To be sure, the absolute value of U.S. investments in Latin America and the Caribbean regions ran toward $71.6 billion, a substantial sum. Yet in the global context, Latin America had less importance to the United States than previously. As Smith states, such trends in trade and investment "meant that in comparison with previous periods the United States would have *less* at stake in its dealings with Latin America—at a time when Latin America would have *more* at stake in the United States."

In the social and cultural realms, by contrast, Latin America has gained in importance to the United States. This conclusion follows from the growing numbers of people with antecedents in Latin America moving into the United States, coming in largest numbers from Mexico, Puerto Rico, and Cuba. By 1990 the U.S. Hispanic population ran to 22.3 million, about 9 percent of the total. This figure marked a 53 percent increase over the 1980 count of 14.6 million, establishing Hispanics among the fastest growing segments in U.S. society. About 60 percent had Mexican origins, 12 percent Puerto Rican, and 5 percent Cuban. Collectively, Hispanics concentrated in four states—California, Texas, New York, and Florida—where they exercised growing influence over popular culture (music), sports (baseball), and politics (especially at the local and state levels).

Such mixed circumstances have raised significant questions over how the United States might deal with Latin America in the future. According to public-opinion indicators in the United States, the prevailing attitudes of other citizens toward Latin Americans still exhibit heavy doses of ignorance, disdain, and indifference. Not many people have felt much need to learn about Latin America or to assist in the resolution of regional problems. Does the same hold true for U.S. leaders? Will they withdraw from the region, seek joint initiatives, or pursue their own perceptions of national interest by essentially unilateral means? Smith makes some preliminary observations.

In the early 1990s an assortment of mutual economic concerns moved to the forefront in U.S.-Latin American relations, constituting a "new economic agenda." The prospect of convergence among economic interests suggested at least a possibility that stronger forms of international cooperation might come about. Such hopes emanated primarily from joint efforts to cope with questions concerning international debt, trade, and environmental protection.

The debt crisis of the 1980s had its origins in the 1970s, when Latin American countries—notably Argentina, Brazil, Mexico, and Venezuela— accepted the risks of negotiating a sequence of high-interest loans with international bankers. Consequently, their international indebtedness rose to unprecedented levels, from $30 billion in 1970 to $240 billion in 1980. Meanwhile, their capacity to make payments on the loans went into eclipse because of a decline in income from the sale of exports in overseas markets. By the early 1980s, Latin Americans were caught in a vicious squeeze; they had to borrow more and more to keep up with their payments on debt service. Between 1975 and 1985, their external debt expanded from $99 billion to $384 billion.

Mexico first experienced the seriousness of the situation in August 1982, when government officials informed U.S. leaders of their incapacity to meet their obligations. To cope with the problem, a sequence of complex negotiations ensued: Mexico took on an additional loan of $3.96 billion from the International Monetary Fund (IMF) and in return agreed to reschedule payments on other loans and to institute a program of economic stabilization by reducing inflation and public-sector deficits. Over the next ten years, other Latin American countries experienced similar calamities, and in each instance the international community responded with the same kinds of measures. The IMF functioned as the source of additional loans. To qualify for them, each country had to accept an austerity program to contain inflation and to cut back on public debt.

Such emergency responses had the positive effect of warding off national bankruptcies but also had an undesirable side. For Latin America the 1980s became "the lost decade" in which "economic and social progress was negligible at best, negative at worst." Smith describes the problem: "Renegotiations and restructuring led to reliance upon continuous lending (and borrowing), which forced the region's external debt up from $242 billion in 1980 to $431 billion by 1990." As a consequence, "economic growth for Latin America came to a virtual halt." Indeed, "by 1989 nearly a third of the region's population lived in poverty . . . up from 27 percent a decade earlier." This grim figure meant that the number of impoverished people in Latin America had increased by 45 to 50 million. "No matter what the measurement, the social reality was clear: for peasants, workers, and downwardly mobile segments of the middle class, the debt crisis had a devastating impact."

The rising levels of poverty and hardship convinced the international financial community that Latin America required fundamental economic reforms. Specific measures for advancing them followed from the prevailing view in Washington that the crisis was attributed to excessive reliance on state intervention and import-substitution strategies. How could Latin Americans generate long-term economic viability? According to an emerging "Washington consensus" the appropriate method was clear: Only the utilization of free-market capitalism could have the desired effects by limiting the role of the state, supporting the private sector, and implementing free trade.

What Smith calls "the mantra of free trade" became an obsessional concern among many leaders in response to the debt crises of the 1980s. In the middle of the decade, Argentina and Brazil began to discuss freeing trade, later including Uruguay and Paraguay in a partnership of four countries. In 1990, Mexico suggested to Canada and the United States the creation of a North American free-trade area, and in the same year, President Bush called for a free-trade zone to encompass the whole of the Western Hemisphere. Seeking to end the economic woes of recent times, the free-trade movement anticipated a process of regional economic integration in which the removal of state barriers would facilitate the exchange of goods, services, capital, and people. *NAFTA*

The most ambitious undertaking was NAFTA, which brought Mexico, Canada, and the United States together in a common endeavor. Taking effect in January 1994, it created one of the two largest trading blocs in the world, with a 1992 population of 370 million and a combined economic production of about $6 trillion, North America could rival the European Union. The agreement promoted free trade among the members by eliminating duties, tariffs, and trade barriers over a period of fifteen years. It also opened Mexico to U.S. investments in various ways: Under its terms, U.S. banks could establish branches in Mexico, and U.S. citizens could invest in Mexico's banking and insurance industries. In fact, for Mexico, NAFTA was primarily about investments. By gaining preferential access to U.S. markets, Mexican leaders hoped to attract significant amounts of foreign capital.

NAFTA elicited strenuous opposition within the United States from organized labor and small businesses. These groups feared a flow of jobs into Mexico, where lower wages beckoned employers seeking to reduce costs. The proponents, in contrast, expected that NAFTA would stimulate exports and enhance U.S. competitiveness. During the presidential campaign of 1992, one candidate, the Texas billionaire Ross Perot, tried to make an issue of the treaty, claiming that it would drain away jobs. The Democratic candidate, Bill Clinton, defended the treaty against such criticism and ended up carrying the day. After the election the House of Representatives and the Senate both endorsed NAFTA by lopsided margins. Whether acceptance of NAFTA will pave the way for larger-scale cooperative endeavors, specifically, the creation of a Western Hemisphere free-trade area, remains a question for the future.

Another issue inviting international cooperation was environmen- *Environt* tal protection. Potential hazards such as the depletion of the ozone layer, the phenomenon of global warming, and deforestation of the Amazon

River basin in Brazil aroused mounting concern. Carbon dioxide emissions from automobiles, industrial waste, acid rain, and the lack of sanitation facilities all threatened public health in Latin America, especially in the great metropolises such as Mexico City, São Paulo, and Santiago de Chile.

The proper means of addressing environmental issues elicited profound differences, especially between the industrialized countries of the North and the developing countries of the South. As Smith notes, "Each side wanted to place its own concerns at the top of the international agenda and to blame the other for its contribution to environmental deterioration." Typically, advocates from the North stressed impending dangers for the future as countries such as China, India, and Brazil underwent the process of industrialization; they also urged the importance of population control. Advocates from the South, in contrast, argued that growing populations in their countries threatened the well-being of the planet much less than the excessive consumption of the industrial countries. They insisted further that the basic problem for the Third World was not its people but its poverty.

How to reconcile such views, distribute the costs, and determine other obligations became immense problems. In 1987 the United Nations World Commission on Environment and Development presented a report in favor of "sustainable development," defined as economic development that "meets the needs of the present without compromising the ability of future generations to meet their own needs." This position established a place to begin, but its vagueness invited an assortment of definitions and interpretations. For example, northern countries usually held southern countries responsible for funding their own environmental protection programs by redistributing resources, reducing military spending, privatizing public enterprises, getting rid of corruption, and revising economic priorities. Southern countries argued that they should not have to pay for problems they did not create; that obligation resided with the North.

For such reasons, many observers anticipated that the United Nations Conference on Environment and Development, held in Rio de Janeiro in June 1992, would precipitate bitter clashes. Dubbed the Earth Summit, this assemblage turned into the largest international conference ever held. It attracted more than 100 heads of state, 8,000 delegates from around the world, 9,000 members of the press, and 3,000 accredited representatives from nongovernmental organizations. Fortunately, the worst expectations failed to materialize. The main accomplishment was the adoption of Agenda 21, which established a plan to guide the policies of governments as they moved into the twenty-first century. Consisting of 40 chapters covering 115 programs in more than 400 pages of text, Agenda 21 addressed a broad range of environmental and developmental issues and sought to institute a partnership between developed and developing countries in search of "sustainable development." A central premise held that both a reduction of poverty in poor countries and an alteration of consumption patterns in rich countries would be necessary steps toward the goal. According to Smith, "Many experts concluded that Agenda 21 represented a workable framework for international collaboration on environmental matters."[24] At the very least, it constituted a departure point, requiring accelerated activity by governments.

Two other issues prominent in the conduct of inter-American relations increasingly appeared impervious to the activities of government: the movement of drugs and the movement of people out of Latin America into the United States without appropriate legal sanctions. Proceeding independent of governmental authority, each has resulted in the creation of large-scale problems between governments. Both can be attributed to economic incentives: The sale of drugs came about in response to consumer demand for hallucinogenic substances; the migration of people occurred in the search for employment opportunities. The U.S. government has considered both phenomena unwelcome, as well as illegal and has sought, so far without much effect, to make them subjects of international regulation.

Drug trafficking, much like alcohol bootlegging in the 1920s, has always resisted governmental control because of the high profits. By the early 1990s, annual sales in the United States amounted to $50 billion per year. The social costs of drug abuse also ran high, calculated at $60 billion per year, partly the result of higher law enforcement costs in such cities as Miami, New York, Chicago, Los Angeles, and Washington. According to many authorities, the fundamental cause resides in consumer demand, yet the U.S. government has concentrated on supply, seeking to suppress the production of illicit drugs throughout the hemisphere. These include marijuana, cocaine, heroin, phencyclidine (PCP), lysergic acid diethylamide (LSD), and methaqualone.

U.S. antidrug measures have consisted of efforts to eliminate sources of supply by destroying crops and laboratories and to interdict shipments into U.S. markets by conducting surveillance at the border and on the high seas. By reducing the flow of drugs into the country, officials hoped to drive prices upward, beleaguer the traffickers, discourage consumption, and push the users out of the market. When public concern over the issue mounted in the 1980s, the Reagan and Bush administrations declared war. Not only was public health at stake but, according to William J. Bennett of the Office of National Drug Control Policy, the issue had become a matter of national security. The war on drugs necessarily placed a heavy emphasis on Latin America. According to some accounts, about 80 percent of the cocaine and 90 percent of the marijuana entering the United States was coming from Latin American countries. Cocaine from the Andean countries—Bolivia, Peru, Colombia, and Ecuador—became an object of special concern.

U.S. efforts to diminish supply produced persistent tension in relations with Latin American countries whose authorities withheld full and enthusiastic cooperation. As some U.S. policymakers understood, Latin American officials had to deal with a profound difficulty. What kind of incentives would encourage economically troubled countries to give up the vast revenues from a lucrative but illegal industry? They had little to gain and much to lose if they accepted the U.S. position on drugs.

Although U.S. antidrug policies failed either to reduce supply or to increase the price, other consequences bore directly on Latin Americans. The drug traffic and campaigns against it exposed the people to high levels of violence and intimidation by either drug traffickers or the authorities or both. In addition, they heightened the risk of corruption among national officials and law enforcement officers by exposing them to drug dealers with lots of money. Also, by investing ever more authority in the armed forces, antidrug activities encouraged militarization, according to critics, thereby posing a threat to new and fragile democracies. Finally, the drug wars complicated U.S.-Latin American relations. When Latin American officials responded to antidrug campaigns, they did so for different reasons, resulting in confusion and incongruity. Smith argues that Operation Just Cause, the U.S. invasion of Panama that led to the ousting of Noriega, in part came about for such reasons.

The movement of people in the Western Hemisphere also took place in many instances without government sanction. The United States, a nation of immigrants, traditionally accepted large numbers of newcomers. Between 1900 and 1910, 8.8 million legal immigrants came into the country, and during the next two decades, about 10 million more. The flow dwindled during the era of the Great Depression and then resumed after the Second World War. Various patterns stand out. Some 2.5 million immigrants entered the country in the 1950s. As the number increased to 6 million in the 1980s, the percentage of immigrants from Europe and Canada declined from 66 percent in the 1950s to 14 percent in the 1980s. This meant an increase of Asians from 6 percent to 44 percent. Legal immigration from Mexico held at 12-14 percent and from elsewhere in Latin America at 26–27 percent.

This changing composition sometimes elicited xenophobic and racist responses in the United States. In California and elsewhere, for example, Mexicans who entered the country without proper documents turned the establishment of immigration quotas into a pointless exercise. While legal entrants into the United States nearly doubled between the 1960s and 1980, vast numbers also came into the country without official authorization and in violation of the law. The exact number defies estimate, but according to demographers, probably some 2.5 to 4 million "illegal aliens" from all parts of the world were residing in the United States in 1992. About 55 to 60 percent of those people came from Mexico.

Within the Western Hemisphere, U.S. immigration policy has always paid special heed to Mexico. From the turn of the century until the 1930s an informal "open border" policy allowed U.S. employers to bring in unskilled Mexican labor to work in agriculture, mining, and construction, building an infrastructure for the Southwest. The first cycle of Mexican migration ended during the Great Depression. A second cycle got under way during the Second World War. Beginning in 1942 the U.S. government allowed temporary Mexican workers, called braceros, to enter the country to compensate for labor shortages. This program continued until 1964. During much of the twentieth century, then, the U.S. immigration quota system in practice often exempted Mexicans from typical discrimination in favor of West Europeans with job skills. Changes in the law during the 1960s expanded official quotas for Western Hemisphere nations and then contracted them a decade later. An annual limit of twenty thousand put in place in 1976 especially worked to the disadvantage of Mexicans, who experienced a "push-pull" effect. The poverty of their country "pushed" them in the direction of el norte, and the attraction of employment in the United States, even in menial capacities, "pulled" them in the same direction.

Seeking to curtail undocumented migration into the United States, the Immigration Reform and Control Act of 1986 attempted to "take control of our borders," in President Reagan's phrase, and to prevent

U.S. employers from "knowingly" giving jobs to Mexicans without proper documents. It also allowed amnesty to undocumented workers who could prove that they had resided in the United States since 1982 and partial amnesty to others who fell into different categories. The legislation obtained mixed results. Because a variety of loopholes existed, employer sanctions had marginal impact on illegal migration.

Since then, a historical shift in the migration of *indocumentados* from Mexico seems to have taken place. Formerly typified by the temporary or seasonal entry of young single males, the migration now features long-term settlement by families, women, and children, suggesting ongoing effects on the society, culture, and politics of the United States. At the end of the century a movement of people out of Latin America is remaking the ethnic structure of large portions of the United States and is operating for the most part beyond the control of the U.S. government.[25]

INTO THE NEXT CENTURY

How should historians appraise the patterns of the past and assess the probable effects on the future? The obvious answer is, with caution and circumspection. While anticipating the possibilities of the next century in U.S.-Latin American relations, historians need to recall the continuities of this one.

For Latin Americans the asymmetries of power, wealth, and influence have posed continual obstacles. Although they have often met this problem with finesse and ingenuity, they have never fully escaped its effects. Vulnerability to events in the outside world, especially in economic relations, appears as a constant in Latin American history. How to maintain functioning economic systems without the requisite resources remains a central puzzle. How can Latin Americans achieve some measure of control over their own destinies while at the same time satisfying the wishes of the Great Powers? No matter how skillfully Latin Americans maneuver, U.S. business and political leaders exercise more control over markets, capital, and technologies—a situation likely to persist into the next century.

For the United States too a continuity of goals and purposes appears probable. Indeed, the basics have not shifted very much since James G. Blaine's formulation of a Pan American policy in 1889. Throughout the era, U.S. leaders wanted trade, resources, and security and, to obtain them, upheld the primacy of their own political and economic interests. The forms of expression changed from time to time, depending upon circumstances. During the past hundred years or so the United States, on the one hand, has tried to encourage Latin American participation in some kind of Pan American system, usually designed to provide incentives for carrying out U.S. preferences. On the other hand, U.S. leaders have acted aggressively in the Western Hemisphere when agitated by perceptions of a foreign threat, posed presumably by the Germans or the Soviets. A sense of menace from the outside seems to have made it easier for them to act upon attitudes characterized by condescension if not outright distaste toward Latin Americans. U.S. definitions of policy have consistently required deference and compliance from Latin Americans, reflecting the actual distribution of power, wealth, and influence. "The Western Hemisphere idea," to the extent that it applies at all, has conveyed a pro-U.S. orientation, constricting the range of choice for Latin Americans.

NOTES

1. Walter LaFeber, *The Panama Canal: The Crisis in Historical Perspective* (New York: Oxford University Press, 1978), 161; John H. Coatsworth, *Central America and the United States: The Clients and the Colossus* (New York: Twayne, 1994), 134.
2. Gaddis Smith, *Morality, Reason, and Power: American Diplomacy during the Carter Years* (New York: Hill and Wang, 1986), 115.
3. Coatsworth, *Central America and the United States*, 132–33, 135–37.
4. Walter LaFeber, *Inevitable Revolutions: The United States in Central America* (New York: W. W. Norton, 1983), 219–26.
5. Coatsworth, *Central America and the United States*, 138–46; Thomas E. Leonard, *Central America and the United States: The Search for Stability* (Athens: University of Georgia Press, 1991), chap. 9.
6. Jeane J. Kirkpatrick, "Dictatorships and Double Standards," *Commentary* 68 (November 1979): 34–45.
7. Ronald Reagan, *An American Life* (New York: Pocket Books, 1990), 239, 360, 471.
8. Coatsworth, *Central America and the United States*, 144–47, 151–59.
9. Michael J. Schaller, *Reckoning with Reagan: America and Its President in the 1980s* (New York: Oxford University Press, 1992), 122, 132; Thomas G. Paterson and J. Garry Clifford, *America Ascendant: U.S. Foreign Relations since 1939* (Lexington, MA: D. C. Heath, 1995), 260–64.
10. Paterson and Clifford, *America Ascendant*, 256–60.
11. Schaller, *Reckoning with Reagan*, 142, 149.
12. Coatsworth, *Central America and the United States*, 164–66, 170–71, 174–78.
13. Mark T. Gilderhus, "An Emerging Synthesis? U.S.-Latin American Relations since 1945," in *America in the World: The Historiography of American*

Foreign Relations since 1941, ed. Michael J. Hogan (New York: Cambridge University Press, 1995), 456–58; Mark T. Berger, *Under Northern Eyes: Latin American Studies and U.S. Hegemony in the Americas, 1898–1990* (Bloomington: Indiana University Press, 1995), chaps. 4–5.

14. Coatsworth, *Central America and the United States*, 180–82.

15. Joseph S. Tulchin, *Argentina and the United States: A Conflicted Relationship* (Boston: Twayne, 1990), 154–58; idem, "The Malvinas War of 1882: An Inevitable Conflict That Never Should Have Happened," *Latin American Research Review* 22, no. 3 (1987): 123–41.

16. Coatsworth, *Central America and the United States*, 181–87; Schaller, *Reckoning with Reagan*, chap. 6; Peter H. Smith, *Talons of the Eagle: Dynamics of U.S.-Latin American Relations* (New York: Oxford University Press, 1996), 176–80.

17. Coatsworth, *Central America and the United States*, 199–200, 202.

18. Michael J. Hogan, ed., *The End of the Cold War: Its Meaning and Implications* (New York: Cambridge University Press, 1992); Lars Schoultz, ed., *The United States and Latin America in the 1990s: Beyond the Cold War* (Chapel Hill: University of North Carolina Press, 1992).

19. Coatsworth, *Central America and the United States*, 207–8, 210, 214–16; Michael L. Conniff, *Panama and the United States: The Forced Alliance* (Athens: University of Georgia Press, 1992), chap. 9.

20. Smith, *Talons of the Eagle*, 218–19.

21. Robert J. McMahon, "Making Sense of American Foreign Policy during the Reagan Years," *Diplomatic History* 19 (Spring 1995): 367–84; Thomas G. Paterson, *On Every Front: The Making and Unmaking of the Cold War*, rev. ed. (New York: W. W. Norton, 1992), 192–93; Paul Kennedy, *The Rise and Fall of the Great Powers: Economic Change and Military Conflict from 1500 to 2000* (New York: Random House, 1987).

22. Smith, *Talons of the Eagle*, 223–24.

23. Abraham F. Lowenthal, *Partners in Conflict: The United States and Latin America* (Baltimore: Johns Hopkins University Press, 1987), 32; Paterson, *On Every Front*, 32.

24. Smith, *Talons of the Eagle*, 224–25, 227, 229–30, 234, 239–41, 243–55.

25. Ibid., 268–77, 281.

SELECT BIBLIOGRAPHY

Adams, Frederick C. *Economic Diplomacy: The Export-Import Bank and American Foreign Relations, 1934–1939.* Columbia: University of Missouri Press, 1976.

Albert, Bill. *South America and the First World War: The Impact of the War on Brazil, Argentina, Peru, and Chile.* New York: Cambridge University Press, 1988.

Ambrose, Stephen E. *Nixon.* 3 vols. New York: Simon and Schuster, 1987–92.

Ambrose, Stephen E., and Richard Immerman. *Ike's Spies: Eisenhower and the Espionage Establishment.* Garden City, NY: Doubleday, 1981.

Ameringer, Charles D. *U.S. Foreign Intelligence: The Secret Side of American History.* Lexington, MA: D. C. Heath, 1990.

Atkins, G. Pope, and Larman C. Wilson. *The Dominican Republic and the United States: From Imperialism to Transnationalism.* Athens: University of Georgia Press, 1998.

Bailey, Thomas A. *A Diplomatic History of the American People.* 9th ed. Englewood Cliffs, NJ: Prentice-Hall, 1974.

Baily, Samuel L. *The United States and the Development of South America, 1945–1975.* New York: New Viewpoints, 1976.

Bastert, Russell H. "A New Approach to the Origins of Blaine's Pan American Policy." *Hispanic American Historical Review* 39 (May 1959): 375–412.

Beezley, William H., and Colin M. MacLachlan. *El Gran Pueblo: A History of Greater Mexico.* 2 vols. Englewood Cliffs, NJ: Prentice-Hall, 1994.

Beisner, Robert L. *Twelve against Empire: The Anti-Imperialists, 1898–1900.* 1968. Reprint, New York: McGraw-Hill, 1971.

———. *From the Old Diplomacy to the New, 1865–1900.* 2d ed. Arlington Heights, IL: Harlan Davidson, 1986.

Bemis, Samuel Flagg. *The Latin-American Policy of the United States: An Historical Interpretation.* 1943. Reprint, New York: W. W. Norton, 1967.

Berger, Mark T. *Under Northern Eyes: Latin American Studies and U.S. Hegemony in the Americas, 1898–1990.* Bloomington: Indiana University Press, 1995.

Beschloss, Michael R. *The Crisis Years: Kennedy and Khrushchev, 1960–1963*. New York: Edward Burlingame Books, 1991.

Bethell, Leslie, and Ian Roxborough. "Latin America between the Second World War and the Cold War: Some Reflections on the 1945–8 Conjuncture." *Journal of Latin American Studies* 20 (May 1988): 167–189.

———, eds. *Latin America between the Second World War and the Cold War: Crisis and Containment, 1944–1948*. New York: Cambridge University Press, 1994.

Blight, James G., Bruce J. Allyn, and David A. Welch. *Cuba on the Brink: Castro, the Missile Crisis, and the Soviet Collapse*. New York: Pantheon Books, 1993.

Boeker, Paul H., ed. *Henry L. Stimson's American Policy in Nicaragua: The Lasting Legacy*. New York: Markus Weiner, 1991.

Bornet, Vaughn David. *The Presidency of Lyndon B. Johnson*. Lawrence: University Press of Kansas, 1983.

Brands, H. W., Jr. *Cold Warriors: Eisenhower's Generation and American Foreign Policy*. New York: Columbia University Press, 1988.

Bulmer-Thomas, Victor. *The Economic History of Latin America since Independence*. New York: Cambridge University Press, 1994.

Burns, E. Bradford. *The Unwritten Alliance: Rio-Branco and Brazilian American Relations*. New York: Columbia University Press, 1966.

———. *At War in Nicaragua: The Reagan Doctrine and the Politics of Nostalgia*. New York: Harper and Row, 1987.

Calder, Bruce J. *The Impact of Intervention: The Dominican Republic during the U.S. Occupation of 1916–1924*. Austin: University of Texas Press, 1984.

Calhoun, Frederick S. *Uses of Force and Wilsonian Foreign Policy*. Kent, OH: Kent State University Press, 1993.

Calvert, Peter, and Susan Calvert. *Latin America in the Twentieth Century*. New York: St. Martin's Press, 1990.

Campbell, Charles S. *The Transformation of American Foreign Relations, 1865–1900*. New York: Harper and Row, 1976.

Cannon, Lou. *President Reagan: A Role of a Lifetime*. New York: Simon and Schuster, 1991.

Cardoso, Fernando Henrique, and Enzo Faletto. *Dependency and Development in Latin America*. Berkeley: University of California Press, 1979.

Carothers, Thomas. *In the Name of Democracy: U.S. Policy toward Latin America during the Reagan Years*. Berkeley: University of California Press, 1991.

Casey, Clifford B. "The Creation and Development of the Pan American Union." *Hispanic American Historical Review* 13 (November 1933): 437–56.

Chilcote, Ronald H., and Joel C. Edelstein, eds. *Latin America: The Struggle with Dependency and Beyond*. New York: John Wiley and Sons, 1974.

———. *Latin America: Capitalist and Socialist Perspectives of Development and Underdevelopment*. Boulder, CO: Westview Press, 1986.

Clark, Paul Coe, Jr. *The United States and Somoza, 1933–1956: A Revisionist Look*. Westport, CT: Praeger, 1992.

Coatsworth, John H. *Central America and the United States: The Clients and the Colossus*. New York: Twayne, 1994.

Cobbs, Elizabeth A. *The Rich Neighbor: Rockefeller and Kaiser in Brazil*. New Haven: Yale University Press, 1992.

Cockcroft, James D. *Latin America: History, Politics, and U.S. Policy*. 2d ed. Chicago: Nelson-Hall Publishers, 1996.

Cohen, Warren I. *Empire without Tears: American Foreign Relations, 1921–1933*. Philadelphia: Temple University Press, 1987.

Cohen, Warren I., and Nancy Bernkopf Tucker, eds. *Lyndon Johnson Confronts the World: American Foreign Policy, 1963–1968*. New York: Cambridge University Press, 1994.

Collin, Richard H. *Theodore Roosevelt, Culture, Diplomacy, and Expansion: A New View of American Imperialism*. Baton Rouge: Louisiana State University Press, 1985.

——. *Theodore Roosevelt's Caribbean: The Panama Canal, the Monroe Doctrine, and the Latin American Context*. Baton Rouge: Louisiana State University Press, 1990.

Combs, Jerald A. *American Diplomatic History: Two Centuries of Changing Interpretations*. Berkeley: University of California Press, 1983.

Conkin, Paul K. *Big Daddy from the Pedernales: Lyndon Baines Johnson*. Boston: Twayne, 1986.

Connell-Smith, Gordon. *The Inter-American System*. New York: Oxford University Press, 1966.

——. *The United States and Latin America: An Historical Analysis of Inter-American Relations*. New York: John Wiley and Sons, 1974.

Conniff, Michael L. *Panama and the United States: The Forced Alliance*. Athens: University of Georgia Press, 1992.

Cottam, Martha L. *Images and Intervention: U.S. Policies in Latin America*. Pittsburgh, PA: University of Pittsburgh Press, 1994.

Cummings, Bruce. *The Origins of the Korean War*. 2 vols. Princeton: Princeton University Press, 1981, 1990.

Dallek, Robert. *Franklin D. Roosevelt and American Foreign Policy, 1932–1945*. New York: Oxford University Press, 1979.

David, Harold Eugene, John J. Finian, and F. Taylor Peck. *Latin American Diplomatic History: An Introduction*. Baton Rouge: Louisiana State University Press, 1977.

DeConde, Alexander. *Herbert Hoover's Latin-American Policy*. Palo Alto, CA: Stanford University Press, 1951.

Delpar, Helen. *The Enormous Vogue of Things Mexican: Cultural Relations between the United States and Mexico, 1920–1935*. Tuscaloosa: University of Alabama Press, 1992.

Divine, Robert A. *Roosevelt and World War II*. Baltimore: Johns Hopkins University Press, 1969.

Dobson, John. *Reticent Expansionism: The Foreign Policy of McKinley.* Pittsburgh, PA: Duquesne University Press, 1988.

Domínguez, Jorge I. *To Make the World Safe for Revolution: Cuba's Foreign Policy.* Cambridge: Harvard University Press, 1989.

Dosal, Paul J. *Doing Business with the Dictators: A Political History of United Fruit in Guatemala, 1899–1944.* Wilmington, DE: Scholarly Resources, 1993.

Dozer, Donald Marquand. *Are We Good Neighbors? Three Decades of Inter-American Relations, 1930–1960.* Gainesville: University Press of Florida, 1961.

Drake, Paul W. *The Money Doctor in the Andes: The Kemmerer Missions, 1923–1933.* Durham, NC: Duke University Press, 1989.

———, ed. *Money Doctors, Foreign Debts, and Economic Reforms in Latin America from the 1890s to the Present.* Wilmington, DE: Scholarly Resources, 1994.

Eisenhower, Milton S. *The Wine Is Bitter: The United States and Latin America.* Garden City, NY: Doubleday, 1963.

Ekirk, Arthur A. *Ideologies and Utopias: The Impact of the New Deal on American Thought.* Chicago: Quadrangle Books, 1969.

Ellis, L. Ethan. *Republican Foreign Policy, 1921–1933.* New Brunswick, NJ: Rutgers University Press, 1968.

Espinoza, J. Manuel. *Inter-American Beginnings of U.S. Cultural Diplomacy, 1936–1948.* Washington, DC: U.S. Department of State, 1976.

Ewell, Judith. *Venezuela and the United States: From Monroe's Hemisphere to Petroleum's Empire.* Athens: University of Georgia Press, 1996.

Falcoff, Mark. *Modern Chile, 1970–1989.* New Brunswick, NJ: Transactions, 1989.

Fausold, Martin L. *The Presidency of Herbert Hoover.* Lawrence: University Press of Kansas, 1985.

Field, James A. "American Imperialism: The Worst Chapter in Almost Any Book." *American Historical Review* 83 (June 1978): 644–83.

Fifer, J. Valerie. *United States Perceptions of Latin America, 1850–1930: A "New West" South of Capricorn?* New York: Manchester University Press, 1991.

Fox, Frank W. *J. Reuben Clark: The Public Years.* Provo, UT: Brigham Young University Press, 1980.

Frank, André Gunder. *Latin America, Underdevelopment or Revolution: Essays on the Development of Underdevelopment and the Immediate Enemy.* New York: Monthly Review Press, 1969.

Freidel, Frank. *The Splendid Little War.* New York: Dell, 1958.

Fry, Joseph A. "William McKinley and the Coming of the Spanish-American War: A Study of the Besmirching and Redemption of an Historical Image." *Diplomatic History* 3 (Winter 1979): 77–98.

Gantenbein, James W., ed. *The Evolution of Our Latin-American Policy: A Documentary Record.* New York: Octagon Books, 1971.

Gardner, Lloyd C. *Economic Aspects of New Deal Diplomacy.* Madison: University of Wisconsin Press, 1964.

Garthoff, Raymond L. *Reflections on the Cuban Missile Crisis*. Washington, DC: Brookings Institution, 1987.

Gelfand, Lawrence E. *The Inquiry: American Preparations for Peace, 1917–1919*. New Haven: Yale University Press, 1963.

Gellman, Irwin F. *Good Neighbor Diplomacy: United States Policies in Latin America, 1933–1945*. Baltimore: Johns Hopkins University Press, 1979.

———. *Secret Affairs: Franklin Roosevelt, Cordell Hull, and Sumner Welles*. Baltimore: Johns Hopkins University Press, 1995.

Giglio, James N. *The Presidency of John F. Kennedy*. Lawrence: University Press of Kansas, 1991.

Gilderhus, Mark T. "Carranza and the Decision to Revolt, 1913: A Problem in Historical Interpretation." *Americas* 33 (October 1976): 298–310.

———. *Diplomacy and Revolution: U.S.-Mexican Relations under Wilson and Carranza*. Tucson: University of Arizona Press, 1977.

———. *Pan American Visions: Woodrow Wilson in the Western Hemisphere, 1913–1921*. Tucson: University of Arizona Press, 1986.

———. "An Emerging Synthesis? U.S.-Latin American Relations since 1945." In *America in the World: The Historiography of American Foreign Relations since 1941*, edited by Michael J. Hogan, 424–61. New York: Cambridge University Press, 1995.

———. *History and Historians: A Historiographical Introduction*. 3d ed. Englewood Cliffs, NJ: Prentice-Hall, 1996.

———. "Founding Father: Samuel Flagg Bemis and the Study of U.S.-Latin American Relations." *Diplomatic History* 21 (Winter 1997): 1–14.

Glade, William. "Latin America and the International Economy, 1870–1914." In *The Cambridge History of Latin America*, vol. 4, *c. 1870–1930*, edited by Leslie Bethell, 1–56. New York: Cambridge University Press, 1986.

Gleijeses, Piero. *The Dominican Crisis: The 1965 Constitutionalist Revolt and American Intervention*. Translated by Lawrence Lipson. Baltimore: Johns Hopkins University Press, 1978.

———. *Shattered Hope: The Guatemalan Revolution and the United States, 1944–1954*. Princeton: Princeton University Press, 1991.

Goldberg, Joyce S. *The "Baltimore" Affair*. Lincoln: University of Nebraska Press, 1986.

Gould, Lewis L. *The Presidency of William McKinley*. Lawrence: Regents Press of Kansas, 1980.

———. *The Spanish American War and President McKinley*. Lawrence: University Press of Kansas, 1982.

———. *The Presidency of Theodore Roosevelt*. Lawrence: University Press of Kansas, 1991.

Green, David. *The Containment of Latin America: A History of the Myths and Realities of the Good Neighbor Policy*. Chicago: Quadrangle Books, 1971.

Greene, John Robert. *The Presidency of Gerald R. Ford*. Lawrence: University Press of Kansas, 1995.

Greenstein, Fred I. *The Hidden-Hand Presidency: Eisenhower as Leader*. New York: Basic Books, 1982.

Grieb, Kenneth J. *The United States and Huerta*. Lincoln: University of Nebraska Press, 1969.

———. *Guatemala Caudillo: The Regime of Jorge Ubico, Guatemala, 1931–1944*. Athens: Ohio University Press, 1979.

Haines, Gerald K. "Under the Eagle's Wing: The Franklin Roosevelt Administration Forges an American Hemisphere." *Diplomatic History* 1 (Fall 1977): 377–88.

———. *The Americanization of Brazil: A Study of U.S. Cold War Diplomacy in the Third World, 1945–1954*. Wilmington, DE: Scholarly Resources, 1989.

Hale, Charles A. "Political and Social Ideas in Latin America, 1870–1930." In *The Cambridge History of Latin America*, vol. 4, c. 1870–1930, edited by Leslie Bethell, 367–442. New York: Cambridge University Press, 1986.

Hall, Linda B. *Oil, Banks, and Politics: The United States and Postrevolutionary Mexico, 1917–1924*. Austin: University of Texas Press, 1995.

Hall, Linda B., and Don M. Coerver. *Revolution on the Border: The United States and Mexico, 1910–1920*. Albuquerque: University of New Mexico Press, 1988.

Hart, John. *Revolutionary Mexico: The Coming and Process of the Mexican Revolution*. Berkeley: University of California Press, 1987.

Hartlyn, Jonathan, Lars Schoultz, and Augusto Varas. *The United States and Latin America in the 1990s: Beyond the Cold War*. Chapel Hill: University of North Carolina Press, 1992.

Healy, David. *Drive to Hegemony: The United States in the Caribbean, 1889–1917*. Madison: University of Wisconsin Press, 1988.

Heinrich, Waldo H. *Threshold of War: Franklin D. Roosevelt and American Entry into World War II*. New York: Oxford University Press, 1988.

Hernández, José M. *Cuba and the United States: Intervention and Militarism, 1868–1933*. Austin: University of Texas Press, 1993.

Hersh, Seymour M. *The Price of Power: Kissinger in the White House*. New York: Summit Books, 1983.

Higgins, Trumbull. *The Perfect Failure: Kennedy, Eisenhower, and the CIA at the Bay of Pigs*. New York: W. W. Norton, 1989.

Hilsman, Roger. *To Move a Nation: The Politics of Foreign Policy in the Administration of John F. Kennedy*. New York: Dell, 1964.

Hilton, Stanley E. *Brazil and the Great Powers, 1930–1939: The Politics of Trade Rivalry*. Austin: University of Texas Press, 1975.

———. *Hitler's Secret War in South America, 1939–1945: German Military Espionage and Allied Counterespionage in Brazil*. Baton Rouge: Louisiana State University Press, 1981.

Hofstadter, Richard. *The American Political Tradition*. New York: Alfred A. Knopf, 1948.

———. *The Paranoid Style in American Politics and Other Essays*. New York: Vintage Books, 1967.

Hogan, Michael J., ed. *The End of the Cold War: Its Meaning and Implications*. New York: Cambridge University Press, 1992.

Hogan, Michael J., and Thomas G. Paterson. *Explaining the History of American Foreign Relations*. New York: Cambridge University Press, 1991.

Humphreys, R. A. *Latin America and the Second World War*. 2 vols. London: University of London Athlone Press, 1982.

Immerman, Richard H. *The CIA in Guatemala: The Foreign Policy of Intervention*. Austin: University of Texas Press, 1982.

Jeffreys-Johns, Rhodri. *The CIA and American Democracy*. New Haven: Yale University Press, 1989.

Johnson, John J. *Latin America in Caricature*. Austin: University of Texas Press, 1980.

———. *A Hemisphere Apart: The Foundations of United States Policy toward Latin America*. Baltimore: Johns Hopkins University Press, 1990.

Jones, Howard, and Randall B. Woods. "Origins of the Cold War in Europe and the New East: Recent Historiography and the National Security Imperative." In *America in the World: The Historiography of American Foreign Relations since 1941*, edited by Michael J. Hogan, 234–69. New York: Cambridge University Press, 1995.

Kagan, Robert. *A Twilight Struggle: American Power and Nicaragua, 1977–1990*. New York: Free Press, 1996.

Karnes, Thomas L. "Hiram Bingham and His Obsolete Shibboleth." *Diplomatic History* 3 (Winter 1979): 39–57.

Katz, Friedrich. *The Secret War in Mexico: Europe, the United States, and the Mexican Revolution*. Chicago: University of Chicago Press, 1981.

———. "Mexico: Restored Republic and Porfiriato, 1867–1910." In *The Cambridge History of Latin America*, vol. 5, c. 1870–1930, edited by Leslie Bethell, 3–78. New York: Cambridge University Press, 1988.

Kaufman, Burton. *Expansion and Efficiency: Foreign Trade Organization in the Wilson Administration*. Westport, CT: Greenwood Press, 1974.

———. *Trade and Aid: Eisenhower's Foreign Economic Policy, 1953–1961*. Baltimore: Johns Hopkins University Press, 1982.

———. *The Korean War: Challenges in Crisis, Credibility, and Command*. New York: Alfred A. Knopf, 1986.

———. *The Presidency of James Earl Carter Jr.* Lawrence: University Press of Kansas, 1993.

Kennedy, Paul. *The Rise and Fall of the Great Powers: Economic Change and Military Conflict from 1500 to 2000*. New York: Random House, 1987.

Kenworthy, Eldon. *America/Américas: Myth in the Making of U.S. Policy toward Latin America*. University Park: Pennsylvania State University Press, 1995.

Kiernan, V. G. *America: The New Imperialism, from White Settlement to World Hegemony*. London: Zed Press, 1978.

Kimball, Warren F. *The Juggler: Franklin Roosevelt as Wartime Statesman*. Princeton: Princeton University Press, 1991.

Kirkpatrick, Jeane J. "Dictatorships and Double Standards." *Commentary* 68 (November 1979): 34–45.

Knight, Alan. *The Mexican Revolution*. 2 vols. New York: Cambridge University Press, 1986.

Krenn, Michael L. *United States Policy toward Economic Nationalism in Latin America, 1917–1929*. Wilmington, DE: Scholarly Resources, 1990.

———. *The Chains of Interdependence: U.S. Policy toward Central America, 1945–1954*. New York: M. E. Sharpe, 1996.

Kyrzanek, Michael J. *U.S.-Latin American Relations*. New York: Praeger, 1985.

Kyvig, David F., ed. *Reagan and the World*. New York: Praeger, 1990.

Lael, Richard L. *Arrogant Diplomacy: U.S. Policy toward Colombia, 1903–1922*. Wilmington, DE: Scholarly Resources, 1987.

LaFeber, Walter. *The New Empire: An Interpretation of American Expansion, 1860–1898*. Ithaca, NY: Cornell University Press, 1963.

———. *The Panama Canal: The Crisis in Historical Perspective*. Rev. ed. New York: Oxford University Press, 1979.

———. *Inevitable Revolutions: The United States in Central America*. New York: W. W. Norton, 1983.

———. *The American Age: United States Foreign Policy at Home and Abroad*. New York: W. W. Norton, 1989.

———. *America, Russia, and the Cold War, 1945–1992*. 7th ed. New York: McGraw-Hill, 1993.

———. *The American Search for Opportunity, 1865–1913*. Vol. 2 in *The Cambridge History of American Foreign Relations*. New York: Cambridge University Press, 1993.

Langley, Lester D. *The Banana Wars: An Inner History of American Empire, 1900–1934*. Lexington: University Press of Kentucky, 1983.

———. *America and the Americas: The United States in the Western Hemisphere*. Athens: University of Georgia Press, 1989.

———. *Mexico and the United States: The Fragile Relationship*. Boston: Twayne, 1991.

Langley, Lester D., and Thomas Schoonover. *The Banana Men: American Mercenaries and Entrepreneurs in Central America, 1880–1930*. Lexington: University Press of Kentucky, 1995.

Lazo, Dimitri D. "Lansing, Wilson, and the Jenkins Incident." *Diplomatic History* 22 (Spring 1998): 177–98.

Leffler, Melvyn P. "Expansionist Impulses and Domestic Constraints, 1921–32." In *Economics and World Power: An Assessment of American Diplomacy since 1789*, edited by William H. Becker and Samuel F. Wells Jr. New York: Columbia University Press, 1984.

Lehman, Kenneth. "Revolutions and Attributions: Making Sense of Eisenhower Administration Policies in Bolivia and Guatemala." *Diplomatic History* 21 (Spring 1997): 185–213.

Leonard, Thomas M. *Central America and the United States: The Search for Stability*. Athens: University of Georgia Press, 1991.

Leuchtenberg, William E. *Franklin D. Roosevelt and the New Deal*. New York: Harper and Row, 1963.

———. *The FDR Years: On Roosevelt and His Legacy*. New York: Columbia University Press, 1995.

Levin, N. Gordon, Jr. *Woodrow Wilson and World Politics: America's Response to War and Revolution*. New York: Oxford University Press, 1968.

Levinson, Jerome, and Juan de Onís. *The Alliance That Lost Its Way: A Critical Report on the Alliance for Progress*. Chicago: Quadrangle Books, 1970.

Lieuwen, Edwin. *Arms and Politics in Latin America*. Rev. ed. New York: Frederick A. Praeger, 1961.

———. *Generals vs. Presidents: Neo-Militarism in Latin America*. New York: Frederick A. Praeger, 1964.

Longley, Kyle. *The Sparrow and the Hawk: Costa Rica and the United States during the Rise of José Figueres*. Tuscaloosa: University of Alabama Press, 1997.

Lowenthal, Abraham F. "United States Policy toward Latin America: 'Liberal,' 'Radical,' and 'Bureaucratic' Perspectives." *Latin American Research Review* 8 (Fall 1973): 3–25.

———. *Partners in Conflict: The United States and Latin America*. Baltimore: Johns Hopkins University Press, 1987.

———, ed. *Exporting Democracy: The United States and Latin America*. Baltimore: Johns Hopkins University Press, 1991.

Macaulay, Neil. *The Sandino Affair*. Chicago: Quadrangle Books, 1971.

Major, John. *Prize Possession: The United States and the Panama Canal, 1903–1979*. New York: Cambridge University Press, 1993.

Marks, Frederick W., III. *Velvet on Iron: The Diplomacy of Theodore Roosevelt*. Lincoln: University of Nebraska Press, 1979.

Martin, Edwin McCammon. *Kennedy and Latin America*. Lanham, MD: University Press of America, 1994.

Martin, Gerald. "The Literature, Music, and Arts of Latin America, 1870–1930." In *The Cambridge History of Latin America*, vol. 4, *c. 1870–1930*, edited by Leslie Bethell, 443–526. New York: Cambridge University Press, 1986.

Martz, John D., ed. *United States Policy in Latin America: A Quarter Century of Crisis and Challenge, 1961–1986*. Lincoln: University of Nebraska Press, 1988.

May, Ernest R. *The World War and American Isolation, 1914–1917*. Cambridge, MA: Harvard University Press, 1959.

———, ed. *American Cold War Strategy: Interpreting NSC 68*. Boston: Bedford Books, 1993.

McAulliffe, Mary S. "Commentary: Eisenhower, the President." *Journal of American History* 68 (December 1981): 625–32.

McBeth, B. S. *Juan Vicente Gómez and the Oil Companies in Venezuela, 1908–1935*. New York: Cambridge University Press, 1983.

McCann, Frank D. *The Brazilian-American Alliance, 1937–1945*. Princeton: Princeton University Press, 1973.

———. "Brazil, the United States, and World War II: A Commentary." *Diplomatic History* 3 (Winter 1979): 59–76.

McCormick, Thomas J. *China Market: America's Quest for Informal Empire, 1893–1901*. Chicago: Quadrangle Books, 1967.

McCullough, David G. *The Path between the Seas: The Creation of the Panama Canal, 1870–1914*. New York: Simon and Schuster, 1977.

McGann, Thomas F. *Argentina, the United States, and the Inter-American System, 1889–1914*. Cambridge, MA: Harvard University Press, 1961.

McMahon, Robert J. "Eisenhower and Third World Nationalism: A Critique of the Revisionists." *Political Science Review* 101 (Fall 1986): 453–73.

———. "Making Sense of American Foreign Relations during the Reagan Years." *Diplomatic History* 19 (Spring 1995): 367–84.

Mecham, J. Lloyd. *The United States and Inter-American Security, 1889–1960*. Austin: University of Texas Press, 1967.

Meyer, Lorenzo. *Mexico and the United States in the Oil Controversy, 1917–1942*. Translated by Muriel Vasconcellos. Austin: University of Texas Press, 1977.

Meyer, Michael C. *Huerta: A Political Portrait*. Lincoln: University of Nebraska Press, 1972.

Morgan, H. Wayne. *America's Road to Empire: The War with Spain and Overseas Expansion*. New York: John Wiley and Sons, 1965.

Morley, Morris H. *Imperial State and Revolution: The United States and Cuba, 1952–1986*. New York: Cambridge University Press, 1987.

———. *Washington, Somoza, and the Sandinistas: State and Regime in United States Policy toward Nicaragua, 1969–1981*. New York: Cambridge University Press, 1994.

Munro, Dana G. *Intervention and Dollar Diplomacy in the Caribbean, 1900–1921*. Princeton: Princeton University Press, 1964.

Neiss, Frank. *A Hemisphere to Itself: A History of U.S.-Latin American Relations*. Translated by Harry Drost. London, 1990.

Newton, Robert C. *The "Nazi Menace" in Argentina, 1931–1945*. Palo Alto, CA: Stanford University Press, 1992.

Niblo, Stephen R. *War, Diplomacy, and Development: The United States and Mexico, 1938–1954*. Wilmington, DE: Scholarly Resources, 1995.

Nixon, Richard M. *Six Crises*. Garden City, NY: Doubleday, 1962.

Offner, John L. *An Unwanted War: The Diplomacy of the United States and Spain over Cuba, 1895–1898*. Chapel Hill: University of North Carolina Press, 1992.

Pach, Chester J., Jr. *Arming the Free World: The Origins of the United States Military Assistance Program, 1945–1950*. Chapel Hill: University of North Carolina Press, 1991.

Pach, Chester J., Jr., and Elmo Richardson. *The Presidency of Dwight D. Eisenhower*. Rev. ed. Lawrence: University Press of Kansas, 1991.

Packenham, Robert A. *Liberal America and the Third World: Political Development Ideas in Foreign Aid and Social Science*. Princeton: Princeton University Press, 1973.

———. *The Dependency Movement: Scholarship and Politics in Development Studies*. Cambridge, MA: Harvard University Press, 1992.

Park, James William. *Latin American Underdevelopment: A History of Perspectives in the United States, 1870–1965*. Baton Rouge: Louisiana State University Press, 1995.

Parrini, Carl. *Heir to Empire: United States Economic Diplomacy, 1916–1923*. Pittsburgh, PA: University of Pittsburgh Press, 1969.

Pastor, Robert A. *Whirlpool: U.S. Foreign Policy toward Latin America and the Caribbean*. Princeton: Princeton University Press, 1992.

Paterson, Thomas G. "Fixation with Cuba: The Bay of Pigs, Missile Crisis, and Covert War against Fidel Castro." In *Kennedy's Quest for Victory: American Foreign Policy, 1961–63*, edited by Thomas G. Paterson, 123–77. New York: Oxford University Press, 1989.

———. *On Every Front: The Making and Unmaking of the Cold War*. Rev. ed. New York: W. W. Norton, 1992.

———. *Contesting Castro: The United States and the Triumph of the Cuban Revolution*. New York: Oxford University Press, 1994.

Paterson, Thomas G., and J. Garry Clifford. *America Ascendant: U.S. Foreign Relations since 1939*. Lexington, MA: D. C. Heath, 1995.

Paterson, Thomas G., J. Garry Clifford, and Kenneth J. Hagan. *American Foreign Relations: A History*. 2 vols. 4th ed. Lexington, MA: D. C. Heath, 1995.

Paterson, Thomas G., and Dennis Merrill, eds. *Major Problems in American Foreign Relations*. 2 vols. 4th ed. Lexington, MA: D. C. Heath, 1995.

Pérez, Louis A., Jr. *Cuba and the United States: Ties of Singular Intimacy*. Athens: University of Georgia Press, 1990.

Perkins, Bradford. *The Great Rapprochement: England and the United States, 1895–1914*. New York: Atheneum, 1968.

Philip, George. *Oil and Politics in Latin America: Nationalist Movements and State Companies*. New York: Cambridge University Press, 1982.

Pike, Frederick. *The United States and Latin America: Myths and Stereotypes of Civilization and Nature*. Austin: University of Texas Press, 1992.

———. *FDR's Good Neighbor Policy: Six Years of Generally Gentle Chaos*. Austin: University of Texas Press, 1995.

Pletcher, David M. *The Awkward Years: American Foreign Relations under Garfield and Arthur*. Columbia: University of Missouri Press, 1962.

———. *The Diplomacy of Trade and Investment: American Economic Expansion in the Hemisphere, 1865–1900*. Columbia: University of Missouri Press, 1998.

Plummer, Brenda Gayle. *Haiti and the Great Powers, 1902–1915*. Baton Rouge: Louisiana State University Press, 1988.

———. *Haiti and the United States: The Psychological Moment*. Athens: University of Georgia Press, 1992.

Poitras, Guy. *The Ordeal of Hegemony: The United States and Latin America*. Boulder, CO: Westview Press, 1990.

Prados, John. *Presidents' Secret Wars: CIA and Pentagon Covert Operations since World War II*. New York: William Morrow, 1986.

Quirk, Robert E. *Fidel Castro*. New York: W. W. Norton, 1993.

Raat, W. Dirk. *Mexico and the United States: Ambivalent Vistas*. Athens: University of Georgia Press, 1992.

Rabe, Stephen G. "The Elusive Conference: United States Economic Relations with Latin America, 1945–1952." *Diplomatic History* 2 (Summer 1978): 279–94.

———. *The Road to OPEC: United States Relations with Venezuela, 1919–1976*. Austin: University of Texas Press, 1982.

———. *Eisenhower and Latin America: The Foreign Policy of Anticommunism*. Chapel Hill: University of North Carolina Press, 1988.

———. "Controlling Revolutions: Latin America, the Alliance for Progress, and Cold War Anticommunism." In *Kennedy's Quest for Victory: American Foreign Policy, 1961–1963*, edited by Thomas G. Paterson, 105–22. New York: Oxford University Press, 1989.

Randall, Stephen J. *Colombia and the United States: Hegemony and Interdependence*. Athens: University of Georgia Press, 1992.

Reagan, Ronald. *An American Life*. New York: Pocket Books, 1990.

Richmond, Douglas W. *Venustiano Carranza's Nationalist Struggle, 1893–1920*. Lincoln: University of Nebraska Press, 1983.

Rock, David, ed. *Latin America in the 1940s: War and Postwar Transitions*. Berkeley: University of California Press, 1994.

Rosenberg, Emily. *Spreading the American Dream: American Economic and Cultural Expansion, 1890–1945*. New York: Hill and Wang, 1982.

Rout, Leslie B., and John F. Bratzel. *The Shadow War: German Espionage and United States Counterespionage in Latin America during World War II*. Frederick, MD: University Publications of America, 1986.

Ruiz, Ramón Eduardo. *The Great Rebellion: Mexico, 1905–1924*. New York: W. W. Norton, 1980.

Safford, Jeffrey J. *Wilsonian Maritime Diplomacy, 1913–1921*. New Brunswick, NJ: Rutgers University Press, 1978.

Sater, William. *Chile and the United States: Empires in Conflict*. Athens: University of Georgia Press, 1990.

Schaller, Michael. *Reckoning with Reagan: America and Its President in the 1980s*. New York: Oxford University Press, 1992.

Schlesinger, Arthur, Jr. *A Thousand Days: John F. Kennedy in the White House.* Greenwich, CT: Fawcett, 1965.

Schmidt, Hans. *The United States Occupation of Haiti, 1914–1934.* New Brunswick, NJ: Rutgers University Press, 1971.

Scholes, Walter V., and Marie V. Scholes *The Foreign Policies of the Taft Administration.* Columbia: University of Missouri Press, 1970.

Schoultz, Lars. *Beneath the United States: A History of U.S. Policy toward Latin America.* Cambridge, MA: Harvard University Press, 1998.

Schuler, Friedrich E. *Mexico between Hitler and Roosevelt: Mexican Foreign Relations in the Age of Lázaro Cárdenas, 1934–1940.* Albuquerque: University of New Mexico Press, 1998.

Schulzinger, Robert D. *Henry Kissinger: The Doctor of Diplomacy.* New York: Columbia University Press, 1989.

Shurbutt, T. Ray, ed. *United States-Latin American Relations, 1800–1850.* Tuscaloosa: University of Alabama Press, 1991.

Sigmund, Paul E. *The United States and Democracy in Chile.* Baltimore: Johns Hopkins University Press, 1993.

Smith, Daniel M. *Aftermath of War: Bainbridge Colby and Wilsonian Diplomacy, 1920–22.* Philadelphia: American Philosophical Society, 1970.

Smith, Gaddis. "The Two Worlds of Samuel Flagg Bemis." *Diplomatic History* 9 (Fall 1985): 295–302.

———. *Morality, Reason, and Power: American Diplomacy during the Carter Years.* New York: Hill and Wang, 1986.

———. *The Last Years of the Monroe Doctrine, 1945–1993.* New York: Hill and Wang, 1994.

Smith, Joseph. *Unequal Giants: Diplomatic Relations between the United States and Brazil, 1889–1930.* Pittsburgh, PA: University of Pittsburgh Press, 1991.

Smith, Peter H. *Talons of the Eagle: Dynamics of U.S.-Latin American Relations.* New York: Oxford University Press, 1996.

Smith, Peter H., and Thomas E. Skidmore. *Modern Latin America.* 2d ed. New York: Oxford University Press, 1992.

Smith, Robert Freeman. *The United States and Revolutionary Nationalism in Mexico, 1916–1932.* Chicago: University of Chicago Press, 1972.

———. "The Good Neighbor Policy: The Liberal Paradox in United States Relations with Latin America." In *Watershed of Empire: Essays on New Deal Foreign Policy,* edited by Leonard P. Liggio and James Martin, 65–94. Colorado Springs, CO: Ralph Myles, 1976.

———. "Latin America, the United States, and the European Powers, 1830–1930." In *The Cambridge History of Latin America,* vol. 4, *c. 1870–1930,* edited by Leslie Bethell, 83–120. New York: Cambridge University Press, 1986.

———. "U. S. Policy-Making for Latin America under Truman." *Continuity: A Journal of History* 16 (Fall 1992): 87–111.

———. *The Caribbean World and the United States: Mixing Rum and Coca-Cola.* New York: Twayne, 1994.

Socolofsky, Homer E., and Allan B. Spetter. *The Presidency of Benjamin Harrison*. Lawrence: University Press of Kansas, 1987.

Sorenson, Theodore C. *Kennedy*. New York: Harper and Row, 1965.

Spector, Ronald H. *Professors of War: The Naval War College and the Development of the Naval Profession*. Newport, RI: Naval War College Press, 1977.

Steward, Dick. *Trade and Hemisphere: The Good Neighbor Policy and Reciprocal Trade*. Columbia: University of Missouri Press, 1975.

Stiller, Jesse H. *George S. Messersmith: Diplomat of Democracy*. Chapel Hill: University of North Carolina Press, 1987.

Stoetzer, O. Carlos. *The Organization of American States*. Westport, CT: Praeger, 1993.

Stuart, Graham H., and James L. Tigner. *Latin America and the United States*. Englewood Cliffs, NJ: Prentice-Hall, 1975.

Stueck, William W. *The Korean War: An International History*. Princeton: Princeton University Press, 1995.

Szulc, Tad. *Twilight of the Tyrants*. New York: W. W. Holt, 1959.

Thorp, Rosemary. "Latin America and the International Economy from the First World War to the World Depression." In *The Cambridge History of Latin America*, vol. 4, *c. 1870–1930*, edited by Leslie Bethell, 57–82. New York: Cambridge University Press, 1986.

———, ed. *Latin America in the 1930s: The Role of the Periphery in World Crisis*. New York: St. Martin's Press, 1984.

Trani, Eugene P., and David L. Wilson. *The Presidency of Warren G. Harding*. Lawrence: Regents Press of Kansas, 1977.

Trask, David F. *The War with Spain in 1898*. New York: Macmillan, 1981.

Trask, Roger R. "The Impact of the Cold War on United States-Latin American Relations, 1945–1949." *Diplomatic History* 1 (Summer 1977): 271–84.

———. "George F. Kennan's Report on Latin America (1950)." *Diplomatic History* 2 (Summer 1978): 307–11.

———. "Spruille Braden versus George Messersmith: World War II, the Cold War, and Argentine Policy, 1945–1947." *Journal of Inter-American Studies and World Affairs* 26 (February 1984): 69–95.

Tulchin, Joseph. *Argentina and the United States: A Conflicted Relationship*. Boston: Twayne, 1990.

Walker, William O., III. "Mixing the Sweet with the Sour: Kennedy, Johnson, and Latin America." In *The Diplomacy of the Crucial Decade: American Foreign Relations during the 1960s*, edited by Diane B. Kunz, 42–79. New York: Columbia University Press, 1994.

Walton, Richard J. *Cold War and Counter-Revolution: The Foreign Policy of John F. Kennedy*. Baltimore: Penguin Books, 1973.

Weis, W. Michael. *Cold Warriors and Coups d'Etat: Brazilian-American Relations, 1945–1964*. Albuquerque: University of New Mexico Press, 1993.

Welch, Richard E., Jr. *Response to Revolution: The United States and the Cuban Revolution*. Chapel Hill: University of North Carolina Press, 1985.

———. *The Presidencies of Grover Cleveland*. Lawrence: University Press of Kansas, 1988.

Whitaker, Arthur P. *The Western Hemisphere Idea: Its Rise and Decline*. Ithaca, NY: Cornell University Press, 1954.

Wilgus, A. Curtis. "James G. Blaine and the Pan American Movement." *Hispanic American Historical Review* 5 (November 1922): 662–708.

Williams, William Appleman. *The Tragedy of American Diplomacy*. Rev. ed. New York: Delta, 1962.

Wilson, John Hoff. *American Business and Foreign Policy, 1920–1933*. Lexington: University Press of Kentucky, 1971.

———. *Herbert Hoover: Forgotten Progressive*. Boston: Little, Brown, 1975.

Wood, Bryce. *The Making of the Good Neighbor Policy*. New York: Columbia University Press, 1961.

———. *The United States and Latin American Wars, 1932–1942*. New York: Columbia University Press, 1966.

———. *The Dismantling of the Good Neighbor Policy*. Austin: University of Texas Press, 1985.

Woods, Randall Bennett. *The Roosevelt Foreign-Policy Establishment and the "Good Neighbor": The United States and Argentina, 1941–1945*. Lawrence: Regents Press of Kansas, 1979.

Wright, Thomas C. *Latin America in the Era of the Cuban Revolution*. New York: Praeger, 1991.

Zubok, Vladislav, and Constantine Pleshakov. *Inside the Kremlin's Cold War: From Stalin to Khrushchev*. Cambridge, MA: Harvard University Press, 1996.

INDEX

Latin American Silhouettes
Studies in History and Culture

William H. Beezley and
Judith Ewell
Editors

Volumes Published

Silvia Marina Arrom and Servando Ortoll, eds., *Riots in the Cities: Popular Politics and the Urban Poor in Latin America, 1765–1910* (1996). Cloth ISBN 0-8420-2580-4 Paper ISBN 0-8420-2581-2

Roderic Ai Camp, ed., *Polling for Democracy: Public Opinion and Political Liberalization in Mexico* (1996). ISBN 0-8420-2583-9

Brian Loveman and Thomas M. Davies, Jr., eds., *The Politics of Antipolitics: The Military in Latin America*, 3d ed., revised and updated (1996). Cloth ISBN 0-8420-2609-6 Paper ISBN 0-8420-2611-8

Joseph S. Tulchin, Andrés Serbín, and Rafael Hernández, eds., *Cuba and the Caribbean: Regional Issues and Trends in the Post-Cold War Era* (1997). ISBN 0-8420-2652-5

Thomas W. Walker, ed., *Nicaragua without Illusions: Regime Transition and Structural Adjustment in the 1990s* (1997). Cloth ISBN 0-8420-2578-2 Paper ISBN 0-8420-2579-0

Dianne Walta Hart, *Undocumented in L.A.: An Immigrant's Story* (1997). Cloth ISBN 0-8420-2648-7 Paper ISBN 0-8420-2649-5

Jaime E. Rodríguez O. and Kathryn Vincent, eds., *Myths, Misdeeds, and Misunderstandings: The Roots of Conflict in U.S.-Mexican Relations* (1997). ISBN 0-8420-2662-2

Jaime E. Rodríguez O. and Kathryn Vincent, eds., *Common Border, Uncommon Paths: Race, Culture, and National Identity in U.S.-Mexican Relations* (1997). ISBN 0-8420-2673-8

William H. Beezley and Judith Ewell, eds., *The Human Tradition in Modern Latin America* (1997). Cloth ISBN 0-8420-2612-6 Paper ISBN 0-8420-2613-4

Donald F. Stevens, ed., *Based on a True Story: Latin American History at the Movies* (1997). Cloth ISBN 0-8420-2582-0 Paper ISBN 0-8420-2781-5

Jaime E. Rodríguez O., ed., *The Origins of Mexican National Politics, 1808–1847* (1997). Paper ISBN 0-8420-2723-8

Che Guevara, *Guerrilla Warfare*, with revised and updated introduction and case studies by Brian Loveman and Thomas M. Davies, Jr., 3d ed. (1997). Cloth ISBN 0-8420-2677-0 Paper ISBN 0-8420-2678-9

Adrian A. Bantjes, *As If Jesus Walked on Earth: Cardenismo, Sonora, and the Mexican Revolution* (1998). ISBN 0-8420-2653-3

Henry A. Dietz and Gil Shidlo, eds., *Urban Elections in Democratic Latin America* (1998). Cloth ISBN 0-8420-2627-4 Paper ISBN 0-8420-2628-2

A. Kim Clark, *The Redemptive Work: Railway and Nation in Ecuador, 1895–1930* (1998). ISBN 0-8420-2674-6

Joseph S. Tulchin, ed., with Allison M. Garland, *Argentina: The Challenges of Modernization* (1998). ISBN 0-8420-2721-1

Louis A. Pérez, Jr., ed., *Impressions of Cuba in the Nineteenth Century: The Travel Diary of Joseph J. Dimock* (1998). Cloth ISBN 0-8420-2657-6 Paper ISBN 0-8420-2658-4

June E. Hahner, ed., *Women through Women's Eyes: Latin American Women in Nineteenth-Century Travel Accounts* (1998). Cloth ISBN 0-8420-2633-9 Paper ISBN 0-8420-2634-7

James P. Brennan, ed., *Peronism and Argentina* (1998). ISBN 0-8420-2706-8

John Mason Hart, ed., *Border Crossings: Mexican and Mexican-American Workers* (1998). Cloth ISBN 0-8420-2716-5 Paper ISBN 0-8420-2717-3

Brian Loveman, *For* la Patria: *Politics and the Armed Forces in Latin America* (1999). Cloth ISBN 0-8420-2772-6 Paper ISBN 0-8420-2773-4

Guy P. C. Thomson, with David G. LaFrance, *Patriotism, Politics, and Popular Liberalism in Nineteenth-Century Mexico: Juan Francisco Lucas and the Puebla Sierra* (1999). ISBN 0-8420-2683-5

Robert Woodmansee Herr, in collaboration with Richard Herr, *An American Family in the Mexican Revolution* (1999). ISBN 0-8420-2724-6

Juan Pedro Viqueira Albán, trans. Sonya Lipsett-Rivera and Sergio Rivera Ayala, *Propriety and Permissiveness in Bourbon Mexico* (1999). Cloth ISBN 0-8420-2466-2 Paper ISBN 0-8420-2467-0

Stephen R. Niblo, *Mexico in the 1940s: Modernity, Politics, and Corruption* (1999). ISBN 0-8420-2794-7

David E. Lorey, *The U.S.-Mexican Border in the Twentieth Century* (1999). Cloth ISBN 0-8420-2755-6 Paper ISBN 0-8420-2756-4

Joanne Hershfield and David R. Maciel, eds., *Mexico's Cinema: A Century of Films and Filmmakers* (2000). Cloth ISBN 0-8420-2681-9 Paper ISBN 0-8420-2682-7

Peter V. N. Henderson, *In the Absence of Don Porfirio: Francisco León de la Barra and the Mexican Revolution* (2000). ISBN 0-8420-2774-2

Mark T. Gilderhus, *The Second Century: U.S.-Latin American Relations since 1889* (2000). Cloth ISBN 0-8420-2413-1 Paper ISBN 0-8420-2414-X

Catherine Moses, *Real Life in Castro's Cuba* (2000). Cloth ISBN 0-8420-2836-6 Paper ISBN 0-8420-2837-4

K. Lynn Stoner, ed./comp., with Luis Hipólito Serrano Pérez, *Cuban and Cuban-American Women: An Annotated Bibliography* (2000). ISBN 0-8420-2643-6

Thomas D. Schoonover, *The French in Central America: Culture and Commerce, 1820–1930* (2000). ISBN 0-8420-2792-0